D1527534

THE BODHISATTVA PATH

BUDDHIST TRADITION SERIES

General Editor
ERNST STEINKELLNER

Joint General Editor
ALEXANDER VAN ROSPATT

Founder Editor
Late ALEX WAYMAN

Editorial Advisory Board
CHR. LINDTNER
KATSUMI MIMAKI
LOKESH CHANDRA
MICHAEL HANN

VOLUME 56

THE BODHISATTVA PATH

Based on the *Ugraparipṛcchā*, a Mahāyāna Sūtra

A Study and Translation by

JAN NATTIER

MOTILAL BANARSIDASS PUBLISHERS
PRIVATE LIMITED • DELHI

First Indian Edition: Delhi, 2007
First Published by the University of Hawai'i Press, 2003
under the title "A Few Good Men*: The Bodhisattva Path according to the Inquiry of Ugra*"

© 2003 INSTITUTE FOR THE STUDY OF BUDDHIST TRADITIONS
All Rights Reserved.

ISBN: 978-81-208-2048-7

MOTILAL BANARSIDASS
41 U.A. Bungalow Road, Jawahar Nagar, Delhi 110 007
8 Mahalaxmi Chamber, 22 Bhulabhai Desai Road, Mumbai 400 026
203 Royapettah High Road, Mylapore, Chennai 600 004
236, 9th Main III Block, Jayanagar, Bangalore 560 011
Sanas Plaza, 1302 Baji Rao Road, Pune 411 002
8 Camac Street, Kolkata 700 017
Ashok Rajpath, Patna 800 004
Chowk, Varanasi 221 001

FOR SALE IN SOUTH ASIA ONLY

Printed in India
BY JAINENDRA PRAKASH JAIN AT SHRI JAINENDRA PRESS,
A-45 NARAINA, PHASE-I, NEW DELHI 110 028
AND PUBLISHED BY NARENDRA PRAKASH JAIN FOR
MOTILAL BANARSIDASS PUBLISHERS PRIVATE LIMITED,
BUNGALOW ROAD, DELHI 110 007

To the memory of

Professor Masatoshi Nagatomi (1926-2000)

scholar, teacher, and friend

Contents

Part Two: Translation

Appendices

Foreword

The *Ugraparipṛcchāsūtra* is a particularly important text for our understanding of the beginnings of Mahāyāna Buddhism. It originated in a monastic milieu prior to the open split between Śrāvakayāna and Mahāyāna Buddhism. Though in the sūtra the Buddha explains to *Ugra,* the interlocutor, the practices and path of the bodhisattva, it differs in many important aspects from the literature that informs our knowledge of Mahāyāna Buddhism. The sūtra neither espouses *śūnyatā* nor any philosophy commonly identified with Mahāyāna Buddhism; nor is it grounded in a particular cult, be it of the *stūpa*, of the book or of celestial Buddhas and Bodhisattvas; nor does it originate in a particular context apart from mainstream monasticism. Rather, the *Ugra*'s portrayal of the bodhisattva ideal is in perfect continuity with Śrāvakayāna Buddhism. The *Ugra* upholds the ideal of the monastic, and, more particularly, of the solitary renouncer who devotes his life to meditative practices pursued in isolation. The sūtra does not challenge the *śrāvaka*'s aspiration as selfish and vain, as happens so famously in the Vimalakīrtinirdeśasūtra; rather, it supplements it with the even loftier ideal of buddhahood, exhorting the bodhisattva to model his spiritual career on that of the Buddha.

It is not possible to discount the picture of emerging Mahāyāna Buddhism afforded by the *Ugra* as peripheral. The sūtra was translated into Chinese no fewer than six times between the second and fifth century, and hence it must have been of enormous importance during that period. However, due to the loss of the Sanskrit original and a bias in the study of Mahāyāna Buddhism towards particular texts, the *Ugra* has so far received scant academic attention. All the more important is the present study of the *Ugraparipṛcchāsūtra* by Prof. Jan Nattier. For the first time, it makes the sūtra available in a carefully annotated translation into a Western language. Nattier translates the Tibetan version of the *Ugra,* the longest and most recent recension of this text. She weaves into her translation deviations from the three extant Chinese translations as well as the Sanskrit fragments handed down as quotations in Śāntideva's *Śikṣāsamuccaya*. Thus, together with the two synoptic tables in Appendix 1 collating the different versions of the *Ugra,* Nattier's translation makes this text accessible comprehensively. The presentation of the text is preceded by an extensive study of the sūtra. First Nattier introduces the *Ugra* and discusses philological and methodological issues pertaining to the handling of the original sources. She then proceeds to place the sūtra within its Buddhist context and offers a thoughtful analysis of its content. Finally, she looks at the *Ugra* in light of our received notion of what Mahāyāna Buddhism is and proceeds to question the validity of these notions.

Prof. Nattier's work is an important contribution to the study of Mahāyāna Buddhism. *A Few Good Men* not only rescues a significant primary source, the *Ugra,* from oblivion, but it also offers a circumspect and penetrating analysis of this text. In the process, Nattier considers the current state of both Western and Japanese scholarship, addresses methodological issues and deals with the prevailing theories on the origins of Mahāyāna Buddhism. Thus this study accomplishes far more than the presentation of an important Mahāyānasūtra that has been much neglected to date. It sheds new light on the incipient phase of Mahāyāna Buddhism and hence is recommended reading for students of Buddhism.

This is the first book in the Buddhist Tradition Series that is no longer appearing under the able editorship of Prof. Wayman. After a long illness, he passed away in New York on September 22, 2004. This is neither the place to recall his significant and always stimulating contributions to different areas in the study of Buddhism, nor is it the occasion to dwell on the dedication with which he promoted the interests and work of a host of students during his long and distinguished career as academic teacher. Suffice it to say here, his death is a big loss to the academic community also because of his work in the field of publishing.

The Buddhist Tradition Series has been edited and accompanied by Professor Wayman since it began in 1987 with Hajime Nakamura's bibliographic survey of Indian Buddhism. With the series Professor Wayman has strengthened the awareness of the Buddhist tradition in India by providing scholars and students with both modern studies in Western languages and classics of scholarship long out of print – all at reasonable costs. Professor Wayman proposed to include only such works that combined "both insight and scholarly excellence." During all these years of service as editor, Professor Wayman took great care to balance the series' program. The included works touch upon almost any aspect of the rich traditions of Buddhism and, at the same time, reflect different styles and developments in present-day scholarship. We gratefully acknowledge the high standards in the series maintained by our respected predecessor and will honour his example by proceeding in a like spirit.

Ernst Steinkellner
Alexander von Rospatt

Preface

This project has had a long history. Its origins can be traced to my initial year as a graduate student at Harvard (1974-75), when I first discovered the pleasures of an in-depth investigation of a Mahāyāna sūtra while writing a paper on the *Aṣṭasāhasrikā-prajñāpāramitā-sūtra* under the direction of Professor Masatoshi Nagatomi. The memory of that experience—including the surprise of finding things in the text which (according to standard textbook definitions of the Mahāyāna) should not be there, and the delight of making a first foray into reading a Sanskrit Buddhist text in the original—has never left me, and indeed virtually all of my work since then could be viewed as a continued attempt to wrestle with questions that arose during that first and very formative year.

A more proximate beginning of this project, however, occurred almost twenty years later, after I had accepted a teaching position at my *alma mater*, Indiana University. A fellow alumnus of IU's Religious Studies program, Daniel J. Boucher (then a Ph.D. candidate at the University of Pennsylvania) shared an interest in the Chinese translator Dharmarakṣa, and together we organized a reading group (subsequently expanded to include IU professors Stephen R. Bokenkamp and Robert F. Campany) to peruse the Buddhist translations of this pivotal figure. Our attention soon fell upon Dharmarakṣa's translation of the *Ugraparipṛcchā-sūtra*, which had particular appeal due to the existence of two other Chinese translations (one earlier, one later) as well as a considerably later Tibetan version which we could call upon for comparison. This small but intrepid group spent countless hours huddled around my kitchen table wrestling with Dharmarakṣa's often inscrutable translation choices, efforts that were rewarded at the end of most sessions by a feast of grilled fish, Boucher's signature guacamole, colossal salads (of which Campany's version won particular acclaim), and—when fortune was especially kind—a sampling of Bokenkamp's fine home-brewed beer.

The group eventually disbanded when Boucher (now at Cornell) accepted a fellowship to study in Japan, and our research interests moved in disparate directions. Boucher (always the pace-car of our group when it came to explaining the Indic antecedents of Dharmarakṣa's peculiar locutions) went on to write a Ph.D. dissertation on Dharmarakṣa's translation idiom, while Bokenkamp and Campany continued to produce important works on various aspects of Chinese religion during the Han and Six Dynasties periods. My own interests remained centered on the use of Chinese sources to understand Indian Buddhism, and the experience of reading portions of the *Ugra* with this stimulating group convinced me that this sūtra could supply vital information on the rise of the Mahāyāna in India that had not yet been adequately mined by scholars. A complete translation of the *Ugra*, I was convinced, could bring this important text into the conversation.

A translation grant from the National Endowment for the Humanities (1995-96), whose generous support I am happy to acknowledge here, made it possible to begin work on this project in earnest, and a first draft of the translation was produced at a tiny desk in Xiaguan, Yunnan, P.R.C., where my partner John McRae was doing research on the religion of the local Bai ethnic group. Since my spoken Chinese was quite minimal, distractions were few, and work on the *Ugra* proceeded with unanticipated efficiency.

Upon my return to the academic fray in North America in 1996 progress slowed considerably, but this was balanced by the opportunity to investigate a wide range of related primary and secondary sources, and above all by the valuable feedback provided by a number of colleagues. Daniel Boucher scrutinized every line of the initial drafts of the introductory chapters, providing critical comments (and additional bibliographical references) that have greatly enhanced the quality of this work. Paul Harrison did the same for the translation, improving the phrasing and saving me from a number of potential mishaps. Stephen Bokenkamp offered invaluable counsel on reading the early Chinese versions of the *Ugra*, while SASAKI Shizuka and Jonathan Silk directed me to important related publications by Japanese scholars. Others whose insights have contributed to the final product are Thanissaro Bhikkhu (who made some excellent stylistic suggestions and offered copious references to related Pāli texts), David Haberman (who took me to task for my original characterization of Hindu *bhakti* and may be slightly happier with the version that appears here), and my colleagues David Brakke and Constance Furey, whose insights into the study of ancient and early modern Christianity, respectively, were extremely helpful in clarifying some of the methodological issues raised here. Gil Fronsdal, Peter Gregory, and two anonymous reviewers offered encouraging comments, and Robert Campany and KARASHIMA Seishi caught some of the last remaining typos and raised a number of issues for further thought. At the eleventh hour Glenn Zuber and Jason

BeDuhn pitched in by offering precise references to Christian and Manichaean materials, respectively, while Ju-hyung Rhi knew immediately how to locate the image that now appears on the cover. Last—and very far from least—Gregory Schopen read through every line of the final draft, offering substantial comments and and catching a number of gaffes that would surely have caused confusion to the reader and embarassment to the writer. To all of these colleagues and friends I am immensely grateful. Any errors that remain, of course, are the sole responsibility of the author.

I would also like to thank the many scholars—most of whom I have never met—whose work is quoted or commented on below. Even in those cases where I have offered critical assessments of their methodology or conclusions, I have benefited greatly from their pioneering work.

This manuscript was originally submitted in 1999 to another press, where after being accepted for publication it languished through mid-2001. I then resubmitted it, at the invitation of series editor Luis O. Gómez, to the University of Hawai'i Press, and I have never regretted that decision. Editor Pat Crosby, in particular, has been a delight to work with, and copy editor Stephanie Chun did a remarkable job with a difficult text. To them and the rest of the staff at the Press, my heartfelt thanks.

Above all I am grateful to my husband, John McRae, who has endured countless hours of speculations on the rise of the Mahāyāna, answered my seemingly endless questions on things Chinese, and read through the entire manuscript, putting a variety of infelicities out of their misery at an early stage. But more than this: his unflagging support and constant companionship mean more to me than I can possibly express.

My only regret is that my teacher, Professor Masatoshi Nagatomi, did not live to see the completion of this work. He would have been amused, I suspect, by the *Ugra*'s seemingly retrograde position on certain issues, and no doubt he would have pushed me to think more deeply on some of the topics discussed below. The field of Buddhist Studies is diminished by his loss. As a very small gesture of gratitude, this work is dedicated to his memory.

Honolulu, Hawai'i
30 June 2002

Abbreviations

AN	*Aṅguttara-nikāya*
Aṣṭa	*Aṣṭasāhasrikā-prajñāpāramitā-sūtra*
AY	An Hsüan and Yen Fo-t'iao
BCSD	HIRAKAWA Akira, ed., *Buddhist Chinese-Sanskrit Dictionary*
BHS	Buddhist Hybrid Sanskrit
BHSD	Franklin Edgerton, *Buddhist Hybrid Sanskrit Dictionary*
Ch.	Chinese
DhA	*Dhammapada Aṭṭhakathā*
Dh	Dharmarakṣa
Dbhv.	*Daśabhūmikavibhāṣā*
DES	Sir Monier Monier-Williams, *A Dictionary of English and Sanskrit*
DN	*Dīgha-nikāya*
GV	*Gaṇḍavyūha*
Jä.	H. A. Jäschke, *A Tibetan -English Dictionary*
Jpn.	Japanese
LC	Lokesh Chandra, *Tibetan-Saskrit Dictionary*
MDPPL	Edward Conze, *Materials for a Dictionary of the Prajñāpāramitā Literature*
MN	*Majjhima-nikāya*
Mvu.	*Mahāvastu*
Mvy.	*Mahāvyutpatti*
MW	Sir Monier Monier-Williams, *Sanskrit-English Dictionary*
Pkt.	Prakrit

Pratyutpanna	*Pratyutpanna-buddhasaṁmukha-avasthita-samādhi-sūtra*
PTSD	Pali Text Society, *Pali-English Dictionary* (ed. T. W. Rhys Davids and William Stede)
R	Ratnakūṭa (version of the *Ugra*, T 310[19])
Rerikh	Yu. N. Rerikh, *Tibetsko-russko-angliĭskiĭ slovar' s sanskritskimi parallelyami*
Sakurabe	SAKURABE Hajime, trans., Tibetan version of the *Ugra*
Śikṣ.	Cecil Bendall, ed., *Śikṣāsamuccaya*
Skt.	Sanskrit
Sn	*Suttanipāta*
SnA	*Suttanipāta Aṭṭhakathā*
SN	*Saṁyutta-nikāya*
T	*Taishō Shinshū Daizōkyō*
Tib	Tibetan translation of the *Ugra*
Tib.	Tibetan
Ugra	*Ugraparipṛcchā-sūtra*

A separate list of conventions, symbols, and abbreviations used only in the translation is provided on p. 206.

PART ONE

ANALYSIS

CHAPTER 1

Introduction

Of the hundreds of Buddhist texts that have come to be classified as "Mahāyāna sūtras," *The Inquiry of Ugra* (*Ugraparipṛcchā*) has been one of the most influential. The *Ugra* was among the first Buddhist sūtras to be transmitted from India to China, and according to traditional catalogues it was translated into Chinese no fewer than six times between the 2nd and 5th centuries CE.[1] By the middle of the 3rd century CE the sūtra had become so popular that K'ang Seng-hui, one of the leading translator-monks of the time, composed both a preface and a commentary to the text. On the Indian side, the **Daśabhūmikavibhāṣā* (a compendium on bodhisattva practice attributed to Nāgārjuna, but surviving only in a Chinese version) contains more lines drawn from this sūtra than from any other source. And as late as the 8th century CE—at least six centuries after its composition, judging by the date of its first Chinese translation—the *Ugra* was still being actively quoted by Mahāyāna scholastics in India, as witness Śāntideva's *Śikṣāsamuccaya* (another instruction manual for bodhisattvas) in which the *Ugra* is one of the most frequently cited texts.

Yet the *Ugra* is virtually unknown in the English-speaking world. Not a single line from the *Ugra* is included in any of the anthologies of Buddhist literature commonly used in colleges and universities (e.g., Burtt 1955, Conze 1959, Conze et al. 1954, de Bary 1969, Lopez 1995, Strong 1995), nor is the sūtra ever mentioned in any of the standard textbooks on the history of Buddhist thought and practice (e.g., Conze 1962, Gethin 1998, Harvey 1990, Robinson et al. 1997). Even in Paul Williams' far more detailed survey of Mahāyāna Buddhism (1989) the *Ugra* is ignored: the titles of more than forty Mahāyāna sūtras appear in the index, but the *Ugra* is not one of them.

In more specialized scholarly venues as well the *Ugra* has been almost entirely neglected. So far as I have been able to determine there has been only one doctoral dissertation written in English on the

---

[1] Technical details on these and other items will be provided in Chapter 2.

subject (Schuster 1976), and only one published journal article, by the same author (Schuster 1985), has appeared. No partial or complete translation has ever been published in English (nor, for that matter, in any other western language).[2] In short, the *Ugra* has fallen from a position of great prominence in early medieval Mahāyāna communities to a status of virtual invisibility in western treatments of Buddhism today.[3]

How did such an influential text come to be so widely ignored? We cannot, of course, point to a single cause that has led to this anomalous situation, nor can we presume to offer an exhaustive enumeration of all the myriad factors that have combined to bring it about; to do so would be to commit one of what Fischer (1970) has aptly termed "historians' fallacies."[4] It would also—if one wishes to invoke Buddhist principles—violate the rich sense of the complex and ultimately indescribable network of causation leading to any particular event that is so characteristic of this tradition. If we set a somewhat more modest goal, however, and attempt simply to sketch the overall contours of the religious and intellectual environment within which Mahāyāna Buddhist scriptures have been received in the West, we may be able to observe a number of factors that seem to be correlated with the neglect of this once-prominent scripture.

We may begin by looking not at the invisibility of the *Ugra* itself, but rather at the prominence of certain other scriptures which have regularly been featured in textbooks and anthologies as well as in more technical studies. When we do so, a distinct pattern begins to appear, for the Mahāyāna sūtras that are the most widely known in the West—works like the *Lotus Sūtra*, the *Heart Sūtra*, the *Diamond Sūtra*, certain other Perfection of Wisdom sūtras (e.g., the versions in 8,000 and 25,000 lines), the larger and smaller *Sukhāvatīvyūha* sūtras, and the *Vimalakīrti*—have certain intriguing features in common. Either they are among the handful of Mahāyāna sūtras

---

[2] Preliminary translations of the three Chinese versions were included in Schuster 1976, but this dissertation has never been published, nor is it available through University Microfilms.

[3] Though the discussion in this chapter will focus on views of Mahāyāna Buddhism that have entered the "mainstream"—that is, that are well represented in textbooks, anthologies of primary sources, and nontechnical reference works—many of the same patterns of emphasis and elision obtain in more specialized studies as well.

[4] See especially Chapter 6, "Fallacies of Causation."

which are still extant in Sanskrit, or they are extremely popular in contemporary Japan, or both. Where these two factors coincide (as they do with virtually all of the above titles), there is an extremely high degree of probability that the sūtra in question will not only be regularly included in anthologies, but that it will have been used as a central interpretive framework in presenting "Mahāyāna Buddhism" to western audiences.

That these two factors should be so strongly correlated with the prominence of a given Buddhist sūtra in western-language publications is not surprising if we consider how the field of Buddhist Studies came to be what it is today.[5] Much of the initial stimulus to the western study of Buddhism came from the encounter by European scholars with Sanskrit and Pāli scriptural texts. The British colonial enterprise in India and Sri Lanka brought to light the existence of both Pāli texts (belonging to the Theravāda school) and a cache of Sanskrit manuscripts preserved in Nepal, both of which drew the attention of British and French scholars already in the first half of the 19th century. Research on Tibetan, Chinese, and Mongolian texts soon followed, but to this day texts written in an Indic language exert a certain hegemony in the field, due in part to the historical accident of their earlier study, but clearly also as a result of the western preoccupation with historical origins. The sense that the Indian texts are the "originals" of which Buddhist texts in other languages (whether translations or local compositions) are simply derivative still prevails, despite the fact that many texts in non-Indic languages predate the surviving Sanskrit and Pāli documents by several centuries.

But if the initial phase of western Buddhist Studies consisted largely of the analysis and digestion of Sanskrit and Pāli texts, an important feature of the second phase of its development (which might be described as extending from the late 19th to the early 20th century; see de Jong 1997) was the beginning of active collaboration between European and Japanese scholars. With the reopening of Japan to foreign contacts in 1868 after two and a half centuries of isolation, Japanese students of Buddhism began to travel to Europe to study Sanskrit and Pāli with leading western scholars. One of the first

---

[5] On this subject see especially Brear 1975, Clausen 1975, Nagao 1979, Kiyota 1984, Wickremeratne 1985, Almond 1986 and 1988, de Jong 1987, Lancaster 1987, Ruegg 1992, Silk 1994b, and Lopez 1995.

to take on such students was F. Max Müller, who published the first western editions of the Sanskrit *Heart Sūtra*, *Diamond Sūtra*, and shorter and longer *Sukhāvatīvyūha* sūtras based on manuscripts preserved in Japan (Müller 1881). The existence of these Sanskrit texts had been made known to him by his students, among whom numbered NANJŌ Bun'yū, who later collaborated with the Dutch scholar Hendrik Kern to produce the first published Sanskrit edition of the *Lotus Sūtra* (Kern and Nanjio 1908-1912).

In addition to the impact of European Indology and early contacts with Japanese scholars, however, there is surely another factor that has contributed to the privileging of certain Mahāyāna sūtras and the obscuring of others in the West. For western readers have not merely been passive recipients of Asian scriptures; they have participated actively in the selection process as well. A second glance at the list of widely quoted sūtras given above—now with an eye toward others that are missing from that list—reveals that they consist not only of those that have survived in Sanskrit and/or been highly valued in Japan, but those that appeal to western cultural preferences as well. The *Sūtra of Golden Light* (*Suvarṇa-prabhāsa*), for example, is extant in Sanskrit and has also been extremely influential in Japan, but its message that guardian deities from various Buddhist heavens will protect a king who patronizes the Dharma holds little relevance for the contemporary western reader. Likewise the *Laṅkāvatāra Sūtra*—also extant in Sanskrit and of some importance in Japan, where it was actively promoted by no less influential a figure than D. T. Suzuki—has garnered far less attention than other sūtras in this category, for its complex discussions of the "three bodies" of the apotheosized Buddha and its repeated statements that this world is nothing but a projection of our own minds have found little favor with pragmatic and this-worldly westerners.

The sūtras that have enjoyed greatest prominence in English-language presentations of Buddhism, by contrast, tend to be those that portray the Buddhist message in terms congruent with certain core western values, such as egalitarianism (e.g., the universal potential for Buddhahood according to the *Lotus*), lay-centered religion (e.g., the ability of the lay Buddhist hero of the *Vimalakīrti* to confound highly educated clerics in debate), the simplicity and individuality of religious practice (e.g., the centrality of personal faith in Amitābha in the *Sukhāvatīvyūha*), and even anti-intellectualism (e.g., the apparent rejection of the usefulness of rational thought in the *Heart Sūtra*, the *Diamond Sūtra*, and other Perfection of Wisdom texts). In sum, certain sūtras appear to have been highlighted above others not only due to the accident of their survival in Sanskrit or to their importance in Japan, but also as a result of their congeniality to contemporary western religious tastes.

To construct an image of Mahāyāna Buddhism in India based on such an obviously skewed selection of sources is clearly inappropriate, yet this is precisely what has happened in western discussions of Buddhism. To choose only a single example: the *Lotus Sūtra*—a text that fulfills all three of the criteria outlined above—has widely been viewed as a typical, even foundational, Mahāyāna scripture. Yet if we compare it with other Indian Mahāyāna sūtras it quickly becomes clear that it is unusual in many respects. Its doctrine of the "one vehicle"—that is, the idea that all Buddhists are destined for Buddhahood and that Arhatship is merely an illusion—flies in the face of the far more widespread Mahāyāna teaching of the "three vehicles" (the idea that Arhatship, Pratyekabuddhahood, and Buddhahood are three quite separate spiritual destinations). Its claim that even a child who builds a stūpa out of sand and offers it to the Buddha will eventually attain Buddhahood himself (i.e., the idea that Buddhahood is easy) contradicts the dominant early Mahāyāna understanding of the bodhisattva path as extremely challenging, even grueling, and suited only for "the few, the proud, the brave." And the famous scene in which Śākyamuni appears in the sky together with a long-dead Buddha of the past, Prabhūtaratna, violates the standard Mahāyāna teaching that there can be only one Buddha per world at a time (not to mention the basic dictum that, for Buddhas as well as Arhats, "extinction is forever"). In sum, when read against the background of other Mahāyāna sūtras it quickly becomes clear that the *Lotus* is far from typical, and that its central role in western-language presentations of Indian Buddhism has more to do with its survival in Sanskrit, its popularity in Japan, and its conformity to western tastes than to its status as a "representative" Indian scripture (which it clearly was not).[6]

If we return now to the case of the *Ugra*, several factors that may have contributed to its obscurity in the West become clear. First, no Sanskrit version of the sūtra itself has survived; the only portions that have been preserved in an Indic language are a dozen or so quotations contained in the Sanskrit *Śikṣāsamuccaya*. Second, it has

---

6 These issues are discussed in detail in Nattier 1997.

little importance in contemporary Japanese Buddhism; to the extent that it is known at all, it is familiar only through citations in the *Shih-chu p'i-p'o-sha lun* (**Daśabhūmikavibhāṣā*), a treatise which had great impact upon the T'ien-t'ai school in China and secondarily upon its offspring, the Tendai school, in Japan. Third, as the reader will soon see, the *Ugra* has little to recommend it to contemporary western tastes. It is far from an egalitarian document: the bodhisattva path is portrayed as a difficult vocation suited only for the few, and those "few" do not seem to include women. Nor (*pace* Schuster) does the text favor laity over monks: becoming a renunciant is said to be an absolute prerequisite for the attainment of Buddhahood, and the lay bodhisattva is urged to "get thee to a monastery" as quickly as possible. The bodhisattva's practice, as described in the *Ugra*, is anything but simple, and the sūtra holds out no promise of the attainment of Buddhahood in this lifetime. On the contrary, the bodhisattva must expect to suffer through thousands of additional lifetimes in order to acquire the merit and knowledge necessary to procure all the qualities that constitute a Buddha. Finally, the *Ugra* contains none of the mind-bending negations that seem to hold a special fascination for 21st-century westerners. Its description of the bodhisattva path offers not rhetorical pyrotechnics but a fairly straightforward (even plodding) program of instruction, urging the bodhisattva to carry out the whole range of traditional Buddhist practices of *śīla* (morality), *samādhi* (meditation), and *prajñā* (wisdom). There are no shortcuts here, no egalitarian and inclusive community, and certainly no validation of the comfortable life of the well-adjusted layman. The *Ugra* is not, by any stretch of the imagination, a "family values" sūtra.

Why, then, should we read such a sūtra? For the scholar of Buddhist history, the answer is clear: the *Ugra* was a highly influential text among Mahāyāna Buddhists in both India and China, and as such was not only preserved and transmitted over many centuries but actively quoted in treatises on the bodhisattva path. Indeed, as we shall see, it appears to be one of the earliest of the bodhisattva scriptures that have come down to us, and as such it offers a particularly valuable window on the process by which the bodhisattva path came to be seen as a distinct vocational alternative within certain Indian Buddhist communities.

For practicing Buddhists, on the other hand, the answer is also straightforward: the authors of the *Ugra* are among the ancestors of the Buddhists of today, and whether one likes what they had to say or not, it will not do simply to ignore their existence. To the extent that the goal of Buddhist practice is described as "seeing things as they are," seeing the past of the Buddhist tradition as it was—and not as we might wish it had been—is a part of that same enterprise. On this point, at least, scholarship and practice coincide.

Whatever our own scholarly and religious preferences, then, the *Ugra* clearly played far too important a role in the development of Mahāyāna Buddhist thought and practice to be allowed to remain in the shadows any longer. By making available a study and translation of this foundational text I hope to bring a once influential but long-silenced voice into the conversation.

* * *

This study is intended, as the preceding lines suggest, for a variety of audiences. At one end of the spectrum are specialists in Buddhist literature, for whom precise philological details are an endless source of fascination and footnotes are their own reward. At the other (and far more thickly populated) end are readers whose interests are more general, including students of comparative religion, members of Buddhist communities, and all those who are curious about the variety of forms Buddhism has assumed over the course of its history. For the latter group complex technical discussions can pose an unwelcome distraction, and with this in mind I have tried to keep the main narrative relatively uncluttered by consigning most of these items to the footnotes. This means that the amount of space taken up by the notes is fairly substantial, but readers who wish to do so may simply ignore them and read only the main text. In a few cases technical matters required a discussion too extensive to be dealt with in footnotes alone. Chapter 2 (on the sources for the study of the *Ugra*) and Chapter 3 (on methodological issues in the study of Buddhist scriptures) contain such materials, and readers for whom these hold little appeal should simply skip them and begin with Chapter 4.

Both generalists and specialists are welcome, of course, to bypass the introduction altogether and proceed directly to the translation, on the basis of which they may wish to construct interpretations quite different than my own.

CHAPTER 2

The Formation of *The Inquiry of Ugra*

The Inquiry of Ugra is an Indian treatise on Buddhist practice, composed by and for men who considered themselves bodhisattvas.[1] It should not, however, be called a "Mahāyāna sūtra"—not, that is, without considerable qualification. Granted, this is the status that has been accorded to the text in subsequent centuries by Buddhists themselves; indeed it has regularly been assigned to a particular division of Mahāyāna sūtras, the *Ratnakūṭa* ("heap of jewels") section, about which more will be said below. But these labels are only retrospective attributions, and it will not help us to understand the world out of which the *Ugra* emerged if we insist on viewing it through the lens of these subsequent understandings. In particular, to call the *Ugra* a "Mahāyāna sūtra" would be likely to elicit in the minds of many readers—though not necessarily on a conscious level, which makes these associations all the more hazardous—the idea that its creators held doctrinal views distinct from those of other contemporary Buddhists, that they were members of a separate Mahāyāna organization or school, or even that they were actively opposed to some competing form of Buddhism known as the "Hīnayāna." But in the case of the *Ugra*, as we shall see, there is no evidence whatsoever that any of these was the case. On the contrary, the author(s) of the *Ugra* present the bodhisattva—and thus themselves—as merely a Buddhist among Buddhists, but nonetheless as one who has chosen the most arduous, and most glorious, of all career paths: the eons-long process of procuring all the qualities that constitute a Buddha.

I will therefore use the term "bodhisattva sūtras," rather than "Mahāyāna sūtras," to refer to those scriptures that discuss the requirements of the bodhisattva path, deferring any assumptions about how the *Ugra* might or might not fit into the category of what 21st-century readers think of as the "Mahāyāna" until we have examined in detail what we find—and perhaps more important, what

1 The exclusively masculine phrasing is chosen advisedly, for reasons to be discussed below.

we do *not* find—within the sūtra itself.[2] Only then can we begin to understand the universe of ideas, activities, and institutional structures within which these early self-proclaimed bodhisattvas lived. First, however, we must consider the nature of the *Ugra* as a literary document: the age of its extant versions, their relationships to one another, and the genre to which it belongs. Having established the place of the *Ugra* within the larger Buddhist textual tradition, we will then be in a position to make appropriate use of its content as one window on a period of significant innovation in Indian Buddhism.

The *Ugra* as a Literary Document

Whether the *Ugra* began its life as a sūtra—that is, whether the person who first formulated what was to become this canonical document deliberately placed his own words in the mouth of the Buddha—we will never know. It is by no means certain that it did: there are examples in the Buddhist canon of texts originally attributed not to the Buddha, but to a particular (and named) individual, which were only gradually subjected to a process of "sūtrafication" during which the standard features of the sūtra genre were added and the Buddha introduced into the text.[3] This is not a trivial issue, for there is a vast

---

[2] In this provisional avoidance of the term "Mahāyāna" I am following in the footsteps of Egil Fronsdal, who used this approach to good effect in his Ph.D. dissertation on the bodhisattva career as portrayed in the early Perfection of Wisdom literature (Fronsdal 1998).

[3] The most striking example of this phenomenon that I have encountered to date is the so-called "Kauśāmbī story," a prophecy of the decline and disappearance of the Dharma that survives in several Chinese, Khotanese, and Tibetan recensions. In the oldest extant version of the tale, an anonymous Chinese translation completed no later than 316 CE and perhaps considerably earlier (T 2029), the prophecy in question is explicitly attributed to a monk named Kātyāyana. The text has neither the form nor the content of a sūtra, and it makes no claim to be *buddhavacana*. Kātyāyana is still the speaker in a somewhat later recension of the tale (T 2028, dated to the period 420-479), though the title of the work has now acquired the word *ching* 經, which serves (among other things) as the Chinese translation of *sūtra*. In still later recensions, however—those contained in the Chinese *Aśoka-avadāna*, the Chinese and Tibetan versions of the *Candragarbha-sūtra*, and the Khotanese *Book of Zambasta*, among others—Kātyāyana has disappeared from the account, and his predictions are now credited to the Buddha (see Nattier 1991, pp. 150-

difference between a text that was originally composed with the pretense to being *buddhavacana*—as at least some of the apocryphal sūtras composed in China, for example, appear to have been—and one that began its literary life more humbly (as the sermon of Bhikṣu So-and-so, for example), and was only gradually upgraded to sūtra

---

157 and 168-204). What we have here, in other words, is clearcut evidence of the gradual assimilation of a popular discourse to the category of *buddhavacana*.

Traces of a similar process can be discerned in *The Perfection of Wisdom in Eight Thousand Lines* (*Aṣṭasāhasrikā-prajñāpāramitā-sūtra*), where the bulk of the preaching in the early chapters is attributed not to the Buddha, but to a monk by the name of Subhūti. This fact is, in itself, unremarkable, since there are many sūtras in which speakers other than the Buddha play a prominent role. But the degree of concern expressed in a number of places in the *Aṣṭa* with establishing the legitimacy of dharma-discourses *not* preached by the Buddha suggests that something more than the use of an alternative speaker as a narrative device is at stake. In the opening lines of the sūtra, before Subhūti has uttered a single word, Śāriputra begins to experience doubts about the legitimacy—that is, the authoritativeness—of what he is about to say. Reading Śāriputra's thoughts, Subhūti replies, "O Venerable Śāriputra, whatever the Blessed One's *śrāvaka*s say, teach, expound, proclaim, set forth, and reveal, all that should be known as the Tathāgata's doing" (*yat kiṁcid āyuṣman Śāriputra bhagavataḥ śrāvakā bhāṣante deśayanti upadiśanti udīrayanti prakāśayanti saṁprakāśayanti, sa sarvas tathāgatasya puruṣakāro veditavyaḥ*, I.4; cf. the much-abbreviated translation in Conze 1973, p. 83). The sūtra admits that the words are those of Subhūti, but grounds their authority in that of the Buddha.

In a number of other passages it continues to be clear that the *Aṣṭa* (or rather, the original discourse out of which the sūtra grew) was viewed not as *buddhavacana* but as the teachings of a particular monk. There is the frankness, first of all, with which the *Aṣṭa* portrays the views of skeptical Buddhists on the subject: "[The teaching of the perfection of wisdom] that you have heard just now is not the word of the Buddha. It is poetry, composed by poets" (*yad etat tvayedānīṁ śrutam, naitad buddha-vacanam | kavikṛtaṁ kāvyam etat*, XVII.328; cf. Conze 1973, p. 202), an objection the *Aṣṭa* attempts to counter by asserting that such criticism is clearly the work of Māra. Even more telling is the technique the *Aṣṭa* uses in another passage to support the authority of its text, where its legitimacy is underscored by the fact that the perfection of wisdom has been preached by other monks named Subhūti in the past: "In these very words, syllables, and letters, monks named 'Subhūti' have taught this very perfection of wisdom, this very exposition (*parivarta*) of the perfection of wisdom" (*ebhir eva nāmabhir ebhir eva padair ebhir evākṣaraiḥ Subhūtināmadheyair eva bhikṣubhir iyam eva prajñāpāramitopadiṣṭā, ayam eva prajñāpāramitā-parivartaḥ*, VIII.199; cf. Conze 1973, p. 147). The text goes on to say that on those occasions Śakras (note the plural here as well) asked questions, and that it

status. Since virtually all of the initial literary, philosophical, and ritual experiments that culminated in the production of what are now known as "Mahāyāna sūtras" took place off-camera—that is, were never documented in written form—it would be rash indeed to assume that a given text known to us today as a sūtra began its life in that format. It has long been recognized in Buddhist Studies circles that most of what we have today as written canonical documents originated as oral texts;[4] it is far less commonly realized that these

---

was at this very spot of earth (*asminn eva pṛthivīpradeśe*) that the perfection of wisdom was pronounced. Nowhere is the claim made that these are the words of Śākyamuni, though an appeal is made to the prestige of the future Buddha Maitreya, who after attaining Buddhahood will preach the perfection of wisdom on this very same site. Finally there is the straightforward exchange between Śāriputra and Śakra in the second chapter: "Where," Śakra asks, "should the bodhisattva-mahāsattva seek the perfection of wisdom?" Śāriputra replies, "He should seek it in [lit. "from"] the exposition of the Venerable Subhūti" (*ayuṣmataḥ Subhūteḥ parivartād gaveṣitavyā*). Śakra then asks by what power (*anubhāva*) and what authority (*adhiṣṭhāna*) Subhūti speaks, and is assured that they are those of the Tathāgata himself (II.44; cf. Conze 1973, p. 100).

We will have occasion to examine the meaning of the key term *parivarta*—which means "exposition" or "discourse" as well as "chapter"—below. For the moment, however, it is sufficient to point out that the *Aṣṭa*'s clear admission that its words are those of Subhūti and not of the Buddha reveals another possible trajectory that the "sūtrafication" process can take: when a given discourse is widely known as the speech of a particular individual, the identity of the original speaker may be maintained, but he can be described as acting under the authorization of the Buddha. The nature of this authorization can, of course, be described in a variety of ways: from the modest claim that because the Buddha's disciples have trained themselves in his teaching (*dharmadeśana*) their own words are authoritative, as asserted by the *Aṣṭa* in its opening chapter (I.4), to the much stronger claims that a given discourse is based on a vision of the Buddha, on a meditative experience, or on a dream. On dreams and visionary experiences as one of the sources of Mahāyāna sūtras see Fronsdal 1998, Chapter 6.

[4] This may be less true of Mahāyāna sūtras than of other Buddhist texts. The fact that many Mahāyāna scriptures encourage their devotees to copy out the text in written form is of course well known. Recently, however, Richard Gombrich has contended that writing is fundamental to the origins of Mahāyāna Buddhism itself: "the rise of the Mahāyana," he contends, "is due to the use of writing" (1990, p. 21). More specifically, Gombrich argues that in a Buddhist community with an exclusively oral canon "any text which is critical of the current teachings or something which is palpably new has no chances of survival" (pp. 26-27)—that is, it would have no chance of being accepted into

oral texts may originally have made no claim to the status of "scripture" (or in the present case, of "sūtra") at all.

For the *Ugra*, it is true, we have no direct evidence of such a process. In the earliest form in which we have it—a Chinese translation dating from the late 2nd century CE—the *Ugra* is already cast in the form of a sūtra, with the Buddha pronouncing virtually the whole of the text. But it is vital that we not treat this earliest extant version as the "original." If we can even hypothesize an "original," it would have been that occasion on which some portion of the words that were to become what we know as the *Ugra* were first verbalized, in all probability in oral rather than written fashion. To this "original" we will never, of course, have direct access. In the four extant versions of the text we have only, as it were, four time-lapse photographs of the sūtra at successive stages of its growth. But even the first of these photographs almost certainly dates from a time well after the initial composition of the text.

Useful as this visual analogy may be, it must be used with caution, for it implies that the evolution of the *Ugra* can be described in linear terms, as changes in the shape of a single entity over time.

---

the canon recited and transmitted by the monastic Sangha. Gombrich's point is provocative and is certainly worthy of consideration, but he is probably being too literalistic in assuming that normative statements concerning how previously unknown sūtras *should* be tested for authenticity constitute evidence that such measures always *were* applied in practice. Even more problematic is the fact that Gombrich's analysis is based on the assumption that only texts considered "canonical" would have been remembered and transmitted within the monastic community. On the contrary, there is every reason to believe that Indian Buddhists had access to a wide range of oral sayings, located at various points along a continuum ranging from texts already accepted as canonical, to popular discourses by a particularly articulate monk or nun, to offhand explanations and useful analogies, to uninspiring sermons that were forgotten almost as soon as they were uttered. It could even be argued that popular discourses *not* attributed to the Buddha but widely acclaimed by the community as valuable and "well-spoken"—*sūkta*, in Pāli and other Prakrits *sutta*, a word which may have been wrongly Sanskritized as "sūtra" (see Walleser 1914, p. 4, n. 1, and Norman 1997, p. 104)—would have met with little resistance from the authorities, and thus would have encountered no significant obstacles to their preservation. More important as a survival mechanism than being set down in writing, in other words, might be a text's very lack of the claim to be *buddha-vacana*. Such popular discourses could subsequently, of course, be upgraded to canonical status, undergoing processes of transformation such as those described in the previous note.

But this is certainly not the case. A single sūtra could be transmitted orally to a number of different people, each of whom might then become the source of his or her own branch of the textual tradition. Subsequently one or more (but not all) of these oral versions of the text might find their way into written form, at which point the possibilities for diffusion—and for new kinds of errors, emendations, and elaborations—would increase still further. Thus the lineage of any single Buddhist sūtra in India might better be described as an immensely complicated family tree, of which photographs of only a few of the ancestors (not all of them belonging to the same branch of the family) have survived.

In the case of the *Ugra*, however, no photograph of *any* Indian ancestor—that is, no complete Sanskrit or Prakrit version of the text—has come down to us. What we have instead are translations based on four different Indian recensions, three of them extant in Chinese and one in Tibetan. Pushing our analogy to its limits, these might be described as four paintings based on four now-lost ancestral photographs, produced by artists of varying levels of expertise using photographs in varying states of preservation. All of this is simply to emphasize an obvious—but often forgotten—fact: that while the vast library of scriptures preserved in Chinese and Tibetan offers an unparalleled resource for the study of Indian Buddhism, they must be used with extreme care, above all with the realization that the Indian texts themselves existed in many different recensions and that much can happen (whether addition, subtraction, modification, or simple incomprehension) in the course of the translation process itself.

In addition to these four surviving translations, the specifics of which will be discussed below, we have a substantial number of citations from what many writers refer to as the "original"—that is, from a Sanskrit version of the text. These citations are contained in a work by Śāntideva, the *Śikṣāsamuccaya*, composed in India during the 8th century CE and preserved in a Nepalese manuscript that has been dated to the 14th-16th century. The inappropriateness of calling these excerpts the Sanskrit "original," however, should be obvious: Śāntideva's citations from the *Ugra* reflect a version of the sūtra that was circulating in India more than half a millennium after its earliest translation into Chinese, and the manuscript copy in which Śāntideva's work has come down to us dates from several centuries after the latest (i.e., the Tibetan) translation of the text. Far earlier, in fact—and considerably more extensive—are the citations preserved in the Chinese text whose Sanskrit title is reconstructed as the

**Daśabhūmikavibhāṣā*, into which a substantial portion of the *Ugra* has been incorporated.[5]

There are, then, a number of pitfalls awaiting the scholar who attempts to make use of sūtra texts to reconstruct the history of Indian Buddhism: first, the facile assumption that what is now presented to us as a canonical sūtra must have originated as a member of that genre; second, treating the multiple extant versions of a given text as if they stood in a direct linear relationship to one another; third, the assumption that the Indian texts that reached China and Tibet (whether in oral or written form) were in sufficiently good condition, and were sufficiently well understood by their translators, to allow us to take these Chinese and Tibetan translations as providing an exact reflection of the content of the underlying Indian version; and finally, the privileging of a late Sanskrit manuscript or citation of a text as representing the "original" by virtue of its language alone. Bearing these brief cautionary notes in mind, we may now proceed to a discussion of our sources: the extant translations of, and citations from, our text.

Versions of the Sūtra

Though no Indian-language text of the *Ugra* has survived, the sūtra has been preserved in four complete translations: three into Chinese (out of a total of six that once existed according to traditional Chinese catalogues[6]) and one into Tibetan. They are listed here with the abbreviations that will be used in the discussion that follows.

---

[5] For further discussion of the *Daśabhūmikavibhāṣā* and the *Śikṣāsamuccaya* see below, pp. 18-20. A small number of citations have also been preserved in two other texts: the *Bodhimārgadīpapañjikā* of Atīśa (11th c.), which quotes two passages from the *Ugra* via their citations in the *Śikṣāsamuccaya* (see Eimer 1978, p. 187); and the *Sūtrasamuccaya* attributed to Nāgārjuna (but certainly not his), which contains one quotation from the sūtra (see Pāsādika 1989, pp. 51-52 [Tibetan text] and p. 218 [Chinese text]).

[6] The *K'ai-yüan shih-chiao lu* 開元釋教錄, a catalogue of translations of Buddhist texts compiled in 730 CE, mentions versions of the *Ugra* by Chih Ch'ien 支謙 (222-228 CE), Po Fa-tsu 白法祖(290-306), and Dharmamitra 曇摩密多 (424-452), in addition to the three extant versions discussed below. See T 2154, 55.627a.

AY *Fa-ching ching* 法鏡經"Dharma-Mirror Sūtra," translated by the Parthian layman An Hsüan 安玄 and the Chinese *śramaṇa* Yen Fo-t'iao 嚴佛調 during the period 180-190 CE (T 322, 12.15a-23a).

Dh *Yü-ch'ieh chia-lo-yüeh*[7] *wen p'u-sa hsing ching* 郁伽迦羅越問菩薩行經 "The Sūtra on the Inquiry of Ugra the *Gṛhapati*[8] Concerning Bodhisattva-Conduct," translated by Chu Fa-hu 竺法護 (Dharmarakṣa), a Yüeh-chih monk from Tun-huang, in the late 3rd or early 4th century CE (T 323, 12.23a-30c).

R *Yü-ch'ieh chang-che hui* 郁伽長者會 "The Section [of the *Ratnakūṭa-sūtra*] on Ugra the *Gṛhapati*," attributed to the Sogdian translator K'ang Seng-k'ai 康僧鎧 (fl. 249-253 CE) but exhibiting translation terminology that is more likely to date from the early 5th century CE or after (T 310[19], 11.472b-480b). On these grounds Hirakawa and others have claimed that this is the lost translation of Dharmamitra 曇摩密多, a translator active in the first half of the fifth century who is credited in some Chinese catalogues with having produced a version of the *Ugra*.[9] While it is possible that this is the case, the identification of this work as that of Dharmamitra cannot be regarded as fully established.[10] Therefore I will simply refer to this translation as the "Ratnakūṭa version," with the understanding that it cannot be the work of K'ang Seng-k'ai.

---

[7] Reading with the variant given in n. 4 to the Taishō edition (12.23a). Since Ugra's name is transliterated within the text itself as *Yü-chia* 郁迦, it may well be that the original reading was *Yü-chia chia-luo-yüeh* 郁迦迦羅越, with the first *chia* then dropped due to its perceived redundancy and the character *ch'ieh* 伽 (also pronounced *chia*) subsequently added to "correct" this omission.

[8] For a discussion of the term *gṛhapati* see below, pp. 22-24.

[9] See Hirakawa 1957b, pp. 160-161.

[10] Though Dharmamitra was active in the early 400s, the first catalogue to credit him with a translation of the *Ugra* is the *Li-tai san-pao chi* 歷代三寶記 (T 2034, 49.92b), which was compiled in 597 CE and lists ten sūtras as his translations. In the *Ch'u san-tsang chi-chi* 出三藏記集, however—which is far more reliable and was completed c. 515 CE—Dharmamitra is credited with only four translations, and the *Ugra* is not one of them (see T 2145, 55 12b-c).

Tib *'Phags-pa Drag-shul-can-gyis zhus-pa zhes-bya-ba'i theg-pa chen-po'i mdo*[11] "The Noble Mahāyāna Sūtra titled *The Inquiry of Ugra*" (Peking 760[19], Derge 63, Narthang 51, Stog Palace 11[19]), translated by Surendrabodhi and Zhang[12] Ye-shes-sde during the late 8th or early 9th century CE.

There is also a translation into Mongolian, produced by Kun-dga' 'od-zer mañjuśrī paṇḍita and Kunga darqan erdeni tai guosi in the early 17th century (Ligeti 811, vol. 52, pp. 333a-373a), titled *Qutuγ-tu Doγšin küčütü-yin öčigsen neretü yeke kölgen sudur*, "The Noble Mahāyāna Sūtra titled *The Inquiry of Ugra*."[13] Since—as is the case with virtually all Mongolian Kanjur texts—this is simply a verbatim translation from the Tibetan, the Mongolian does not represent a distinctive recension and thus has only occasionally been consulted here.

In addition to these complete translations of the sūtra, extensive citations from the *Ugra* are also contained in two other works, one extant only in Chinese and the other surviving in Sanskrit (as well as in Chinese and Tibetan translations).

Dbhv. The **Daśabhūmikavibhāṣā*, Ch. *Shih-chu p'i-p'o-sha lun* 十住毘婆沙論 (T 1521, 26.20a-122c), attributed to Nāgārjuna[14] and translated into Chinese by Kumārajīva

[11] For variants in the Tibetan title see below, pp. 27-31.

[12] The official title *Zhang*, which appears in the colophons to the Stog Palace and Narthang editions, has been replaced by the solely religious title *ban-de* "paṇḍita" in the Peking and Derge editions.

[13] Or rather, "The Inquiry of Ferocious-and-Powerful" (*Doγšin küčütü*). Though Ugra's name is translated in this way in the title of the sūtra, within the body of the text it is simply transliterated in Mongolian script as *Ugra*. This discrepancy suggests that the text has undergone some editorial emendation in the course of its transmission.

[14] There is good reason to be suspicious of this attribution. Near the beginning of the text, for example, in reply to a question about whether even those who have just experienced the arising of the spirit of enlightenment (*bodhicitta*) should be called "bodhisattvas," the author answers in the affirmative and then offers the following example: "It is like the case of a *bhikṣu* who, though he has not yet attained enlightenment (*wei te tao* 未得道), is still called a monk (*tao-jen* 道人)" (26.21a6-7). This explanation, however, makes sense only in Chinese, where *tao-jen* "person of the Way" served as one of

during the period 402-412 CE. Large segments of the *Ugra* have been incorporated into Chapters 14-17 and 32 of this compendium. In contrast to the more famous case of the *Ta chih-tu lun* 大智度論 (T 1509)—where the virtually word-for-word correspondence between the text of the sūtra being commented upon (the *Perfection of Wisdom in Twenty-Five Thousand Lines*) and the Chinese translation of that same text by Kumārajīva (T 223) has aroused suspicions that the commentary might be the work not of the purported author Nāgārjuna, but of Kumārajīva himself—in the present case there are only the most tangential correspondences in wording between the passages of the *Ugra* as cited by the commentator and their counterparts in any of the three extant Chinese translations. There is no evidence, in other words, that Kumārajīva consulted any of these three texts (the third of which may not yet have been completed during his lifetime) in the course of his translation of this commentary.[15]

Śikṣ. Śāntideva's *Śikṣāsamuccaya*, composed in the eighth century CE and preserved in Sanskrit in a Nepalese manuscript dating from the 14th-16th century. The text was translated into Tibetan (Pek. 5336) in the late 8th or early 9th century by Jinamitra, Dānaśīla, and Ye-shes-sde, and into Chinese (T 1636, 32.75b-145a) during the period 1058-1072 CE by Jih-ch'eng 日稱 and Fa-hu 法護 (*Dharmapāla). The citations found here, though much more limited in extent than those contained in the *Shih-chu p'i-p'o-sha lun*, are of particular interest since they provide (despite their late date) our only direct access to an Indic-language version of the text. They also offer clear evidence of the popularity of the sūtra in at least some circles in India several centuries after its

---

several expressions for "Buddhist monk," and *te tao* "attain the Way" was one of several equivalents for "to attain enlightenment." It cannot possibly be, in other words, a translation from the Sanskrit. At the very least, therefore, we must assume that the **Daśabhūmikavibhāṣā* as we have it includes explanatory interpolations added in China. For further discussion see Hirakawa 1957a.

[15] It is possible, of course, that he did have access to one or more of the Chinese translations that have not survived (see above, n. 6).

> composition, for this is one of the scriptures most frequently quoted by Śāntideva in his *Śikṣāsamuccaya.*

These versions of the *Ugra* have received varying degrees of scholarly attention to date. No published translation of the version of An Hsüan and Yen Fo-t'iao or of Dharmarakṣa exists in any language, though preliminary English translations of both formed part of a dissertation by Nancy Schuster (1976). The Chinese version of the text that has been most widely used in East Asia is that found in the *Ratnakūṭa* section of the canon; thus it is only this version, of the three extant Chinese translations, that was selected for inclusion in the *Kokuyaku issaikyō* in a semivernacular Japanese translation (Nagai 1932). An English translation of R was also included by Schuster in her dissertation. Another English translation (presumably of R) was prepared by the group of Taiwanese translators responsible for Garma C. C. Chang's *A Treasury of Mahāyāna Sūtras* (1983) but was not included in the published version.[16] For the Tibetan the sole modern-language version is a Japanese translation by SAKURABE Hajime (1974). No translation of the Mongolian version, to the best of my knowledge, has been attempted.

For citations from the *Ugra* in other texts, an annotated Japanese translation of the *Shih-chu p'i-p'o-sha lun* (**Daśabhūmikavibhāṣā*) by URYŪZU Ryūshin (1994-1995) is now available. For the *Śikṣāsamuccaya* we have a complete Sanskrit edition published by Cecil Bendall a century ago (Bendall 1897-1902), together with an English translation begun by Bendall himself and completed by W. H. D. Rouse after Bendall's death (Bendall and Rouse 1922).[17] The citations from the *Ugra* contained in the Sanskrit *Śikṣāsamuccaya* are also given in transliteration in MOCHIZUKI Ryōkō's study of the Mahāyāna *Mahāparinirvāṇa-sūtra* (Mochizuki 1988).[18]

---

[16] According to the editor's introduction (p. ix) a translation of the entire *Ratnakūṭa* section of the Chinese canon was completed by 1976, but only a portion of these texts could be included in the published text. Even those that were included are generally abridged versions (though the editor has kindly indicated where text is missing by the presence of ellipses). An interesting study could be done of which texts (and which passages) were and were not included; no doubt these choices reflect much that is of interest in contemporary Taiwanese Buddhism.

[17] This translation is now quite dated and is greatly in need of revision.

[18] For the Sanskrit citations see pp. 247-310. Mochizuki's study includes also a transliteration of the corresponding passages of the *Śikṣāsamuccaya* in

In addition to these extant works, Chinese catalogues report that in the 3rd century CE a commentary on the sūtra was composed by K'ang Seng-hui 康僧會. Unfortunately the commentary itself has not been preserved; the preface to the text, however, is extant.[19]

The Name "Ugradatta"

Readers familiar with the *Ugra* only through Śāntideva's citations may be wondering why its main character has been referred to in this discussion exclusively as "Ugra" and not as "Ugradatta," the name by which the scripture is arguably better known in both Japan and the West. In the extant Sanskrit version of the *Śikṣāsamuccaya* the text is referred to on nine occasions as the *Ugradattaparipṛcchā*[20] and another thirteen times as the *Ugraparipṛcchā*.[21] There is no discernible pattern to these variations: all but one of Śāntideva's citations correspond to passages found in extant versions of the sūtra,[22] and the variant titles occur in seemingly random sequence within the *Śikṣāsamuccaya* itself. All we can say, therefore, is that in the Sanskrit *Śikṣāsamuccaya* there is an unexplained fluctuation in the form of the title.

Within the body of the sūtra itself, however—that is, within the translations preserved in both Chinese and Tibetan—there is not a trace of anything that can be associated with the longer name "Ugradatta." In AY the name of the main character is translated by the single character *Shen* 甚, literally "very, extremely"—a seemingly odd choice, but surely an attempt to convey the meaning of Ugra's Sanskrit name ("terrible, ferocious"). In both Dh and R the name Ugra is transliterated rather than translated (as *Yü-chia* 郁迦 and *Yü-ch'ieh*

Tibetan (based on the Peking and Derge editions), a Japanese translation of the Sanskrit and Tibetan passages, and the parallel passages from the three Chinese translations of the *Ugra* (R, Dh, and AY).

[19] See T 12.15a and 55.46b-c.

[20] See Bendall 1897-1902, 18.18-19.1, 37.7, 78.7, 180.1, 180.14, 193.3, 196.7, 198.1, and 290.1.

[21] See Bendall 1897-1902, 11.2, 120.3, 131.10, 136.1, 144.1, 144.5, 145.10, 146.5, 147.20, 192.11-12, 267.12, 271.9, and 315.14.

[22] The sole exception is a citation of the *Ugraparipṛcchā* at 144.1, which does not parallel material in any extant version of the sūtra. For other sūtra citations in Śāntideva's work that have no parallels in the extant versions cf. Pagel 1995, pp. 23-24, n. 68.

郁伽, respectively), while in the Tibetan version Ugra is translated as *Drag-shul-can* "ferocious" or "possessing ferocity," just as prescribed by the *Mahāvyutpatti*.[23] In short, all extant versions of the sūtra are unanimous in supporting the reading of the name as simply "Ugra." The name "Ugradatta" thus appears to represent only a late (and apparently quite peripheral) Indian development.[24]

The Epithet *Gṛhapati*

If the name "Ugradatta" thus turns out to be an unimportant element in the nomenclature of our text, things are certainly otherwise with the term *gṛhapati* (literally "house-lord"). This term—which I have thus far left untranslated—is ubiquitous in our text, used both as an epithet to describe Ugra and his dozen or so male companions and as a term of address when Ugra is spoken to directly. In two of the three Chinese translations of the sūtra the word *gṛhapati* (translated as *chang-che* 長者 or transliterated as *chia-lo-yüeh* 迦羅越)[25] even

---

[23] See *Mvy*. no. 2949. The name of the sūtra itself is also given in a separate entry as Skt. *Ugra-paripṛcchā* = Tib. *Drag-shul-can-gyis zhus-pa* (no. 1396).

[24] Interestingly, there is evidence that the form "Ugradatta" made a relatively late appearance even within the *Śikṣāsamuccaya* itself. In the Tibetan translation of this compendium this longer form of the name appears only once (Tib. *Drag-shul-can-gyis byin-pa* [Peking 80b7, Derge 69a2], cited in Mochizuki 1988, p. 271). Curiously, at this point the extant Sanskrit text reads *Ugraparipṛcchā*, not *Ugradatta-paripṛcchā*.

[25] It should be pointed out that the strange equation of Ch. *chia-lo-yüeh* with Skt. *kulapati* given in Soothill and Hodous 1937 (316a) and widely repeated in Western secondary literature (e.g., Coblin 1983, p. 241, no. 15; Schuster 1985, p. 29) is erroneous. This is even on the surface a phonetically unsatisfying equivalent, since the term in question would have been pronounced something like **kɾa-la-wuat* in Early Middle Chinese (see Pulleyblank 1991, pp. 143, 203, and 388; Coblin [*loc. cit.*] reconstructs a pronunciation of *kra-la-ɣjwat*). In any event, the equation of *chia-lo-yüeh* with *gṛhapati* is easily documented. The term appears occasionally in Mokṣala's late 3rd century translation of the *Pañcaviṁśati-sāhasrikā-prajñāpāramitā-sūtra* (T 221, e.g., 8.3b28-29 and 10c14-15), where it can be shown by a comparison with the extant Sanskrit text to be the equivalent of *gṛhapati* (Dutt 1934, 25.6 and 94.16). It also appears at least once (12.27b17) in Dharmarakṣa's translation of the *Ugra*, again in a context where it can be established with certainty (this time via a comparison with the Tibetan) that the underlying Indian term was

appears in the title, a fact which—as we shall see— is of considerable importance for reconstructing the history of the text.

The term *gṛhapati* itself would seem at first glance to be entirely unproblematic, for it is one of the few Buddhist technical terms about which there is considerable consensus among English-language translators. Whether working from Sanskrit *gṛhapati* or its Pāli counterpart *gahapati*, such translators have almost universally rendered this expression as "householder." Not surprisingly, this has created the impression that the epithet *gṛhapati* refers, above all, to the lay (i.e., nonmonastic) status of the person in question.

Yet a review of the literature in which this epithet occurs makes it abundantly clear that this is not the case. First of all, the term is applied exclusively to those of considerable financial means; Edgerton (BHSD 214b) even suggests the translation "capitalist." Second, in a number of instances in both the Pāli canon and in the bodhisattva sūtra literature the term appears in a list of caste names, either in a threefold list of which the first two members are *kṣatriya* and *brāhmaṇa* (in that order) or in a twofold list where the first element is *brāhmaṇa*.[26] Third, as the Pali Text Society's dictionary points out, the occupation most often associated with the *gahapati* is that of merchant or guild leader (Pāli *seṭṭhi*, Skt. *śreṣṭhin*; see PTSD 248a-b). Indeed, so closely linked are these two terms that a single Chinese expression, *chang-che* 長者 "elder, eminent man, person of substance" is used as the regular equivalent of both.[27] Fourth, it is

---

gṛhapati. Though the equivalence with Skt. *gṛhapati* is thus assured, the pronunciation of the Chinese transliteration suggests that it was actually based on a Prakrit form such as **gharapati* or even **gharavati* rather than directly on the Sanskrit. For the form *ghara* "house" (though not the compound expression) in Buddhist Hybrid Sanskrit see BHSD 220a, and cf. Pischel 1955, §365; for examples of the term *grahavati* in Kharoṣṭhī-script Prakrit inscriptions see Kino 1957. (I am grateful to Daniel Boucher for bringing Kino's work to my attention.)

[26] For an illuminating discussion of several such instances see Fick 1920, especially Chapter 9. Particularly noteworthy are the many instances in which it is said that a bodhisattva, after reaching a certain stage of advancement or performing a particularly good deed, will henceforth be born either among the gods or in great *kṣatriya*, *brāhmaṇa*, or *gṛhapati* families (see for example the Sanskrit *Pañcaviṁśatisāhasrikā-prajñāpāramitā-sūtra* [Dutt 1934], pp. 25.5-7, 64.9-11, 80.8-9, 94.15-16, and *passim*).

[27] For a discussion of this expression with numerous examples see May 1967.

useful to recall that the *gṛhapati* is one of the seven jewels of the *cakravartin*, in which context the term appears to mean "treasurer" or "financial advisor." Fifth, at least in the bodhisattva sūtras I have examined, the word is applied exclusively to adult males; one can be the "son of a *gṛhapati*" or the "wife of a *gṛhapati*," but the term is not applied to these dependents directly.[28] Thus it would seem that *gṛhapati* implies not only the social status acquired at birth (which would be shared by the members of one's family), but a certain degree of personal occupational stature as well. At a minimum, then, it seems necessary to conclude that this term as used here and in other early bodhisattva sūtras indicates not merely a generic lay person, but someone who is a "man of substance" or "leading citizen," though not a member of the *kṣatriya* or *brāhmaṇa* caste.[29]

In addition to his distinguished social and financial status Ugra is, of course, a householder as well. But this status is expressed in our text by other terms. Foremost among these is Skt. *gṛhin* (lit. "houseman," translated into Tibetan as *khyim-pa* and into Chinese as *tsai-chia* 在家 and *chü-chia* 居家). Not only in our text, but in every Indian text I have consulted thus far, it is this term or its equivalent[30]—and never the word *gṛhapati*—that serves as the opposite of *pravrajita* (lit. "gone forth"; Tib. *rab-tu byung-ba*, Ch. *ch'u-chia* 出家, *ch'ü-chia* 去家, etc.), i.e., of the renunciant or monastic way of life. The word *gṛhapati* is thus not an indicator of simple householder status but rather of significant social and financial standing, and it would have been applied only to a relatively limited segment of the lay Buddhist population.

---

[28] In Pāli sources this restriction does not seem to hold, as there are a number of occurrences of the feminine form of the term (*gahapatānī*), e.g., in *Aṅguttaranikāya* II, 57 and III, 295. The PTSD editors note, however, that the feminine form never occurs without being paired with its masculine counterpart (248a).

[29] For a rich discussion of the varied meanings of *gṛhapati* and other status terms in Indian Buddhist texts see Chakravarti 1987, especially pp. 65-93. Part of what has made the meaning of the term *gṛhapati* so elusive to readers less careful than Fick and Chakravarti, I suspect, is the fact that it is a hybrid term, referring both to a caste status immediately below that of the *kṣatriya* and *brāhmaṇa* levels (and thus forming a part of what would later be classified as the *vaiśya* caste) and to the achieved social and financial prominence of the individual in question.

[30] Other expressions sometimes used in this sense are *gṛhavāsa* and *gṛhastha*, both meaning "home-dweller."

There is of course another expression used in reference to lay Buddhists (and one that does not, interestingly, occur in our text): the term *upāsaka* (fem. *upāsikā*), which is now increasingly recognized to be not a generic term for supporters of the Buddhist community who happen not to be monks or nuns, but a very precise category designating those lay adherents who have taken on specific vows.[31] The word *upāsaka/-ikā* is thus best understood as a term applied to dedicated members of a "lay auxiliary" of the monastic community,[32] and not to the broader group of all those favorably inclined toward Buddhism who have not left the household life. The fact that the etymology of the term suggests "those who serve"—i.e., who assist and attend the full-time renunciants who comprise the *bhikṣu-* and *bhikṣuṇī-saṁgha*—should also serve as a reminder that these dedicated lay Buddhists did not constitute a free-standing community, but were rather adjunct members of particular monastic organizations.

Ugra as Literary Character: Precedents in Earlier Texts

The sūtra known as *The Inquiry of Ugra* is not the only Buddhist text in which a character named Ugra makes an appearance. On the contrary, there are numerous other texts—preserved in Pāli as well as in Chinese and Tibetan—in which a character named Ugra (Pāli *Ugga*) is either mentioned in passing or plays a major role. A number of such figures appear in Pāli sources, though they belong to different

---

[31] This point was made several decades ago; see La Vallée Poussin 1925 and 1927.

[32] It is surely in this context that the standard reference to "white-robed (*avadāta-vassana*) lay people" is to be understood, since the wearing of white clothing in India has often signified (in both ancient and modern times) a degree of renunciation midway between that of the householder who indulges freely in all the pleasures of the senses and the *saṁnyāsin* who has left all worldly ties behind. Thus we find white clothing viewed both as the proper dress for widows and as the appropriate attire of lay people who are taking on special obligations during a period of religious observance. White garments are also worn by those who are renunciants but are less than fully ordained, a practice that is continued today by some Theravāda communities in Southeast Asia. Even in the Jain tradition, where white robes are worn by the full-time renunciants of the Śvetambara school, such clothing can still be viewed as a compromise category between the ordinary dress of the layman and the nakedness of the strict Digambara ascetics.

eras (some living in the time of various Buddhas of the past, others appearing as contemporaries of Śākyamuni) and inhabit different towns; all are described as wealthy and influential men, and most are given the title *gṛhapati*. In one case we clearly have two variants of a single story: Ugga of Hatthigāmaka (*Aṅguttaranikāya* 4.212-216) and Ugga of Vesāli (4.208-212) are both described as possessing "eight wonderful and marvelous qualities."

The fact that the Ugra portrayed in these stories is not only an outstanding layman but a *gṛhapati* as well has led a number of scholars to conclude that *The Inquiry of Ugra* is actually based on one or more of these earlier texts. Mochizuki (1988, p. 223) describes this earlier literature as the "prototype" of our sūtra, and asserts that *The Inquiry of Ugra* "is a Mahāyānized version of the *Ugragṛhapati-sūtra* of the *Madhyamāgama*."[33] Schuster (1985, pp. 50-51) claims that *The Inquiry of Ugra* is "borrowing directly from a body of earlier literature on Ugra the householder" but that the particular versions of the tale used by our Mahāyāna authors have been lost. Hirakawa (1990b, p. 108) is somewhat more cautious, suggesting only that our sūtra presents its main character "in the guise of the *gṛhapati* [Jpn. *chōja* 長者] made famous in the Āgama sūtras."

It is true that all of these Ugras are portrayed—like the character in our text—as outstanding Buddhist laymen, but it is not at all clear that any of these Āgama or Nikāya texts can be described as a genuine "prototype" of *The Inquiry of Ugra*. Those who would argue for this scenario must contend with one particularly recalcitrant fact: not a single line of any of these earlier canonical sūtras has an exact parallel in our text. If these texts had any influence at all on the formation of our sūtra, it must certainly have been in the form of a catalyst rather than as a direct textual prototype.

The Title of the Sūtra

Of all the elements of Buddhist sūtra literature in India, only the opening formulas of homage are more fluid than titles. It is not clear just when such formulas came to be considered a standard part of the Mahāyāna sūtra genre,[34] but the fact that no such salutations appear

---

33 Mochizuki's reference is to T 26, 1.479c-481b.

34 Such formulas do occur with some frequency in the Sanskrit manuscripts from Gilgit (c. 5th-6th century CE), but their content often diverges from the

in Chinese sūtra translations suggests (though it certainly does not prove) that these formulas were not, at the time when Buddhist scriptures first began to be translated into Chinese, considered a necessary part of the sūtra itself.[35] Even after such formulas came to be considered standard, they exhibited tremendous volatility in content, even within the manuscript copies and translations of a single text.[36]

Since no Sanskrit or Prakrit manuscript of the *Ugra* has come down to us, we do not know what forms its opening salutation may have taken in India. But its translations are quite typical: while none of the Chinese versions has any opening salutation, the Tibetan carries a standard one (found in perhaps the majority of sūtras in the Kanjur) reading "Homage to all the Buddhas and bodhisattvas" (*sangs-rgyas dang byang-chub sems-dpa' thams-cad-la phyag 'tshal-lo*). The Mongolian, as a translation from the Tibetan, follows suit, but adds

---

formulas given in the translations of the same texts in the Tibetan Kanjur (Gregory Schopen, personal communication, 1996).

[35] The fact that Chinese sūtra translations (the majority of which were translated before 700 CE) never contain such an opening formula, while their Tibetan counterparts (most of which were translated after that date) virtually always do, raises the question of whether the practice of placing such salutations at the beginning was a relatively late development in the formation of the Mahāyāna sūtra genre in India.

[36] A single example will suffice to illustrate the degree of this fluctuation, though many more could be adduced. In the Sanskrit manuscript of the (longer) *Heart Sūtra* edited by F. Max Müller (1881), the opening salutation reads *oṁ namaḥ sarvajñāya*, "Oṁ! Homage to omniscience." Later Sanskrit manuscripts of the same sūtra from Nepal, however, open with a completely different salutation: Conze's text Na reads *oṁ namo āryaprajñāpāramitāyai*, "Oṁ! Homage to the noble perfection of wisdom," while versions Nb, Nc, Ne, Ni, and Nm as well as Ce (the Sanskrit portion of a polyglot edition from China, c. 17th century) add the word *bhagavatyai* "to the Blessed One (f.)" after *ārya* (see (Conze 1967b, p. 149, n. 1). The Tibetan translation of the sūtra found in the Tantra section of some (but not all) editions of the Kanjur follows the latter, but lacks any equivalent of the word *ārya* (Tib. *bcom-ldan-'das-ma-la phyag 'tshal-lo*). The translation contained in the Prajñāpāramitā section (in all Kanjur editions), by contrast, opens with the more generic formula found at the beginning of dozens (if not hundreds) of other sūtras, including the *Ugra*: "Homage to all the Buddhas and bodhisattvas" (*sangs-rgyas dang byang-chub sems-dpa' thams-cad-la phyag 'tshal-lo*; for the Tibetan versions see Silk 1994a). In contrast to the great variety exhibited by these Sanskrit and Tibetan texts, no Chinese version of the sūtra contains any opening salutation at all.

before the Sanskrit, Tibetan, and Mongolian titles an additional formula of homage that is part of the distinctive Mongolian Kanjur tradition.[37]

As to the titles themselves, Buddhist sūtras (especially those texts that would come to be identified as "Mahāyānist") appear to have circulated in India under a variety of names, a fact that has sometimes posed obstacles to modern scholars in their identification.[38] Even within the texts themselves we have evidence of this practice. In the closing lines of many sūtras, Ānanda (or another member of the audience) asks the Buddha under what name the sermon just preached should be remembered. In most cases the Buddha replies with not one title but several alternatives. The *Ugra* itself contains such a passage: toward the end of the sūtra Ānanda asks about the name of the text and is given three quite different titles in reply.[39] One of these, "The Inquiry of Ugra,"[40] corresponds to the name by which the sūtra is most widely known.

The earliest extant version of the *Ugra* (AY) provides us with an excellent example of the malleability of sūtra titles, for it is labeled "The Dharma-Mirror Sūtra" (Ch. *Fa-ching ching* 法鏡經)—a name which is totally unique, reflects nothing of the content of the text, and in all probability originated in China.[41] Among the remaining versions of the text, however, we find relatively close agreement. The Tibetan is titled "The Noble Mahāyāna Sūtra called *The Inquiry of*

---

[37] See Nattier 1994.

[38] A classic example is the text now generally known as the *Kāśyapa-parivarta*, which is cited in Indian sources as the *Ratnakūṭa-sūtra* (see Pedersen 1980, p. 62) but is known by a variety of other titles in Chinese (see T. Nos. 310[43] and 350, 351, 352).

[39] See §33A of the translation. This exchange is found in all four extant versions of the text, with slight variants in the form of the titles.

[40] So Tib and AY; Dh and R read "The Inquiry of Ugra the *Gṛhapati*."

[41] It is not unusual for Chinese translations of Buddhist sūtras to have titles that bear no resemblance to those of their Sanskrit or Tibetan counterparts. In the present case, the image of the mirror—a much-used metaphor in Chinese religious and philosophical writings, yet rarely referred to in Indian Buddhist works—suggests that the title of AY was coined with a Chinese audience in mind. (It is particularly noteworthy that the title *Fa-ching ching* is not one of those suggested to Ānanda by the Buddha in the closing lines of the sūtra in AY's version.) See however Wayman 1974 and 1985 for the use of mirror imagery in Indian texts, and in particular the reference to the "Mirror of Dhamma" in the Pāli *Mahāparinibbāna-sutta* (16.2.8ff.). I would like to thank Gregory Schopen and Paul Harrison for calling these references to my attention.

Ugra,"[42] while Dharmarakṣa has "The Sūtra on the Inquiry of Ugra the *Gṛhapati* concerning Bodhisattva Conduct." Finally, in the Chinese *Ratnakūṭa* version of the text, where the forty-nine sūtras assigned to this category are classified as individual collections or sections within the *Ratnakūṭa* as a whole, our text is called "The Section (*hui* 會) on Ugra the *Gṛhapati*."

The slightly longer title found in Dh was probably coined in China, for it has no analogue elsewhere, and indeed the addition of extra words for clarification is one of the hallmarks of Dharmarakṣa's translation style.[43] One element in his title, however, offers unexpected clues to the history of the text. The epithet *gṛhapati*, which is present in the titles of both Dh and R, is unknown among Tibetan editions of the *Ugra* until it makes a sudden (and quite visible) appearance in the version of the Peking edition contained in the Ōtani reprint edition: here the term *gṛhapati* has been added to the transliterated Sanskrit title after the initial carving of the woodblock, a correction made quite transparent by the cramped shape of the inserted letters.[44] The fact that this word is an interpolation (and not a "correction" inserted as the result of consulting an actual Sanskrit manuscript) is confirmed by a mistake in the word order: the Tibetan editors have erroneously placed the word *gṛhapati* before Ugra's name, rather than after it where it would belong.[45] The Tibetan translation of the title was emended at the same time, for here the word *khyim-bdag* (the Tibetan equivalent of *gṛhapati*) is inserted—like its Sanskrit counterpart—in letters that are unusually small. In fact, we can be even more specific about when this change took place. The Mongolian version, which generally exhibits readings intermediate between those of the earliest Peking printing ("P1" or K, completed in 1692 CE) and the version that served as the basis of the

---

[42] There are, however, some slight but telling variants in the Tibetan title, as discussed immediately below (pp. 29-31).

[43] See Boucher 1996.

[44] Tibetan Buddhist texts were traditionally printed (when they were not simply copied by hand) using "immovable type": the letters were carved onto woodblocks, each of which contained one page of text (i.e., one folio side). When errors in carving were identified, corrections were made on the block itself, rather than redoing the entire block from scratch. On this technology see von Staël-Holstein 1933 and Eimer 1980.

[45] Word order in Sanskrit is of course rather flexible, but in every instance that I have seen in a Sanskrit or Pāli text this epithet comes after, not before, the personal name.

Ōtani reprint edition ("P3" or Q, completed in 1720) and thus was presumably based on the intermediate Peking printing ("P2"), contains no equivalent of the word *gṛhapati* in either the Sanskrit or the Tibetan title (nor, of course, in the Mongolian). Thus we can infer that these insertions were made no earlier than the time of the third printing of the Peking edition, in other words, around the year 1720.[46] This modification was made, in other words, in a version of the Tibetan canon produced in the Chinese capital, and at the apogee of Manchu control of Tibet.[47]

The presence or absence in the title of a single epithet—and a word which, in any event, occurs frequently within the body of the text—might seem a trivial matter, and indeed it has no bearing whatsoever upon the content of the text. Its importance is on another level altogether: it contains a valuable trace of the influence of Chinese editorial practices on Buddhist scriptural collections in Tibet. On the one hand, there is no evidence that any Indian version of the *Ugra* ever contained the word *gṛhapati* in its title;[48] on the other, there is no Chinese version of the text (with the exception of the anomalous AY) that does *not* contain this epithet. The term *gṛhapati*, in other words, was treated in China as an integral part of the title of the sūtra from the late third century onward. Thus the Chinese texts offer the only known prototype from which the Tibetans, in the early

---

46 For the abbreviations K and Q (and a convenient discussion of the known editions of the Tibetan Kanjur and their relation to one another) see Harrison 1992d. The abbreviations P1, P2, and P3—which indicate that we have a series of printings from a single set of woodblocks, albeit with periodic emendations—are my own. The Ōtani edition (Q or P3) in fact includes materials belonging to more than one vintage; see Imaeda 1977.

47 The significance of the fact that this version of the Tibetan canon was produced in China (from the carving of the first set of woodblocks in 1410 through the production and multiple printings from a second set of blocks from the late 17th century on) is often overlooked by those who wish to minimize the importance of Chinese influence on Tibetan culture. In the Peking edition the mark of Chinese editing is clearly visible, in everything from page numbers (which are given in Chinese as well as Tibetan) to the Chinese "running heads" (in most cases, section titles) in the margins. That in the course of the production of a Tibetan canon under Chinese (or later, Manchu) sponsorship some comparison of the content of individual Tibetan texts with their Chinese counterparts should have been made is not, in retrospect, surprising.

48 The citations contained in Śāntideva's *Śikṣāsamuccaya* (our only Indic-language source in this matter), at any rate, never include this epithet as part of the title.

18th century, could have borrowed this additional element of the title.[49]

But the presence of the term *gṛhapati* in the name of the text in later recensions of the *Ugra* is not our only evidence for Chinese influence on the Tibetan text. On the contrary, the very section of the canon to which the *Ugra* has been assigned—the *Ratnakūṭa* division—is a classification that appears to have originated in China. At this point, therefore, we must consider the significance of the fact that the *Ugra* has been classified as part of the *Ratnakūṭa* literature.

The *Ugra* as a *Ratnakūṭa* Text

In both of the extant canons in which it appears—i.e., the Chinese and the Tibetan[50]—the *Ugra* is classified as a sūtra belonging to the *Ratnakūṭa* class.[51] The antiquity of this categorization, however, is still far from clear. Though something called the "Ratnakūṭa" is quoted in certain Indian Buddhist texts (e.g., the *Mahāyāna-sūtrālaṁkāra* and the *Śikṣāsamuccaya*), in all such instances the citation in question has been shown to be taken from just one of the sūtras now classified as a part of that group, i.e., the *Kāśyapa-parivarta*. Thus there is every reason to think that the name

---

[49] The actual scenario may be even more complicated. The *Ugra* is one of a hundred or so scripture titles listed in the *Mahāvyutpatti* (a Sanskrit-Tibetan dictionary compiled in Tibet during the first half of the 9th century); its Sanskrit title is given as *Ugraparipṛcchā* and the corresponding Tibetan as *Drag-shul-can-gyis zhus-pa* (no. 1396). But the *Ugra* also appears in the earliest known catalogue of Tibetan Kanjur texts, the *Ldan-kar-ma* (compiled in the late 8th or early 9th century); here the title is given as *Khyim-bdag Drag-shul-can-gyis zhus-pa*, "The Inquiry of Ugra the *Gṛhapati*" (see Lalou 1953, p. 320, no. 43). The fact that no extant Tibetan version of the sūtra prior to the P3 (Q) edition replicates this version of the title suggests that—if a Tibetan translation of the sūtra ever carried this title—it was lost at an early date. The *Ldan-kar-ma* itself was clearly compiled with reference to Chinese scriptural catalogues, and it is possible that we are seeing here an emendation made only to the listing in the *Ldan-kar-ma* catalogue and not (at this point) to the translation of the sūtra itself.

[50] It is also so classified in the Mongolian canon, whose limitations as an independent witness, however, are noted above (p. 18).

[51] For the following discussion I have drawn heavily on the very useful materials collected in Pedersen 1980. For more extended discussions see Sakurabe 1930, Nagao 1973, and Pagel 1995, pp. 53-78.

"Ratnakūṭa" was used in India only in reference to this single text, and not as the name of a scriptural collection. Strong corroborating evidence that a *Ratnakūṭa* collection was unknown in India even as late as the 8th century CE is offered by the *Śikṣāsamuccaya*, where a number of texts now classified as belonging to the *Ratnakūṭa* (e.g., the *Akṣayamati-paripṛcchā*, the *Rāṣṭrapāla-paripṛcchā*, the *Sukhāvatīvyūha*, and of course the *Ugra* itself) are cited by their individual titles alone, while quotations from what is now known as the *Kāśyapaparivarta* are labeled "from the *Ratnakūṭa*." The fact that such a well-educated scholar-monk as Śāntideva knew of the *Ratnakūṭa* only as a particular sūtra and not as the title of a collection of texts strongly suggests that no such collection was circulating in India during his time.

In a Tibetan source of approximately the same date the existence of a *Ratnakūṭa* collection is also conspicuous by its absence. As von Staël-Holstein pointed out several decades ago, the *Mahāvyutpatti* (early 9th century) gives the names of several individual texts now classified as parts of the *Ratnakūṭa* section, but gives no indication that its compilers were aware of any collection by that name.[52] The *Ldan-kar-ma*, on the other hand—supposedly a catalogue of Buddhist scriptures translated into Tibetan by the late 8th century, but considered by many to be of a somewhat later date—provides an entire list of the contents of the *Ratnakūṭa-sūtra*. The evidence from our Tibetan sources, in sum, suggests that the notion of a *Ratnakūṭa* "collection" was just beginning to make itself felt in this region by the beginning of the 9th century.[53]

In Chinese sources, on the other hand, references to a *Ratnakūṭa* collection—as opposed to an individual sūtra by that name—begin to appear in the second half of the 7th century, with a report in the biography of Hsüan-tsang that a group of translator-monks had requested that he translate the *Ratnakūṭa*.[54] Hsüan-tsang is said to

---

[52] See von Staël-Holstein 1926, p. xvi. On the *Mahāvyutpatti* itself see above, n. 49.

[53] It is important to note that, of these two sources, the one that does know of a *Ratnakūṭa* collection—the *Ldan-kar-ma*—is the same one that betrays significant Chinese influence. The same pattern may be observable in the treatment of the title of the *Ugra* itself; the *Ldan-kar-ma* registers it in a form resembling the Chinese (i.e., including the epithet *gṛhapati*), while the *Mahāvyutpatti* does not. Cf. above, n. 49.

[54] Supposed references to a *Ratnakūṭa* "collection" in Kumārajīva's translation of the **Daśabhūmikavibhāṣā* (T 1521) have led a number of Japanese

have protested that it was far too long, making it clear that the *Ratnakūṭa* under discussion was not the *Kāśyapaparivarta* alone (which would certainly not have intimidated so prolific a translator) but a considerably larger body of texts.

The actual translation and assembly of the entire *Ratnakūṭa*

---

and western scholars to assert that a group of sūtras known as the *Ratnakūṭa* existed already in India prior to the date of this translation (early 5th century CE). The situation is, however, not so straightforward. In only two instances can the text be construed as indicating that a given sūtra is part of a larger entity called the *Ratnakūṭa*, and one of these is an erroneous attribution. In one case, a citation is attributed to a text called the *Pao-ting ching Chia-yeh p'in* 寶頂經迦葉品 (26.118c13), understood by most scholars as "the Kāśyapa chapter of the *Ratnakūṭa-sūtra*," while the other the citation is said to be found "In the *Ratnakuṭa-sūtra*, Chapter 30, 'Akṣayamati Bodhisattva'" (*Pao-ting ching-chung Wu-chin-i p'u-sa ti san-shih p'in* 寶頂經中無盡意菩薩第三十品, 26.50a9-10). The latter, however, is peculiar, since the material quoted actually occurs not in the *Akṣayamati-paripṛcchā-sūtra*, which belongs to the *Ratnakūṭa* collection (see T 310[45]), but in the *Akṣayamatinirdeśa*, which comprises the twelfth division (*p'in* 品) of the *Mahāsaṁnipāta-sūtra* (T 397), which includes vols. (*chüan* 卷) 28-30 of that text. This raises the possibility that references to the *Kāśyapaparivarta* and to the *Akṣayamati* as "parts" of the *Ratnakūṭa* were added not by the original composer of the *Daśabhūmikavibhāṣā*, nor even necessarily even by Kumārajīva, but by a later editor who thought he recognized these titles as part of the *Ratnakūṭa* collection.

Elsewhere the text again quotes from what appears to be a "Kāśyapa chapter" (*Chia-yeh p'in* 迦葉品, 26.118c25), which would seem to indicate that this sūtra was being treated as part of a larger work. But much confusion has also been created by the facile assumption that the term *parivarta* (usually translated as *p'in* by Kumārajīva) must always be understood in the sense of "chapter." This is of course one of its meanings, but the term is also used simply in the sense of "discourse" or "exposition," as references in the *Aṣṭasāhasrikā-prajñāpāramitā-sūtra* to the "discourse of the noble Subhūti" (II.44) or to the "discourse on *prajñāpāramitā*" (VIII.199), for example, make clear. The term is also used in standard references to the three turnings (or, reading *parivarta* in the sense suggested here, "three expositions") and twelve aspects of the Four Noble Truths (*triparivartaṁ-dvādaśākāraṁ*; cf. BHSD 329a), where once again the meaning "chapter" would clearly be inappropriate.

In sum, when a text is labeled *parivarta*—as in the case of the *Kāśyapaparivarta*—there is no need to assume that this implies that it was viewed as a chapter or subset of a larger work. On the contrary, the most basic meaning of *parivarta* is simply "exposition." A discourse or exposition may, of course, later be incorporated into another work, at which point the *parivarta* in question does become a "section" of something else.

collection did not take place until some four decades later, under the supervision of the south Indian monk Bodhiruci at the request of emperor Chung-tsung, the son and successor of Empress Wu. Working with a team of assistants, Bodhiruci was able to complete the project during the years 706-713 CE. Of the forty-nine sūtras included in Bodhiruci's collection a substantial number had already been translated into Chinese, and in twenty-two cases Bodhiruci simply accepted an existing translation into his collection. The remaining twenty-seven sūtras were either newly translated or re-translated by Bodhiruci and his team.

It is to Bodhiruci, then, that we owe the present arrangement of the texts in this collection. And this is true not just of the Chinese version, but of the Tibetan *Ratnakūṭa* as well. As Marcelle Lalou has shown, the structure of the Tibetan version of this collection matches that of the earlier Chinese version exactly,[55] and in fact several of the individual texts it contains were translated not from Sanskrit, but from Chinese.[56] There is thus every reason to believe that the Tibetan *Ratnakūṭa* collection was arranged using the Chinese version as its

---

[55] See Lalou 1927. Lalou notes that in the Peking xylograph (Q) and Berlin manuscript editions the sequence of two groups of texts (nos. 17 and 18 and nos. 44 and 45, respectively) are reversed with respect to their sequence in the Chinese canon. The Narthang, Derge, and Stog Palace editions, however, as well as the *Ldan-kar-ma* catalogue, all follow the Chinese order. For the *Ldan-kar-ma* listings see Lalou 1953.

[56] Texts explicitly labeled as translated from the Chinese are nos. 7 (Skt. **Varmavyūhanirdeśa* according to the reconstruction given in the Peking edition, but this is surely an error on the part of the Tibetans; the underlying Sanskrit title was probably something like **Saṁnāha-saṁnaddha-nirdeśa*; note also that the Stog Palace edition gives no Sanskrit title), 13 (**Āyuṣman-nandagarbhāvakrāntinirdeśa*, again a reconstruction; the Stog Palace edition gives no Sanskrit title), 14 (**Nandagarbhāvakrāntinirdeśa*, a text closely related to 13 and virtually identical in title), and 40 (**Vimalaśuddhā-dārikā-paripṛcchā*; reconstructed as *Vimalaśraddhāparipṛcchā* in the Peking edition, but no Sanskrit title is given in the Stog Palace edition). All four of these texts are credited to the translator Chos-'grub (Ch. Fa-ch'eng 法成), who translated both Chinese texts into Tibetan and Tibetan scriptures into Chinese. On his life and work see Ueyama 1967-1968, as well as the summary of Ueyama's work in Demiéville 1970, pp. 47-62. It is worth noting that in the Peking edition (Q) all references to Chos-'grub, and to the Chinese basis of these translations, have been deleted; in the Derge edition only nos. 7 and 14 (the latter only in the catalogue, not in the colophon itself), and in the Stog Palace edition nos. 7, 13, and 40, are so labeled.

prototype, and that where Indian versions of the requisite texts were unavailable Chinese versions were used as the basis for the Tibetan translations in order to fill in the perceived "missing pieces."

There is one additional piece of evidence within the Tibetan texts themselves—evidence which has not yet been considered, to the best of my knowledge, by *Ratnakūṭa* specialists—of the degree to which the Chinese *Ratnakūṭa* collection served as the basis for its Tibetan counterpart. In the most archaic versions of the *Ugra* that I have examined—the Stog Palace and Narthang editions—the title appears at the end of the text in the following form:

> From the *Āryamahāratnakūṭa-dharmaparyāya* in one hundred thousand chapters, the chapter titled *The Inquiry of Ugra*, the Nineteenth Assembly, is completed *('Phags-pa Dkon-mchog brtsegs-pa chen-po'i chos-kyi rnams-grangs le'u stong phrag brgya-pa-las Drag-shul-can-gyis zhus-pa'i le'u zhes bya-ste | 'dus-pa bcu-dgu-pa rdzogs-so).*

But the word "assembly" (Tib. *'dus-pa*) is rather unexpected here. It is not one of the terms ordinarily used in Tibetan literature to mark a section, chapter, volume, or any other division of a text, and its meaning in this context seems unclear.

A quick glance at the titles of the sūtras contained in the Chinese *Ratnakūṭa* collection, however, provides an immediate solution to this problem, for *'dus-pa* is surely nothing other than a translation of the character *hui* 會 "assembly," a term which appears at the end of the title of each of the individual sūtras in the Chinese *Ratnakūṭa* collection. What the Tibetans have done, in other words, is to label the individual sūtras just as the Chinese did—as individual "assemblies" within a larger collection—despite the fact that the term *'dus-pa* in this sense has neither a visible Sanskrit antecedent nor any currency in Tibetan literary usage.[57]

This telling detail is invisible in the more recent (that is, the more editorially emended) versions of the Tibetan texts, where it is either eliminated or replaced by the more standard term "chapter" (Tib. *le'u*). We are thus indebted to the conservatism (or perhaps the simple

---

[57] Even in Chinese the word *hui* as a label for sections of a larger scriptural collection is rather unexpected. Was there some confusion between *parivarta* "discourse, chapter" and *parivāra* "assembly, entourage"? Or was the use of *hui* in this sense simply Bodhiruci's own invention, without any Indian antecedent at all? (I would like to thank Jonathan Silk for suggesting the latter possibility.)

oversight) of the editors of the Stog Palace and Narthang recensions of the *Ugra* for the preservation, whether deliberate or inadvertent, of this valuable clue.[58]

The Evolution of the Text over Time

With four complete recensions of the sūtra at our disposal, ranging in translation date from the late second century to the late eighth or early ninth century CE, we are in an ideal position to observe the growth and development of the *Ugra* over a period of more than half a millennium. Moreover, the fact that there is no evidence for any interdependence among these four versions—that is, no indication that any of the four translators consulted the work of any of the

---

[58] The word *'dus-pa* has been replaced by *le'u* in the Derge and London editions, while it has simply been eliminated in P3. It is difficult to determine whether it was present in an earlier printing of the Peking edition; although there is a large blank space at this point in the text, which would ordinarily serve as an indication of an erasure, there are large empty spaces before many of the phrases on this folio. It is extremely unfortunate that volume 53, which would have contained the *Ugra*, is one of the five volumes (29, 45, 53, 59, and 61) that were missing from the P1 edition when it was purchased for the Harvard-Yenching library.

In other *Ratnakūṭa* texts the distribution of the presence or absence of the word *'dus-pa* as part of the title is seemingly random: according to Sakurabe's tabulations, in the Peking (P3) edition the word appears *only* in the titles of texts 13, 14, and 20, while in the Narthang edition it appears in the titles of all of the texts *except* nos. 1, 3, 5, 6, 8, 9, 10, 22, 23, and 39—that is, in all of the remaining thirty-nine texts (Sakurabe 1930, p. 171). In the Stog Palace edition, by my own count, the word *'dus-pa* appears in the titles of forty texts, that is, in all except nos. 1, 5, 6, 8, 9, 10, 22, 23, and 30. There is considerable similarity in this respect between the Narthang and Stog Palace editions, no doubt reflecting their shared membership (at least in this instance) in the western branch of the Kanjur textual family.

The distribution of the texts that do and do not contain the word *'dus-pa* is hard to explain, but the fact that the overwhelming majority of texts in the most archaic recensions (Stog Palace and Narthang) do contain this term raises the possibility that it was originally used in all titles, but was dropped (either inadvertently or through deliberate emendation) in certain instances by an editor or copyist. In any event, the use of the term *'dus-pa* seems to make clear once again the extent of the dependence of the Tibetan *Ratnakūṭa* section on its Chinese counterpart.

others—allows us to consider them as four independent witnesses documenting the shape of the sūtra at several distinct points in the course of its development in India. As noted above, it is vital that we bear in mind that these four extant versions do not necessarily stand in a linear historical relationship to one another; there is no reason to think that the Indian text used by Dharmarakṣa, for example, was a direct lineal descendant of the version translated by An Hsüan and Yen Fo-t'iao. On the contrary, it is far more likely that the four extant Chinese and Tibetan translations were based on Sanskrit or Prakrit versions stemming from several different branches of the textual family tree. Yet it is striking that when the four surviving versions of the sūtra are arranged in chronological order, their length varies from the shortest (AY) to the longest (Tib) in exact accord with their chronological age.[59] This can serve as a general indicator, at the very least, of the overall direction of development of the text in India: like other sūtras for which we have multiple exemplars, the *Ugra* was clearly expanded, rather than abbreviated, over time. While on rare occasions a passage found in an early version seems to have dropped out of one or more of the later texts, there is no evidence that editors of later versions of the text deliberately removed material found in earlier recensions.

What we see in the *Ugra*, then, is a gradual process of accretion, with new elements being continually added to older ones. Like a geologist analyzing the relative ages of a series of sedimentary layers, the textual analyst can thus identify older and newer strata in the text based on the level at which each item was added.[60]

---

[59] That is, with the chronological age of their translations. It should also be noted, of course, that the age of the translations—which is the only "age" to which we have direct access—does not necessarily parallel the relative ages of the Indian texts upon which these four translations were based. For further discussion of the problems in establishing the date of the Indian texts see below, pp. 41-45.

[60] Here we must remember that we are dealing with a somewhat more complex situation: not merely a single line of textual transmission is involved, but remnants of several different branches of the family. Cf. above, "The *Ugra* as a Literary Document," for further discussion.

Structure and Genre

Even as the text of the *Ugra* was gradually expanded, its overall structure remained remarkably consistent, making it possible to generate a synoptic chart of parallel passages in the four versions of the text with little difficulty (see Appendix 1). There is only one major instance of rearrangement: in the oldest version of the sūtra (AY) Ugra and his companions request ordination as monks at the end of the sūtra, but this event takes place in the middle of the sūtra in all three of the later translations. In Dh, R, and Tib, in other words, the ordination scene occurs at the point of transition from the discussion of the practices of the lay bodhisattva to the section dealing with the life of his renunciant (i.e., monastic) counterpart.

One can see why an Indian editor might have thought it more reasonable to have these lay Buddhists undergo monastic ordination prior to being taught the practices proper to the renunciant bodhisattva, but the fact that the arrangement found in AY is the earlier one is made clear by several inconsistencies that appear in the later recensions as a result of the shift in the sequence of this scene. Even after his apparent ordination, Ugra continues to be addressed throughout the second half of the sūtra as "Eminent Householder" (*gṛhapati*), an epithet that would be inappropriate to a monk.[61] Moreover, when Ugra's companions are next mentioned (in §30), they too are referred to not as monks but as *gṛhapati*.[62] The editor who thought the ordination should be moved to the middle of the sūtra, in other words, failed to make the corresponding changes in the latter part of the text that would have been necessary to ensure consistency, thus leaving clear traces of his activity for the 20th-century scholar to discern.[63]

---

61 For a discussion of this issue see Chapter 3, p. 62 and n. 20.

62 Dh attempts to salvage the situation by adding "who had left home and shaved off their beard and hair" (12.30a26-27), but no such phrase is found in R or Tib.

63 Still another trace of editorial activity—and one that must predate the composition of any of the extant recensions—may perhaps be found in the anomalous fact that Ugra remains a householder even at the end of the sūtra, despite the fact that in all extant versions of the text (wherever they place the ordination scene) he *and* his companions request, and receive, monastic ordination. Was the passage praising Ugra for what he is able to accomplish added after the passage describing his ordination, once again without the corresponding editorial changes being made?

With respect to its overall structure, then, as well as in countless textual particulars, AY clearly represents the most archaic extant version of the text. We must remember that this does not mean we can refer to AY (or even to the lost Indian text upon which it was based) as the "original"; whatever the first version of what was to become the *Ugra* may have been, it will forever remain inaccessible to us. What we can do, though, is to use AY as a baseline text for comparison with the other available versions, and from this perspective the existence of this very early translation will prove to be of immense value. Though (as noted above) we do not know in what form the *Ugra* began its literary life, in all its extant versions the *Ugra* fits squarely within the genre of the Buddhist sūtra as we know it.[64] The text contains the standard opening and closing formulas, from "Thus have I heard" at the beginning to the favorable reaction of the audience at the end. Again like most sūtras, the *Ugra* is structured as a dialogue between the Buddha and one of his disciples, in this case the wealthy lay bodhisattva Ugra, whose question offers the catalyst for the Buddha's remarks. Virtually the entirety of the sūtra, in fact, is placed in the mouth of the Buddha himself, with Ugra and his companions adding only brief and occasional remarks.

Though some Buddhist sūtras were composed either in verse or in a combination of verse and prose, there is no indication in the extant Chinese or Tibetan translations that any Indic version of the *Ugra* contained passages that were metric in form. There is also no evidence that the recensions of the text that circulated in India contained any section or chapter divisions. While the Tibetan translation is divided into three *bam-po*s, or "sections," none of the three Chinese versions has such subdivisions. Likewise only one of the four extant versions—the translation by Dharmarakṣa—includes chapter divisions or chapter titles. Since the addition of extra terms and labels for clarity is one of the hallmarks of Dharmarakṣa's translation style,[65] the eight chapter titles found in his version of the text are almost certainly his own contribution.

The content of the text, however, falls rather naturally into two sections: an opening section discussing practices appropriate for the lay bodhisattva (comprising approximately 58 percent of the text in

---

[64] For a concise statement of the difference between Buddhist and brahmanical understandings of the "sūtra" genre see Gombrich 1990, p. 23; on the etymology of the term as used by Buddhists see above, n. 3.

[65] See Boucher 1996.

AY and Dh and approximately 65 percent of the two later translations), and a second section detailing practices the renunciant (i.e., monastic) bodhisattva should pursue.[66] Like most sūtras the *Ugra* is highly prescriptive, setting forth norms of conduct for the ideal practitioner in both categories.

In overall length the sūtra is quite modest in size, amounting to approximately two and a half times the length of the *Vajracchedikā*, almost exactly the same as the larger *Sukhāvatīvyūha*, and half the length of the *Vimalakīrtinirdeśa*. The printed text of the earliest extant version (AY) amounts to some 7⅓ pages in the Taishō edition; Dh occupies 8 pages, while R runs to 8⅓. The Tibetan version (whose pagination varies from one version of the Kanjur to another) is in

---

66 Schuster (1985, p. 40) contends that these two sections were originally independent texts, using the following line of argument:

> It appears that the Mahāyāna UPP [*Ugraparipṛcchā*] was formed by binding together two separate *sūtras*, each of which was composed using materials from certain older pre-Mahāyāna texts.... I think the two Mahāyāna sūtras, on lay *bodhisattva* and *pravrajita*, were joined together at a very early date in the evolution of the Mahāyāna, probably not long after both were composed. And I think this was done so that the two bodhisattva paths could be presented as equally viable alternatives, quite complementary to each other.

While this is an interesting theory, Schuster is arguing mainly on the basis of her own intuition; the only solid evidence she presents is the fact that following each of these two parts of the sūtra the reaction of the audience is described, a feature that commonly appears at the end of a sūtra (or, of course, at the end of a particular discourse within a sūtra). One argument against the suggestion that the two parts of the sūtra originated as independent texts is the fact that the first section, dealing with the practices of the lay bodhisattva, continually encourages him to adopt as much as he can of the monastic lifestyle and ultimately to seek full ordination. As such this section would seem rather incomplete without the second part of the sūtra, which describes in detail the monastic life to which the lay bodhisattva should aspire. It should also be noted that in all extant versions of the text Ugra asks the Buddha to tell him about the conduct of both the householder and the renunciant at the outset.

Be that as it may, Schuster's suggestion that the motive for bringing two originally separate works together as one sūtra was to show that the lay and renunciant options are "equally viable" is dramatically out of keeping with the main themes of the sūtra. As we shall see, the *Ugra* makes it clear that becoming a monk is a prerequisite for the attainment of Buddhahood, and that the lay bodhisattva's objective should be to escape from worldly life as soon as he possibly can.

turn slightly longer than R. What we see in these four versions, in other words, is a gradual increase in the length of the sūtra over the centuries as a result of the addition of various interpolations.[67]

Date and Provenance

It may seem strange to some readers—especially those used to working with Chinese sources, where precisely dated documents abound—that a discussion of the date and provenance of the *Ugra* has been deferred until this point. Yet the fact is that, as with most Indian religious texts, we have very little information on the circumstances under which the *Ugra* was composed. Like all Buddhist texts now classified as Mahāyāna sūtras, the *Ugra* is—at least in its present form—attributed to the Buddha himself. Yet it contains numerous ideas that were clearly unknown in the Buddha's time (above all the notion of the bodhisattva path itself), making it obvious that this is a pseudepigraphic attribution. What, then, can we say with confidence about the actual time and place of its composition?

In assessing the date of an Indian Buddhist text we have, in general terms, three types of evidence at our disposal: external evidence, internal evidence, and language. External evidence includes citations from, references to, commentaries on, and translations into another language of the text in question. Such evidence is useful for historical reconstruction, of course, only to the extent that the external source itself can be dated. (Very often the only datable external source available to us is the date of the first translation of the text into Chinese.) If any one or more of these items is available, it can provide us with a *terminus ad quem* for the existence of the scripture in question in India. This does not tell us, of course, about the actual date of its composition; it merely points to the date prior to which the scripture must have come into existence.

Internal evidence includes the mention within the text of known (and datable) historical figures and events, as well as clear dependence upon, or quotation from, another (likewise datable) source. More difficult to evaluate is another kind of internal evidence: the ideas, practices, and historical circumstances that the text presupposes as background. What, in other words, must we assume to already be in existence for the text as we have it to make sense? In

---

67 On this process of accretion see Chapter 3, pp. 51-59.

asking this question we are attempting to establish a relative chronology by placing the content of the text in a sequential relationship with that of other known Buddhist scriptures. It is important to realize, however, that even when it is possible to establish a plausible sequence in the development of certain ideas and practices—that the idea of the bodhisattva's becoming "irreversible" from full enlightenment at a certain point in his career preceded the development of the full-blown ten-*bhūmi* system, for example, or that the idea of the bodhisattva path preceded the critique of that path using the rhetoric of negation—these developments may well have occurred at vastly different rates in different geographical locations. Thus to say that the world of thought and practice portrayed in the *Ugra* (for example) is conceptually prior to that of the *Aṣṭasāhasrikā-prajñāpāramitā-sūtra* (for example), as I will argue in Chapter 7 below, does not demonstrate conclusively that the former was actually composed prior to the latter. Rather, it signifies only the fact that in the *Aṣṭa* we find an understanding of the bodhisattva path that presupposes what we find in the *Ugra* but has undergone further developments. If the *Aṣṭa* was composed in an area where the understanding of the bodhisattva path was evolving quite rapidly, while the *Ugra* came from an area where it was proceeding far more slowly, it would be entirely possible for the *Aṣṭa* to be more conceptually "advanced" and yet older in chronological terms.

Finally, where an Indic-language manuscript is extant, the date of its language or script may also offer useful data for estimating the date of composition of the text. In general the direction of development in Indian Buddhist literature has been from the use of a variety of Prakrits (that is, vernacular languages) to Buddhist Hybrid Sanskrit (perhaps best described as partially Sanskritized Prakrit) to grammatically correct classical Sanskrit. For this reason, the existence of a manuscript of a given text in a Prakrit language (e.g., Gāndhārī) or in Buddhist Hybrid Sanskrit is generally taken as evidence of its relative antiquity.

It is true that the existence of a Prakrit or BHS version of a given scripture constitutes a fairly strong argument for the composition of the text prior to the Gupta period (4th-6th centuries CE), when the prestige of classical Sanskrit led to the production of most Buddhist literature in that language.[68] But we must once again bear in mind the

---

[68] There was, however, a return to the use of Prakrit in the 6th or 7th century and after for the composition of tantric literature.

importance of regional variations, as well as the impact of differing sectarian preferences. The Sarvāstivādins, for example, appear to have adopted classical Sanskrit prior to some other Buddhist schools, while the Theravāda tradition adopted the Pāli language (a kind of "artificial Prakrit")[69] as its official "church language,"[70] and texts continued to be composed in it down to the 19th century.[71] There is also some evidence, though it is far from conclusive, that the Dharmaguptaka school (at least until the early centuries CE) favored the use of Gāndhārī.[72]

It is clear that texts originally composed in Prakrit or in BHS could be, and were, subsequently Sanskritized, and that verses—by virtue of their metric requirements—were more resistant than prose to such emendation. Thus the fact that the verse portions of the *Lotus Sūtra* (for example) are in a more archaic language than the corresponding prose sections does not necessarily mean, as scholars once believed, that the verse sections were composed first.[73] As the

---

[69] See von Hinüber 1982.

[70] On Buddhist use of "church language" in general see Nattier 1990.

[71] See Norman 1983a, pp. 181-192.

[72] For a brief listing of some items that have been adduced to support this hypothesis see Bernhard 1970, pp. 59-60. Not all of these items hold up to careful scrutiny, however; cf. Boucher 1996, pp. 106-107, and Boucher 1998, especially pp. 473-474.

[73] In fact there is considerable evidence of the reverse. In the case of the *Kāśyapaparivarta*, for example, the vast majority of the verse sections found in the Sanskrit manuscript (9th-10th centuries CE), the Tibetan translation (c. 800 CE), and the fourth and final Chinese translation (985 CE), have no parallel at all (whether in verse or in prose) in the earlier Chinese translations (dating from the 2nd-5th centuries CE). This suggests that the original text of the *Kāśyapa-parivarta* was almost entirely in prose, and that the verses—with the exception of those in §§136 and 137, which do have parallels in the earlier translations—were added later. (Cf. de Jong [1977], who concludes more broadly that in this text "the verse parts are later than the prose parts" [p. 255].) Likewise the portions of the *Avataṁsaka-sūtra* which exist in translations dating from the 2nd-4th centuries CE (T 280, 281, 282, 283, and 284) lack the verse sections found in the two later (and far longer) Chinese translations of the text (T 278 and 279, dating from the early 5th and late 7th centuries, respectively).

It is possible, of course, that these two texts are anomalous, but should a broader comparative study confirm that it was a general trend for verse sections to be added to sūtras originally composed in prose, this phenomenon should then be considered within the broader context of Indian literary practices at the time. To what extent, for example, might this practice reflect the rising prestige

substantial manuscript finds have now conclusively demonstrated, the entire sūtra was once written in BHS (and perhaps, though this is far from certain, existed earlier in Gāndhārī).[74] More recent manuscripts, in which the prose portions are written in relatively good Sanskrit, simply illustrate that these passages were more successfully updated than the verse.

In sum, language can only be used with great caution to establish the relative chronology of a given Buddhist text. Paleography can provide somewhat greater precision, but it must be remembered that such evidence can only establish the date of a particular copy—and not of the composition—of a given text.

Taken together, evidence of these three types can be used as a general indicator of the approximate date of the *Ugra*. Our first firm date comes from external evidence: the fact that the sūtra was translated into Chinese by An Hsüan and Yen Fo-t'iao during the period 180-190 CE The other pieces of external testimony available to us—citations from the *Ugra* in Kumārajīva's 5th-century translation of the **Daśabhūmikavibhāṣā* and in Śāntideva's 8th-century *Śikṣā-samuccaya*—are considerably later, and thus provide no useful additional evidence.

As to internal evidence, the *Ugra* mentions no historical events or figures whatsoever, with the exception of the Buddha and some of his contemporaries (e.g., Ānanda and Anāthapiṇḍada). On the more complex issue of the relative chronology of its content, however, a few observations may be made. First of all, one of the characters in the text (albeit a minor one) is the bodhisattva Maitreya, which suggests that the *Ugra* was composed some time after Maitreya's identity as the future Buddha had become well known. Since Maitreya is among the myriad figures represented on the coins of King Kanishka, the emergence of his cult must be dated prior to that time.[75] In other respects, however, the *Ugra* seems far more primitive in content than other sūtras that were translated into Chinese at approximately the same time. There is no reference, for example, to any of the "celestial bodhisattvas," such as Avalokiteśvara and

---

of the Hindu epic and later purāṇic literature (the genre which resembles Mahāyāna sūtras most closely), which are entirely metrical in form?

[74] For a discussion of some of the evidence for and against a Gāndhārī prototype for the earliest Chinese translation of the *Lotus Sūtra* see Boucher 1998.

[75] There is still no consensus on the reign dates of King Kanishka, but most scholars assign him to the late 1st or early 2nd century CE.

Mañjuśrī, within the body of the text; such figures appear only in the list of members of the audience at the beginning, and these "frame sections" are often among the last to be added (and the first to be updated). There are no references to women as bodhisattvas, or for that matter as Buddhist practitioners of any kind; the expression "gentleman or lady" (*kulaputra vā kuladuhitṛ vā*) appears only at the beginning (and, in the later recensions, again at the end) of the text, and thus it may be a relatively late (and formulaic) addition.[76] There is no indication that the bodhisattva path is accessible to all, nor could it by any stretch of the imagination be described as "easy"; there are no shortcuts, such as worshipping the sūtra itself (as in the *Aṣṭasāhasrikā-prajñāpāramitā-sūtra*) or visualizing Amitābha or other celestial Buddhas (as in the *Pratyutpanna-buddha-saṁmukha-avasthita-samādhi-sūtra*) to speed one along the path to Buddhahood. Finally, there is little evidence that the authors of the *Ugra* were concerned about the possible pitfalls of the bodhisattva path—not, at least, to the extent of using the language of negation and non-reification (as in the *Aṣṭa* or the *Vajracchedikā*) to critique wrong attitudes toward that path. In sum, in terms of its content the *Ugra* appears to be one of the most primitive of the bodhisattva-vehicle sūtras translated into Chinese prior to 200 CE.[77] Thus if we posit the beginning of the 2nd century CE as the latest possible date for the composition of the Indian texts in this group, we might wish to assign a slightly earlier date to the *Ugra*, given that it seems to be conceptually less developed than the rest. A not unreasonable date for its composition would be the 1st century BCE, assigning some of the clearly more developed texts (e.g., the *Aṣṭa*, the *Pratyutpanna*, and the *Akṣobhya-vyūha*) to a century or so later.

But if the precise date of composition of the text remains elusive, we have even less to go on when it comes to determining the place of its origin. The *Ugra* contains no geographical data whatsoever (with the exception of its stereotypical, and therefore uninformative, location near the city of Śrāvastī). The few clues to the language of the text that can be coaxed from its earliest Chinese translations suggest that the underlying language was almost certainly not Sanskrit, but a Prakrit vernacular (as would in fact be expected at this

---

[76] The formula occurs in §2B and C, and (in Dh, R, and Tib, but not in AY) again in §32B.

[77] For a detailed discussion of these and other items not found in the *Ugra* and their significance for the dating of the text see Chapter 7 below.

early date).[78] Given this exceedingly sparse information, it seems unlikely that we will ever be able to say anything specific about the region where the *Ugra* was composed.

Finally, though the once-thriving industry of attempting to locate the "origins of the Mahāyāna" within a particular Nikāya school is no longer fashionable (and with good reason), it is nonetheless worth pausing to take note of the one clue within the text which might point to at least the possibility of its circulation in a particular monastic environment. The *Ugra* refers to the recitation of four types of texts: sūtras (*dharma*), vinaya, abhidharma (*mātṛkā*), and a *bodhisattva-piṭaka*.[79] If this refers—as seems likely—to a canonical collection in four sections, we should note that the only Buddhist nikāya known to have had such a canon is the Dharmaguptaka school.[80]

Interestingly, this information harmonizes with (or at least does not contradict) another small piece of data that might point to the identity of the monastic lineage within which the *Ugra* was formed. In §23 the two earliest versions of the sūtra (AY and Dh) contain a version of the four "noble traditions" (*āryavaṁśa*s) that is attested, in the non-Mahāyāna sources that have been examined by scholars thus far,[81] only in the Chinese translation of the Dīrghāgama (T No. 1), a

---

[78] The most notable example is found in the name of Ugra himself, whose transliterations in Dh and R as *Yü-chia* 郁迦 and *Yü-ch'ieh* 郁伽, respectively, suggest an underlying **Ugga* rather than *Ugra*. (Cf. the transliterations *Yü-ch'ieh-luo* 郁伽羅 *and Yü-chia-luo* 郁迦羅, both of which occur in the **Daśa-bhūmikavibhāṣā* [T 1521, at 26.61b18 and 57b19, respectively], which clearly represent the Sanskrit form *Ugra*.) In addition, the apparent confusions between "seven" and "one hundred" (see §8B, n. 184) and between *dhūta* (in the term *dhūtaguṇa*) and "satisfied" (see §22A, n. 479) would more easily take place in Prakrit than in Sanskrit.

[79] For further discussion of the significance of this passage and the exact terminology used in the various versions see below, Chapter 4, pp. 80-81.

[80] See Bareau 1955, p. 296. The Bahuśrutīyas are also said to have had a canon that included a *bodhisattva-piṭaka* (based on the list given in the *Satyasiddhiśāstra*, which some scholars consider to be a Bahuśrutīya text), but that list includes five sections, not four. On the various meanings of the term *bodhisattva-piṭaka* see most recently Pagel 1995, pp. 7-36. The fact that our text lists four sections of a Buddhist canon, does not, of course, imply that there were not other versions of the canon circulating in the Buddhist communities at the time. The information contained in the *Ugra* tells us only about the shape of the canon that was current in the community out of which this sūtra emerged.

[81] I am drawing in particular on the survey provided in Takasaki 1967.

text generally assigned to the Dharmaguptaka school, as well as in two relatively late Pāli commentaries. In the later Chinese translation (R), by contrast, the list has been changed to a format that is uniformly attested in sources thought to be Sarvāstivādin and is also standard in Theravādin *sutta* texts.[82] (The Tibetan version contains a combination of both lists.) Taken together with the evidence concerning the shape of the canon related above, this pattern suggests—though it certainly does not prove—that the *Ugra* may have circulated in Dharmaguptaka circles at an early point in its history. The fact that later translations of the text contain an altered version of the list points to the likelihood that a sūtra formulated in one Nikāya community was subsequently being adopted by others, where certain changes would be made in accord with the recipient communities' textual recitation traditions.

In sum, in light of the meager evidence available to us it seems likely that the environment within which the *Ugra* was originally formulated will forever be hidden from view. But if the conditions under which the sūtra was born remain invisible, its childhood and youth—that is, the subsequent phases of its growth and development over time—are relatively well documented. In the following chapter we will consider some of the changes that have taken place in the content of the sūtra from the earliest to the most recent extant recensions, considering as we do so the methodological tools that will be necessary to evaluate the significance of these changes.

---

82 On these sources see below, Chapter 5, pp. 128-129.

CHAPTER 3

The *Ugra* as a Historical Source: Methodological Considerations

The Inquiry of Ugra offers us a unique window into a number of aspects of Buddhist life at the time when the sūtra was composed. Before making use of the information it provides, however, we must first consider several methodological issues involved in using scriptural sources to reconstruct social history. First of all, not all portions of the *Ugra* are of the same age; certain passages were clearly added after the bulk of the text had already been composed. How can such interpolations be identified, and what literary processes led to these additions? Second, the *Ugra* makes no pretense to be an objective historical source; rather, it is a highly prescriptive text, offering a whole range of injunctions concerning how the householder and renunciant bodhisattvas should conduct themselves. Given the evident agenda of its author(s), can we trust the *Ugra* to provide us with any valid historical information at all? If so, what procedures can we use to separate reflections of what Buddhists actually thought and did from the wishful thinking of the authors? Third, the *Ugra* is utterly silent about certain matters that we might expect it—as a member of the category of bodhisattva sūtras—to discuss. How should we interpret these absences, and what procedures should we use to evaluate their significance? Finally, the challenge of mining the *Ugra* for information about the history of Indian Buddhism is compounded by the fact that no version of the sūtra has survived in any Indic language. Rather, our only access to the text (aside from the passages cited in Śāntideva's 8th-century *Śikṣāsamuccaya*) is through its translations into Chinese and Tibetan. But to what extent can these translations be relied upon to provide an accurate reflection of the content of their Indian antecedents?

In the following discussion we will consider each of these issues as they bear on our understanding of the *Ugra*. The procedures described below, however, should apply to the study of other Buddhist scriptures, and they may prove also to be applicable to a wide range of non-Buddhist literature as well.

The Problem of Textual Stratification

The fact that many—perhaps most—Buddhist sūtras contain passages that were added after the initial composition of the text has long been recognized by specialists in the field. Yet what constitutes a valid procedure for identifying such interpolations has been far from clear. In many cases scholars have simply followed their own intuition, employing a method that could be characterized (only somewhat facetiously) as "If I like it, it's early; if I specialize in it, it's *very* early; if I don't like it at all, but it's in my text, it's an interpolation!" Referring to attempts by various scholars to stratify the texts in the Pāli canon, Rupert Gethin aptly observes:

> Many of the criteria employed by Winternitz, Law and Pande only work if one is already prejudiced as to the nature of early Buddhism. If one feels at the outset that the Buddha, being, as it were, a reasonable sort of chap, taught a simple ethical doctrine uncluttered by myth, legend and magic, then it is a fairly straightforward matter to stratify the Nikāyas accordingly. But in fact, given what is known of Indian thought from, say, the early Upaniṣads, there is no *a priori* reason why the earliest Buddhist thought should not have contained mythical, magical or "unscientific" elements, or—if we need to go back one stage further—why the Buddha himself should not have employed such elements in his own teaching. In fact there seems every reason to suppose that he would have.[1]

The stratification of texts based on personal preference has not, of course, been limited to studies of the Pāli canon. Comparable procedures can be found in the work of Edward Conze, the great pioneer of Prajñāpāramitā studies whose work has contributed so much to the understanding of this literature in the West. In his study of the formation of the *Aṣṭasāhasrikā-prajñāpāramitā-sūtra*, for example, Conze draws attention to several passages in which the celestial Buddha Akṣobhya appears. And he does not hesitate to declare them interpolations: "A set of four additions [to the *Aṣṭa*] can be inferred," he writes, "*from the fact that the name of Akṣobhya occurs in them.*"[2] To be fair, Conze does go on to note that these passages are missing from the verse counterpart to the *Aṣṭa*, the

---

[1] Gethin 1992, p. 11.

[2] "The Composition of the *Aṣṭasāhasrikā Prajñāpāramitā*," in Conze 1967b, pp. 168-184 (p. 172, emphasis added).

Ratnaguṇa-saṁcayagāthā (though much that Conze considered "original" in the *Aṣṭa* is missing from that text as well). From the way his argument is structured, however, it is clear that his principal basis for declaring these passages to be interpolations is the nature of their content, and not their presence or absence in another text. In Conze's mind, it would seem, such "devotional" passages simply could not have been composed by the same person who was responsible for the more philosophical sections of the text, those that deal (in Conze's terminology) with the "Absolute," and with emptiness.

This example, together with Gethin's comments cited above, should alert us to the fact that one commonly used method for identifying certain textual layers as interpolations—a perceived discrepancy between (to put it crudely) intellectual sophistication and devotional credulity—is fraught with dangers. The gap between the subtleties of Prajñāpāramitā philosophy and the naïveté of devotion to a celestial Buddha or bodhisattva, which seemed so self-evident to Conze, would not have been obvious at all to (for example) the 7th-century Chinese Buddhist pilgrim Hsüan-tsang, who was not only one of the leading scholars and translators of the Prajñāpāramitā literature of his day, but also one of Maitreya's most fervent devotees.[3] To judge a particular passage to be an interpolation based upon our own sense of what constitutes a "discrepancy" implies that we fully comprehend what would, and what would not, have seemed coherent to the Buddhists of that time. More often than not, this is an illusion.

There are other procedures, however, which—if used with caution—can help us to identify the presence of later layers even when we have only a single exemplar of a text. One such approach is to use structural and stylistic criteria to identify noticeable breaks within a text. When there is a clear interruption of the narrative, for example, and the discussion resumes after the end of the suspected interpolation, we are almost certainly in the presence of an addition to an existing text. Likewise when there is a noticeable difference between the language, grammar, or style of a particular passage and

---

[3] When Hsüan-tsang was captured by pirates who intended to sacrifice him to the godess Durga and was granted his request for a few moments to collect his thoughts before his death, he used this time not to meditate on the emptiness of all phenomena, but to visualize the future Buddha Maitreya in the Tuṣita heaven. For an insightful discussion of this event see Eckel 1992, pp. 132-134. Indeed, Eckel's entire book serves as a vivid lesson in the lack of boundaries between "high" and "popular" religion as seen by medieval Indian and Chinese Buddhist thinkers.

the surrounding material, we may suspect that there has been an interpolation here as well.[4]

A far more reliable procedure, however, is to compare a range of versions of a single text—in the case of Buddhist texts, including both the extant Indic-language copies, if any, and all available Chinese and Tibetan translations—to identify passages that are present in some, but not all, of these recensions. Where such passages are present only in the later version(s) of the sūtra in question, we can conclude with some measure of confidence that they are indeed interpolations.

In the case of the *Ugra* we are fortunate to have four extant versions—three preserved in Chinese and one in Tibetan—and it is therefore a straightforward procedure to identify passages in the later version(s) that have no parallels in the earlier one(s). Accordingly, in the discussion that follows we will employ only this method of identifying interpolations, and will not need to resort to any of the less reliable procedures discussed above.

Types of Interpolations in the *Ugra*

Most passages in the *Ugra* that can be identified as interpolations—that is, items which are absent from AY but present in one or more of the later versions—are extremely brief, sometimes consisting of only one or two words. A few, however, are quite extensive:

- the majority of §13, in which the (male) lay bodhisattva is instructed to think of his wife in highly negative terms—as a crocodile, a black snake, a demon, and so on—in order to free himself from any affection for her;
- the entirety of §19, in which a series of contrasts is drawn between the household and the renunciant life, all to the detriment of the former;
- the entirety of §31, in which Ugra makes an offering to the Buddha and the latter describes how the householder bodhisattva can emulate the life of the renunciant while still living at home;
- §32A and B, in which the Buddha smiles and sends forth a

[4] For a technical discussion of some of these issues (applied to modern rather than classical literature) see Morton 1978.

multicolored ray of light, provoking Ānanda to ask for an explanation; and

a substantial portion of §33, in which the qualities of the sūtra itself are praised in extravagant terms and devotion to *The Inquiry of Ugra* is said to be even more beneficial than making offerings to the stūpas of past Buddhas or to the living Buddhist community of the present.

What is intriguing about these interpolations, however, is that most of them—including the very long additions in §§13, 19, and most of 31—add no new conceptual material whatsoever to the sūtra. That is, they simply reiterate, with additional words or examples, ideas already present in AY. It is only in the last two examples (§§32-33) that we meet with genuinely new concepts and elements of the plot. We will return to a consideration of the significance of these additions below. What should be noted at this point, though, is that these instances aside, the vast majority of the interpolations found in later versions of the *Ugra* can be characterized as trivial in content, adding nothing new to the message of the text.

But if most of the interpolations in the *Ugra* are so trivial, why did some unknown editor (or far more likely, a whole series of such editors) go to the trouble of adding them at all? At this point we must confront an issue that plays a major role not just in the study of Buddhist sūtras, but in the field of Indian religious literature as a whole: what forces lead to the insertion of new material into an existing religious text? Or to put it another way, what is the motive of the interpolater who seeks to add his (or, at least theoretically, her) own ideas to an already authoritative scripture?

This is surely the most natural way for a western-trained scholar to put the question, but to phrase our inquiry in this way is to smuggle in, at the outset, two assumptions about how interpolation works: first, that an interpolator adds to a text in order to express new and creative ideas; and second, that interpolation is necessarily a conscious act. However, an examination of interpolated passages in the *Ugra*—as well as in a whole range of other Buddhist sūtras—reveals an immense body of evidence to counter these assumptions. Even a brief cataloguing of these passages will make it clear that to assume a "creative individual author" as the driving force behind interpolations in Buddhist scriptures is to import a model that is foreign to most of the literary processes that have shaped the production of Indian religious texts.

With the exception of the few substantial passages noted above, most of the items in the *Ugra* that can be identified as interpolations fall into one of the following (sometimes overlapping) categories.

Multiplication of epithets. Buddhist texts abound in long sequences of essentially synonymous expressions, and such repetitiveness—which may stem in part from the oral genesis of this literature—was clearly viewed as a virtue and not a vice in the Indian literary environment. Thus it is not surprising that one of the most common types of expansion seen in Buddhist scriptures is the multiplication of epithets. The *Ugra* is not nearly as effusive in this respect as, say, the Prajñāpāramitā texts, and this small clue may point to its production and subsequent transmission in a different literary environment. Nonetheless, it does contain a few examples of this phenomenon, such as the following:

§2A: AY and Dh have translations only of "Bhagavat," while R and Tib add "the Tathāgata, the Arhat, the Samyak-saṁbuddha";

§25I: All three Chinese versions state that wilderness-dwelling means "to dwell with the mind fully calmed," to which the Tibetan alone adds the roughly synonymous epithet "fully purified."

Such multiplication of epithets adds no new conceptual content to the text, but serves merely to reinforce existing ideas.

Completion of a standard list. As even beginning students are well aware, Buddhist literature also abounds in a wide variety of lists—the Four Noble Truths, the five *skandha*s, the six perfections, the eightfold path, and so on. A second type of interpolation widely seen in Buddhist scriptures is the result of the completion of such standard lists. That is, when only the initial term of a well-known list appears in an early version of a given text, we may find that in later recensions the names of the remaining items are added as well. For example:

§3D: Here the head-word is *śrāvaka-yāna*, the sole vehicle mentioned in the three Chinese versions. The Tibetan, however, adds "the *pratyekabuddha* vehicle or the great vehicle," thus completing the standard list of three.

§10A: AY refers only to "giving" (Skt. *dāna*), but Dh expands this term into the full list of the six perfections (*pāramitā*). Tib and R, however, take the word *dāna* as the head-word of an entirely different list, viz. giving (*dāna*), discipline (**dama*), self-restraint (**saṁyama*), and gentleness of character (**sauratya*).

Recall of a passage from elsewhere. It is not unusual for Buddhist scriptures (particularly bodhisattva sūtras) to make explicit reference to other scriptures, occasionally even citing them directly.[5] Far more common in sūtra literature, however, is the incorporation of well-known passages without attribution. The *Ugra* abounds in instances of this phenomenon, such as the following:

§1A: While the three Chinese versions state only that the Blessed One "was teaching the Dharma" (**dharmaṁ deśayati sma*), Tib alone adds a standard list of epithets known already in the Pāli canon, describing the Dharma as "good at the beginning, good in the middle, good at the end, good in meaning, good in letter, uncontaminated, complete, pure, and spotless."[6]

§3D: In a discussion of how the bodhisattva should relate to *śrāvaka*s, the *Ugra* reminds its audience that when bodhisattvas have attained Buddhahood they too will teach others to cultivate the qualities of a *śrāvaka* (*śrāvaka-gūṇa*). AY, Dh, and Tib go on to say that the bodhisattva, when encountering *śrāvaka*s, should therefore not cause them any trouble or disrespect them. R alone, however, reads "his heart does not dwell among them." This quite divergent reading bears a strong resemblance to a passage that occurs in the *Aṣṭasāhasrikā-prajñāpāramitā-sūtra*, also in a discussion of how a bodhisattva should relate to *śrāvaka*s, which

---

[5] The *Rāṣṭrapāla-paripṛcchā-sūtra*, for example, cites an extensive series of *jātaka* tales (for the Sanskrit text see Finot 1901, 21.9-27.18, and cf. the English translation in Ensink 1952, pp. 22-28). This passage is not included, however, in the earliest version of the sūtra, translated into Chinese by Dharmarakṣa (T 170).

[6] Cf. DN I.62; SN I.105, IV.315; AN II.147 and 208, and so on. Note the peculiar fact that the term *brahmacarya* occurs first in the standard form of this list in the Tibetan, while in Pāli it appears at the end.

> reads *ye 'pi Subhūte śrāvakagūṇāḥ tān api sa jānāti, na tatrāvatiṣṭhate* (p. 433; cf. Conze's translation, p. 253). In §4C below R again diverges from the other versions by inserting this same phrase, likewise when the "qualities of the *śrāvaka*" have just been mentioned. In both cases it seems certain that in R—or in the Indic text upon which it was based—this phrase was "recalled in" from another source (not necessarily the *Aṣṭa*, of course), elicited by the mention of the *śrāvaka-guṇa*s.

In some cases we even find the recall of material that occurs elsewhere in the same text, a phenomenon we might label somewhat facetiously as "self-plagiarism":

> §6B: Here AY (alone) repeats material that occurred earlier in §2D, likewise following a reference to not abandoning one's vow to attain Buddhahood: "[he will be] faultless in conduct in this life, and distinguished in future lives."

What all of the above interpolation types have in common (and it should be noted that there is considerable overlap among these categories) is that they are based not on creativity, but on memory: that is, they involve the interpolation into a text of material that has already been standardized elsewhere. Specifically, they all appear to be provoked by the presence of one or more "trigger words," terms that could elicit the memory of another word, phrase, or list that had followed in another context. Such automatic recall need be neither creative nor voluntary; indeed, it seems likely that many of these interpolations were not conscious at all.

Filling in the blanks. This type of interpolation is less transparently based on memorization, but is in fact quite closely related to the categories given above. Here the transmitters of the text seek simply to fill in all perceived absences in the text, either by providing extra transitional material or by repeating qualifiers attributed to the first item in a given list to apply to each of the remaining items as well. (A particularly striking example of this latter procedure may be found in the *Perfection of Insight in One Hundred Thousand Lines* [*Śatasāhasrikā-prajñāpāramitā-sūtra*], part of whose considerable bulk is derived from its propensity to repeat every statement with respect to each of the ten directions!) The net effect of interpolations of this sort is to smooth the flow of the narrative by filling in all perceptible gaps. Virtually all of this supplemental material, however, is entirely formulaic, occurring at such points in countless other Buddhist texts. Once again it seems likely that what we have is not an author (or editor)'s creative inspiration, but the ongoing background rhythms of a memorized oral tradition. Even in a text as short as the *Ugra*, we find countless examples of this phenomenon, such as:

§1B: Here R and Tib, but not AY or Dh, add "And having assembled there" after stating that Ugra and his attendants had gone to where the Blessed One was.

§2A: R and Tib, but again not AY or Dh, insert "When he had spoken thus" after Ugra's question and before the Buddha's reply.

§23A-E: One of the most dramatic examples of this procedure occurs in the section dealing with the four noble traditions (*āryavaṁśa*), where a long series of exhortations—to be content with any old robe, not to make extraordinary efforts to obtain a robe, not to be attached to the robe one obtains, and so on—is repeated for each of the noble traditions in turn in R and Tib, but does not occur at all in AY or Dh. This is, however, quite standard material, known for example from texts in the Pāli canon.[7]

Reiteration with additional examples. All of the above examples consist of interpolations that add nothing that is genuinely new in content; indeed it could be argued that there are not four distinct categories at all, but only a single category consisting of "adding what follows" in another text. To put it another way, all four types of interpolations could be described as varieties of "filling in the (perceived) blanks"—blanks that would have been perceived by the reciter, whether consciously or unconsciously, on the basis of other memorized material. The *Ugra* also contains, however, amplifications of a fifth type, which show at least a minimal degree of genuine

---

7 See the *Vaṁsa-sutta* in the *Aṅguttaranikāya* (II, 27-28) and the *Saṅgīti-sutta* in the *Dīghanikāya* (III, 224-225). For a discussion of these and other parallel texts see Chapter 5, pp. 128-129.

innovation. Additions of this sort are new in verbalization but not in content: that is, they do not diverge from any of the assumptions found elsewhere in the text, but simply reiterate those points with additional illustrations.

It is tempting (and it may well be correct) to conclude that additions of this sort are the result of the use of a memorized version of the text in preaching, during the course of which the preacher felt inspired to add additional examples for emphasis or clarification. Such supplemental flourishes might then find their way into future recitations of the text, one or more of which could eventually be recorded in writing.

§13J-GG: Following a passage in which the lay bodhisattva is told to cultivate a whole series of negative images of his wife (as a crocodile, a black snake, and so on; §13A-I), R and Tib—but not AY or Dh—go on to give a long series of additional examples.

§19: R and Tib—but not AY or Dh—insert a series of contrasts illustrating the superiority of the renunciant life over that of the householder. This passage, too, adds nothing that is conceptually new, since its promonastic perspective is entirely in keeping with the point of view expressed elsewhere in the text (see especially §9). Rather, it is the specific images and examples that are new, and they may well reflect the exegetical repertoire of a particular preacher.[8]

§25J: In a passage in which the renunciant bodhisattva living in the wilderness is told to reflect that grasses, shrubs, and trees also live there but are not afraid since they lack any notion of "self," Dh alone adds to the list of wilderness-dwellers "wild oxen, elephants, and horses."

Addition of genuinely new material. In the overwhelming majority of cases the interpolations we find in later versions of the *Ugra* add little that diverges from what was already found in earlier versions of the text. As noted above, however, there are a few

[8] Cf. the comments of Edward Conze (1958, pp. 51-52) on the latter part of the *Vajracchedikā*, where patterns of negation already established earlier in the sūtra are repeated almost *ad nauseum* with progressively less compelling examples.

instances in which we find new material that seems to represent genuine innovation:

§32A-B: The Buddha smiles and sends forth a multicolored ray of light, prompting Ānanda to ask the reason for this event. This entire sequence is missing, however, from AY.

§33B-E: Here the *Ugra* praises its own value as a text and declares that remembering and reciting this scripture is more meritorious than offerings of other kinds; in other words, we find here the kind of language that is associated with "the cult of the book."[9] The entirety of this long passage is missing from AY, however, and thus it appears to be a later addition to the text.

These sections certainly seem, at first glance, to be the result of authorial creativity, for they have no parallels elsewhere in the text and introduce ideas, incidents, or motifs that are genuinely new to the text. But even these passages prove, upon closer investigation, to be based on the recall of material from elsewhere. The Buddha's smile and Ānanda's question (§32A and B), for example, though new to the *Ugra*, are stereotypical events described in the same formulaic language in dozens (if not hundreds) of other sūtras.[10] Likewise the extravagant praise of the sūtra itself (§33B-E) is entirely commonplace, occurring at the end of countless bodhisattva texts.

In sum, the vast majority of interpolations found in the *Ugra* can best be explained as having emerged within an oral context, and of these a substantial proportion seem to be the result of the recall of previously memorized texts. It may seem strange that orally-based interpolations should still occur many centuries after an extensive collection of written scriptures had come into being, yet the notion (often an unconscious assumption on the part of modern scholars) that texts travel on a one-way street from oral to written form is clearly inapplicable to the Indian situation. Though the apparent taboo against recording religious texts in writing had already been

---

[9] For a detailed discussion of this issue see below, Chapter 7, pp. 184-186.

[10] A quick perusal of the English translation of selections from the *Ratnakūṭa* collection edited by Garma C. C. Chang (1983), for example, netted the following examples (and there may well be more): pp. 18 (sūtra #21), 39 (#31), 92-93 (#33), and 216 (#11, with Maitreya rather than Ānanda making the inquiry).

broken as early as the 1st century BCE,[11] the memorization of scriptures has continued to be a central element in Buddhist communities down to today. An oral text can be dictated and recorded by one or more scribes; a written text can be memorized and then recited orally. The boundary between oral and written Buddhist texts was clearly an open one, with frequent border crossings in both directions.[12]

The Possibility of Omissions and Abbreviations

In the above discussion I have portrayed all material that appears in later versions of the *Ugra* but not in earlier ones as the result of interpolation. But, the reader may well ask, is it not also possible that the earlier texts have simply omitted or abbreviated material that was transmitted in its entirety in the later translations? How are we to distinguish between an interpolation in a longer version and an omission in a shorter one? Why should we not assume, for example,

---

[11] The fact that the writing down of Buddhist texts first took place at the fringes of the Indian cultural sphere has not, it seems to me, received sufficient attention. In the Sri Lankan sources we are given clear indications that it was a perceived situation of crisis—widely interpreted as due to war and famine, but perhaps more likely (as suggested in Collins 1990) competition among contending monastic centers—that led to the taking of this radical step. On the Indian mainland, perhaps even more striking is the fact that in the absence of any Indian word meaning "written religious text" a foreign term—the Iranian loan word *pustaka*, meaning "leather" (a common writing material in the Iranian world)—was adopted to designate these strange new objects. The use of the term *pustaka* suggests (though it certainly does not prove) that the practice of writing down scriptures in mainland India may have been introduced from the Iranian world—that is, from the far northwest. If this is the case, the picture that emerges is of the practice of writing down Buddhist scriptures beginning at two opposite edges of the Buddhist world, both of them far removed from what was then the brahmanical heartland. Indeed this is not unexpected, in retrospect, when we consider the fact that writing was actually considered polluting (and thus utterly inappropriate for recording religious literature) by brahmanical thinkers. See for example the *Aitareya-āraṇyaka* edited by A. B. Keith (1919), where writing is listed along with meat-eating, sexual intercourse, and contact with blood as an impure activity after which one must abstain from Vedic study (p. 158, line 5; English translation on pp. 301-302).

[12] For an illuminating discussion of similar phenomena in the Islamic world (and elsewhere) see Graham 1987.

that AY—whose version lacks most of what we have suggested is interpolated material—simply found much of the *Ugra*'s repetitive language too cumbersome, and excised it to suit the literary tastes of a Chinese audience?

It is often asserted—not just by modern scholars—that Chinese translators, in particular, were inclined to abbreviate Indian Buddhist texts. Indeed some were accused of doing so by their compatriots, for instance Tao-an 道安, who criticized Mokṣala 無羅叉 and Chih Yüeh 支越 (= Chih Ch'ien 支謙?) for condensing and altering the style of their Indian sources.[13]

In modern scholarship the translations of Kumārajīva, in particular, have been treated as suspect in this regard.[14] But where Kumārajīva's work can be compared with an extant Indic manuscript—that is, in those rare cases where part or all of a text he translated has survived in a Sanskrit or Prakrit version—a somewhat surprising result emerges. While his translations are indeed shorter in many instances than their extant (and much later) Sanskrit counterparts, when earlier Indic-language manuscript fragments are available they often provide exact parallels to Kumārajīva's supposed "abbreviations."[15] What seems likely to have happened, in sum, is that Kumārajīva was working from earlier Indian versions in which these expansions had not yet taken place.

In sum, there are two factors to consider in evaluating the likely direction of development—that is, whether to suspect abbreviation in one text or expansion in another—in a given Chinese or Tibetan text. First, when we have both earlier and later recensions of a given sūtra it is generally the case that the later text will be the longer one. There are exceptions, of course, and many of these involve interpolations arguably added in China; but by and large growth rather than shrinkage seems to be the norm. Indeed the *Ugra* offers a textbook example of this phenomenon, for in stair-step fashion the text increases in size with each new translation.

Second, when relatively early Indic-language manuscripts are available for comparison, Chinese translators can sometimes be

---

[13] See Tao-an's comments in a preface preserved in Seng-you's *Ch'u san-tsang chi-chi* 出三藏記集 T. 2145, 55.52c10-19).

[14] For what may be the *locus classicus* of this idea see Ōcho 1958.

[15] An excellent example is the *Vajracchedikā-prajñāpāramitā-sūtra*, where Kumārajīva's version appears to be abbreviated when compared with the late Sanskrit texts edited by Müller (1881), but corresponds quite closely to the earlier (5th-6th century) Sanskrit texts.

proven to be in agreement with these earlier versions (and thus acquitted of the charge of having abbreviated their texts). The contents of the Schøyen collection of Buddhist manuscripts, which includes text ranging from the 2nd to the 9th century in date and includes fragments of several Mahāyāna sūtras, promise to provide us with priceless new comparative data in this regard.[16]

We are justified in taking it as a general rule of thumb, then—though hardly as an ironclad principle—that Buddhist scriptures (and in particular bodhisattva sūtras, whose mode of transmission may have been somewhat different from that of earlier canonical texts) tend to grow rather than to shrink over time.[17] Where we do find occasional omissions, they can often be shown to be the result of a copyist's error, skipping from a phrase found in one line to identical wording below.

Moving Pieces: Alterations in the Sequence of the Text

An additional change that can occur in the process of transmission of a text is that the order of individual components of the text will be altered over time. An excellent example of wholesale rearrangement is offered by the larger *Sukhāvatīvyūha*, a text whose contents have been so scrambled that a heroic effort is required to establish a comparative table of the various versions.[18] A much smaller-scale but likewise well-known example can be found in the *Lotus Sūtra*, where Śākyamuni entrusts the text to his audience at the end of the sūtra (Chapter 27) in the extant Sanskrit version, but considerably earlier

---

[16] For the first of an important series of volumes in which these manuscripts are edited and translated see Braarvig 2000.

[17] Edward Conze's reference to one group of Prajñāpāramitā sūtras—including the *Suvikrāntavikrāmi-paripṛcchā*, the *Saptaśatikāprajñāpāramitā*, and the *Vajracchedikā*—as "abbreviations" (Conze 1978, pp. 56-74) has created a misleading impression. These texts are not in fact shortened versions of other works but rather new compositions which restate some of the same themes found in earlier Prajñāpāramitā texts. The *Heart Sūtra*, which does indeed borrow most of its content from other sources and which Conze places in this same category (*ibid.*, pp. 67-74) is a more complicated case; for a detailed discussion see Nattier 1992.

[18] Happily such an effort has been made by KAGAWA Takao, who has produced an extremely valuable synoptic edition of the Sanskrit, Chinese, and Tibetan versions of the text (Kagawa 1984).

(in Chapter 22) in Kumārajīva's Chinese version. In many more cases, however, we see no rearrangement at all, with the sequence of elements remaining intact even as a whole range of interpolations are added.[19]

In general the *Ugra* has followed this latter pattern, and the fact that its overall sequence has been retained over the centuries makes the task of constructing a synoptic table of its extant versions (see Appendix 1) quite straightforward. There is one segment of the text, however, which has undergone a noteworthy migration, appearing at the end of the earliest version (AY) but in the middle—at the point of transition from the lay to monastic sections of the sūtra—in the others. This is the scene in which Ugra and his friends request and receive ordination as *bhikṣus*, declaring that they have well understood the Buddha's teaching of the superiority of the monastic over the lay estate.

An understandable response to this situation would be simply to treat the earliest extant version as representing the original sequence, but are there any more reliable indications of whether or not this is in fact the case? Fortunately, as mentioned in the previous chapter the editors who chose to move the location of this passage have left clear fingerprints, allowing us to track their activity with relative ease. For throughout the latter part of the sūtra, which deals with the life of the renunciant bodhisattva—that is, after the ordination scene in Dh, R, and Tib, but before it in AY—Ugra is repeatedly referred to as "Eminent Householder" (*gṛhapati*). Such a title is, however, completely inappropriate to a renunciant, as it refers to a man's status in lay society.[20] By failing to remove these signs that Ugra was

---

[19] A particularly interesting example is the evolution of the *Aṣṭasāhasrikā-prajñāpāramitā* into the *Pañcaviṁśati-sāhasrikā* through what we might call the "club sandwich" style of textual formation: with exception of the final chapters (30-32 in the Sanskrit version) of the *Aṣṭa*, which have no counterpart in the Sanskrit *Pañca* and apparently circulated separately before being incorporated into the *Aṣṭa* (see Kajiyama 1989, p. 15), the latter consists of the *Aṣṭa* "sliced" like a loaf of bread and then layered with "fillings" introduced from other sources. Very little of the text of the *Aṣṭa* has been altered in the process, and only rarely does a crumb of the "bread" seem to have dropped out. The *Pañca* is thus not simply related to the *Aṣṭa*; it *is* the *Aṣṭa*, with the addition of a number of layers of new material.

[20] See for example the *Potaliya-sutta* (MN I.359-368, corresponding to T 26[203], 1.773-775), where a wealthy *gahapati* objects to being addressed by this title by the Buddha, for he believes (wrongly, as it turns out) that he has

originally still a layman in the latter part of the sūtra, the editors have left us a clear indication that the sequence found in AY, where the ordination scene occurs at the end, is the original one.

This single alteration aside, the overall structure of the *Ugra* has remained remarkably stable over time. A comparative study of Buddhist texts that have suffered major alterations vs. those that have not might yield interesting results; in the meantime, we may simply note that the *Ugra* clearly belongs in the "relatively unaltered" category.

Extracting Historical Data from a Normative Source

Like most Buddhist scriptures the *Ugra* is above all a prescriptive document, composed by Buddhists seeking to establish (or at the very least, to reinforce) certain norms of thought and practice within their own religious community. To take their statements as providing a literal portrait of life in that community would thus be to commit a fundamental methodological error: the error of reading normative statements as if they were descriptive. The commission of this error has a long history in otherwise respectable Buddhist Studies circles, above all in studies of the Vinaya, where the monastic rules have all too often been taken as descriptions of the way monks and nuns actually behaved.[21] On the contrary—as we shall see—such prescriptions are frequently evidence of precisely the opposite.

Yet if we are to say anything at all about the early history of the bodhisattva path, we will be forced to use normative sources, for—at least at this early date—these are the only sources we have. Gregory Schopen has argued that references to something that can be construed as a self-consciously "Mahāyāna" community do not appear in inscriptions prior to the 4th century CE,[22] and it is only at the end of that century that our first nonscriptural source on the presence of bodhisattvas in India, the travel narrative of the Chinese pilgrim

---

given up all worldly things. On the term *gṛhapati* as such see Chapter 2, pp. 22-24.

[21] For some illuminating examples see the sources cited in Schopen 1991. Though the scholars whose writings he cites are mostly European (with a sprinkling of South Asians and North Americans), the same pattern obtains in the work of East Asian scholars as well.

[22] See the discussion in Schopen 1979b.

Fa-hsien, is composed.[23] Prior to this time we have the evidence of certain statues labeled "bodhisattva,"[24] yet without an accompanying narrative it is hazardous at best to draw any conclusions as to what these figures represent. Where we have no extended inscriptional context for a bodhisattva image, there are at least four interpretive possibilities: (1) that it represents the historical Buddha Śākyamuni prior to his enlightenment; (2) that it represents the future Buddha Maitreya in his (still to be actualized) final life; (3) that it represents one or another of the so-called "celestial bodhisattvas," such as Avalokiteśvara or Mañjuśrī, to whom the devotee can appeal for assistance in the present; or (4) that it represents a generic ideal, to be actualized by the practitioner himself.

Well before the 4th century, however, substantial numbers of scriptural texts advocating the bodhisattva path (known retrospectively as "Mahāyāna sūtras") were being composed, eleven of which had already been translated into Chinese by the end of the 2nd century CE.[25] It is fair to say that it is only by consulting these sources that we will have any hope of painting a picture, however sketchy, of the world out of which the idea of the bodhisattva path emerged. To eliminate these sources from consideration merely because they are predominantly normative in content would be to exclude an immensely rich body of material. What is necessary, therefore, is the careful use of these sources, recognizing their nature as prescriptive texts but at the same time using them, as appropriate, to extract historical data. Though our primary concern in this study is to make use of the data contained in one particular bodhisattva sūtra, it should be noted that the same considerations apply to virtually the

---

[23] See Legge 1886.

[24] The first images explicitly labeled "bodhisattva" appeared no later than the beginning of the Kushan period. In the earliest images from the greater Mathura region (north-central India), the bodhisattva is generally represented as a monk; for two examples see Huntington 1985, plates 8.29 (the so-called "Bala bodhisattva" from Sārnāth, which is generally interpreted as a representation of Śākyamuni) and 8.34 (a bodhisattva image from Ahicchatrā, which can be identified as Maitreya by its inscription). Images from the Gandhāra region (the far northwest of the subcontinent), by contrast, generally represent bodhisattvas in princely garb (e.g., the Kushan-period image of Maitreya from Takht-i-Bāhī; see Huntington 1985, plate 8.15).

[25] This figure includes only those sūtras which are still extant and for which the identity of the translator (and thus the date) is assured. For a discussion of these early translations see Harrison 1987.

entire range of Buddhist literary texts.

To separate the descriptive from the prescriptive is, of course, no easy task. The following observations are intended as general guidelines for those working with scriptural texts. To the extent that they provide valid operating principles, they should be equally applicable to both Buddhist and non-Buddhist materials.[26]

The principle of embarrassment.[27] When an author reveals, in the course of a discussion, something that is quite unflattering to the group or the position that he or she represents, there is a high degree of probability that the statement has a basis in fact. When the authors of the *Perfection of Insight in Eight Thousand Lines* admit, for example, that many Buddhists did not accept the Prajñāpāramitā literature as genuine scripture, or the authors of the *Lotus Sūtra* describe some members of the audience as getting up and walking out when the message of the *Lotus* was first preached, it seems extremely likely that these portrayals of nonacceptance by the broader Buddhist community reflect the actual reaction to the ideas contained in these texts at the time of their composition.

Examples of this phenomenon are also found in earlier Buddhist literature. In the *Mahāvagga* section of the Vinaya, for example, we are told that during the Buddha's lifetime monks in the city of Kosambī (Skt. Kauśāmbī) became embroiled in a quarrel so bitter that they actually came to blows, and as a result were criticized by the public at large. When the Buddha attempted to mediate the dispute the feuding monks told him to leave them alone and let them settle their own affairs.[28] Such a narrative hardly paints a positive picture of the members of the early Buddhist community—nor of the degree of authority of the Buddha himself! Accordingly, we may accept this passage as offering evidence that even during the Buddha's own lifetime there were quarrels and disputes within the mendicant community.

A similarly unflattering portrait of the community appears in a

---

[26] The following principles have been formulated primarily for use in analyzing texts that are exhortational in style. Other genres—hagiography, for example, or ecclesiastical history—might require modifications in some of these techniques.

[27] I would like to thank my colleague David Brakke for bringing this term (commonly used in New Testament studies) to my attention.

[28] Vinaya I.341-342; English translation in Horner 1951, vol. 4, pp. 488-489.

Pāli Vinaya passage where we are told that on full and new moon days—the traditional occasions for religious assembly in India—the Buddha's disciples did not gather like other religious groups, and thus missed an opportunity to draw an audience from among the laity. At the suggestion of King Bimbisāra the Buddha agreed to convoke an assembly on these occasions, but the monks did nothing but sit around like "dumb hogs." Once again they were criticized by the general public, and the Buddha instituted the biweekly recitation of the *prātimokṣa* rules (as well as the giving of dharma-talks) in response.[29] Here too we no doubt have the traces of an actual incident (or series of incidents) reflecting the Buddhist community's gradual adjustment to prevailing norms as the result of public pressure. Such a story—in which Buddhist monks are described as falling short of societal expectations—would hardly have been viewed as flattering to the Buddhist community, but was presumably too widely known to be denied.

The principle of irrelevance. A second situation in which we may draw with some confidence on data found within a normative text occurs when incidental mention is made of items unrelated to the author's primary agenda. When the author of the *Jarāmaraṇa-sutta* of the *Saṁyutta-nikāya* presents the Buddha as stating, in the course of a general discussion of the transitoriness of life, that not even the members of great *khattiya* houses, great *brāhmaṇa* houses, or great *gahapati* houses can escape from old age and death,[30] he is not attempting to make a point about the importance of the caste system, much less about the order in which these social groups are ranked. Rather, he is merely drawing on a well-known list to illustrate the fact that even the most privileged members of society are not exempt from human mortality. Such an illustration would not work if his audience were not already familiar with this list, and to alter its usual sequence would only have distracted the listeners from the point being made. We may therefore conclude that this list reflects a known aspect of social life in India at the time, on which the author could conveniently draw for an example.

In similar fashion, when the author of the *Ugra* tells us, in the

---

[29] Vinaya I.101-102; English translation in Horner 1951, vol. 4, pp. 130-132.

[30] SN I.71; for an English translation see Rhys Davids and Sumangala Thera 1917, p. 97.

course of a discussion of how the bodhisattva should use his worldly belongings, that the bodhisattva should bestow wealth upon his male and female slaves (*dāsa* and *dāsī*), he is not making an argument for or against the institution of slavery, but is merely revealing that it exists. He is also letting us know, again inadvertently, that the category of "bodhisattva" included at least some individuals of considerable wealth. To conclude that this passage provides evidence that bodhisattvas actually *did* bestow wealth upon their servants and slaves, however, would be to go too far, for here the author is using clearly prescriptive language, a subject to which we will now turn.

The principle of counterargument. It is in this category that we meet with prescriptive statements of the type that have, with surprisingly frequency, been interpreted as if they were documenting actual fact. But it should be obvious, at least in retrospect, that when we encounter statements of the type "One should *not* believe X" or "One should *not* do Y" there must have been some reason for the author to argue against them. That is, these statements—far from revealing what people actually did *not* believe or do—can serve as evidence that at least some members of the community were involved in the offending practices, hence the author's need to argue against them.[31]

Yet there is an important difference between items in this category and those in the previous two, for despite their prescriptive character these statements do offer evidence that at least some members of the Buddhist community—at a minimum, the author himself—considered them worthy of upholding. The existence of a rule against killing, for example, hardly constitutes evidence that monks and nuns were widely involved in this activity. With prescriptive statements we are thus dealing with a more complex situation: in these cases there is some difference of opinion or conduct within the community, and the author of a given text is taking a particular position on the issue.

There are numerous examples of such prohibitions in the *Ugra*, many of which may reveal the existence of beliefs or practices within

---

31 Indeed, the Vinaya rules as they have come down to us make this explicit in their discussion, for each rule is portrayed as having been formulated in response to a situation in which an offense (in the view of some members of the community) had been committed. To prevent others from doing the same thing in the future, the Buddha (according to these narratives) instituted the rule in question.

the Buddhist community that our authors were trying to stamp out. When the text argues that a lay bodhisattva should not show any disrespect to a monastic *śrāvaka*, surely this suggests that such slights were in fact taking place. Likewise when our text prescribes that a layman, upon arriving at the monastery for a visit, should first prostrate himself at the entrance and only then go within, surely this tells us that some were entering more casually, without pausing to make this deferential gesture. The sūtra does not, on the other hand, tell us that the layman *should* go to the monastery; it simply assumes that he does, thus providing an example of our previous category.

The principle of corroborating evidence. If we were dealing with sources from another context—from the Roman Empire in the 2nd century, say, or from late medieval Japan—one of the first things we would look for would be other sources that could confirm or deny the picture of the religious community presented in our text. In the Indian case, however, this is rarely an option. Sometimes we have surviving artistic or archaeological evidence (including inscriptions) from approximately the time in question; more often, however, we do not—or, due to uncertainty about the date and provenance of the sūtra with which we are concerned, we simply cannot determine the degree of relevance of these materials. Some early inscriptions have survived, but though they are of significant value they are limited in content and highly formulaic in style. As a result they offer only a limited range of information on beliefs and practices that might (or might not) correlate with what we see in scriptural texts.[32] And the most obvious corroborating source—information gleaned from contemporary narrative histories—is simply not available, for the writing of history in the strict sense does not begin in India until the 12th century, with the composition of Kalhaṇa's *Rājataraṅgiṇī*. In sum, most of the time we will be constrained to work primarily from scriptural texts themselves if we are to have any hope of beginning to understand the wide range of forms of belief and practice that Buddhism has taken over the course of its history in India.

It is increasingly recognized, of course, that even our reading of such undatable and unlocalizable materials can benefit from cross-

---

[32] Gregory Schopen has argued that such inscriptions, these limitations notwithstanding, are far more important for understanding what Buddhists in India actually thought and did than are the vast numbers of surviving scriptural texts. For a critical assessment of this view see below, Chapter 5, pp. 103-105.

fertilization from other disciplines, chief among them anthropology, archaeology, and epigraphy. Even data widely separated from our Indian sources in time and place—anthropological reports from contemporary Southeast Asia, for example—can help to raise new questions, and alert us to previously unseen issues, when we return to our texts with these insights.[33] As long as we cannot locate most of our sūtras—including the *Ugra*—precisely in either space or time, the most we can hope to accomplish is to gain a rich sense of the Buddhist thought and practice embodied in each of these sources, ultimately with the possibility of better understanding the relationships among these highly disparate texts.

Ex Silentio: The Interpretation of Absence

A difficulty of a another kind emerges when, on a certain issue, our text has nothing at all to say. What are we to make of the fact that, for example, the *Ugra* never mentions the cult of the stūpa, the ten stages (*bhūmi*) of the bodhisattva path, or the doctrine of the "one vehicle" (*ekayāna*)? Buddhist exegetes—like their counterparts in other religious traditions—have felt quite free to read these concepts into earlier texts where they do not occur, but the historian must be more cautious. There are at least three possible explanations for an author's silence on a particular idea or practice: (1) the item in question was too well known to require explicit mention and was simply assumed as background; (2) the item was completely unknown to the writer, either because it developed at a later time or because it was still unknown in his particular locale; and finally, (3) the author was quite familiar with the item in question, but considered it so unacceptable, or so foreign to his understanding of Buddhism, as to be unworthy of his attention. It is also possible, of course, that the author knew of the item in question but simply considered it uninteresting.[34]

How, then, can we determine which of these three possibilities is most likely in a particular case? In each case we will need to ask at least three questions. First, is this missing item required in order for

---

[33] See for example the discussion by Paul Harrison of what he variously refers to as "close reading" or "textual anthropology" (Harrison 1995, especially pp. 53-54).

[34] I would like to thank Gregory Schopen (personal communication, 2001) for calling this fourth possibility to my attention. Such apparent lack of interest may of course be due to its irrelevance to the particular topic at hand.

what we *do* have in the text to make sense? Second, does our text contain what appears to be a less-developed version—a precursor, in other words—of an item on which it is silent? And third, does the item in question conflict with any position the author *does* hold? If we answer the first question in the affirmative, we may conclude that we are in the presence of a silence of the first type: that the item in question was simply taken for granted and thus not seen by the author as requiring any special comment. If we answer yes to the second, we may infer that the item in question developed after the time of our text, and that the less-developed form we actually see in the sūtra was all that was known to the author. Finally, if the answer to the third question is positive, we may conclude that the author *may* have known of the absent item and rejected it, but here further evidence is required, and we will have to return to the text to try to identify traces of some familiarity with, or indirect criticism of, the item in question.

We will return to the question of the *Ugra*'s silences in Chapter 7, where we will examine a number of items one might expect to find in a "Mahāyāna sūtra" that are missing from our text. At that point we will apply the procedures that are only sketched briefly above to assess the significance of these silences.

A Distant Mirror: Studying Indian Buddhism through Chinese and Tibetan Texts

The *Ugra*, like most Indian bodhisattva scriptures, has not come down to us in any Indic-language version. Our only access to this text—aside from the citations from it preserved in the *Śikṣā-samuccaya*—is thus through admittedly derivative Chinese and Tibetan sources. But to what extent do these translations really provide an accurate reflection of the content of their underlying Indic texts? The problem is particularly acute in the case of early Chinese translations, for these works—often produced by translators whose expertise in Sanskrit or Prạkrit was limited at best—can contain an appalling number of mistakes. When Dharmarakṣa, for example, confuses the Prakrit verb *bhonti* "they are" with the noun *bodhi* "enlightenment" in his translation of the *Lotus Sūtra*,[35] how can we possibly place any confidence in his text?

---

[35] On this confusion see Boucher 1998, p. 479, with references in n. 45 to additional examples given in Karashima 1992.

The short answer, of course, is that we cannot. In any given instance a translator (or more properly a translation committee, for in contrast to modern scholarly practice these texts were almost never produced by a single individual working alone) may have misread an ambiguous Kharoṣṭhī-script character, misheard a Sanskrit word recited by a *sūtra-dhara* with a Tokharian accent, or misconstrued an unfamiliar Prakrit grammatical form. In short, when reading any given line of a Chinese Buddhist sūtra—excepting perhaps those produced by someone like Hsüan-tsang, who is justifiably famous for his accuracy—we have a roughly equal chance of encountering an accurate reflection of the underlying Indian original or a catastrophic misunderstanding.[36]

But lest we give up on this vast treasury of sources prematurely, we must note that the preceding statement holds true only if such texts are treated in isolation. If, on the other hand, we have multiple translations of a given work—which is often the case, given that the Chinese regularly preserved older translations even when a newer rendition had been produced—we are in a completely different situation. By using a number of different translations (particularly if they date from different periods and do not exhibit dependence upon one another) we can generally triangulate back to the meaning of the underlying Indic text. This does not—it must be emphasized—mean that we can reconstruct the exact wording of the so-called "original," for there is far too much variety in translators' choices (and this applies even to the far more mechanical Tibetan versions) to allow us the luxury of such certainty. And in any event, it is unlikely that any two translations would have been based upon precisely the same Indic text. Yet the application of this triangulation procedure does allow us to determine with a far higher degree of confidence the overall meaning and, to a more limited extent, some of the actual vocabulary used in the underlying text.

The *Ugra* abounds in passages that illustrate the usefulness of this procedure, and this is the method I have followed—using all extant versions of the sūtra—throughout my translation of the text. But perhaps a single example will suffice to demonstrate the value of this

---

36 To some extent this also applies to the Tibetan translations, though they date from a later period when better reference works were available and were more often the product of collaboration with Indian (as opposed to Central Asian) informants. Even here, however, we frequently encounter visual, grammatical, or (less commonly) aural misunderstandings, which must be compensated for with recourse to other extant versions of a given text.

method. In the section of the text that discusses the practices of the renunciant bodhisattva, such a bodhisattva is told that he should reflect on his reasons for dwelling in the wilderness (*araṇya*). After considering the fact that wilderness-dwelling alone does not make one a *śramaṇa*—after all, robbers and wild animals also inhabit the forest without making any spiritual progress—the bodhisattva is told to realize that his reason for being there is to accomplish the following (§25A):

AY: the *śramaṇa*'s seeking 息心求

Dh: the *śramaṇa*'s meaning 沙門之義

R: the *śramaṇa*'s meaning-benefit 沙門之義利

It would be easy to throw up one's hands in despair at this point and to conclude that all three versions are incomprehensible. Yet the technique of triangulation offers us a way out. For all three of the words chosen by the translators—*ch'iu* 求 "seek," *i* 義 "meaning," and *li* 利 "benefit"—reflect aspects of a single Indian term, the word *artha*, which can mean "objective" (i.e., what one seeks) and "meaning" as well as "benefit."[37] Read in this light, the passage now makes sense: the bodhisattva lives in the forest in order to accomplish the objective (*artha*) of the *śramaṇa*, that is, to attain enlightenment.

The Tibetan, not surprisingly, confirms this interpretation, for it uses the term *don*, which is the standard Tibetan equivalent of the word *artha* and carries the whole range of meanings of the latter. Yet there are also cases (though certainly far less numerous) where the reverse is the case, and it is a Chinese version that helps to illuminate the meaning of the Tibetan.

In sum, whenever we have only a single extant translation of a given sūtra—particularly if that version is in Chinese—we must be extremely cautious about drawing any conclusions about Indian Buddhism on the basis of such an uncertain foundation. Yet when we have a variety of recensions of a given text to work with, the odds of commiting a grievous error of interpretation are greatly reduced. Clearly the absence of an Indic text is a far from ideal situation, yet the Chinese and Tibetan texts can still be used as sources for Indian Buddhism, provided they are used together and with utmost care.

---

37 Cf. MW 90b-c, where these and several other meanings are given.

CHAPTER 4

The Institutional Setting

One of the most controversial topics in recent studies of the bodhisattva path is the nature of the community out of which this distinctive form of Buddhist practice emerged. Was the idea of the bodhisattva vehicle the product, as HIRAKAWA Akira (e.g., 1957b, 1963, 1987, 1989, 1990b) has contended, of a lay-centered community of believers who gathered at reliquary mounds (*stūpa*) containing the remains of the Buddha? Or did it develop, as the work of scholars such as SHIZUTANI Masao (1957, 1974), Paul Harrison (1987, 1995), and SASAKI Shizuka (1995, 1997a) strongly suggests, within traditional monastic organizations? Should this new form of practice be understood as a liberalizing "reform movement" that stood in tension with a more conservative sangha—as virtually all the standard encyclopedias and textbooks would have it—or was it an elite subset within the monastic establishment, demanding even more of its devotees than did the traditional *śrāvaka* vehicle? Was the bodhisattva path a movement of "engaged Buddhists" (to use the contemporary Franco-Vietnamese expression coined by Thich Nhat Hanh) concerned with bettering the conditions of life in this world, or were its proponents advocating even greater withdrawal from society than were their *śrāvaka* counterparts? In short, what can we say about the institutional basis, the social environment, and the cultic setting out of which the bodhisattva movement grew?

In attempting to answer these questions we will be drawing mainly on evidence associated with what was described in the previous chapter as "the principle of irrelevance": that is, items the *Ugra* does not argue for or against, but simply mentions in passing as part of the background. If the *Ugra* were to tell us, for example, that a householder bodhisattva *should* visit the monastery (*vihāra*), we might well suspect that many bodhisattvas were not doing so; conversely, if it were to exhort the householder bodhisattva *not* to visit the monastery, we could infer that some, at least, were making a practice of frequenting monastic centers. If, however, the sūtra simply states (as in fact it does) that *when* the lay bodhisattva visits the *vihāra* he should conduct himself in a certain way, the sūtra is revealing that visits to the monastery by lay Buddhists were standard practice.

Incidental remarks of this sort, in other words, will supply us with the majority of the data to be analyzed in this section.

Defining Categories: Household vs. Renunciant Life

We may begin with an aspect of the Buddhist community, as seen by the writers of the *Ugra*, that is embedded within the very structure of the text itself: the fundamental distinction between the home-dwelling Buddhist (*gṛhin*), on the one hand, and the renunciant or monastic practitioner (*pravrajita*, lit. "gone forth") on the other.[1] So basic is this distinction that the entire sūtra is constructed around it: a discussion of practices appropriate to the householder bodhisattva comprises the first part of the sūtra, while the latter part is devoted to an enumeration of practices to be undertaken by the renunciant bodhisattva. The *Ugra* does not argue for, or even reflect upon, the fact of this distinction; it simply accepts it as a matter of course. The bifurcation of the Buddhist community into householder and renunciant practitioners may thus be viewed as part of the very fabric of the world within which the *Ugra* was produced.[2]

---

[1] The Indian terms can be established with certainty, thanks to the citations preserved in Śāntideva's *Śikṣāsamuccaya*.

[2] In light of the fact that the distinction between home-dwelling and renunciant bodhisattvas is not only a major element of the plot, but determines the very structure of the sūtra itself, it is astonishing to read the claim in Hirakawa 1990b that "in the *Ugra* the distinction between the home-leaving (*shukke* 出家) and the home-dwelling (*zaike* 在家) [bodhisattva] is not clear" (p. 136). The only evidence Hirakawa offers in support of this statement is the fact that after the ordination of Ugra and his friends they continue to be addressed as *gṛhapati*, a term which (as Hirakawa rightly points out) is applicable only to lay people. Hirakawa goes on to argue that this ordination ritual did not result in their becoming *bhikṣu*s in the normal sense (i.e., ordained monks associated with a particular nikāya; p. 137) and ultimately that according to the *Ugra* "Bodhisattva Buddhism, even when one is engaging in strict practice, is fundamentally 'dwelling at the household level' " (p. 177).

There is, however, a much more straightforward solution to the problem of why Ugra and his friends continue to be called *gṛhapati* after their apparent ordination. In the earliest extant version (AY) the ordination scene appears at the end of the sūtra; in the later versions (Dh, R, and Tib), by contrast, it has been shifted to the middle. The editors who made this change, however, neglected to take the appropriate "touch-up" measures elsewhere in the text to ensure consistency. In sum, the fact that these characters are called *gṛhapati* in the

The division between renunciant and householder was not, of course, a new development in the time of the *Ugra*, nor was it the exclusive property of the Buddhist community. Already in the time of the Buddha the category of the *śramaṇa* (non-brahmanical renunciant) was well established; in this larger context to be a Buddhist monk or nun was simply to be a particular type of *śramaṇa*.[3] The fact that Buddhists are divided into home-dwelling and home-leaving categories in the *Ugra* thus does not tell us anything specific about the concerns of its compilers, except perhaps that they had no quarrel with this traditional division; rather, it simply reflects an institutional feature of Indian religious life at large.

The *Ugra* was evidently intended for an audience consisting exclusively of bodhisattvas, for it never addresses non-bodhisattvas (whether lay or monastic) directly. Non-bodhisattva laity, in fact, are never even mentioned; non-bodhisattva monks do appear, but only in contexts in which the bodhisattva is being instructed on how he should treat them. Nuns (or for that matter, female practitioners of any kind) never appear at all. Thus it is important to realize at the outset that the *Ugra* will not provide us with a complete portrait of the Buddhist community of its time, but will only refer to those segments of that community with which its authors expected its target audience to interact. Our discussion will therefore focus only on the three segments of the Buddhist community that actually appear in our text: male lay bodhisattvas, male monastic bodhisattvas, and male monastics who are not on the bodhisattva path.

Lay Bodhisattvas

More than half of the *Ugra*, as we have seen, is devoted to instructions to the lay bodhisattva. Most of this material (not surprisingly) is prescriptive in character, and will be dealt with in the following chapter. What is of concern to us here is information of a different kind: the data conveyed in passing about the nature of the community to which the lay bodhisattva belonged. We may begin with a negative observation: there is no mention in the text of groups of lay bodhisattvas gathering at any place, for any purpose; indeed

second half of the text is simply a reflection of the fact that, in the original version, they had not yet been ordained. For a more detailed discussion of this issue see above, pp. 62-63.

[3] On the category of *śramaṇa* as such see Jaini 1970.

there is not a trace of anything that could be construed as a "congregational" community with strong horizontal bonds of shared practice and mutual encouragement among bodhisattvas of roughly equal status. The only interactions between individual lay bodhisattvas and other Buddhists portrayed in the sūtra are vertical relationships, that is, interactions with ordained monks who by definition are superior to them in status.[4] The picture that emerges is not one of a mutually supportive community of bodhisattvas, but of individual lay bodhisattvas practicing more or less in isolation—separate spokes of a wheel, as it were, whose hub was the monastic community.[5]

These interactions between the lay bodhisattva and his monastic counterparts are described in the *Ugra* in some detail. It is taken for granted, first of all, that the lay bodhisattva will visit the monastery (§18A);[6] the sūtra never prescribes that he should do so, but simply sets forth the proper conduct to engage in when he does. It is also assumed that he will have the opportunity to learn the specific specializations of the various monks within the monastery, ranging from vinaya specialist to meditator to administrator (§20C). The fact that the lay bodhisattva is urged to emulate the conduct of these various specialists insofar as he is able (§§20C, E), and that he is warned not to reveal what takes place within the monastery to those outside its walls (§20D), suggests that he would have had considerable access to information on the particulars of monastic life.

---

[4] Superior, in other words, in terms of religious vocation. On the variety of hierarchical systems used by Indian Buddhists in this period (including vocation, spiritual achievement, gender, and *yāna*) see Nattier 1996. The lay bodhisattva is also portrayed as encouraging those in his community to adhere to the Dharma in a general sense (see below, pp. 77-78), but it is not clear whether these recipients of his exhortations are in any sense "Buddhist." Whatever their religious affiliation, once again no individual or ongoing relationship between them and the bodhisattva is portrayed.

[5] Because so many 20th-century Buddhist groups in the West (and some new Buddhist organizations in other westernized countries, such as Sri Lanka and Japan) are congregational in character—stressing fraternal relations among equals and even, in some cases, meeting in the homes of lay practitioners rather than at temples or monasteries—there has been a notable tendency on the part of some scholars (especially Americans and Japanese) to read this contemporary model back into earlier centuries. The *Ugra*, however, provides absolutely no support for such a scenario.

[6] On various translation terms for "monastery" see below, pp. 90-93.

All of these relationships, however, are described in quite impersonal terms. The lay bodhisattva is portrayed as interacting with a whole range of monastic practitioners, but not as establishing a special relationship with any one of them. There is nothing resembling the strong guru-disciple bond that would later become normative in tantric Buddhism; indeed, on the one occasion when an explicit reference is made to the lay bodhisattva's teachers, the term for "teacher" appears in the plural (§4B).[7] For the authors of the *Ugra*, it would seem, the lay bodhisattva's interactions with the monastic community take place in what might be described as "corporate" terms, not involving the formation of a close personal attachment to any particular individual.

The sūtra also provides considerable detail about the home life of the lay bodhisattva. It assumes, first of all, that he will be a husband and father, and the intensity of the sūtra's insistence that he cultivate revulsion for his wife and indifference toward his son suggests that these family bonds were viewed by the *Ugra*'s authors as dangerously strong.[8] Not only the bodhisattva's immediate family members but a large number of others are included in the picture, including his parents, paid workers, and male and female slaves.[9] Ugra and his companions—the only lay Buddhists who actually appear in the text, aside from the large group of servants who accompany them—are portrayed as men of considerable means, each arriving in the presence of the Buddha accompanied by a retinue of five hundred attendants. Indeed they are labeled as belonging to a specific social category: that of the *gṛhapati*, a member of the wealthiest and most influential segment of what was to become the *vaiśya* caste.[10]

The lay bodhisattva portrayed in the *Ugra* is thus a typical family man (typical, that is, of a certain highly privileged stratum of Indian society), living at home and interacting with the organized monastic community on occasion. But even as he is urged to minimize his ties with his wife and children, he is told to interact with more distant members of his town or village and exhort them to take up Buddhist practice (§8A). Like a physician who, if he fails to cure even one

---

[7] Two additional mentions of teachers—likewise in the plural—appear only in the Tibetan (§§5C and 6B).

[8] See below, Chapter 5, pp. 115-117.

[9] One of the longest lists occurs in §5A. On the issue of slavery in Buddhist sūtra literature see Silk 1992.

[10] On the term *gṛhapati* see Chapter 2, pp. 22-24.

person of an illness, will be blamed by the local people, if the bodhisattva fails to admonish even one being and as a result that being is born into one of the evil destinies, the bodhisattva will be held responsible by the Buddhas themselves (§8D).

These are of course prescriptive statements, and we might hesitate to take them seriously were it not for the fact that the text offers specific advice for what the bodhisattva should do when his activities as "dharma-monitor" do not meet with success. If after as many as seven attempts ("one hundred" in the two earliest translations) the beings who are the target of his exhortations do not respond, he is told to direct great compassion toward them and to recall that it is for the sake of unruly beings like these—not for those who are already advanced in morality and insight—that he has taken the bodhisattva vow (§8B-C).

Once again it should be noted that the relationships described here are hierarchical ones, in this case with the bodhisattva as the senior figure urging less devoted Buddhists (or even non-Buddhists) to improve themselves. Indeed one wonders whether such interactions would have led to a "relationship" at all; it seems equally likely that the neighbors and associates of such a bodhisattva would merely have perceived him as a nuisance.

Be that as it may, it is clear that for the authors of the *Ugra* the bodhisattva's possibilities in this world are represented as consisting of two quite unequal options: his present situation in the home (portrayed as deeply disadvantageous to his religious pursuits), on the one hand, and his eventual ordination as a *bhikṣu*, either in this life or in a future one, on the other. No third alternative is either advocated or criticized, nor is the bodhisattva assigned to a "middle category" between these two. Rather, he is described in the terms traditionally applied to the *upāsaka*,[11] and is urged to abandon this second-class status for that of the ordained monk as soon as he is able.

---

[11] Given the amount of space devoted in the *Ugra* to discussing the activities of the home-dwelling bodhisattva, it is striking that the words *upāsaka* (masc.) and *upāsikā* (fem.)—usually taken to be the ordinary terms for "lay Buddhist"—never appear in the text. At first glance we might suspect that the householder bodhisattva and the *upāsaka* belong to different categories, but a closer look suggests another possibility. An *upāsaka* is not simply a "non-monastic Buddhist"; rather, the term refers to a specific category consisting of lay Buddhists (one might better use the terms "lay brother" and "lay sister") who are particularly diligent in their Buddhist practice (cf. above, Chapter 2, nn. 31 and 32). Specific activities are generally associated with becoming an

Monastic Bodhisattvas

Just as the lay bodhisattva is portrayed in our text in terms consistent with the traditional role of the *upāsaka*, so the renunciant bodhisattva appears in the *Ugra* as a particular type of monk. He is described as wearing monastic robes (§24A), interacting with his *ācārya* and *upādhyaya* (§§24E, 26B), and taking part in an assembly where he will meet with others whom he should treat with respect regardless of their level of monastic seniority (§26A). In a particularly interesting passage (to which we will return below) the *Ugra* lists four characteristics which, if possessed by a renunciant bodhisattva, entitle him to engage in solitary practice in the wilderness (*araṇya*) rather than the monastery (§25K). Taken as a whole, the offhand remarks provided by the *Ugra* about the renunciant bodhisattva's life conform with what we would expect of a *bhikṣu* belonging to any Nikāya community.

Conversely, the *Ugra* contains no criticism of *bhikṣus* as such, which if present might have constituted evidence that the renunciant bodhisattvas comprised an independent order distinct from that of ordained monastics. Indeed, far from criticizing the *bhikṣu* or trying to play down his role in the community, a major concern of the authors of the *Ugra* seems to have been to ensure proper respect for all Buddhist monks, be they *śrāvakas* or bodhisattvas (e.g., §§3D, 17A-C, 20F).

---

upāsaka, that is, taking the three refuges, observing the five ethical precepts, frequenting the monastery in order to hear teachings and make offerings, and taking extra vows on festival or *uposatha* days (which in essence involve emulating monastic behavior). Moreover, the role of the *upāsaka*, as the etymology of the term ("one who serves") would imply, is to associate with and to be of service to the monastic community.

All these activities, from serving and paying respects to ordained monks (whether or not they themselves are bodhisattvas) to taking refuge, upholding the ethical precepts, and observing the *uposatha* day, are mentioned in connection with the householder bodhisattva in the *Ugra*. Moreover, there is no criticism of *upāsakas* as such, nor are lay bodhisattvas ever explicitly contrasted with lay Buddhists of any other type. The most reasonable explanation for the absence of the term *upāsaka*, therefore, would seem to be that to the authors of the *Ugra* it was self-evident that all householder bodhisattvas belonged to this category. Just as one would hardly need to add the epithet "Catholic" when describing a Carmelite nun to a Roman Catholic audience, just so the authors of the *Ugra* may have considered it quite redundant to specify that a home-dwelling bodhisattva was also an *upāsaka*.

Most significant for our purposes, however, is the following passage, which contains a detailed list of the various specialties in which members of the monastic community might be engaged. Upon entering the monastic precincts, the layman is told, he should reflect as follows:

> Which monk is a learned one? Which monk is a Dharma-preacher? Which monk is a Vinaya-holder? Which monk is a Mātṛkā-holder? Which monk is a Bodhisattva-piṭaka-holder? Which monk is a wilderness-dweller? Which monk lives on almsfood? Which monk dresses in rags from the dustheap, has few desires, is satisfied [with what he has], and lives in seclusion? Which monk does yogic practice? Which monk practices meditation? Which monk belongs to the bodhisattva vehicle? Which monk is in charge of repairs? Which monk is the administrator? Which monk is the overseer? (§20C)[12]

Several things are noteworthy about this passage, but we may begin with the observation that the member of the bodhisattva vehicle is only one of several types of monks the layman might meet. Just as the other items on this list are specialties engaged in by one or more—but not all—of the monks in a given monastery, so being a bodhisattva was clearly an optional pursuit. The picture the *Ugra* provides conforms, in other words, with the information supplied by Chinese travelers some centuries later: that bodhisattva and non-bodhisattva monks could and did live together within a single monastery.[13]

This passage also contains an important clue to the possible Nikāya affiliation of the group that produced the *Ugra*: the fact that its authors knew of a canon consisting of four sections, which included (in addition to the standard "three baskets" of sūtra, vinaya, and abhidharma literature) a *bodhisattva-piṭaka*.[14] Since the only

---

[12] For a synoptic chart of the specific terms used in the Chinese and Tibetan versions see Appendix 3.

[13] For reports by Chinese travelers of "mixed" Mahāyāna and "Hīnayāna" monastic communities see the accounts by Fa-hsien 法顯 (Legge 1886, e.g., p. 41) and Hsüan-tsang 玄奘 (Beal 1906, vol. 2, pp. 133, 208, etc; for a tabulation of his figures see Lamotte 1988b, pp. 540-543). Hirakawa, however (1990b, pp. 128-129 and *passim*), argues on essentially *a priori* grounds that this would have been difficult if not impossible; for an evaluation of his arguments see below, pp. 84-86.

[14] R alone offers a different list, consisting of *sūtra* (*fa* 法), *vinaya*, *āgama* (sic! *a-han* 阿含), and *bodhisattva-piṭaka*. Given the concord of the other three versions, it seems certain that the word *āgama* is simply an error made in the

Nikāya school which is explicitly described in surviving literature as possessing such a canon is the Dharmaguptaka school, this bit of evidence points to the possibility (though hardly the certainty) that the *Ugra* was a product of a Dharmaguptaka monastic order.

Whatever the Nikāya affiliation of its authors, however, the overall picture that the *Ugra* presents is quite clear. It describes a monastic community in which scriptures concerning the bodhisattva path were accepted as legitimate canonical texts (and their memorization a viable monastic specialty), but in which only a certain subset of monks were involved in the practices associated with the Bodhisattva Vehicle. The bodhisattva path thus appears as an option elected by some members of the monastic community, while others (in all probability the majority) continued to follow the traditional *śrāvaka* path.[15]

The issue of the relationship between advocates of these two vehicles as portrayed in the *Ugra* will be discussed in the following section. First, however, we must pause to consider an issue we have already treated in the case of the lay bodhisattva: what the sūtra can tell us about the monastic bodhisattva's interactions with other Buddhists.

Were we to focus on the prescriptive portions of the text, the most striking aspect of the *Ugra*'s discussion of the renunciant bodhisattva would be its insistence that, under ideal circumstances, he

---

course of transmission of the text, probably based on an earlier *abhidharma*, which would be the equivalent of the word *mātṛka* which seems to underlie the other versions.

[15] Our text contains no information on whether all reciters of the *bodhisattva-piṭaka* were themselves bodhisattvas, or for that matter, whether all bodhisattvas participated in the memorization and transmission of such texts. Complete identity of the two groups should not be assumed (as does Hirakawa, 1990b, p. 132), though doubtless there was considerable overlap between the two. In the *Aṣṭasāhasrikā-prajñāpāramitā*, for example, we find references to bodhisattvas who did not accept the Perfection of Wisdom sūtras as legitimate (e.g., viii.178ff., xi.234ff.). Conversely, the same text urges *śrāvaka*s and bodhisattvas alike to study the *prajñāpāramitā* texts (i.6) and states that while not all beings will comprehend these teachings, those who have attained Arhatship will (ii.40). The *Akṣobhyavyūha-sūtra*, too, recommends that members of the Śrāvakayāna as well as the Bodhisattvayāna listen to and recite this text (Stog Palace reprint ed., 36.178-182) and promises that by doing so they will be able to attain Arhatship quickly, perhaps even within this very life (179-180). For references to still other statements of this kind see Pagel 1995, p. 8, n. 5.

should not interact with anyone at all. He is told that he should "be happy alone" (§24D), that he should "not mix with householders or renunciants" (§27A), and that he should "not be in close contact with many people" (§25C). The Buddha states that this general rule should be followed whenever possible, but that under certain circumstances fraternizing with others is allowed: the renunciant bodisattva may do so in order to listen to the Dharma, to "mature beings," to revere the Tathāgata, or to associate with those whose "spirit of Omniscience" (*sarvajñacitta*) is uncontaminated (*loc. cit.*). Aside from these occasions, the renunciant bodhisattva should remain apart from all human contact.

This is, of course, the voice of the narrator, and in insisting that the bodhisattva keep his personal interactions to a minimum he is revealing (by the principle of counterargument discussed in Chapter 3) that such contacts were in fact taking place. We will return to these prescriptive passages in the following chapter; our concern at present, however, is to see what the *Ugra* can tell us about the kinds of interactions in which renunciant bodhisattvas were actually involved. Two such instances are explicitly mentioned in our text: first, the renunciant bodhisattva's contact with lay almsgivers, and second, his participation in monastic assemblies.

The first of these is dealt with fairly briefly, in the course of an exhortation to the bodhisattva to remain even-minded (i.e., impartial) toward all the beings he meets on his alms-rounds and to use the begging encounter as an opportunity to induce those who do not give him alms to embark on a life of renunciation (§24B). The same passage concludes with a statement by the Buddha that the renunciant bodhisattva may accept a special invitation to a meal if (and only if) he is able to "benefit both self and other" by so doing. These comments offer us a small window into some of the issues that renunciant bodhisattvas actually encountered in dealing with others: their own all-too-human tendency to favor certain lay people (especially the more generous donors) over others, the fact that they were sometimes rebuffed by the householders from whom they sought alms, and finally the fact that there was some degree of controversy within the Buddhist community over whether it was proper for the renunciant bodhisattva to take a meal in a lay person's home.

The renunciant bodhisattva's interactions with other monastic Buddhists receive a somewhat more detailed discussion. He is described as entering an assembly for the purpose of listening to the recitation of texts, and there he can expect to encounter his teacher (*ācārya*) and preceptor (*upādhyaya*) (§26A). These are well-known monastic titles, the latter referring to the teacher who presides over a novice's ordination and continues to instruct him for several years afterwards.[16] In the same passage the bodhisattva is told that he should show proper respect to all those in the assembly, regardless of whether they are elders (*sthavira*), of middle rank (*madhya*), or junior (*navaka*)—again, a well-known set of seniority levels within Buddhist monastic communities.[17] The text goes on to say that when he approaches his teacher or preceptor he should do so with decorum and mindfulness, and that he should fulfill the wishes of these two figures "out of desire for the Dharma" (§26B). The picture presented here is that, unlike the lay bodhisattva who appears not to have special relationships with particular individuals in the monastic community, the renunciant bodhisattva does, and these individuals are the traditional teacher and preceptor of Nikāya communities. That they are viewed as a source of the Dharma—that is, not simply as bureaucratic officials but as teachers—is strongly suggested by the reference to his "desire for the Dharma" quoted above.

The *Ugra* goes on, however, to single out a particular individual to whom the renunciant bodhisattva should offer special veneration: the teacher who recites even a single verse dealing with the perfections (*pāramitā*) of the bodhisattva (§26C).[18] The sūtra speaks in extravagant terms of the degree of reverence that such a teacher should receive (§26C-D), suggesting that those individuals could—and, in the view of the narrator, should—receive particular veneration. It is not difficult to discern the seeds of eventual disruption of harmony within the monastic community that are inherent in such a prescription.

---

[16] On these titles see Sasaki 1997b and 1997c.

[17] The terminology can be established with certainty thanks to the citation preserved in the *Śikṣāsamuccaya*. For examples of the same usage in Pāli (*thera-bhikkhu, majjhima-bhikkhu, nava-bhikkhu*) see PTSD 310a-b.

[18] Our text does not state explicitly that these are identical with the *bodhisattva-piṭaka* reciters referred to above (§20C), but because the content of the teachings mentioned in §26C are the same as those described in a more detailed discussion of the role of the *bodhisattva-piṭaka* reciter that occurs earlier in the text (§20E), there is good reason to think that they were.

Bodhisattvas and *Śrāvaka*s in the Buddhist Community

The *Ugra* provides a fairly detailed picture of the place of the renunciant bodhisattva within the larger community of ordained *bhikṣus*. Yet some scholars have insisted that this could not be what the *Ugra* intends to convey. By far the most influential of these voices is that of HIRAKAWA Akira, who in a long series of publications, most recently in the revised edition of his *Shoki daijō bukkyō no kenkyū* (*Studies in Early Mahāyāna Buddhism*) (1989 and 1990b), has argued that such a living arrangement would be difficult, if not impossible. His reasoning is as follows: "Between the various Nikāyas," he writes, "differences of doctrine and faith were not very striking. But between the Great Vehicle and the Small Vehicle, both doctrinal differences and differences in faith were great" (1990b, p. 128). Citing a passage from the **Daśabhūmikavibhāṣā* that warns the bodhisattva against "falling to the level" of the Śrāvaka and Pratyekabuddha Vehicles and describes such a fall as the "death of the bodhisattva," he concludes that people of the Bodhisattvayāna "abhorred (*ken'o* 嫌悪) and disdained (*besshi* 蔑視)" the Śrāvakayāna (*loc. cit.*). "Even in Japanese Buddhism," Hirakawa goes on to observe, "monks of different creeds (*shūshi* 宗旨) do not live in the same temple" (p. 129). Thus Hirakawa finds it difficult to conceive of the possibility that renunciant bodhisattvas could live in a "mixed temple" that included both *śrāvaka*s and bodhisattvas (*loc. cit.*).

Such reasoning, however, is based on a category mistake: a confusion between the Mahāyāna as a school of thought, on the one hand, and as a religious vocation on the other. To argue as Hirakawa does requires that we think of these early bodhisattvas as belonging to a distinctive doctrinal or philosophical school, not merely as carrying out one option for religious practice that was viewed as valid (though certainly not as obligatory) by their monastic fellows. To be sure, a number of philosophical schools associated with the label "Mahāyāna" (e.g., the Mādhyamika, the Yogācāra, and the Tathāgatagarbha, as well as the often less systematic schools of thought centered around particular sūtras) would eventually arise both in India and elsewhere. Yet within the *Ugra* itself we find no evidence whatsoever that this had yet taken place.[19] On the contrary, the term "Mahāyāna"—when it is used at all, which in fact is quite rarely—has one meaning and

---

[19] For a discussion of the meaning of the term "Mahāyāna" as used in the various versions of the *Ugra* see below, Chapter 8.

one meaning only: the pursuit of the bodhisattva path culminating in Buddhahood.

Hirakawa's argument that *śrāvaka*s and bodhisattvas could not easily live together because of "differences in doctrine and faith" thus requires that we import into the *Ugra* an assumption for which the text itself offers no evidence whatsoever: the idea that bodhisattvas differed from their *śrāvaka* counterparts in their doctrinal or philosophical beliefs. What we actually see in the sūtra, however, is not differences in "doctrine and faith" but a difference in vocation, just as a Catholic priest or nun—while clearly following a higher and more demanding calling—is no different in matters of belief (though perhaps more sophisticated) than his or her lay counterparts. The difference is thus not a matter of religious affiliation, much less of "doctrine and faith" as Hirakawa would have it, but of the selection of a particular lifestyle among a number of such options—that is, of a vocation. And the bodhisattva vocation, despite its relative newness, appears in the *Ugra* as being accepted as legitimate, and indeed admired, by the larger *śrāvaka* community.

It is in this context that we must interpret the warnings against "falling to the level" of the *śrāvaka* or the *pratyekabuddha* that Hirakawa adduces as evidence that members of the bodhisattva vehicle despised these other vehicles. Here too we are dealing with a methodological error, in this case with a failure to consider the context within which these remarks are made. First of all, it must be noted that these exhortations not to fall to the (clearly lower) level of the *śrāvaka* or *pratyekabuddha* are consistently made by bodhisattvas to bodhisattvas—that is, these are statements made by and for Buddhists who have already undertaken the strenuous path leading to Buddhahood. What this implies is that we are dealing here with a type of "in-house" discourse, which is not necessarily intended to be universal in its implications. To urge someone who is already on the bodhisattva path not to abandon his vocation is not at all the same thing as urging all Buddhists to become bodhisattvas. A careful reading of the texts that Hirakawa quotes shows that none of these passages are addressed to the Buddhist community at large; on the contrary, they are addressed only to those who have already elected to pursue the bodhisattva vocation.

What we are seeing, in other words—to change to an academic analogy—is something like a conversation that might take place between an advisor and an aspiring Ph.D. student who expresses doubts about his ability to complete his degree. The advisor might well encourage her student not to give up and take a "mere" terminal M.A., but to accept the challenge and strive for the highest and most distinguished attainment—the Ph.D. degree. Or to use a Catholic analogy once again, just as the mission of an ordained priest is to serve a community made up largely of those who have a different (i.e., a lay) vocation, so that of the Ph.D.—should he actually manage to land an academic post—is to help others attain what are admittedly lower, but still admirable, goals: the B.A. and M.A. degrees.

The authors of the *Ugra*, then—like the authors of numerous other bodhisattva scriptures which have likewise been misread as disparaging or rejecting the *śrāvaka* path—are expressing their commitment to a difficult and delicate task: that of encouraging and supporting those who have undertaken the bodhisattva vocation, while at the same time attempting to preserve harmony within a Buddhist community that now offers its members two quite distinct, and unequal, religious goals. While the bodhisattva vocation is consistently portrayed as the highest and most excellent option, the *Ugra* and other bodhisattva sūtras of roughly comparable vintage (e.g., the *Aṣṭasāhasrikā-prajñāpāramitā*, the *Akṣobhyavyūha*, and the *Kāśyapaparivarta*, to mention only a few) stop short of recommending it to all Buddhists.[20] Indeed, the equation found in so many contemporary Japanese and western writings between the "Mahāyāna" (i.e., the pursuit of the bodhisattva path oneself) and the notion of *ekayāna*, or "one vehicle" (the idea that the *śrāvaka* path is unacceptable or unreal and that all Buddhists should pursue the bodhisattva path) is strikingly absent from this literature. The widespread assumption that Mahāyāna and *ekayāna* are synonymous is not based on the earliest (or the most numerous) bodhisattva scriptures, but is rather the result—I strongly suspect—of reading Indian bodhisattva literature in the aggregate through the hermeneutical lens of the *Lotus Sūtra*, a text which played a central role in East Asian scriptural interpretation but whose status was far less important, and perhaps even marginal, on the Indian subcontinent itself.[21]

Be that as it may, the fact that bodhisattvas and *śrāvaka*s coexisted within a single Buddhist community (as clearly implied in the *Ugra* and in other early bodhisattva scriptures) does not imply

---

[20] The *Kāśyapaparivarta* does make this move, however, in its later translations; see §4 in von Staël-Holstein 1926.

[21] For a preliminary discussion of this issue see Nattier 1997.

that there were not significant problems with this arrangement. It is easy to imagine the kinds of tensions that could arise between, say, a junior monk who had just embarked on the bodhisattva path and an elder who had been following the traditional *śrāvaka* path for many years. Who should receive greater respect from the monastic community (and from potential lay donors): the young bodhisattva or the senior *śrāvaka*? What if the latter is not only an elder, but has actually attained stream-enterership or even Arhatship? How might such a person feel toward a newly ordained bodhisattva who—by his very choice of vehicle, however modest his speech and conduct might be—was proclaiming, in essence, that the path to Arhatship was not good enough for him? Even when the lines of authority and respect are quite clear, there are infinite possibilities for rivalry and oneupsmanship in communal religious situations, as any reader who has actually lived in such an institution will attest. When we add to this generic difficulty the fact that (according to many self-proclaimed Mahāyāna sūtras) even a bodhisattva who has just experienced the arousal of *bodhicitta* should be viewed as superior to an Arhat,[22] the possibilities for jealousy and friction become quite evident.

But we need not rely on imagination alone. In several passages the *Ugra* expresses concern about tensions between members of the bodhisattva and *śrāvaka* vehicles, thus revealing that such tensions were indeed a problem in the community to which its authors belonged. Particular care is taken to ensure that the lay bodhisattva not show any disrespect to the monastic *śrāvaka*. He is explicitly told

---

[22] There are countless examples of such statements in sūtras dealing with the bodhisattva path. See for example the **Vimaladattā-sūtra*, which proclaims that all bodhisattvas, from the first moment of *bodhicitta* until the final attainment of Buddhahood, are superior to Arhats and Pratyekabuddhas (T 338, 12.96b4-6; cf. T 310[33], 11.563a22-23, and the Tibetan version in Peking [Ōtani] 760[33], vol. 24, 111.1.4-5). An even more radical stance is taken in the **Aśokadattā-sūtra*, where the twelve-year-old daughter of King Ajātaśatru refuses to rise and bow to a group of Buddhist monks because she is a bodhisattva, while they are mere *śrāvaka*s! (T 337, 12.84b2ff.; cf. T 310[32], 11.550c8ff. and the Tibetan version in Peking 760[32], vol. 24, 96.4.7ff.) Even the *Kāśyapaparivarta*—which almost certainly belongs to an earlier layer of literature than either of the sūtras just cited—makes a similar assertion, contending that "Even a bodhisattva who has just aroused the spirit of enlightenment (*bodhicitta*) for the first time surpasses all the Arhats and Pratyekabuddhas" (§85).

that he should not look down on those monks who are not candidates for Buddhahood (i.e., who are on the *śrāvaka* path), recognizing that when he becomes a Buddha in the distant future he too will preside over a community of *śrāvaka*s (§3D). The job description of a Buddha, in other words, is to ensure that others will succeed in following the *śrāvaka* path to Arhatship.[23] To despise those who are following that path at present would thus be to undermine the very purpose of the bodhisattva's own endeavors. Even if a monk has fallen far short of the prescribed conduct of the *śramaṇa* (a term our text uses as a generic category for renunciant religious practitioners, including Buddhist monks), the lay bodhisattva should not criticize or despise him, but should recall that the monastic robe itself is the "banner of sages" (**ṛṣi-dhvaja*) and that the Buddha forbade criticizing others (§17A-C). All the inhabitants of the monastery—not just the monk who happens to be a member of the bodhisattva vehicle—are portrayed as worthy objects of reverence, and as persons whose activities and attitudes he should strive to emulate (§20C and E). In the case of a monk who is sick, the home-dwelling bodhisattva is told that he should attempt to cure him of that sickness "even by means of his own flesh and blood" (§20F). There is no indication here that the lay bodhisattva should reserve this kind of service for monks who are on the bodhisattva path.

Similar injunctions, as we have seen, are directed toward the monastic bodhisattva: he should show respect for all *bhikṣus*, regardless of their level of seniority (§26A), and he should show proper veneration to his own teacher and preceptor (§26A-B). When he returns to the monastery after a period of time spent in solitary practice in the wilderness, he should not (despite his relatively exalted status as a bodhisattva) expect to receive special service from others (§26A). Once again, the attempt of the authors seems to be directed toward ensuring that the bodhisattva's aberrant—that is, unusually distinguished—status will not result in pride on his part and a

---

[23] This very simple fact—which is a fundamental assumption in the earliest bodhisattva literature—has long been overlooked by both Japanese and western scholars, due in large part (I suspect) to the inordinate influence of the *Lotus Sūtra* and its radical new doctrine of the "one vehicle." This doctrine, while central to East Asian Buddhism almost from the outset, required many centuries to gain even a modicum of acceptance in India. For an extended discussion of the doctrine of the three vehicles as understood in the *Ugra* and other early bodhisattva scriptures see Chapter 6, especially pp. 138-141, and Chapter 7, pp. 174-176.

disruption of harmonious relationships within the community. What the authors reveal, in so doing, is a growing sense of the possibility that the distinction between *śrāvaka*s and bodhisattvas could lead to an intolerable degree of veneration for the latter, and a corresponding slighting of the former, within a still unified monastic community.[24]

The *Vihāra* and the Wilderness

One of the types of monks that the lay bodhisattva is told he might meet within the monastic compound is rather unexpected: the wilderness-dweller, or *āraṇyaka*. A long discussion is devoted to wilderness-dwelling in the latter section of the sūtra, and it is clear that the authors of the *Ugra* are enthusiastic advocates of this practice. What seems surprising, though, is the fact that the householder bodhisattva, when visiting a *vihāra*, expects to meet the wilderness-dwelling bodhisattva there.

Indeed there have been extended discussions—almost all of them in Japanese, and all of them written either by or in reaction to the work of HIRAKAWA Akira—about whether a *vihāra* is referred to here at all. Before discussing the relationship portrayed in the *Ugra* between wilderness-dwelling monks and their *vihāra*-dwelling counterparts, therefore, we must pause to consider this question in detail.

Hirakawa's theory of the lay origins of the Mahāyāna. In an extensive series of publications beginning nearly half a century ago (Hirakawa 1957b) and culminating in his *magnum opus* of 1968 (reissued in slightly updated form as Hirakawa 1989 and 1990b), Hirakawa has argued that the "Mahāyāna" arose not within a traditional monastic environment, but in lay-centered communities of bodhisattvas who congregated at stūpas. For Hirakawa this scenario involves not only the institutional independence of such groups from the traditional monastic establishment and their freedom from standard monastic observances (e.g., the *prātimokṣa*) but the cultivation of positive new practices—above all, devotion to the Buddha—as well. In sum, for Hirakawa the emergence of something

---

[24] By this time there were, of course, a number of distinct ordination lineages (*nikāya*), but what I am suggesting is that difference of vehicle (that is, the *śrāvaka* vs. the bodhisattva path) did not yet constitute the basis for a separate institutional structure. For further discussion see below, Chapter 8.

known as the "Mahāyāna" involved not only the pursuit of the alternative goal of Buddhahood, but the formation of a separate community with a distinctive set of beliefs and practices as well.[25]

Using the *Ugra* as one of his sources, Hirakawa has constructed a theory describing a gradual shift from a lay-centered community of bodhisattvas, independent of existing monastic communities and assembling at stūpa sites, to a later "monasticized" form of Mahāyāna Buddhism in which renunciant bodhisattvas began to emulate their non-bodhisattva counterparts, even taking up formal ordination and the observance of the monastic rules. In other words, while the bodhisattva "movement" was at first institutionally independent, over the course of time it gradually accommodated itself to the monastic establishment. Specifically, Hirakawa argues that the Chinese word *miao* 廟, used in two early Chinese sūtra translations (one of them AY's version of the *Ugra*) to label the place where bodhisattvas congregated, refers to a "stūpa-temple" (Jpn. *tōji* 塔寺), while terms such as *seng-fang* 僧坊, *seng-ch'ieh-lan* 僧伽藍, *ching-she* 淨舍 that occur in parallel passages in later translations of the same sūtras refer to a *vihāra* or *saṁghārāma*. This change in vocabulary, Hirakawa contends, reflects the gradual transition from an indepen-dent stūpa-centered Mahāyāna community to a later "monasticized" Mahāyāna organization.[26]

---

[25] For the most recent statement of this position see Hirakawa, 1990b, especially pp. 189-255. A convenient summary of the main points contained in this volume and a discussion of some of the logical problems with Hirakawa's hypothesis can now be found in Sasaki 1995 (in Japanese) and 1997a (in English).

[26] In his earliest work (1957b) Hirakawa seems to suggest that only the vocabulary changed, while the institutional setting remained the same. By the time an English translation of his ideas first appeared in print (Hirakawa 1963), however, he had shifted to seeing this change in terminology as reflecting an actual adjustment by Mahāyānists to the monastic conventions of "Nikāya Buddhism."

Hirakawa's path to this conclusion is rather convoluted. His inquiry begins with the observation that, according to certain passages in the *Daśabhūmika-vibhāṣā*, renunciant bodhisattvas (*ch'u-chia p'u-sa* 出家菩薩) are said to reside either at a location referred to as *t'a-ssu* 塔寺 or in the wilderness (*araṇya*). In an attempt to determine the referent of the term *t'a-ssu* Hirakawa turns to another text translated by Kumārajīva, the *Saddharmapuṇḍarīka-sūtra*, which has an extant Sanskrit counterpart. Here he finds three occurrences of the expression *t'a-ssu*, two of which correspond to the word *stūpa* (or *dhātu-stūpa*) in the surviving Sanskrit, and the other of which corresponds to *vihāra*. Hirakawa

Hirakawa is quite right in pointing out that the vocabulary does change over time, and if this did indeed reflect changing conditions in India (rather than simply the changing preferences of Chinese translators) it would certainly be a major discovery. But there are methodological problems with his hypothesis at every turn. First of all, the hypothesis is based on a precariously small body of data: Hirakawa cites only four sources (the *Ugra*, an early translation of part of the *Avataṁsaka-sūtra*, the *Saddharmapuṇḍarīka-sūtra*, and the **Daśabhūmikavibhāṣa*), and identifies only two texts in which a shift from *miao* 廟 to terms clearly meaning "monastery" can be documented. But there are serious (indeed, fatal) flaws in both of these citations. In the case of the *Avataṁsaka*, Hirakawa argues that in the earliest translation (by Chih Ch'ien 支謙, 222-229 CE) the term *miao* (which in fact occurs in the compound expression *tsung miao* 宗廟) is a translation of stūpa, while the terms *seng-fang* 僧坊 and *seng-ch'ieh-lan* 僧伽藍 found in the corresponding passage in the two later Chinese versions (T 278 and 279, dating from 418-422 and 695-699 CE, respectively), as well as the expression *dge-'dun-gyi ra-ba* found in the Tibetan (c. 800 CE), reflect a shift from stūpa to "monastery" (*saṁghārāma*). As Sasaki has pointed out, however (1995, p. 51; 1997a, pp. 104-105), a discussion that unquestionably refers to a stūpa occurs in a subsequent passage in the same sūtra, and here Chih Ch'ien uses not the controversial word *miao* but rather *t'a* 塔, the ordinary Chinese word for *stūpa* (10.449b14-15).

There is likewise strong evidence against Hirakawa's assertion that *miao* translates the word *stūpa* in AY's *Ugra*. As with Chih

---

rejects this third example, arguing that *t'a-ssu* is not an acceptable translation of *vihāra* and that Kumārajīva must have been working from a different text. Based on the two remaining examples, Hirakawa concludes that whenever the expression *t'a-ssu* occurs in a translation by Kumārajīva, the underlying Indic term must be *stūpa*.

At this point Hirakawa turns for further illumination to the *Ugra* (which *Dbhv.* is quoting when it uses the term *t'a-ssu*) and to the *Avataṁsaka-sūtra* (*Hua-yen ching* 華嚴經), since *Dbhv.* also quotes from the *daśabhūmi* section of that sūtra, leading Hirakawa to conclude that *Dbhv.* "must also have a connection with the religious life of the believers of that sūtra" (a dubious move in methodological terms). It is in these two texts that he notes the use of the term *miao* 廟 in earlier translations paralleling a variety of terms which clearly mean "monastery" in the later ones, as discussed in the main text above. For a detailed discussion of the terminology adduced by Hirakawa see the articles by Sasaki cited in the preceding note.

Ch'ien's *Avataṁsaka*, the term *miao* occurs in AY in contexts where other versions of the sūtra all clearly read "monastery" (in this case, based on an underlying *vihāra* rather than *saṁghārāma*). Since AY contains no discussion of *stūpa*s at all,[27] we cannot use the same approach that Sasaki did to see how AY might translate this term. What we do have, however, is a passage in which the terminology points to a play on words using the term *vihāra*. When the lay bodhisattva finally enters the monastery (AY *miao*, Tib. *gtsug-lag khang* = Skt. *vihāra*), after cultivating the proper attitude of reverence he should reflect as follows:

> This is a place for dwelling in emptiness (Tib. *stong-pa-nyid-la gnas-pa'i gnas*, Skt. **śūnyatā-vihārāvāsa*). This is a place for dwelling in the signless (**animitta-vihārāvāsa*). This is a place for dwelling in the wishless (**apraṇihita-vihārāvāsa*). It is a place for dwelling in loving-kindness (*maitrī*), compassion (*karuṇā*), sympathetic joy (*muditā*), and equanimity (*upekṣā*). (§18A)

These last four items, of course, are the meditational states known as the *brahma-vihāra*s, thus continuing—or perhaps originally eliciting—the play on this word.[28]

Even without this philological evidence, however, the *Ugra*'s descriptions of those who dwell at the *miao* (in AY's rendition) and of the events that take place there make it clear that we have here not a new stūpa-based community, but a traditional—indeed, quite ordinary—Buddhist monastery. As we have already seen, the *Ugra* provides a long list of monastic specialists, ranging from vinaya specialist to meditator to administrator whom the lay bodhisattva might encounter at this place.[29] An impartial reading of this list leads convincingly to the conclusion that AY's term *miao* is simply an early

---

27 On this striking absence see below, Chapter 7.

28 Just as this work was going to press I stumbled across a statement in the *Gaṇḍavyūha* that is virtually identical to the beginning of this passage. Here (in reference to Maitreya's tower) the *Gaṇḍavyūha* reads: *ayaṁ sa śūnyatānimitta-apraṇihita-vihāra-vihāriṇām āvāsaḥ* (469.25), which might be translated (following Edgerton in BHSD 505a) as "This is the abode of those who dwell in the state of emptiness, the signless, and the wishless." Though the context and the meditational states mentioned are different, this is surely an echo of the same well-known saying, and it serves to confirm the suspicion that the underlying Indic text of the *Ugra* did indeed contain the word *vihāra*.

29 §20C (for the complete list see Appendix 3).

translation of *vihāra*. Certainly there is nothing in the Chinese use of the word *miao* to suggest that it would not have been an appropriate choice.[30]

In sum, Hirakawa's contention that the "Mahāyāna" emerged out of a cult of the stūpa finds absolutely no support in the *Ugra*. On the contrary, the sūtra provides copious evidence in support of the opposite theory: that the bodhisattva path was developed, as an optional religious vocation, within the confines of the traditional monastic community.

Ray's theory of the forest origins of the Mahāyāna. More recently an American scholar, Reginald Ray, has put forth a theory quite different than Hirakawa's, suggesting that the bodhisattva path emerged among forest-dwellers who devoted themselves to intensive meditation (Ray 1994). Like Hirakawa, Ray contends that the Mahāyāna arose outside the confines of the monastic establishment, but in contrast to Hirakawa's assertion that the laity played a key role Ray suggests that the first bodhisattvas were renunciants who were even more stringent in their religious practice than settled monks. Ray's argument assumes a fundamental dichotomy between ordained monastics (living in monasteries, concerned above all with the study of texts and adherence to the precepts, and neglecting actual practice and realization) and forest renunciants (devoting themselves to strenuous religious cultivation, above all to the practice of meditation). Contending that the standard "two-tiered model" which divides the Buddhist community into laity and monastics neglects an equally important third category of the forest renunciant (p. 433), Ray proposes a threefold model consisting of laity, settled monastics, and forest renunciants (p. 438ff.; cf. pp. 15-43 and *passim*). He views the two-tiered model as merely reflecting "certain dominant monastic ways of conceiving Buddhism within the Theravāda" (p. 433), and argues that it has led to the invisibility of the forest renunciant as a

---

30 Noting that "in China the term *miao* 廟 refers to the ancestral hall where people worshipped the wooden tablets of their ancestors," Hirakawa asserts that "the original [Indic] word must have indicated an object of worship." He goes on to say that the only appropriate candidates are *stūpa* and *caitya*, and that in the present instance he believes (for reasons that are not explicitly stated) that the underlying term must have been *stūpa* (see Hirakawa 1990b, p. 190; for an English citation see Sasaki 1997a, p. 104).

distinct religious type. "[T]he amplification of the forest voice," Ray writes, "has been the primary goal of this study" (p. 434).

While Ray provides copious evidence of the importance of the forest renunciant from earliest Buddhism to the present, it is in the emergence of the Mahāyāna (and again later of the Vajrayāna) that he sees this "third order" as playing a pivotal role. After surveying a number of bodhisattva sūtras in which he argues that wilderness-dwelling is privileged (pp. 251-292), Ray concludes that "the Mahāyāna from the beginning was primarily a forest tradition, *entirely non-monastic in character*" (p. 407, emphasis added).[31]

Ray has certainly succeeded in demonstrating that the *araṇya* (a term I prefer to translate as "wilderness" rather than "forest," to reflect that fact that it was viewed as a frightful place and not as a site for pleasant encounters with nature) plays a major role in a number of early bodhisattva sūtras, one of which is the *Ugra* itself. Yet it is far less clear that in any of these texts the *āraṇyaka*, or wilderness-dweller, is being treated as belonging to a category separate from that of the ordinary monk. In the *Ugra*, in fact, it is evident that the wilderness-dwelling bodhisattva is considered to be a particular kind of monk, albeit an especially diligent one. He appears in a list of monastic specialties as one of the people the lay bodhisattva can expect to meet in the monastery (§20C). He is described as making occasional trips back from the wilderness to take part in the life of the monastic community, even as he is urged to return to the wilderness as soon as possible (§24E). Finally, the *Ugra* offers a list of four conditions under which it is permissible for a monk to dwell in the wilderness (§25M). Taken together, these passages make it absolutely clear that the wilderness-dwelling bodhisattva was considered a member of the order of *bhikṣu*s even during the long periods of time

[31] It is not clear that all the sources adduced by Ray in this connection can legitimately be described as "pro-wilderness" texts. The *Ratnaguṇasaṁcaya-gāthā*, for example, uses the motif of the village (and indeed, the city) as a positive image (e.g., vii, §1; x, §3-4) while speaking of the wilderness as "full of famine and disease" (xix.8). The closely related *Aṣṭasāhasrikāprajñāpāra-mitāsūtra* takes an even stronger antiforest stance, referring to wilderness-dwelling as "the detachment recommended by Māra" (xxi.391). A reexamination of the representation of the wilderness-dwelling bodhisattva in the sources cited by Ray (drawing in all cases on the sūtras themselves and not merely on their citations in other works) is clearly to be desired. Finally, several of Ray's sources represent a fairly late layer of bodhisattva literature and thus are not relevant to a discussion of the initial emergence of the bodhisattva path.

he spent outside the monastery. The repeated mentions of the conditions under which he may return to the *vihāra*, and how he should conduct himself when he does so, make it clear that despite his intensive program of ascetic practice he remained within the orbit of the monastic community.[32] The wilderness-dweller as portrayed in the *Ugra*, in sum, is not independent of the monastic establishment, but is on a "long leash" (as it were) connecting him to the community within which he was ordained.

Ray's hypothesis that the bodhisattva path emerged among wilderness-dwelling renunciants thus comes closer to the mark than does Hirakawa's (at least as far as the *Ugra* is concerned), for he recognizes that the emergent bodhisattva vocation reflects an environment of strict asceticism, not a liberalized (or lay-influenced) community. Both scholars, however, fall into the trap of painting a monolithic portrait of "monastics" and then using this representation as evidence that the originators of the bodhisattva path must have come from outside their ranks. For Hirakawa, an assumed identity between *bhikṣus* and *śrāvakas* prevents him from considering the possibility that the renunciant bodhisattva portrayed in the *Ugra* could be an ordained monk;[33] for Ray, the assumption that settled monks and nuns have no time for meditation leads him to see all mentions of meditation in the wilderness as referring to individuals who had no connection to the monastic establishment.[34] In both cases

[32] Ray states that according to the *Ugra* "the *bodhisattva* who has left the world must reflect that the forest life was ordained by the Buddha,' and that in following the forest life 'there is fulfillment of the Pure Law" (p. 407). What he is actually citing, however, is not the *Ugra* itself but the *Śikṣāsamuccaya*'s quotation from it (Bendall 1897, 110.17-19; English translation in Bendall and Rouse 1922, p. 193), and the brevity of the quotation has led to a misunderstanding. Whereas Ray understands this passage as stating that the bodhisattva is *required* to live in the forest, in the sūtra itself it is clear that the opposite is intended: under certain conditions wilderness-dwelling is permitted, but if these conditions are not met the renunciant bodhisattva should remain in the monastery.

[33] For a detailed critique of this assumption see Sasaki 1995 and 1997a.

[34] It is interesting to note the extent to which the images of the type of community that must have produced the "Mahāyāna" held by Hirakawa and Ray, respectively, are reflective of the authors' own religious commitments. For Hirakawa—a member of the first school of Japanese Buddhism to abolish celibate monasticism in favor of a married priesthood (the Jōdo Shinshū school) and a citizen of the only Buddhist country in which the observance of the Vinaya has died out—it seems self-evident that the Mahāyāna must have begun

the point that the *Ugra*'s authors were trying to convey is lost from view: that the renunciant bodhisattva is simply a particular type—indeed, an exemplary type—of monk.[35]

Gender Issues

The reader will have noticed that in our discussion thus far we have made use of exclusively masculine pronouns, in reference both to the lay bodhisattva and to his monastic counterpart. There is, unfortunately, good reason for this: not a single woman practitioner of the Dharma—whether lay or monastic, whether a candidate for Arhatship or for Buddhahood—ever appears in the text of the *Ugra*. Aside from a pair of formulaic references near the beginning of the sūtra to "gentlemen and ladies" (*kulaputra* and *kuladuhitṛ*) who desire to practice the bodhisattva path (§2B-C), which may have been late additions to the text,[36] there is never any mention of the possibility that a woman might be a genuine Buddhist devotee.

But this is not merely a matter of silence. Though no individual female chararcter ever appears in the sūtra, there are numerous generic mentions of women, virtually all of them in reference to the wife of the male lay bodhisattva, and she is consistently portrayed as an obstacle to the religious practice of the male. She is portrayed as an object of clinging (§9C) and as a possible stimulus to wrong action on the bodhisattva's part (§12C). The bodhisattva is told to view her as a "denizen of the Avīci Hell" (§6A) and to train himself to conceive of

---

as a lay movement, and that the *pratimokṣa* was replaced by a shorter list of rules. For Ray—a disciple of the late Chögyam Trungpa, whose "crazy wisdom" brand of Tibetan tantra focused on meditation as the central (often sole) religious practice—the Mahāyāna is seen as emerging from a nonconformist group of dedicated meditators who avoided falling into the trap of spending too much time on observing the precepts and textual study, as their settled monastic counterparts did. In both cases the concept of "Mahāyāna" seems to have functioned as something of a Rorschach test, reflecting not so much the actual content of the texts they were studying but the authors' own religious views.

35 It is worth noting that the *Ugra*'s image of the wilderness-dweller is very much in harmony with the understanding of the role of the "forest monk" in contemporary Thai Theravāda (see Tambiah 1984), though the monks described by Tambiah—unlike those portrayed in the *Ugra*—live in groups.

36 A second occurrence of this phrase appears in §33C of the Tibetan version, but has no parallel in any other translation of the text.

her (together with his other relatives, employees, and slaves) as not really "his" (§12A). Lest he continue to feel any residual attachment to his marital partner even after these depersonalizing reflections, the lay bodhisattva is given a long list of negative thoughts he should cultivate toward his wife, ranging from a crocodile to a demon to a guardian of hell (§13A-HH). Quite tellingly, the word "wife" appears in the middle of a list of property which the bodhisattva might or might not succeed in obtaining (§12A). In sum, the bodhisattva's wife is portrayed as an object and an obstacle, and the possibility is never even considered that she might be a serious Buddhist practitioner (much less a bodhisattva) in her own right.

The statements just enumerated are of course largely prescriptive, and as such they will be considered in greater detail in the following chapter. What is clear from the overall pattern of discourse in the *Ugra*, however, is that when its authors thought of bodhisattvas, they had only male Buddhists in mind. All of the characters named as part of the audience for the Buddha's discourse to Ugra are male, as are both the lay and the monastic bodhisattvas the sūtra describes. Women are, in sum, entirely absent from the *Ugra*'s portrait of the ideal bodhisattva, and when ordinary women do appear in the sūtra (as a category, it must be emphasized, not as individuals), they are portrayed in a decidedly negative light.[37]

This is of course not a stance unique to the *Ugra*, for in much earlier Buddhist literature it is also common to find descriptions of women as temptresses, together with instructions for detaching oneself from lust.[38] But what is noteworthy is that while these earlier texts are addressed to a male monastic audience, in the *Ugra* the instructions to cultivate negative thoughts toward women are all addressed to the lay bodhisattva, not to his renunciant counterpart. That such instructions should be necessary becomes entirely understandable when we recognize that the authors of the *Ugra* believed that the lay bodhisattva should be completely celibate (§§7A[3] and 31B[2]).

The *Ugra* is hardly unique, of course, in its negative attitude toward women. As Paul Harrison has shown in his survey of the

---

[37] The only exception to this rule is the special category of parents. The *Ugra* in two places points to lack of respect for one's father and mother as a fault (§8A and §9B), though the first of these appears only in the later translations (R and Tib).

[38] The best discussion of this issue can now be found in Wilson 1996.

earliest bodhisattva scriptures to be translated into Chinese, women are generally afforded a distinctly second-class status in these texts; in some, it seems, the authors were reluctant to concede that they could be bodhisattvas at all.[39] Even in sūtras in which (unlike the *Ugra*) women appear as positive characters, it is admitted that being female is a serious disadvantage to religious practice, and that in order to become a Buddha a woman must be transformed into a male.[40] That some particularly capable women are portrayed as changing their gender on the spot serves as evidence not that the gender of an enlightened being did not matter (*contra* Schuster 1981 and Paul 1985),[41] but that it mattered so much as to be nonnegotiable.[42]

---

[39] Harrison (1987, pp. 76-77) notes that in the *Pratyutpanna*, for example—which, it should be noted, is considerably more inclusive of women than is the *Ugra*—nuns and laywomen are never described as bodhisattvas (though their male counterparts are), but only as *mahāyāna-saṁprasthita*, "set out in [or perhaps only "set out *for*"?] the Mahāyāna." Harrison cites numerous other passages from these sūtras which reveal a negative attitude toward women (pp. 77-79), an attitude which he concludes "is clearly demonstrable throughout these early texts" (p. 77).

[40] There is a standard set of five roles for which a woman is ineligible: Buddha, Māra, Indra, Brahma, and a world-ruling emperor (*cakravartin*). There is, in addition, the problem of the "thirty-two marks" that are said to characterize the physical body of a Buddha (as well as the *cakravartin*), one of which is a sheathed or retractable penis.

[41] Both Schuster and Paul seem to view these accounts—inexplicably, in the view of this writer—as providing evidence for the growing spiritual equality of women. Schuster states that these sūtras "argue for the spiritual and intellectual equality of women" (p. 26) and that the transformation of females into males "is a narrative theme which was probably developed by Mahāyānist writers in order to confront traditional Buddhist views of the spiritual limitations of women" (p. 54), while Paul prefaces her scriptural citations with the statement that "the 'transformation of sex' (*parivṛttavyañjana*) plays an important role in advocating a more equitable social order" (p. 170).

[42] Were we dealing with the simple irrelevance of gender here, we would surely expect a parallel body of stories in which men change to the female form. This does not happen, however—with the exception of the story of the goddess and Śāriputra in the *Vimalakīrti*, in which their original bodies are eventually retrieved—in any Buddhist source I have been able to locate. The changes of women (or even more commonly, little girls) into males are regularly accompanied by the statement that the newly attained male form shows how close the former female is to Buddhahood, simply reinforcing the fact that a male body was considered a prerequisite for Buddhahood.

Once we begin to take the antifemale rhetoric of these early bodhisattva sūtras seriously, we can discern a substantial body of corroborating evidence indicating that the emergence of the goal of Buddhahood (as opposed to Arhatship) brought with it a perceptible drop in women's status in those circles that embraced it. We might note, first of all, that unlike earlier terms for Buddhist practitioners (e.g., *upāsaka*, *bhikṣu*, and *arhant*), the words "Buddha" and "bodhisattva" have no feminine forms (though these would have been perfectly easy to construct in Sanskrit or Prakrit). One might dismiss this as a philological fluke were it not for the fact that female bodhisattvas (and of course female Buddhas) are almost entirely absent from the artistic record prior to the tantric period.[43] Nor is a single female character—to the best of my knowledge—ever registered in the long list of names of celestial bodhisattvas (from Avalokiteśvara to Mañjuśrī to Samantabhadra) who appear in the opening passages of so many sūtras.

Once again this is not simply a matter of omission or oversight, for the first bodhisattva images to appear in India are decidedly masculine in appearance, often sporting mustaches and well-muscled bodies in addition to the ornaments befitting a prince.[44] Likewise the virtues associated with the bodhisattva in early scriptures advocating this path would almost all have been culturally scripted as masculine in the Indian environment, from the ability to endure physical pain inflicted by others (the sense in which *kṣānti* is most commonly used in early bodhisattva stories) to taking on the "armor" of the bodhisattva vow (*saṁnāha*) to the cultivation of exertion (*vīrya*, a

---

43 So much has been made of images of the bodhisattva Tārā and of the personified representations of the *prajñāpāramitā* that the virtually total absence of images of female bodhisattvas prior to the Pāla period has been, apparently, completely overlooked.

44 The representation of bodhisattvas in princely garb has been widely misunderstood as an indication of the increased status of the laity. Reading these images in conjunction with the surviving texts (rather than "free-associating" in isolation), it becomes immediately evident that these images represent particular bodhisattvas—most often Maitreya, in the earliest images—in their final lifetimes. Since the script for the attainment of Buddhahood is patterned on the life of Śākyamuni, it is assumed that every Buddha-to-be must be born into a wealthy family where he will grow to young manhood before finally renouncing the world. These statues, in other words, tell us absolutely nothing about the status of ordinary lay people; what they represent is a very small number of individuals whose lives replicate that of Śākyamuni.

word whose resemblance to the English word "virile" is etymological, not accidental). In such a pervasively male-oriented environment, the observation made by Gregory Schopen (1988-1989, pp. 164-165) that the appearance of evidence for the "Mahāyāna" as a distinct institution in Indian inscriptions is correlated with a sharp drop in the proportion of women donors takes on a new and quite transparent significance.

It is ironic, then, that while the "Mahāyāna" is often portrayed in 20th-century publications as more welcoming of women than earlier Buddhism had been, the reality appears to have been the opposite. While the highest goal of Arhatship was, in early Buddhism, completely accessible to women, the goal of Buddhahood was not. Thus as certain groups of Buddhists—including those responsible for the production of the *Ugra*—began to shift their efforts toward becoming Buddhas, the status of women in the Buddhist community appears to have suffered a precipitous decline.

Conclusions: Bodhisattvas in Their Nikāya Contexts

We have in the *Ugra*, in sum, a window into Indian Buddhism at a time when the bodhisattva path had already emerged as a distinct option but was not yet the basis for a separate religious institution. We are not seeing, it is essential to note, the initial appearance of this vocation; already by the time of the *Ugra*—and of all the other bodhisattva scriptures that have drawn scholarly attention to date—the existence of the bodhisattva path was already taken for granted. The initial experiments in religious thought and practice that led to its formulation had already taken place off-camera, so to speak, in an "intertestamental period" between the closing of the canons of the various Nikāya Buddhist lineages and the composition of the earliest "Mahāyāna" sūtras.[45] The bodhisattva sūtras that are available to us today merely show us the representations of this ideal at various

---

[45] Though the various Nikāya Buddhist canons were theoretically closed at a relatively early date, there is substantial evidence to indicate that even after this time certain adjustments were made to their content. What I am referring to here is simply the inclusion of entirely new scriptures, something we do not seem to find (regardless of later editorial emendations and interpolations) in the Āgama or Vinaya sections of the canons of any of the Nikāya schools.

stages in its subsequent development, of which—I would argue—that found in the *Ugra* is one of the earliest.[46]

Though the *Ugra* takes it for granted that both laity and monastics (*male* laity and monastics, that is) can pursue the bodhisattva path, the center of gravity of the text is clearly located within the monastic community. The lay bodhisattva is treated as an exemplary *upāsaka* (though the term itself does not appear), while his monastic counterpart is portrayed as the most diligent of monks. Ideally the lay bodhisattva should emulate his monastic counterpart, seeking ordination as soon as he is able; the monastic bodhisattva, for his part, should ideally engage in solitary self-cultivation in the wilderness.

While the *Ugra* describes a still-united community in which monastic bodhisattvas live and practice side by side with their non-bodhisattva fellows, there is already a clearly felt sense of the potential hazards of this situation, and both lay and monastic bodhisattvas are urged to try to preserve harmony within the community. In both cases there seems to be a clear awareness on the part of the *Ugra*'s authors that the new bodhisattva vocation could lead to arrogance on the part of those who had undertaken it and to jealousy on the part of those who had not. That the text urges both laity and monastics to take steps to undercut these tensions suggests that the *Ugra* represents a point in the development of the bodhisattva ideal when (in its own community, at least) these tensions were palpable, but had not yet reached the breaking point.

One potential solution to the problem of multiple vocations—the "one-vehicle" stance presented in the *Lotus Sūtra*—is conspicuously absent from the *Ugra*. The two vehicles are consistently presented here as distinct paths leading to two distinct and quite separate goals,[47] of which the requirements for Buddhahood were far more rigorous than those for Arhatship. The latter, though admittedly a less glorious destination, is still portrayed as a viable—indeed, quite admirable—goal.

---

[46] For a detailed discussion of the evidence supporting this claim see Chapter 7.

[47] I am excluding from consideration the *pratyekabuddha-yāna*, a shadowy ideal which was never (so far as available evidence indicates) actually practiced by living Buddhists. For a brief discussion of the place of this vehicle in the *Ugra* and further references to secondary studies see below, Chapter 6, p. 139-140 and n. 6.

We have already pointed out that bodhisattva-monks are portrayed as residing within the larger (largely *śrāvaka*) monastic community. But it is worth noting as well that the *Ugra* provides no evidence even of a subgroup—a bodhisattva "club" or "interest-group" (*gaṇa*)—within the larger community. Neither lay nor monastic bodhisattvas are ever portrayed as joining together in any group activity or organization; rather, they are represented as practicing on their own, though consulting on occasion with those above them in the religious hierarchy.

Finally, we should recall that in the largely non-bodhisattva monastic community the *Ugra* describes, a group of scriptures dealing with the bodhisattva path—referred to as a *bodhisattva-piṭaka*—are being memorized and transmitted by monastic specialists. Though the *Ugra* provides no table of contents for this new *piṭaka*, it would be hard to find more convincing evidence of the gradual emergence of the bodhisattva path, and of the literature associated with it, within the Mainstream Buddhist community.

In sum, the bodhisattva is portrayed in the *Ugra* as an elite member of a traditional Buddhist community, striving for a higher ideal than most of his fellows even as he attempts to prevent this discrepancy in status from becoming unduly disruptive. We see a community in tension, but not yet in fission, struggling to accommodate this new religious option in its midst.

CHAPTER 5

Bodhisattva Practices: Guidelines for the Path

The *Ugra*, as we have seen, structures its discussion of the bodhisattva path around a division between two distinct categories of practitioners: the home-dwelling bodhisattva (*gṛhin*), on the one hand, and the renunciant or monastic bodhisattva (*pravrajita*) on the other. So fundamental is this distinction that the authors of the sūtra never refer simply to generic practices appropriate to all bodhisattvas; rather, the entire discussion of practice—that is, the entire normative list of what the ideal bodhisattva should do—is divided into two categories based on the lay or monastic status of the bodhisattva in question. In reviewing the *Ugra*'s prescriptions for bodhisattva conduct it will therefore be necessary to observe these same distinctions, beginning with the preliminary practices appropriate to the lay bodhisattva and then moving on to the more demanding practices reserved for the monk. As we shall see, there is considerable continuity between the two, due mainly to the fact that the lay bodhisattva is enjoined to emulate, to the fullest extent that his life in the household will allow, the way of life of his monastic counterpart.

Before we begin our exploration of these practices, however, we must pause for a moment to recall the nature of our sources. The *Ugra*, like all Buddhist sūtras, is an avowedly normative document: that is, its authors were not concerned with documenting what their fellow Buddhists were actually doing, but with prescribing how the ideal Buddhist *ought* to behave. In the previous chapter we generally bypassed these prescriptive remarks, focusing instead on passing comments by the *Ugra*'s authors that could provide us with clues to the structure and internal dynamics of the Buddhist community in which they lived. In this chapter, however, we will shift our attention to the prescriptive passages themselves, in an attempt to discern what the *Ugra*'s authors thought a bodhisattva should be like.

But what is the value, to the historian, of such prescriptive statements? Taking a strong antiscriptural stance, Gregory Schopen has contended recently that they tell us far less than is usually supposed. Contrasting the texts contained in the Pāli canon with the data preserved in the inscriptional record, which he contends "records or reflects at least a part of what Buddhists—both laypeople and monks—*actually practiced and believed,*"[1] Schopen attempts to minimize the value of the canonical materials, arguing that they record only "what a *small atypical part* of the Buddhist community *wanted* that community to believe or practice."[2]

Such statements—though phrased in extreme terms and certainly overstating the degree to which inscriptions reflect the "actual" beliefs and practices of living Buddhists—were helpful correctives in an environment in which scholars tended to read the Pāli canon and other scriptural sources as a literal record of the ideas and practices of the Buddha and his descendants. But at this stage in the development of the field it may be time to allow the pendulum of opinion on the value of canonical texts to return to a more moderate position between the extremes of uncritical acceptance and hypercritical rejection. But to allow this to happen, we must first raise a simple question: just what do these prescriptive statements actually tell us?

First of all, it is important to recognize that the act of constructing and attempting to inculcate an ideal is, like the commissioning of an inscription, one of the things that Buddhists actually *do*. And the surviving bodhisattva sūtras, which contain a voluminous record of some of these attempts, offer impressive evidence of the amount of energy that certain Buddhists devoted to this activity. Indeed these documents make it clear that a wide range of individuals, holding a wide range of opinions, were involved in this project, for these sūtras are as notable for their variety as the inscriptional record is for its monotony.[3] At the very least, therefore, we must concede that the production of scriptures concerning the bodhisattva path was an activity pursued with great vigor by a significant number of individuals over a substantial period of time.

But there were other Buddhists, in addition to the composers of these texts, who were involved as well. The very fact that these sūtras have survived tells us that many generations of Buddhists considered

---

[1] Schopen 1991, p. 2 (emphasis added).

[2] *Op. cit.*, p. 3 (emphasis added).

[3] Though Schopen has argued that inscriptions and not canonical texts reveal the true sentiments of actual Buddhists, it seems important to point out that the surviving dedicatory inscriptions on which he bases his argument are remarkably limited in both content and form. The fact that such a large body of material is so utterly formulaic suggests that we should perhaps view it not as a reflection of actual Buddhists' beliefs and practices, but rather as a record of what they thought it acceptable—or perhaps even obligatory—to carve.

them to be worth preserving, for an oral text does not survive unless it is memorized and recited to others, while a written text cannot withstand the voracious climate of India unless it is copied and recopied at frequent intervals. Texts of either variety that did not win some degree of community approval thus had few if any prospects for survival.

Not all canonical texts were equally influential, of course, and the extent to which Buddhists accepted and attempted to implement any particular version of the bodhisattva ideal is a question for which we will never be able to offer a fully satisfactory answer. But this does not force us to conclude that the version of this ideal advocated by the authors of the *Ugra* represented the views only of a "small atypical part" (to borrow Schopen's phrase) of the Buddhist community. Both the practices and the attitudes prescribed in the *Ugra* continued to be echoed in other Buddhist scriptures down through the centuries, suggesting that the vision it articulates was widely shared. At the very least, therefore, what we have in the *Ugra* is one expression of what was to become a very durable ideal.

Finally, it is worth recalling that even an unactualized ideal can play a significant role in the life of a community. While few Theravāda Buddhists today, for example, would claim to have met an Arhat (much less to be one), the goal of Arhatship still serves as a point of reference and as an ultimate, if distant, value for members of that tradition. This does not of course imply that most Theravāda Buddhists expect (or even want) to attain that goal, either in this or in a proximate lifetime. Nonetheless, the mere awareness of that goal overshadows the life of the ordinary Theravāda Buddhist in myriad ways, from the subtle inculcation of a distrust for human passions to the stimulation of a flourishing market in amulets.[4] At the very least, therefore, we must allow for the possibility that the image of the bodhisattva presented in the *Ugra* and in countless other bodhisattva sūtras served as an ongoing point of reference, not only for those who aspired to that status themselves but for hosts of others who admired them.

What we will be exploring in this chapter, therefore, is not the extent to which Buddhists actually carried out the practices outlined here, but the way in which the *Ugra*'s authors chose to represent the

---

[4] On the thriving interest in amulets blessed by forest monks in Thailand—and especially by those who are believed to be Arhats—see Tambiah 1984, especially pp. 258-273.

bodhisattva ideal. And one of the noteworthy features of this representation is that it is profoundly continuous with the ideals of the earlier tradition. The overwhelming majority of the practices recommended in the *Ugra*—whether for lay or monastic bodhisattvas—were already well-established elements of the *śrāvaka* path. Indeed it is the overarching theme of renunciation and detachment, which is so characteristic of early Buddhism in general, that pervades the *Ugra*'s discussion of both lay and monastic bodhisattva practices. Where the *Ugra* diverges from earlier sources it is not so much through discarding traditional practices as through adding new ones, which are often even more stringent in their requirements than the earlier ones had been.

THE LAY BODHISATTVA

The course of conduct prescribed for the householder bodhisattva by the authors of the *Ugra* includes practices of a variety of types: ritual actions, such as taking refuge in the three jewels; ethical practices, such as observing the distinctive list of "eleven precepts" found here and in a number of other Buddhist texts from approximately the same period; and cultivating a proper attitude, which consists above all in fostering detachment from the things (and the people) of this world. Since virtually the entire sūtra consists of prescriptions for how the bodhisattva should live, to enumerate each and every one of these would be simply to replicate the entirety of the text. Instead, we will highlight only those practices that are treated at some length, and which seem to have been regarded by the authors of the *Ugra* as central.

Taking Refuge

The *Ugra* begins its discussion of the practices required of the lay bodhisattva with one of the most traditional Buddhist activities of all: taking refuge in the Buddha, the Dharma, and the Sangha. There is of course nothing new in this formula, but what is distinctive about the *Ugra*'s presentation is the way in which it adapts the understanding of the three refuges to the specific requirements of the bodhisattva career. In taking refuge in the Buddha, for example, the bodhisattva is urged to focus not on the Buddha himself but on his own future

Buddhahood: "I must attain the body of a Buddha," he is told to reflect, "ornamented with the thirty-two marks of the Great Man (*mahāpuruṣa*)" (§3B). Specifically, taking refuge in the Buddha means exerting himself to acquire the roots of goodness (*kuśalamūla*) that will result in the attainment of those marks (§3B), as well as being unswerving in his determination to reach his goal (§4A). The exhortations to uphold and to practice the Dharma that comprise the *Ugra*'s discussion of taking refuge in the second jewel offer little that is new, but the distinctiveness of the bodhisattva's vocation is again manifested in the treatment of taking refuge in the Sangha. Even as he honors and respects the sangha of *śrāvaka*s, the bodhisattva is reminded to preserve his own determination to follow another path (§3D). One way of succeeding in performing this mental balancing act, the bodhisattva is told, is to bear in mind that when he becomes a Buddha in the future he too will preside over a sangha of *śrāvaka*s (§3D).[5]

What is perhaps most striking about the *Ugra*'s prescription for the way the lay bodhisattva should take the three refuges is not what it says, but what it does not say. For—contrary to what one might expect of a "Mahāyāna" sūtra—there is no discussion whatsoever of cultivating devotion for the Buddha, or for that matter, of cultivating any relationship with him at all.[6] On the contrary, even in the context of the discussion of "taking refuge in the Buddha" (which would seem to have afforded an obvious opportunity to discuss the practitioner's relationship with the Buddha) the authors of the *Ugra* simply urge the bodhisattva to focus on becoming a Buddha himself. In sum, the *Ugra*'s treatment of the three jewels seems designed not to elicit an attitude of reliance on the Buddha or other exalted figures, but an energetic dedication to attaining the qualities of a Buddha oneself.

The Eleven Precepts

The next practice recommended to the bodhisattva is also of an entirely traditional type: the observance of a group of basic "training rules" (*śikṣāpada*) or moral precepts (§7). Various lists of precepts for laity are well known in Buddhist sources, above all the five

---

[5] For a discussion of the implications of this statement see Chapter 4, pp. 87-89.

[6] For a detailed discussion of this issue see below, Chapter 6, pp. 156-170.

precepts (*pañcaśīla*) to be practiced by the *upāsaka* and *upāsikā* and the more generic list of ten good deeds (*daśakuśalakarmapatha*), which appears not only in Buddhist sources but also in the *Laws of Manu* and the *Mahābhārata*.[7] The *Ugra* begins its discussion of ethical behavior by exhorting the lay bodhisattva to observe the five precepts, but goes on to enumerate a total of eleven: (1) not taking life, (2) not taking what is not given, (3) no sexual misconduct, (4) no lying, (5) no consumption of intoxicants, (6) no slander, (7) no harsh speech, (8) no idle chatter, (9) no covetousness, (10) no malice, and (11) no wrong views. It is easy to see what has happened here: this list is the result of a merger of the *pañcaśīla* with the longer list of the ten *kuśala-karmapatha*s. Since all of the items in the first group are included in the latter, with the exception of the precept against taking intoxicants, the resulting total is eleven.

Unexpected as the number eleven may be (and the number itself is not mentioned in the *Ugra*), this same list of eleven precepts also occurs elsewhere in Buddhist literature, and may have been far more widely used than has been recognized to date.[8] It appears, for example, in the earliest Chinese version of the *Perfection of Wisdom in Eight Thousand Lines* (*Aṣṭasāhasrikāprajñāpāramitā*), translated by Lokakṣema in the late 2nd century CE,[9] as well as in the Sanskrit and Tibetan versions of the same text.[10] In contrast to the *Ugra*, which prefaces this list with a reference to the five precepts, the *Aṣṭa* promises ten, but in both cases the same set of eleven is given. A slightly different version of the hybrid list occurs in the *Mahāvastu*, where the prohibition against alcohol is included (in this case as the fourth item in the list), but the total of ten is maintained by omitting

---

[7] For references see Hirakawa 1963, p. 76, nn. 111 and 112.

[8] This topic is discussed in greater detail in Nattier 2002.

[9] T 224, 8.454b28-29. Later Chinese translations of the same text by Chih Ch'ien and Kumārajīva have apparently "corrected" this anomaly, including only the more expected list of ten *kuśala-karmapathas*. The versions of the same text subsequently produced by Hsüan-tsang do not provide a full list of precepts, but rather mention the first and tenth items only (in T 220[4], 7.826a17ff.) or simply refer to the "ten good deeds" (in T 220[5], 7.901a2ff.).

[10] *Aṣṭa* xvii.324 (cf. Vaidya 1960, pp. 161.20-162.3 and Conze 1973, p. 200), here with the precept on intoxicants in fourth place and lying listed fifth—that is, with these two items reversed from the sequence given in the *Ugra* and in Lokakṣema's *Aṣṭa*. The Tibetan version (Peking [Ōtani] 734, vol. 21, 135.3.3-8) agrees with the Sanskrit.

one of the vocal offenses, namely, "harsh speech" (*pāruṣya*).[11] In sum, it appears that the practice of combining the five precepts (*pañcaśīla*) and the ten good deeds (*daśakuśalakarmapatha*) into a single list was quite common, and that it is not necessary to treat these occurrences as simply "erroneous" or "inadequately translated" (as Hirakawa describes the list of eleven that occurs in Lokakṣema's version of the *Aṣṭa*) or as forming "a completely separate lineage" (as he writes of the identical list that appears in the *Ugra*).[12]

Of the eleven precepts that are listed in the *Ugra*, the third and the fifth—dealing with sexual misconduct and the use of intoxicants, respectively—receive by far the most attention, suggesting that their interpretation may have been the most controversial. It is noteworthy that the authors of the *Ugra* take an extremely conservative position on the third precept but an unusually liberal stance on the fifth. In interpreting the precept against sexual misconduct, the *Ugra* requires the bodhisattva not only to avoid sexual contact with women other than his wife, but also that he attempt to withdraw even from marital relations with his own spouse. Thinking of his wife as loathsome and as characterized by impermanence, suffering, the absence of self, and impurity, he should reflect to himself: "I should not act on my desires even by inclining my mind toward them; how much less should I enter into the actual conjunction of the two sexes or into erotic love? No, I should not do so" (§7A[3]).[13] Here we see quite clearly the

---

[11] See *Mvu.* ii.99.5-12. The substitution of "ignorance" (*avidyā*) for "covetousness" (*abhidhyā*) as the eighth item in the list is presumably the result, as Edgerton has suggested, of textual corruption (BHSD 170b-171a). Elsewhere in the *Mahāvastu* (i.107.13-15) the standard list of ten *karmapatha*s, without the inclusion of the precept on intoxication, is given. It may even be a version of the same list that we find in the Chinese indigenous scripture *Fan-wang ching* 梵網經 (commonly referred to by the reconstructed Sanskrit title **Brahmajala-sūtra*), which gives a list of ten grave offenses (**pārājika*) beginning with the *pañcaśīla* and concluding with an additional five items, most of which seem to correspond to elements of the *daśakuśalakarmapatha*s (for this list see Pagel 1995, p. 172, n. 248).

[12] On the *Aṣṭa* see Hirakawa 1963, p. 75. On the *Ugra* see Hirakawa 1990b, p. 112; cf. p. 127, where Hirakawa asserts that the *Ugra* does not set forth the ten *karmapatha*s, and that with respect to the ethical precepts it belongs to a different lineage from such sūtras as the *prajñāpāramitā* texts (*sic!*) and the *Daśabhūmika-sūtra*.

[13] This was evidently a well-known saying; the same statement is repeated in §31B(2) below, and is also cited (perhaps on the basis of the *Ugra* itself) in *Pratyutpanna* §16M.

extent to which the lay bodhisattva is instructed to emulate the conduct of the monk. The ideal is to avoid any sexual contact whatsoever, thus maintaining complete celibacy even while living at home.

In its explication of the fifth precept, by contrast, the *Ugra* takes what could be construed as a far more liberal stance. After issuing the standard warnings against the consumption of alcohol, and stipulating that the bodhisattva should not "get drunk, or crazy, or ill-mannered, or foolish in his speech" (§7A[5]), the authors raise an interesting ethical dilemma: given that the bodhisattva is expected to observe not only the standard ethical precepts, but the six perfections (*pāramitā*) as well, what should he do if someone asks him for a drink? The list of five (or eleven) precepts requires the practitioner to avoid alcohol, while the first *pāramitā* requires him—in the *Ugra*'s interpretation, at any rate—to give others whatever they may desire (*loc. cit.*). The result is a classic case of a conflict between two different ethical injunctions. In this case the *Ugra* argues that the practice of *dāna-pāramitā* must take precedence over the avoidance of alcohol, and that when asked to supply someone with alcohol the bodhisattva should comply. While doing so he should attempt to induce clear-mindedness in those who are the recipients of his gift, but whether or not he is successful in this endeavor the overriding principle is clear: "To fulfill all their desires is to carry out in full the bodhisattva's perfection of giving" (*loc. cit.*). Thus on the topic of intoxicants the *Ugra* takes a stance that is considerably more liberal than that advocated in certain other bodhisattva scriptures.[14]

There is little that is distinctive in the *Ugra*'s discussion of the other nine precepts,[15] with perhaps the exception of the fact that it repeatedly emphasizes maintaining a proper state of mind in addition to fulfilling the formal (i.e., vocal or physical) requirements of the first eight items. (The last three, as in the standard list of ten *kuśala-karmapatha*s, are all mental in character in and of themselves.) In sum, what we have here is simply an adoption by partisans of the bodhisattva path of a list of ethical precepts that had long been

---

[14] See for example *Pratyutpanna* §11B, which argues that the bodhisattva should *not* give alcohol to others.

[15] Hirakawa contends that the *Ugra*'s treatment of the first precept is quite divergent from that of earlier Buddhism (1990b, p. 112 and p. 178, n. 16, referring the reader to his own *Genshi bukkyō no kenkyū* [1964], p. 406ff., for details), as well as from the treatment of this precept in the list of the *daśa-kuśala-karmapatha*s in the *prajñāpāramitā* sūtras.

current in Buddhist circles, with only minor emendations in the strictness with which the rules are to be observed.

The Practice of Giving

In addition to the traditional lists of five and ten precepts, the *Ugra* also assumes, as we have seen, the existence of a newer list of guidelines for practice: the six "perfections," or *pāramitā*.[16] These practices are enumerated briefly at four points in the sūtra (§§11G, 25L, and 26C, as well as in an aberrant form in §8A), and the set of six is mentioned (but the individual items not named) in two other places (§§20E, 25B). Nowhere, however, does the sūtra do more than devote a line or two of discussion to each of these items, and it is only in the section dealing with the activities of the lay bodhisattva that one perfection is singled out for special attention: the practice of giving, or *dāna*.[17]

Interestingly, however, in its quite lengthy discussion of giving (comprising the whole of §§10-11 and revisited in §15), the act of *dāna* is not treated as a *pāramitā*—not, that is, except in a single line of a section dealing with interaction with beggars (§11G), in which all of the six *pāramitā*s are enumerated. In fact, in the opening discussion of *dāna* (§10A) two recensions of the text treat the act of giving as the first item in an altogether different list of practices, namely, "giving (*dāna*), discipline (*dama*), self-restraint (*saṁyama*), and gentleness of character (*sauratya*)."[18] Nor does the sūtra ever go on to discuss the other five *pāramitā*s in comparable detail. In sum,

---

[16] On the etymology of this term as understood in India and elsewhere see below, Chapter 6, p. 153, n. 35 and the references cited there.

[17] Schuster has argued that an emphasis on giving for renunciant as well as householder bodhisattvas is a unique feature of AY, distinguishing it from the later Chinese translations (1976, p. 330; the same claim is made in Schuster 1985, p. 50). This is, however, simply the result of a misreading of the Chinese: the expression *shih-hsing* 施行 used in reference to the activity of the renunciant bodhisattva simply means "conduct," not—as translated by Schuster (1976, p. 117 and *passim*)—"*dāna*-practice." When the compound is correctly interpreted simply as "conduct," the apparent distinction between earlier and later Chinese translations disappears.

[18] So in R and Tib; AY has *dāna* alone, while only Dh gives the list of the six *pāramitā*s in what is certainly an interpolation; see the discussion of this passage in Chapter 3, pp. 53-54 and in the translation at §10A, n. 217.

dāna seems to be portrayed as a freestanding religious activity that is valid in itself, not requiring association with the list of six bodhisattva practices for its significance.

This is, of course, precisely the way that giving was treated in earlier Buddhism, where it was also viewed as a practice eminently suited for the laity. But there are important ways in which the *Ugra*'s discussion of *dāna* diverges from descriptions found in other Buddhist sources. First, while the object of giving recommended in most Buddhist texts is the monastic community itself,[19] in the *Ugra* the focus of the discussion is on gifts to ordinary beggars. That the lay bodhisattva will make contributions to members of the monastic community is clearly assumed, and is mentioned in passing on occasion,[20] but a detailed discussion is reserved for the lay bodhisattva's interactions with nonreligious beggars. And despite their extremely low status in Indian society, these beggars are portrayed here in entirely positive terms: the bodhisattva is told that he should view the beggar as his teacher (§11A), as his attendant (§11D), and as an opportunity to put the Buddha's teachings into practice (§11C). By thinking of the beggar in this way, each encounter will result in the reduction of the bodhisattva's passion (*rāga*), aversion (*dveṣa*), and delusion (*moha*) (§11E) and will afford him an opportunity to practice all six of the perfections (§11G).

In a section that may originally have followed more closely on the heels of §11 than it does in the extant recensions, the text goes on to prescribe how the bodhisattva should react when he does not merely see a beggar, but is asked by one for a specific one of his possessions (§15). If at all possible, the sūtra states, the bodhisattva should simply give the beggar what he wants (§15A). But if he cannot bring himself to do so, he is enjoined to apologize to the beggar, explaining to him in extremely polite terms that he is only a beginner in the Mahāyāna (one of the few places in the sūtra where this term occurs) and that he is still subject to grasping and to thoughts of "me" and "mine" (§15A). He should also ask the beggar to forgive him, promising that in the future he will fulfill not only the beggar's desires but those of all sentient beings (§15B).

---

[19] An important distinction is made in some sources between gifts made "to the Buddha" (i.e., to a stūpa or other symbolic or figurative representation of the Buddha) and "to the Sangha" (i.e., to the monastic community). On these two types of gifts and the rules governing their disposition see Hirakawa 1963, pp. 98-100.

[20] See for example §§17A, 20F, and 20D.

The fact that our text offers such specific prescriptions for how the bodhisattva should deal with situations in which he fails to live up to this demanding ideal—an embarrassing admission, we should note, which requires that we pay close attention to the information it conveys—suggests that the practice of giving away all of one's possessions was taken quite seriously by the lay bodhisattvas to whom the sūtra was addressed. This must surely have made them the target of special imprecations by beggars and others as soon as word spread that a certain individual had embarked on the bodhisattva path. One also wonders—and the *Ugra* does not tell us—what the dynamics of intrafamily debates might have been when the husband and father of a wealthy *gṛhapati* family undertook to put these prescriptions into the practice. Under these circumstances it would not be surprising if the ideal (at least) of a peaceful monastic life seemed an attractive option indeed.

Be that as it may, these passages point to another way in which the *Ugra*'s treatment of *dāna* diverges from that of Mainstream sources: that it takes quite seriously the idea that the lay practitioner should, if at all possible, not merely give of his surplus but relinquish all that he owns.[21] We are clearly dealing here with a radical extension of what was expected of the ordinary *upāsaka*, for the ideal toward which the bodhisattva was expected to strive is represented as generosity on a dramatic scale, moving in the direction of the heroic acts of *dāna* described in the *jātaka* tales.[22]

---

[21] The long discussion in §10 concerning the disadvantages of owning property and the advantages of giving one's belongings away represents a noticeable departure from the financial advice offered in the *Siṅgālavāda-sutta*, where Siṅgālaka is told that the layman should "gather wealth just as the bee gathers honey," and is further advised that he should divide his income into four parts: one to be used for immediate enjoyment, two to be invested, and the last to be saved for a rainy day (DN iii.192; for an English translation cf. Walshe 1987, p. 466, §26). The *Ugra* is clearly taking a far more radical position, once again demonstrating that the ideal bodhisattva, as seen in this text, is en route to becoming a monk.

[22] It should be noted, however, that nowhere in the *Ugra* is the lay bodhisattva urged to make the most extreme sacrifice of giving up his "body and life." There may be a reflection of this theme in the portion of the sūtra dealing with the life of the renunciant bodhisattva, where it is said that the bodhisattva who lives in the wilderness accomplishes the cultivation of the *dāna-pāramitā* by "having no regard for his body and life" (§25L[1]), but nothing more explicit than this ever occurs in the sūtra. For an insightful study

Important as the donation of one's property may be—and it is no exaggeration to say that this is central to the *Ugra*'s portrait of the lay bodhisattva's life—it is ultimately subordinated to an even more valuable activity. "If I make offerings as numerous as the sands of the Ganges River for many days, and give away all my possessions," the bodhisattva is instructed to think, "those actions will be surpassed by the mere thought of becoming a renunciant in the well-taught Dharma and Vinaya" (§20A). In the end, even the extreme acts of generosity recommended to the lay bodhisattva are dwarfed by the importance of monastic ordination. To put it bluntly: the most valuable act that the lay bodhisattva can carry out is to abandon his lay status altogether.

The Transformation of Merit

One of the by-products of these acts of generosity—not only according to bodhisattva sūtras, of course, but in Mainstream Buddhist scriptures as well—is the generation of merit (*puṇya*), which under normal circumstances would lead to a better rebirth (and perhaps also to rewards in this life) for the individual in question. Like many other bodhiṣattva sūtras, however, the *Ugra* urges the lay practitioner not simply to let nature take its course, but to intervene directly in the karmic process. Specifically, he is instructed to perform the mental act of transferring his merit from (as it were) one karmic bank account to another, so that it will contribute not to his rebirth in heaven or to other worldly rewards, but to his future attainment of Buddhahood.

It is important to note that the *Ugra* is not recommending the "transfer of merit" in the sense in which that expression is most commonly understood—that is, diverting its benefits from one recipient to another. On the contrary, in the *Ugra* this act of transferral (*pariṇāmaṇā*) results not in a change of beneficiary, but in a change in the kind of reward that will accrue to the bodhisattva himself.[23] Other beings will of course benefit from this transformation, but only in the distant future when the bodhisattva has

---

of the bodhisattva's "gift of the body" as portrayed in the *jātaka* and *avadāna* literature see Ohnuma 1997.

[23] For a helpful discussion of this distinction (though not with reference to the *Ugra*) see Kajiyama 1989, especially pp. 10-13.

succeeded in becoming a Buddha and is at last in a position to perform the ultimate service of rediscovering the Dharma and teaching it to others.

The bodhisattva is repeatedly told that whenever he performs an activity that is likely to result in the production of merit—whether giving a gift (§§4E, 11F, 11G[6]), observing the ethical precepts (§7B), or the very act of taking the triple refuge itself (§3A)—he should redirect that merit toward his eventual attainment of Buddhahood. Other Buddhist texts go on to prescribe elaborate rituals involving rejoicing in the merit of others, then transforming the resulting merit (resulting from one's own act of rejoicing) into full enlightenment for oneself,[24] but such a complicated scenario is not presented here. The *Ugra* simply assumes that it is possible to change the outcome of one's own merit by willing to do so, and urges the bodhisattva to make that effort.

Detachment from People and Things

If there is any single theme that pervades the whole of the *Ugra*, it is the importance of cultivating an attitude of detachment. This is of course one of the hallmarks of the life of the renunciant, and it is surely in the *Ugra*'s treatment of the lay bodhisattva's family relations that the origins of Buddhism as a *śramaṇa* tradition can be most clearly discerned. Those who expect to find in the bodhisattva path a model for a type of Buddhism that celebrates "family values" will find little in the *Ugra* to support that view. Admittedly the bodhisattva is urged to show respect for his parents, and to bestow wealth (which the text stipulates must be earned in accordance with the Dharma) upon his wife, children, employees, and slaves (§5A). But this

---

[24] So for example in the *Aṣṭasāhasrikā-prajñāpāramitā-sūtra* (Vaidya 1960, p. 70.17-18): *evaṁ anumodya anumodanā-sahagataṁ puṇyakriyāvastu anuttarāyāṁ samyaksaṁbodhau pariṇāmayāmi iti.* A different understanding of this practice is found in the *Upāli-paripṛcchā-sūtra*, where the bodhisattva is instructed to rejoice in his own meritorious deeds! (T 310[24], 11.516a22-29; for an English translation see Chang 1983, p. 266, but note that the translators' rendition of the act of transferral of the resulting roots of goodness as the bodhisattva's statement that he will "dedicate them to [the universal attainment of] supreme enlightenment" alters the meaning of the text, which—like the *Ugra*—does not suggest that the "supreme enlightenment" in question is to be achieved by anyone other than the bodhisattva himself).

fulfillment of his duties certainly does not extend to the deepening of an affective relationship with his family members. On the contrary, the *Ugra*'s authors urge the bodhisattva to sever all emotional ties to his wife and children, with the ultimate aim of leaving home altogether to pursue the vocation of the monk.

In an extended series of contrasts between the household and the renunciant life, the bodhisattva is encouraged to see "the faults of living at home," a place which should be viewed as (among other things) a city made of sand (§9C), a net of thorns (§9E), and a constant source of troubles (§9F).[25] Of particular concern to the authors of the *Ugra*, however, are the dangers of love (especially erotic love) for another human being. The text devotes considerable attention, therefore, to prescribing certain meditative practices which should be cultivated by the bodhisattva to counter any affection he might feel for his own son or, above all, for his wife.

Toward his son, the bodhisattva is then instructed to cultivate certain attitudes which will result in eliminating excessive (i.e., partisan) affection for him (§14). Thinking to himself that "*bodhi* belongs to the bodhisattva who does not make distinctions," he should view his son as an enemy of his religious practice (§14A). Then shifting to a different approach, the authors suggest that the bodhisattva use the fondness he feels toward his son as the basis for generating loving-kindness (*maitrī*) toward all beings, reminding himself that "all beings have been my sons" (§14C). Thus his son is in no way special, and should not be the object of particular affections. Aside from the one mention of viewing his son as an enemy, the overall tone of this section is one of detachment: ideally the bodhisattva "should act in such a way as to be a friend or an enemy to no one" (§14D).

When it comes to the bodhisattva's wife, however, the tone of detachment disappears, and it seems clear that the authors of the *Ugra* viewed the marital bond as a serious threat. In a long series of triads (which were steadily expanded over the centuries, from six sets in AY to thirty-three in Tib) the bodhisattva is presented with groups of "three thoughts" with which he should regard his wife (§13). He should view her, for example, as impermanent, unreliable, and changeable (§13A), as impure, stinking, and disagreeable (§13C), as an ogre, a demon, and a hag (§13E). The rhetoric becomes ever more

---

[25] This theme is discussed at even greater length in R and Tib, which include a lengthy interpolation not found in AY or Dh on this topic (§19).

strident in later recensions, as the bodhisattva is taught to see his wife as a whole series of evil creatures (e.g., §§13U and 13X). There is never for a moment the suggestion that she might be his companion in the practice of the Dharma; on the contrary, this possibility is explicitly rejected in §13B, where the bodhisattva is told that his wife is his companion for enjoyments in this life, but not in suffering, or in experiencing the ripening of actions, or in the life of the next world. Viewing his wife as the root of all harm and as the source of all bad actions (§13HH), the bodhisattva would surely be well prepared to receive the advice offered later in the text: that he should, as soon as he is able, abandon the householder's life for that of the renunciant (§§18A, 20A). As we shall see, the requirements of the ideal of isolation are even more stringent for the bodhisattva who has undergone ordination as a monk.[26]

The *Triskandhaka* Ritual

One liturgical practice that could be carried out by the bodhisattva at home is singled out for attention in the *Ugra*: a ritual known as the *triskandhaka*, or "three sections" (§16). In AY the ritual begins with bowing to the Buddhas of the ten directions, then rejoicing in the merits of all those who have sought Buddhahood in the past (§16A). The sūtra then states that three times during the day and three times during the night the bodhisattva should recite the "three-part dharma" (*san-p'in ching-shih* 三品經事),[27] that is, the *triskandhaka-dharma*. He should confess and repent of all the evil he has committed in former lives, and he should seek the forgiveness of all the Buddhas. For the sake of the Dharma he should grieve and be remorseful about his past offenses (§16B).

Dh follows the same basic format, but adds that after calling to mind all the Buddhas of the ten directions the bodhisattva should purify his body, speech and mind, practice universal loving-kindness, and then bring to mind all good roots (presumably those that have been accumulated by others, though Dh is not explicit on this point). He should then recite the three-part dharma (*san-p'in fa-ching* 三品法經), abandon all evil conduct, and repent of "the eighty things" (it

---

[26] See below, pp. 132-135.

[27] On the renditions of this term in the extant Chinese and Tibetan translations of the *Ugra* see n. 29 below.

things" (it is not stated what these are). He should rejoice in the major and minor marks (possessed by all Buddhas), turn the Dharma-wheel of the Buddhas [*sic*!], and rejoice in the turning of the wheel by the Buddhas. Dh goes on to say that "through such limitless conduct, he himself will receive a [Buddha]-field where the span of life cannot be measured."

R agrees that the ritual begins with purifying the deeds of body, speech, and mind (though neither he nor Dh specifies how this is to be done), practicing loving-kindness, and rejoicing in all the good roots that have been accumulated. The bodhisattva should then chant the three-division dharma (*san-fen fa* 三分法). Singlemindedly repenting of all his bad deeds and resolving not to do them again, he then rejoices in all good deeds, brings together in his mind all of the major and minor marks, and entreats the Buddhas to turn the Dharma-wheel. He desires that the Buddhas live long, and expresses the hope that "by accumulating deep roots of goodness, may my own Buddha-world be thus." The version found in Tib is virtually identical.

It is noteworthy that all four versions of the sūtra begin the discussion of the *triskandhaka* by stating that this ritual is to be performed if the bodhisattva has no access to the three jewels—that is, if the bodhisattva is isolated from a Buddhist community. Accordingly, the audience before which the confession is performed does not consist of one's flesh-and-blood fellow Buddhists but of "all the Buddhas of the ten directions" (§16A).[28] This is an unexpected scenario, given the close links between the bodhisattva and the Buddhist sangha described in other parts of the sūtra, and it seems reasonable to assume that this framework was simply taken over by the compilers of the *Ugra* from its original source: a text (to which the sūtra explicitly refers) known as the *Triskandhaka*.[29]

---

[28] Note that this is a different conception from that of the thirty-five "Buddhas of confession" before whom the repentance ceremony is performed in the *Upāli-paripṛcchā*. The latter are named individually, and are not associated with any particular direction in space. The *Upāli*—which represents a considerably later layer of sūtra literature than the *Ugra*—also takes a different stance on the situation in which a confession of this type should be performed, reserving it for the most serious offenses.

[29] It is important to note that the *Ugra* never refers to this text as a "sūtra," *contra* the contention of Hirakawa (1989, p. 115) that it does. Hirakawa makes much of the fact that the titles given to the *Triskandhaka* in AY and Dh both include the word *ching* (the standard Chinese translation of "sūtra"), and

There is, of course, a sūtra contained in the Tibetan canon that bears the title *Triskandhaka*, but it is quite unlikely that this text is the same as the one these early bodhisattvas were urged to recite.[30] SHIZUTANI Masao has suggested that the *Ugra* is actually referring to the confession contained in the *She-li-fu hui-kuo ching* 舍利弗悔過經 (T 1492),[31] a text attributed to An Shih-kao but probably dating from the 3rd century or after.

Whatever the identity of the *Triskandhaka* to which the *Ugra* refers, it is clearly a text intended for recitation. There is nothing to

---

concludes that "there was at an early time the practice of reciting the *Triskandhaka-sūtra*, revering the Buddhas of the ten directions, and repenting" (*loc. cit.*). While he is surely correct that the practice of reciting such a text was early (earlier than the *Ugra*, at any rate), it would be misleading to suggest that the text in question was considered a sūtra. What must be noted here is the fact that the term *ching* is also used by both translators as the equivalent of the word "dharma"; indeed, AY does so elsewhere in this very text, at §§1A and 3D. Moreover, in referring to the *Triskandhaka* both AY and Dh use not simply the word *ching* alone but compound expressions (*ching-shih* 經事 and *fa-ching* 法經, respectively), both of which point even more clearly toward an underlying *dharma* rather than *sūtra*. (I strongly suspect that Dh's *fa-ching* is a copyist's hypercorrection of an original *ching-fa* 經法, an expression he occasionally uses to render the word *dharma* when it refers to a "teaching" or "text.") Finally, both R and Tib use straightforward equivalents of *dharma* (*fa* 法) and *dharmaparyāya* (*chos-kyi rnam-grangs*), respectively. In sum, there is every reason to think that the underlying Indian text referred simply to a *dharma*-text in general—not to a "sūtra" in the narrow sense—named *Triskandhaka*.

Schuster, by contrast, errs in the opposite direction, contending that "[n]one of the Chinese translations seem to be naming a text called *Triskandhaka*, and even the Sanskrit of the Śikṣ. does not clearly name it as a text" (1976, p. 194). The problem, however, lies not in the *Ugra* itself but in her rendition of these titles, translating AY's *san-p'in ching-shih* 三品經事 (for example) as "the three classes of Sūtra-matters" and Dh's *san-p'in fa-ching* 三品法經 as "the Dharma-Sūtras (in) 3 classes" (p. 205). In fact, the titles found in AY, Dh, and R are all quite legitimate translations of an Indic **triskandhaka-dharma*, "Dharma-[text] consisting of" (or perhaps only "referring to") "three sections."

[30] *'Phags-pa phung-po gsum-pa zhes-bya-ba theg-pa chen-po'i mdo*, **Ārya-triskandhaka-nāma-mahāyāna-sūtra*, Peking (Ōtani) 950, Derge 384, Stog Palace 60. For a brief synopsis of the content of the text see Python 1981, pp. 182-183. As Shizutani (1974, p. 121) observes, the content of the Tibetan *Triskandhaka* clearly reflects a later stage of literature, and could not be the text to which the *Ugra* refers.

[31] Shizutani 1974, pp. 118-126.

imply that it existed in written form in the time of the *Ugra*; indeed, there is no mention of writing in the *Ugra* at all.[32] In this regard it is interesting to note that even as late as the 8th century CE Śāntideva refers to what is to be done with *Triskandhaka* not as "writing" or "reading" but as *pravartana*, a term which might best be translated here as "performance."[33] We are thus clearly dealing with a liturgical text which was used to structure a formal ritual of confession.

The *Ugra* provides no hint as to the actual content of the confession itself.[34] Most versions of the sūtra seem to suggest that the bodhisattva merely recalls and repents of his own past misdeeds (specifying that those committed in former lives, which the bodhisattva cannot remember, are also included). Dh's enigmatic reference to "the eighty matters," however, raises the possibility that a specific list of possible offenses was invoked. If Shizutani is correct that the *She-li-fu hui-kuo ching* (or a similar text) corresponds to the *Triskandhaka* mentioned in the *Ugra*, this would imply that such a list was used, for this scripture does include a catalogue of evil deeds. First distinguishing between offenses motivated by passion (*rāga*), aversion (*dveṣa*), and delusion (*moha*), or committed through acts of the body, speech, or mind, the text then goes on to enumerate several categories of specific offenses, including one group that corresponds fairly closely to the five *ānantarya* offenses,[35] a second that

---

32 On writing and the "cult of the book" see Chapter 7, p. 185.

33 Cf. PTSD 442b, s.v. *pavattana*.

34 Barnes (= Schuster) contends that the occasion for practicing the *Triskandhaka* ritual is that "the bodhisattva is unable to make a free gift to a stranger" (Barnes 1993, p. 4)—in other words, that the confession is performed in response to the bodhisattva's failure to give to a beggar as described in §15A-B. There is no internal evidence in the *Ugra*'s discussion of the *Triskandhaka*, however, that its authors intended the confession to be connected in any way to its instructions on how to deal with beggars. I strongly suspect that Barnes' interpretation has resulted from her misreading of the expression *shih-hsing* 施行 as "*dāna*-practice" rather than simply "action" or "practice" in general (cf. above, n. 17), leading her to read the beginning of the confession itself in AY's version as "I freely repent of all wicked actions *relative to giving*" (Barnes 1993, p. 5; emphasis added).

35 These five offenses—which are said to result in immediate rebirth in the Avīci hell—are usually said to be (1) killing one's mother, (2) killing one's father, (3) killing an Arhat, (4) causing a schism in the Sangha, and (5) causing a Buddha to bleed. (The crime of "killing a Buddha" is said to be impossible to commit, and thus is not included in the list.) The list given in the *Hui-kuo ching* is almost identical, with a difference in sequence and the addition of an

corresponds exactly to the ten good deeds (*daśa-kuśala-karmapatha*) discussed above, and a third involving crimes of property against Buddhist religious sites or communities.[36]

It is also impossible to tell from the rather brief treatment in the *Ugra* what is meant by the "three sections" to which the title of the *Triskandhaka* refers. Following the discussion found in later sources, scholars have generally assumed that these are (a) repentance, (b) rejoicing in the merit of others, and (c) requesting the Buddhas to teach the Dharma.[37] Not all of these three items, however, are attested in the earliest version of the *Ugra* (AY), which lacks any mention of requesting the Buddhas to teach. Even more important, in all extant versions of the sūtra the practice of rejoicing in the merit of others is said to precede the recitation of the *Triskandhaka*, rather than being contained within it. In sum, what relationship if any there might be between the "three sections" known to Buddhist scholiasts of later centuries and those referred to in the *Ugra* cannot be established with certainty.[38]

The Necessity of Becoming a Monk

Though there are a number of practices that can be carried out by the beginning bodhisattva while he is still trapped in the life of the householder, it is clear throughout the sūtra that the lay state is inferior to that of the monk. The sūtra repeatedly contrasts the household life with that of the renunciant to the stark disadvantage of

---

offense against the Dharma: "desiring to harm the Buddha or defame the Dharma, splitting the *bhikṣu-saṃgha*, killing an Arhat, and killing one's mother and father" (24.1090a19-20).

[36] See T 1492, 24.1090b1-13.

[37] See Śantideva's *Śikṣāsamuccaya*, p. 290, and the *Ta chih-tu lun* 大智度論, 25.110a2-10 and 25.495b9-11. (The latter passage does not explicitly mention the *Triskandhaka*, but Shizutani [1974, pp. 118-119] is probably correct in assuming that the three *p'in* 品 described there are a reference to the same three items.)

[38] The structure of the *She-li-fu hui-kuo ching* suggests at least two other possible interpretations of the word *triskandhaka*: first, that the three "heaps" or "sections" in question correspond to offenses committed under the influence of *rāga*, *dveṣa*, and *moha*, respectively; and second (and in my view more likely), that they refer to the three categories of offenses committed through deeds of body, speech, and mind.

the former (§§9, 19), and in its interpretation of the lay bodhisattva's practices clearly recommends that he emulate the monk (*passim*).

That the authors of the *Ugra* were strong supporters of the renunciant life (or more specifically, of leaving home to become a Buddhist monk) is most explicitly stated in the sūtra's categorical denial of the possibility of attaining Buddhahood as a layman. "No bodhisattva who lives at home," the sūtra states emphatically, "has ever attained Supreme Perfect Enlightenment (*anuttara-samyaksaṁbodhi*)" (§18A). The authors then remind their listeners that all previous Buddhas—not only Śākyamuni, but all of his predecessors—have left home for the wilderness (*araṇya*), and it is there that they have awakened to Buddhahood (*loc. cit.*).

This does not imply, however, that the layman should simply leave home and set out for the wilderness on his own. Such a move would be both appropriate and necessary for one who is on the brink of attaining Buddhahood (as in the paradigmatic case of the young Siddhārtha himself), but such cannot be the case in the present age. As we shall see, the *Ugra* shares with the vast majority of Indian Mahāyāna scriptures the assumption that it is not possible to attain Buddhahood in this lifetime, for the very fact that the Buddhist teachings are currently available in this world precludes such an attainment.[39] Thus what is necessary for the bodhisattva practitioner is not to embark on a solitary and unaffiliated life of religious practice, but to take advantage of the existence of the Sangha by becoming ordained.

The *Ugra* does not content itself merely with exhorting the lay bodhisattva to seek ordination, however, but weaves the ideal of renunciation into the very fabric of the narrative. In all four extant versions of the sūtra—at the end of the text in AY, and in the middle of the text in the three later recensions—Ugra and his companions proclaim that they have understood the Buddha's teaching of the superiority of the monastic life over that of the householder, and they unanimously request ordination. After a rather perfunctory attempt to dissuade them by pointing out the difficulties of the monastic life, the Buddha accedes to their request, and (again in all four versions) asks two of those present to ordain them: the well-known bodhisattva Maitreya, and a quite obscure bodhisattva named All Pure Conduct.[40]

---

[39] For a detailed discussion of this issue see Chapter 6, pp. 142-143.

[40] AY *i-ch'ieh hsing ching k'ai-shih* 一切行淨開士, Dh *chu-hsing ch'ing-ching p' u-sa* 諸行清淨菩薩, R *i-ch'ieh ching p'u-sa* 一切淨菩薩, Tib *spyod-*

The main characters thus embody in action the message the sūtra has been teaching throughout: that ordination as a monk is vital to success on the bodhisattva path.

Once again, however, Hirakawa finds it difficult to believe that the text means what it says. Because the sūtra refers only to "shaving off the hair and beard" and does not use the full technical vocabulary used to describe ordination in the Vinaya, he claims, "it must certainly have meant something different than the act taught in the Vinaya of going forth and receiving the full precepts of a monk" (Hirakawa 1990b, p. 136). Hirakawa also contends that "the fact that it is Maitreya and All Pure Conduct bodhisattva who confer the *pravrajita* precepts on Ugra and the rest shows that it was not a conferral of precepts that took place within a Nikāya Buddhist vihāra" (p. 137). If this were the case, Hirakawa argues, "it would be impossible to ignore the senior *bhikṣus* living there and to have Maitreya bodhisattva and All Pure Conduct bodhisattva confer the precepts" (*loc. cit.*). The fact that Maitreya and All Pure Conduct officiate at the ordination ceremony, in other words, means that Ugra and his friends "are not becoming *bhikṣus* attached to Nikāya Buddhism" (*loc. cit.*).

There are a number of problems with this argument, but the most glaring is a genre mistake: Hirakawa seems to expect a sūtra to speak of ordination in the same way that the Vinaya does. Were this a Vinaya text, we would of course expect to find the precise use of technical and legal language that is characteristic of that genre of Buddhist literature. To expect the authors of a sūtra to focus on these details, though—and to assert that if they do not do so, monastic ordination as a *bhikṣu* could not be meant—would be comparable to claiming that if a fairy tale states that its hero and heroine "got married and lived happily ever after," but provides no details on the performance of a ceremony, something other than a legal marriage must be implied!

The same problem obtains in Hirakawa's discussion of the identity of the preceptors at the ordination, for the characters

---

pa thams-cad rnam-par dag-pa. The underlying Indic term is obscure. Schuster interprets this as a plural and suggests that "'All the Bodhisattvas of Pure Conduct' or 'all the Pure Bodhisattvas' may be a particular group or class of bodhisattvas" (1976, p. 258), but I can see no justification for doing so; the context—in which this name is paired with that of Maitreya—certainly suggests that a particular individual was intended. The Tibetan version, at any rate, cannot be interpreted in this way, but must be read as referring to a single bodhisattva all of whose actions are pure.

Maitreya and All Pure Conduct are just that: narrative characters. Composing their text hundreds of years after the death of the Buddha, the authors of the *Ugra* had no difficulty in placing these figures in the presence of the Buddha, nor with treating them as members of the community of those he had ordained. While a Vinaya specialist like Hirakawa might worry about the precise positions of Maitreya and All Pure Conduct within the monastic hierarchy, the composers of the *Ugra* clearly did not.[41]

What we are concerned with in this discussion, it must be emphasized, is not whether bodhisattvas were actually being ordained as *bhikṣus* at the time the *Ugra* was composed, for establishing historical fact is not our primary concern in this chapter. Rather, the question here is whether the authors of the *Ugra* meant to convey the idea that Ugra and his friends underwent a standard ordination procedure as Buddhist monks—that is, whether they viewed traditional Nikāya Buddhist ordination as a part of the bodhisattva ideal. And there is overwhelming evidence that they did. As we have seen, the sūtra consistently praises the monastic way of life, urges lay bodhisattvas to support their monastic confrères, and forbids them to criticize a monk even if he is actually guilty of an offense. While still in the lay state bodhisattvas are exhorted to emulate monastic behavior (including the observance of complete celibacy), and it is stated emphatically that no lay person has ever attained Buddhahood. Finally, the very fact that Ugra and his friends are portrayed as requesting (and receiving) ordination underscores the centrality of the monastic vocation in the minds of the *Ugra*'s compilers.

Equally important, however, may be what the text does *not* say, for if the *Ugra*'s authors had been trying to argue for a radically new type of ordination, resulting in membership in a new institutional entity (as Hirakawa proposes), we would surely expect some hint of this in the text. More than that, we would likely find a spirited argument in favor of this innovation and/or a defense against anticipated (or actual) objections. The fact that the *Ugra* gives not the

---

41 For Hirakawa the problem is even greater: because he begins with the assumption that the terms *bhikṣu* and *śrāvaka* are synonymous, and thus that a bodhisattva cannot be a *bhikṣu*, the scenario of Ugra and his friends being inducted into a Nikāya monastic community by two bodhisattvas is incomprehensible. There are, of course, significant difficulties with equating *bhikṣu* and *śrāvaka* in this literature; for a discussion of this issue see Sasaki 1995, pp. 37-41, and 1997a, pp. 89-94.

slightest indication that it is advocating a move away from traditional monasticism points to an obvious conclusion: it was not.

Yet Hirakawa has not been alone in finding it difficult to accept the fact that the *Ugra* places such a high value on the monastic life. The few western scholars who have discussed the *Ugra* in print have generally done the same.[42] Schuster asserts that "Ugra is more virtuous than a thousand people who go forth, because he chooses to remain in the world for tne sake of others" (1985, p. 38), while Pagel contends that according to the *Ugra* "it is the lay bodhisattva [not the monk] who comes closest to the realisation of Buddhahood" (1995, p. 112). This tendency to elide the *Ugra*'s emphatic support of traditional Buddhist monasticism is a fascinating subject in itself, for these modern readings reveal a great deal more about contemporary Japanese and western attitudes toward sexuality, monastic celibacy, and the family (and, of course, toward that elusive entity known as "Mahāyāna Buddhism") than they do about Indian values in the time of the *Ugra*.

There is, however, one brief and problematic passage in the sūtra which has surely fueled such interpretations, and which (if read in isolation from the rest of the text) could lead the unwary reader to conclude that the *Ugra*'s authors did indeed favor the layman over the monk. In the final lines of the sūtra Ānanda suddenly turns to Ugra and questions the appropriateness of his remaining in the lay state (§32C). Ugra's reply varies considerably in the different recensions of the sūtra, but all versions agree on one thing: that he has chosen to remain a layman not for his own benefit, but for the good of others (§32C). The Buddha confirms the validity of Ugra's statement, remarking that "not one renunciant bodhisattva in a thousand possesses the good qualities this eminent householder has" (§32D).[43]

That something has gone awry here is evident, however, for Ugra has recently been ordained according to all four versions of the sūtra; thus for him to appear at this point as a layman is completely

---

[42] The sole exception that I am aware of is Richard Robinson, who recognizes that according to the *Ugra* "the household life is inferior to the monastic life" (Robinson 1965-1966, p. 30). Robinson proposes a fourfold typology of "laicizing" and "monachizing," on the one hand, and "secularizing" and "asceticizing" on the other (pp. 25-26). Though the distinctions between laicizing and secularizing and between monachizing and asceticizing are not (in my view) fully articulated, there is much food for thought here.

[43] So in AY and Tib; Dh and R read "hundreds of thousands of renunciant bodhisattvas."

incongruous. Likewise unexpected is the Buddha's extravagant praise of Ugra's lay status in response to Ānanda's query, given the fervent advocacy of monasticism found throughout the rest of the sūtra. Whatever the explanation for its presence, this strange pericope ends as abruptly as it began: Ānanda makes no response either to Ugra's statement or to that of the Buddha, but merely asks by what title this sūtra should be remembered (§33A).

The jarring contrast between this passage and the rest of the sūtra—in particular, the incongruity of Ānanda's asking Ugra to defend his choice of the lay life when in fact he has just been ordained—raises the question of whether this passage was composed by a different hand. Since this episode occurs in all versions of the sūtra, if it is indeed an interpolation it must have been added at a relatively early date. But who would have inserted a passage so at odds with the rest of the text, and for what purpose?

It is highly unlikely that this riddle will ever be resolved satisfactorily, but two points should be noted before conceding defeat. First, the person responsible for inserting this passage made no attempt to cover his tracks; the incongruities (both narrative and conceptual) between this episode and the rest of the sūtra are starkly visible in all versions of the text. And second, despite the comments of the scholars cited above, even in this passage the *Ugra* does not actually elevate the role of the householder above that of the renunciant. The Buddha speaks in praise not of householder bodhisattvas in general, but *of Ugra as an individual.* The subject here is thus not the value of the lay status in general, but the virtues of a particular man.

There is, as we have seen, a group of sūtras in the *āgama* (or *nikāya*) section of the canons of various schools that deal precisely with this topic: the so-called "Ugga suttas" (preserved in both Pāli and Chinese) in which the Buddha praises an eminent householder named Ugra (or Ugga) for his outstanding qualities.[44] None of the extant sūtras dealing with a character by this name contains an exact parallel to the passage in the *Ugra* with which we are concerned, yet the contents of our pericope would be entirely at home in such a text. All of these sūtras focus on the good qualities of a particular layman named Ugra, and all include a passage in which he is explicitly praised. Given the fact that only a small fraction of the literature of the so-called "eighteen schools" has survived, it is possible that an

---

44 See Chapter 2, pp. 25-26.

"Ugga sutta" that has not come down to us was the source of the passage subsequently interpolated into the *Ugra*. It must be emphasized, however, that the scenario just described is only a theoretical possibility.

Whatever the source of this episode, it is clear that its praise of Ugra as an individual is not sufficient grounds for treating the entire sūtra as exalting the lay life over that of the monk. On the contrary, the presence of this somewhat anomalous exchange merely serves to highlight the consistency with which the monastic life is praised elsewhere in the sūtra. There can be no question that the authors of the *Ugra*—if not necessarily the author of this particular passage—viewed monastic vows as an essential part of the bodhisattva path.

THE MONASTIC BODHISATTVA

Once the pivotal step of being ordained as a *bhikṣu* has been taken, the practitioner is now in a position to undertake even more strenuous religious practices. The *Ugra* singles out four of these—some formalized, some not—for special attention: the four noble traditions, living in the wilderness, avoiding contact with others, and maintaining humility. In this section we will explore the *Ugra*'s representation of each of these in turn. Once again we will find little that is new here, though the *Ugra*'s authors expect the bodhisattva to carry out these traditional practices in even more scrupulous fashion than his *śrāvaka* counterparts.

The Four Noble Traditions

The four "noble traditions" (*āryavaṁśa*)[45] are a set of practices well known in Nikāya Buddhism, and it is possible that these were widely

---

[45] The word *ārya* is easily translated as "noble," but it is more difficult to know what to do with the word *vaṁśa* in the context of this well-known list of four things with which a monk should be content. Edgerton understands the compound in the sense of "attitudes (literally, 'stocks,' sources) of the Buddhist saint" (BHSD 105a), while the PTSD renders it as "noble family" (78a). The Chinese *Dīrghāgama* (see below) approximates the latter with its rendering *hsien-sheng tsu* 賢聖族 "noble clan," as does the Tibetan version of the *Ugra*, which uses the standard form *'phags-pa'i rigs* (*Mvy.* no. 2371). R has "noble types" 聖種, while Dh reads simply "good and noble [things]" 賢聖. AY, here

known already in the period of primitive Buddhism.[46] References to them are found in both the Pāli *nikāyas* (i.e., the sutta section of the canon) and in the corresponding *āgamas* of other schools. While the list always consists of four elements, there are differences as to the content of the fourth. All of the available sources agree on the first three items of the list: (1) contentment with any robe he may receive, (2) contentment with any almsfood, and (3) contentment with any lodging (or bedding; the term is *śayanāsana*). In all cases what is intimated is that the monk should avoid the more luxurious possibilities of monastic life: receiving ornate robes from the laity, being invited to specially arranged dinners, and living in a relatively comfortable monastic abode. On the contrary, the monk who follows these guidelines will emulate the life of the earliest members of the Buddhist tradition, the wandering renunciants who had not yet settled into fixed dwelling places and were totally dependent upon individual donations for their livelihood.

It is when we come to the fourth item that we find interesting differences among the sources belonging to various schools. According to the version found in Sarvāstivādin and in canonical Theravādin sources, the fourth *āryavaṁśa* is "delighting in cutting off (Pāli *pahāna*, Skt. *prahāṇa*) and cultivation (*bhāvanā*)"—that is, delighting in cutting off or abandoning bad qualities and in cultivating good ones.[47] According to the other version, found in the

---

as elsewhere, seems to understand *vaṁśa* exclusively in the sense of "text," and renders this expression as "holy texts" (*sheng tien* 聖典).

[46] The term "primitive Buddhism" refers to the period of time prior to the emergence of distinct monastic ordination lineages, or *nikāyas*; on this usage and its ancestry see Nattier 1991, p. 9, n. 1.

[47] The *Vaṁsa-sutta* in the *Aṅguttaranikāya* (II, 27-28) and the *Saṅgīti-sutta* (itself a sort of mini-*Aṅguttaranikāya*, featuring a graduated series of numerical lists) of the *Dīghanikāya* (III, 224-225) both offer very close parallels to what we have here in the *Ugra*. In both versions the fourth item in this sequence is renunciation (*pahāna*) and meditative cultivation (*bhāvanā*). For an extended discussion of the treatment of the four noble traditions in Pāli sources (including extracanonical literature and inscriptions) see Malalasekera 1937, vol. 2, pp. 89-92, s.v. *ariyavaṁsa*.

A second group of sources, all of them associated with the Sarvāstivāda school, contain the same rendition of the fourth *āryavaṁśa*. This group includes the Chinese translation of the *Madhyamāgama* (T 26, 1.563c5; note that this is a rather garbled translation) as well as the *Abhidharmakośa* (VI, §7c-8d), which gives the fourth item as *prahāṇa-bhāvanā-rāmatā*. A Sanskrit version of the *Saṅgīti-sūtra* (likewise believed to belong to the Sarvāstivāda school) has

Chinese translation of the *Dīrghāgama* (generally attributed to the Dharmaguptaka school) as well as in two later Theravāda commentaries, the fourth noble tradition parallels the first three in form: "contentment with any medicine."[48]

Interestingly, precisely the same split in the understanding of the fourth *āryavaṁśa* is reflected in the various recensions of the *Ugra*. In the two earliest recensions (AY and Dh) we find "contentment with any medicine," while R (together with the citations preserved in the **Daśabhūmikavibhāṣā*, 26.116b24) refers to "delighting in cutting off and delighting in cultivation." (The Tibetan version deals with this discrepancy by simply merging the two lists, thus yielding a total of five *āryavaṁśa*s, though it consistently refers to them as "four.") This variety points to the possibility—indeed, the likelihood—that the *Ugra* circulated in more than one Nikāya community in India, and that this passage was adjusted to conform to local usage when the sūtra was transmitted across sectarian lines. More specifically, the fact that the two earliest recensions of the *Ugra* exhibit a version of this list that is associated with the Dharmaguptaka school (among others) harmonizes in an interesting way with the evidence provided by the *Ugra*'s reference to a collection of canonical texts in four sections, a list which is mentioned (among sources identified to date) only in connection with the Dharmaguptakas.[49]

Whatever the monastic lineages that served as the sources for the *Ugra*'s versions of this list, the overall implication of its discussion of the *āryavaṁśa*s is clear: the ideal way of life for the renunciant

---

survived, but it is unfortunately quite fragmentary at this point; enough of the text is present, however, to allow us to determine that the fourth *āryavaṁśa* was given here as "delight in renunciation and cultivation," not "contentment with medicine" (see Stache-Rosen 1968, p. 97). For additional references to the *āryavaṁśa*s in Sārvastivādin śāstra literature see the sources cited in Hirakawa 1990b, p. 184, n. 120.

[48] See the *Mahāniddesa* (II, 497) and the *Cullaniddesa* (p. 106), as well as the version of the *Saṅgīti-sutta* contained in the Chinese translation of the *Dīrghāgama* (T 1, 1.51a1-8). Strangely, however, the Gāndhārī *Saṅgīti-sūtra* found in the British Library collection of Kharoṣṭhī manuscripts, which have been provisionally identified as belonging to the Dharmaguptaka school, has a version of the four *āryavaṁśa*s which differs from the (supposedly Dharmaguptaka) Chinese Dīrghāgama and agrees more closely with the form of the list found in certain Pāli sources (Richard Salomon, personal communication, 1998).

[49] See above, Chapter 2, p. 46 and n. 80.

bodhisattva is one of utmost simplicity, in which even the belongings permissible to a monk are kept to a minimum. As a set, the noble traditions—like the ascetic practices known as the *dhutaguṇas*,[50] which overlap with them to a certain extent—reflect the more ascetic end of the spectrum of Buddhist monastic practice. That is to say, they have generally been viewed as an ideal appropriate to the few rather than as a norm that all monastic Buddhists should be expected to observe. The fact that the *Ugra* advocates their practice by renunciant bodhisattvas in general suggests that, once again, its authors viewed the bodhisattva as someone who should be the most stringent practitioner within his category: the lay bodhisattva should emulate the monk, while the monastic bodhisattva should emulate the strictest forest renunciant.

Wilderness-Dwelling

By far the longest discussion in the portion of the sūtra describing the renunciant bodhisattva's practices is devoted to the virtues of wilderness-dwelling (§§24D-E, 25A-M). It is clear that the authors of the *Ugra* were enthusiastic advocates of this practice, and they spare no efforts in pointing out its many advantages. Living in the wilderness affords an opportunity to cultivate a whole range of practices, from mastering the paranormal powers (*ṛddhi*) to practicing the six kinds of mindfulness (*anusmṛti*) to carrying out the requirements of the eight-fold path (§25B-C). Above all, the bodhisattva who lives in the wilderness will come to understand the truth of no-self in direct fashion: he will realize that all fears arise from grasping at the idea of a "self" (§25H). By noting that grasses, shrubs, and trees also live in the wilderness but do not experience the fear that he does, the bodhisattva will be able to answer the question "who is afraid here?" by realizing that there is no self and that fear is only a mental construction (§25J). Not only does one succeed in maintaining one's spirit of enlightenment (*bodhicitta*) and in preserving one's roots of goodness (*kuśala-mūla*), one is also praised by the Buddhas (§25K). The bodhisattva is also told that the wilderness-dweller can cultivate the six perfections with little

---

[50] The best discussion in English of the twelve (sometimes thirteen) *dhutaguṇaṣ* is Ray 1994, pp. 293-323, which now supersedes the much shorter treatment in Dayal 1932, pp. 134-140. For greater detail see Dantinne 1991.

difficulty (§25L). In sum, the wilderness is portrayed as the ideal setting for mastering virtually the whole repertoire of bodhisattva practices.

On occasion it may be necessary for even the most serious wilderness practitioner to return to the monastery temporarily, and the *Ugra* allows the bodhisattva to do so under certain restricted conditions. The most commonly mentioned reason is to listen to the Dharma (§§24E, 26A, 26C); some versions of the sūtra also mention conferring with his teacher (*ācārya*) or preceptor (*upadhyāya*), or having an illness diagnosed (§24E).[51] It is clear, however, that these are exceptions to the rule, and that the renunciant bodhisattva should return to the wilderness as soon as he is able (*loc. cit.*).

Although the most dedicated renunciant bodhisattvas are urged to devote themselves to practice in the wilderness, not everyone is permitted to embark on this rigorous course. The *Ugra* stipulates four conditions under which living in the wilderness is appropriate: (1) if the bodhisattva is learned and able to remember what he has heard; (2) if he has many defilements (*kleśa*) and needs to devote himself to their purification; (3) if he has attained the five paranormal powers and is able to mature non-human beings such as gods, *nāga*s, and *yakṣa*s; (4) and if he knows the saying "the Buddha has sanctioned wilderness-dwelling" (§25M). While the import of this last item is less than transparent, the overall message is clear: certain members of the monastic community may undertake the strenuous training of the wilderness life, but such extreme practices are not appropriate for all.

Even if some renunciant bodhisattvas may not yet be ready for these practices, it is clear that the authors of the *Ugra* view them as central to the bodhisattva path. Indeed the sūtra offers one of its most categorical statements on precisely this issue: "all the bodhisattvas who have attained Buddhahood in the past," we are told, "did so after dwelling in the wilderness" (§25G). Without this practice, in other words, Buddhahood itself will be impossible to attain.

Not all bodhisattva scriptures agreed on the importance of wilderness-dwelling; some even reject life in the wilderness as "the detachment recommended by Māra."[52] The *Ugra*, however, falls squarely within the pro-wilderness camp.

---

[51] These additional items are mentioned in Dh, R, and Tib, but not in AY. For a somewhat longer list of acceptable motives for interacting with others see §25E (discussed immediately below).

[52] See for example *Aṣṭa* xi.392.

Avoiding Contact with Others

A key element of life in the wilderness is its isolation: that is, that the bodhisattva will be able to avoid all contact with other human beings. For those who are used to thinking of the bodhisattva as a kind of "social Arhat"—compassionate toward others, concerned for the welfare of all beings, and expressing that concern in concrete and constructive activities in society—the portrait of the bodhisattva presented in the *Ugra* will seem foreign indeed. Yet this portrait was clearly widely held, and the expectation that a bodhisattva's compassion should be manifest in the world here and now appears to have been largely unknown in medieval India. On the contrary, the renunciant bodhisattva is commonly exhorted to withdraw from society to an even greater extent than most of his *śrāvaka* monastic counterparts. Once again, what we are seeing in the *Ugra*'s portrait of the ideal bodhisattva is a traditional model writ large: the bodhisattva should emulate the *śrāvaka* monk's isolation from society, but with even greater thoroughness and determination.

The most explicit (and illuminating) discussion of the necessity of isolation from others is found in §25E, where the renunciant bodhisattva is told that he should avoid all close contact with others.[53] He is told to think to himself "I should not bring forth the roots of goodness for just one being; rather, I should bring forth the roots of goodness for all beings."[54] The isolation of the bodhisattva, in other words, is seen as a tactical investment in his future: the strenuous practices in which he is presently engaged will eventually enable him to benefit all beings when he finally becomes a Buddha and can teach others far more effectively than he could do now as a mere (unenlightened) monk.

There are, however, a few things that cannot be accomplished in the forest, and the *Ugra* allows four exceptions to its ideal of perpetual isolation. The bodhisattva may go into town (specifically, he may visit a monastery) in order to listen to the Dharma, to mature beings, to worship the Tathāgata, and to associate with others "whose

---

[53] Cf. §27A, where the bodhisattva is told that he "should not mix with either householders or renunciants"—in other words, that he should not interact with any human beings at all.

[54] This passage was misunderstood by Bendall and Rouse, who read "it is not mine to cultivate the roots of good in a single being" (p. 190; for the Sanskrit text see *Śikṣ.*, p. 196, lines 7-8). For further discussion see n. 568 to the translation (§25E).

spirit of Omniscience is uncontaminated" (§25E).[55] In a subsequent discussion of proper deportment when taking part in a monastic assembly only the first of these items is singled out for attention (§26A). At the same time, the bodhisattva is reminded that he should not seek service or donations from others while he is visiting the community (§26A-B).

It is noteworthy that nowhere in the *Ugra*'s discussion of wilderness-dwelling is there ever a mention of the bodhisattva interacting with (or even encountering) other human beings in the forest. The bodhisattva is told to reflect that robbers and outcastes, as well as a variety of wild animals, live in the wilderness, but this is only a theoretical issue; the only beings with whom the wilderness-dwelling bodhisattva is described as actually interacting are non-human ones: the gods, *nāga*s, *yakṣa*s, and *gandharva*s who may be taught by the bodhisattva who has attained the five paranormal powers (*ṛddhi*) (§25M[3]). For the writers of the *Ugra*, it would seem, the notions of "wilderness" and "community" are utterly incompatible.[56]

But if the bodhisattva's vocation involves compassion for others,[57] how can the avoidance of the company of other beings (especially other human beings) be justified? The *Ugra*'s authors seem to be aware of this potential objection, for in a brief mention of the practice of *dhyāna*—commonly associated with life in the wilderness—the authors adopt a slightly defensive tone, asserting that the bodhisattva is "not indifferent to the maturing of beings, but devotes himself to amassing the roots of goodness" (§25L[5]). The renunciant bodhisattva's business at this stage in his life, in other words, is to acquire the many prerequisites for Buddhahood,[58] not to

---

[55] For a discussion of the implications of this passage see above, Chapter 4, pp. 81-82.

[56] On the persistence of this theme in contemporary Thai Buddhism see Tambiah 1984, especially Chapter 6.

[57] On the place of compassion (*karuṇā*) in the *Ugra* see below, Chapter 6, pp. 145-146.

[58] The task of attaining these prerequisites was immense. Opinions varied on the length of time required to complete all the prerequisites for Buddhahood, but one common figure was three *asaṁkhyeya* kalpas and one hundred *mahākalpa*s. See for example the *Ta chih-tu lun* 大智度論 (T 1509), 25.86c-87c and the French translation in Lamotte 1944-1980, vol. 1, pp. 246-255. According to this treatise each of the thirty-two marks of a Buddha is "adorned with one hundred merits." Each one of these merits, in turn, is the equivalent of

give whatever small measure of assistance he might presently (as a still unenlightened being) be able to offer to others.

That the *Ugra*'s position on this issue was not unique—indeed, that it represents a broad consensus in Buddhist circles at the time—can be inferred from a passage in the *Ta chih-tu lun* in which a questioner objects to the bodhisattva's seeming disregard for the welfare of other beings. "For the Bodhisattva," the questioner asserts, "the rule is to save all beings; so why does he keep himself apart, in the woods and the swamp, in solitude and in the mountains, preoccupied only with himself and abandoning beings?"[59] Surely this is the same image of the solitary bodhisattva, locked in intensive retreat and avoiding human company altogether, that we see in the *Ugra*. And the treatise-writer's reply is quite telling: "Even though it is true that the bodhisattva is physically far away from living beings, his mind never abandons them."[60] The text goes on to say that once the bodhisattva has sought out meditational absorption (*samādhi*) and has attained true insight (*prajñā*), he will then be in a position to save others. It then offers the analogy of a person who withdraws from familial obligations in order to undergo a course of medical treatment, but returns to normal interactions once the treatment is complete. In a more modern context one might point to the example of the beginning medical school student who devotes herself night and day to solitary study, cutting herself off from family and friends and withdrawing from normal social interactions, but with the ultimate aim of being able to use the skills she is acquiring to accomplish the healing of others.[61]

The idea that a bodhisattva's compassion toward others is to be expressed in concrete terms only in the distant future seems not to have been an unusual position. In the *Bodhicaryāvatāra*—widely

---

the amount of merit necessary to become a *cakravartin* (according to some sources cited by the *Traité*), Indra (according to others), or Māra, the chief of the Paranirmitavaśavartin gods (according to yet another opinion). Some authorities gave even more immense equivalents, such as "the collective merit of all beings at the end of the kalpa," which is the amount of merit that results in the re-formation of a *trisāhasramahāsāhasra* world-system after a period of dissolution (25.87b; cf. Lamotte, vol. 1, pp. 250-251).

[59] T 1509, 25.180b18-19; cf. Lamotte, vol. 2, p. 984. I would like to thank Reginald Ray for bringing this passage to my attention.

[60] T 25.180b20.

[61] This analogy is especially apt because ambition, as well as compassion, is clearly a requirement for success.

acclaimed as a work extolling the compassion of the bodhisattva—Śāntideva takes a comparable stance. While the third through sixth of the perfections (*pāramitā*) are allotted an entire chapter each (Chapters 6-9), the first two—giving and morality, arguably the most interpersonal items on the list—are dispensed with in a mere six verses (5.9-14). And Śāntideva goes out of his way to define the bodhisattva's practice of these perfections as a purely mental act. Giving (*dāna*) is described not as donating real things to real people, but as "the mental attitude of relinquishing everything to all people" (5.14). (Śāntideva goes on to say that this explains why it is that, if the Buddhas of the past all fulfilled the perfection of giving while they were bodhisattvas, the people of this world are still poor!) The same approach is applied to the cultivation of morality (*śīla*), which he defines as "the mental attitude of abstaining from worldly actions" (5.11).

In sum, the *Ugra*'s representation of the ideal monastic bodhisattva as an isolated cultivator of perfection is not at all exceptional, but is part of a long tradition in Indian Buddhist thought. What remains to be demonstrated is where and when—if indeed at all—we find exceptions to this rule in Indian Buddhism.

Maintaining Humility

Having taken on the greatest challenge that the Buddhist repertoire has to offer—the task of becoming a fully enlightened Buddha—the bodhisattva had yet another challenge to face: the danger of spiritual pride. The potential for arrogance on the part of the practitioner who is striving for such a glorious goal is a theme that pervades the earliest bodhisattva literature, and various coping tactics are recommended in order to aid the bodhisattva in dealing with this threat. One of the best known (though its significance in this context has not, I believe, been fully recognized) is the rhetoric of negation: the use of negative language to undermine reification, and thus the very conceptual basis for pride, in what the bodhisattva is undertaking.[62]

---

[62] See for example the *Aṣṭa* and the *Vajracchedikā*, in both of which the initial negations (found in the earlier parts of the extant sūtras, which are also thought by Edward Conze to represent the oldest layers of these two texts) are directed not at "dharmas" or at things in general, but at the bodhisattva and the practices in which he is engaged. It is my strong suspicion that this "rhetoric of negation" first emerged as a tactical attempt to undercut the potential for

The *Ugra*, however, generally employs more modest countering tactics. The renunciant bodhisattva is reminded that he should conduct himself with respect toward others whenever he enters a monastic assembly (§26A), and that he should act with courtesy and propriety toward other monks regardless of their level of seniority (*loc. cit.*). Above all, he should not expect—or try to elicit—service from others, and should remind himself that even the Buddha did not require service (Skt. *upasthāna*) for himself (§26A-B). The bodhisattva should not, in other words, view himself as a superior being who merits service and devotion from his fellow Buddhists. On the contrary, it is he who should show veneration toward his teachers (§26A-B), and in particular toward anyone who provides him with teachings concerning the bodhisattva path (§26C).

Most fundamentally, though, the *Ugra* appeals to a teaching that has been present in Buddhism from the outset: the idea of "no self" (*anātman*) (§25J). If the self is nothing but an artificial mental construction, then all notions of "self" and "other"—and thus all judgments of one's own superiority, as a bodhisattva, to others who are not on that path—are called into question. In the final analysis, the *Ugra* seems to suggest, there are simply no grounds for viewing himself (since the "self" is only a fiction) as superior to anyone else.

In sum, what the *Ugra*'s authors are clearly trying to do is to counteract the possibility that bodhisattvas might view themselves as superior to other members of the Buddhist community. That this was not a groundless concern is evident in many other sūtras, where it is claimed that even a beginning bodhisattva is superior to an Arhat, or where those on the *śrāvaka* path are referred to in derisive tones as "Hīnayānists."[63] Both of these attitudes are entirely absent from the *Ugra*. Though the bodhisattva is indeed striving for a glorious goal, his practice involves ensuring that its reflected glory not serve as grounds for constructing an inflated sense of self. Ultimately, with the attainment of Buddhahood, he can expect to experience what it would be like to live in this world with no sense of "selfhood" at all.

---

bodhisattvas' arrogance, and was only later generalized to what came to be considered a new (anti-abhidharma) ontology.

63 For several examples of the former see above, Chapter 4, n. 22. Examples of the latter are too numerous to cite, thus making the total absence of such remarks from the *Ugra* particularly noteworthy. For further discussion of this issue see below, Chapter 7, pp. 172-174.

CHAPTER 6

The Structure of the Bodhisattva Career: Implicit Assumptions

Though *The Inquiry of Ugra* is structured as a dialogue between the Buddha and one of his disciples, this format (as is so often the case in Buddhist sūtras) is essentially a pretext allowing the Buddha to issue a set of guidelines for the attainment of enlightenment. As we have seen in the previous chapter, the authors of the sūtra provided copious specific prescriptions for how bodhisattvas, both lay and monastic, should conduct themselves. These prescriptions, however, were formulated within the context of a preexisting set of ideas concerning the overall structure of the path to Buddhahood: its duration, the distinctive stages that comprise it, and particular events that signal its inception, solidification, and completion. The authors also held very specific ideas about the nature of the goal: what it means to become, and to be, a Buddha. In this chapter we will attempt to bring together various hints contained in the *Ugra* as to the overall structure of the bodhisattva path.

The methods used in this enterprise will necessarily be more speculative, and the results more tentative, than those set forth in the preceding chapters. Precisely because a certain general picture of the bodhisattva path was taken for granted by the *Ugra*'s authors, it is never spelled out in detail; instead, the sūtra addresses only those aspects of the path which its authors felt were in need of emphasis or clarification. Our task in this chapter, therefore, will bear a certain resemblance to the children's game of "connecting the dots": by drawing together certain items that do appear (or at least are alluded to) in the sūtra, we may begin to discern the shape of those that do not, thus enabling us to construct a tentative portrait of the way in which the *Ugra*'s authors viewed the bodhisattva enterprise as a whole.

Such an exercise necessarily entails tolerating a moderate degree of uncertainty, a fact that may be frustrating to those readers used to dealing with sources about which more conclusive things can be said. Despite the frustrations, though, I believe that this is a valuable, even vital, step. For the alternative is not simply to abstain from sketching such a portrait altogether, but to allow our reading of the *Ugra* to be shaped by certain presuppositions that may never be brought to consciousness and tested against what we actually find (and do not find) in this sūtra. The following, in sum, represents a preliminary attempt to describe the larger body of assumptions concerning the bodhisattva path held by the authors of the *Ugra*—many of which may differ significantly from the dominant assumptions about that path held by scholars and practitioners of Buddhism today. If the exercise carried out in this chapter is successful, it will not be so because the picture given here is proven definitively, but because it will provide a plausible, if necessarily provisional, portrait against which the assumptions of other early bodhisattva scriptures can also be tested and compared.

The Three Vehicles: Separate Paths to Separate Goals

While the bodhisattva career is clearly the central concern of the *Ugra*'s authors, the sūtra takes for granted the existence of other paths as well. Indeed, the very use of the term "great vehicle" (which occurs in all versions of our text) presupposes the existence of one or more alternative vehicles that were viewed as less exalted. While it would be hazardous to assume that in every instance where we find *ta-tao* 大道 "great Way" or *ta-sheng* 大乘 "great vehicle" in one of the Chinese translations the corresponding Indic version read *mahāyāna*,[1] the fact that every one of the extant versions of the *Ugra* contains several occurrences of the expression "great vehicle" strongly suggests that by the time the sūtra was composed this epithet was already well established.[2]

---

[1] The fact that Chinese translations often read "great Way" or "great vehicle" where surviving Indic-language versions have *bodhisattvayāna*—or vice versa—has long been noted; see for example Harrison 1987, pp. 72-73 for examples drawn from the translations of Lokakṣema. Whether this phenomenon is interpreted as reflecting variations in the Indian textual tradition itself or a certain license on the part of the Chinese translators, it reveals that the two expressions were widely viewed as interchangeable. For further discussion of the implications of the use of the term "Mahāyāna" see below, Chapter 8.

[2] Expressions equivalent to "great vehicle" occur in §§1B, 2B, 2C, 3D (only in the later editions), 5B, 15B, 20C (Dh only; the other versions read "bodhisattva vehicle"), and 20E (Tib only). In particular, it seems likely that the long series of statements involving the term "great vehicle" in §2B employed

It has sometimes been suggested that the very use of the term *mahāyāna* points to the emergence of the bodhisattva "movement" as a separate institution or organization.[3] The evidence provided by the *Ugra*, however, strongly suggests that this is not the case. As we have seen in Chapter 4, the *Ugra*'s authors locate the vocation of the bodhisattva squarely within the larger Buddhist (mostly *śrāvaka*) community, and the fact that they felt free to use the expression "great vehicle" under these circumstances demonstrates that the term does not require a separate institution as its base. That is to say, the use of the expression "great vehicle" implies only that the path of practice to which it refers is viewed as especially exalted, not that its practitioners comprised a separate religious organization.[4]

As we have seen, the path of the *śrāvaka* is mentioned with considerable frequency in the *Ugra*, both as something the bodhisattva himself should avoid falling into and as a path that he will teach to others once he becomes a Buddha.[5] The *pratyekabuddha* vehicle, by contrast, is mentioned only rarely. This is hardly surprising, for there is no evidence that actual Buddhists, in any Asian culture, ever considered themselves practitioners of the *pratyekabuddha* path.[6]

---

the term *mahāyāna* and not *bodhisattvayāna* in the Indic recensions, as the latter would have led to wording that would have been extremely cumbersome even by Indian literary standards.

[3] See for example Harrison 1987, who states that "The rarity of the terms *mahāyāna* and *bodhisattvayāna* [in Chinese Buddhist translations dating from the 2nd century CE] already invites the conclusion that at this stage there was no rigid division of the Buddhist Sangha into two hostile camps to the extent that the modern understanding of the terms 'Mahāyāna' and 'Hīnayāna' implies" (p. 73). I am in complete agreement with Harrison that the rarity of the term "Hīnayāna" does have this implication; I am far less certain that the presence of the terms *mahāyāna* and *bodhisattvayāna* can be taken as evidence that a division into "hostile camps" has begun. For further discussion see below, Chapter 7, p. 174, n. 6.

[4] Given that all extant versions of the *Ugra* freely use the expression "great vehicle," it is noteworthy that no equivalent of the corresponding term *hīnayāna* ("low vehicle" or "inferior vehicle") occurs in any Chinese or Tibetan version of the text. For a discussion of the significance of this absence see below, Chapter 7, pp. 172-174.

[5] References to the *śrāvaka* path occur at §§3D, 4C (four times), 5B, and 19G (twice).

[6] There are various definitions of the *pratyekabuddha* in Buddhist texts, but one of the most common characterizations is that this figure becomes enlightened without the aid of a teacher and does not teach what he has

Like other bodhisattva sūtras, the *Ugra* contains no instructions on how to become a *pratyekabuddha*, nor does it warn the practitioner against straying onto that path. There is, in other words, no active discussion of the *pratyekabuddha* vehicle as an actual path of practice, whether positively or negatively portrayed. Finally, even the small number of references to this vehicle that do appear would seem, for the most part, to have been added after the initial composition of the text; only one passage mentioning the *pratyekabuddha* occurs in all four extant versions.[7] The authors of the *Ugra*, in sum, do not present this path as being practiced by living members of the Buddhist community.

But if the *pratyekabuddha* path was not seen by the authors of the *Ugra* as a viable option for the Buddhist practitioner, the *śrāvaka* path emphatically was. Like a great many other Indian bodhisattva sūtras—perhaps even the majority of such texts—the *Ugra* assumes that the *śrāvaka* path is a legitimate form of practice, leading to a goal of Arhatship that differs in important ways from Buddhahood. Ironically, the fact that the *śrāvaka* path was seen as capable of resulting in this attainment—indeed, that an energetic practitioner might reach Arhatship in this very lifetime—posed a problem for practitioners of the bodhisattva path. Many (if not most) of the practices undertaken by the bodhisattva were the same as those carried out by candidates for Arhatship, which meant that there was a danger, at least for advanced bodhisattvas, of accidentally attaining enlightenment as an Arhat. The fact that the *Ugra* assumes—again, like the vast majority of Indian bodhisattva scriptures—that once

---

discovered to others (a "no-input, no-output Buddha," as it were). The masculine pronoun is used advisedly; I am unaware of any references in Buddhist literature to a female *pratyekabuddha*, and in K'ang Seng-hui's translation of the *Liu-tu chi-ching* 六度集經 (T 152) the *pratyekabuddha* is added to the traditional list of five things a woman cannot become (3.38c19-20). For further discussion see Kloppenborg 1974, Collins 1992, and Norman 1983b.

The rare instances of the assertion that a particular living person is a *pratyekabuddha* or a candidate for that state would seem to prove the rule that this was not viewed as a genuine option for Buddhist practice, for they seem to occur in the context of critiques of rival teachers (for two examples in the Ch'an and Zen tradition see McRae 1986, p. 35 and p. 284, n. 62) or more mildly, in contexts in which the relative superiority of one monk over another is being claimed (for an example from contemporary Thailand see Tambiah 1984, p. 86).

[7] See §5B. The only other references to the *pratyekabuddha* path in the sūtra occur in §§3D (Dh and Tib only) and 4C (Dh only).

enlightenment has been attained (whether as an Arhat or as a Buddha) the practitioner will never again be subject to rebirth means that an Arhat is forever ineligible for Buddhahood.[8] Even the attainment of the status of stream-enterer—at which point one has a maximum of seven more lives to live—would disqualify the bodhisattva from the attainment of Buddhahood, for seven lifetimes is not nearly enough to attain all the merit (*puṇya*) and knowledge (*jñāna*) that are required. The bodhisattva is thus involved in something of a "balancing act," carrying out the practices of his *śrāvaka* correligionists while attempting to stave off what would be their natural result.[9]

The *Ugra* takes for granted, in sum, the existence of two separate but overlapping options for Buddhist practice, leading to two separate and unequal goals: the *śrāvaka* path leading to the enlightenment (limited but genuine) of an Arhat, and the bodhisattva path leading to the far greater enlightenment of a Buddha. But Buddhahood is not characterized by an increase in insight alone. The *Ugra* also presumes (as did Buddhists in general) that the attainment of Buddhahood also involves the development of a unique body, ornamented with the marks (*lakṣaṇa*) of the Great Man (*mahāpuruṣa*).[10] To become a Buddha is thus, in a very concrete and physical sense, to transcend the ordinary bounds of the human species. The necessity of acquiring the massive amounts of merit required to produce such a body was one of the factors contributing to the unimaginably long duration of the bodhisattva path.[11]

---

[8] It is this assumption that makes the passages in the *Lotus Sūtra* in which Śāriputra, Maudgalyāyana, and other well-known Arhats of the Buddha's time receive predictions of their future Buddhahood so unexpected, and which probably made them quite shocking to listeners of the time.

[9] See below, "Tactical Skill."

[10] See for example §§3B and 16B (the latter in R and Tib only). On the quest for physical perfection in Mahāyāna scriptures see Graham 1998. For a Theravāda discussion of these distinctive marks see the *Lakkhaṇasuttānta* (DN iii.142ff.).

[11] On various calculations of how many merits were required to attain each mark (*lakṣaṇa*) see above, Chapter 5, pp. 133-134, n. 58.

The Impossibility of Attaining Buddhahood in This Lifetime

Though the *Ugra*'s authors clearly assume that it is possible—at least for some members of the Buddhist community—to embark upon the bodhisattva path here and now, this does not imply that it is possible to become a Buddha in this lifetime. As we have seen, the attainment of Buddhahood requires the acquisition of a tremendous stock of merit, which can only be acquired by carrying out the practices of the bodhisattva over an uncountable number of lives. Indeed the sūtra repeatedly reminds its audience of the tremendous burden the bodhisattva has taken on: the burden of remaining in *saṁsāra*, and thus in an inescapably painful embodied form, until all the qualities of a Buddha are attained.[12]

But it is not only the necessity of attaining these massive quantities of merit that makes the attainment of Buddhahood in this lifetime impossible. For a Buddha is, by definition, a person who discovers the way to enlightenment by himself. Attaining awakening without benefit of a teacher, he then proceeds to teach others what he has found. Ironically, this means that it is impossible to become a Buddha in a world in which Buddhism is already known, for to do so would be a contradiction in terms. The widespread assumption that there can be only one Buddha per world-system at a time is thus only the most extreme case of a more general assumption: that while the bodhisattva path can of course be pursued within the context of a living Buddhist community, Buddhahood itself can only be attained in a world that has no knowledge (or memory) of the Buddhist religion. After spending millions of lifetimes preparing for that goal, the bodhisattva must therefore be born in his final life into a world devoid of Buddhism, where he will rediscover its truths for himself.[13]

For the authors of the *Ugra*, then—as for the vast majority of proponents of the bodhisattva path in India, down to the final extinction of Buddhism on the subcontinent—the attainment of Buddhahood was inevitably viewed as something that could only be

---

[12] See for example §§2C (one occurrence) and 5B (three occurrences).

[13] Even the well-known story of the dragon king's daughter found in the *Lotus Sūtra*, where a young *nāga* girl changes into a man and attains Buddhahood on the spot, exhibits at least a vestigial awareness of this tradition, for she does not become enlightened here in this Sahā world but in another world-system, the Vimalā world in the south (see *Saddharmapuṇḍarīka-sūtra*, Kern and Nanjio 1908-1912, p. 265.6-7).

accomplished in a future life. It is important to point out, however, that this does *not* imply that the bodhisattva deliberately seeks to defer his own enlightenment. While the *Ugra* does state that the bodhisattva voluntarily remains in *saṁsāra* far longer than would be necessary if he were a candidate for the enlightenment of an Arhat (§2C), this is not a deliberate postponement of his own awakening; on the contrary, it is simply a result of the vast amount of time necessary to attain all the prerequisites of Buddhahood. As Paul Williams has pointed out (1989, pp. 52-54), the idea that a bodhisattva should delay his own Buddhahood is not found in Tibetan Buddhism—one of the major forms of Mahāyāna Buddhism in the world today—and is, in addition, *prima facie* incoherent, for it suggests that Buddhas are inferior to bodhisattvas, and moreover that (since all others must be placed in nirvāṇa before the bodhisattva attains it himself) there can be only one bodhisattva (p. 52). There is nothing in the *Ugra* to suggest that any such postponement is meant,[14] and on the contrary, in one passage the *Ugra* refers explicitly to the idea that the bodhisattva should practice in such a way that he will "quickly attain Supreme Perfect Enlightenment" (§20B). Lest we radically misunderstand the spiritual task in which these pioneering bodhisattvas were engaged, it is vital that the idea of a bodhisattva "postponing" his enlightenment not be read into texts that do not contain it.[15]

---

[14] The one passage that might be construed as an exception to this statement occurs in §8B, where the lay bodhisattva is instructed to devote himself to exhorting the spiritual underachievers of his town. Specifically, he is told to recall that it is for the sake of such "wild and unruly beings" that he has taken on the bodhisattva vocation, and that he should vow not to attain Supreme Perfect Enlightenment until he has brought them to maturity. What is at issue here, though, is not an eons-long deferral of enlightenment, but the bodhisattva's own dedication to guiding a particular group of beings, in his own hometown, along the path. Whether such "spiritual monitoring" tactics would have been welcomed by those beings, of course, is another matter.

[15] A glaring example of this error can be found in Carol Meadows' translation of Āryaśūra's *Pāramitāsamāsa* (1986). In a discussion of the intense and isolated meditation practice which the bodhisattva should undertake, the text reads ... *lokahitāvekṣī buddhabhāvagataspṛhaḥ* | *kuryāt sātatyayogena dhyānārambhasamudyamam* (5.10) "Thus taking into consideration the welfare of the world, and being eager (*spṛha*) to attain the state of a Buddha, he should set about rousing himself to meditation through constant practice (*yoga*)." Meadows, however, translates "Thus taking into consideration the welfare of the world, *without* [*sic*!] the eager desire to reach the state of a Buddha [immediately], he should set about the undertaking of meditation by means of

Motivations for the Bodhisattva Path

It is not merely the immense length of time necessary to complete the bodhisattva path, but also the specific requirements of that path, that make the idea of attaining Buddhahood such a daunting prospect. Using a script provided at least in part by the *jātaka* stories, early bodhisattvas seem to have understood that the path to Buddhahood required not only strict adherence to the moral precepts, rigorous meditation practice, and a life of renunciation, but many lifetimes of heroic self-sacrifice as well. Tales like the "Hungry Tigress" *jātaka* (in which Śākyamuni in a former life, as a young prince, sacrifices himself to feed a starving tigress and her cubs), the *jātaka* of the *ṛṣi* Kṣāntivādin (in which a sage is systematically dismembered by an angry king), or the *jātaka* of the hare (in which a generous rabbit throws himself into a fire to provide dinner for a hungry brahman) illustrated an extreme version of generosity which—if not necessarily practiced by the bodhisattva in this life—was surely seen as awaiting him in the next.[16] Given that the *jātaka* tales were considered to relate actual incidents in previous lives of Śākyamuni Buddha, and that bodhisattvas were attempting to retrace Śākyamuni's steps in order to attain Buddhahood themselves, the use of these tales as a source of guidelines for practice must surely have been widespread.[17]

---

uninterrupted yoga" (p. 223; emphasis added). Assuming this widespread notion that the bodhisattva should postpone his own enlightenment, Meadows has supplied a negative which is absent from the Sanskrit text, thus producing a translation with exactly the opposite meaning from the original.

[16] Exhortations not to take injunctions to sacrifice literally, or to avoid sacrificing oneself in circumstances that do not warrant it, serve as good evidence that at least some bodhisattvas were taking these prescriptions quite literally. Śāntideva, for example—even while noting that a bodhisattva may be fearful, thinking "I shall have to sacrifice a hand or a foot or something" and "I shall be cut up, split apart, burned, and split open for innumerable billions of aeons" (*Bodhicaryāvatāra*, 7.20-21; Crosby and Skilton 1996, p. 68), and while urging the bodhisattva to begin by giving "only vegetables and the like at first" and gradually work up to the point "that one is even able to give up one's own flesh" (7.25, p. 69)—tries to restrain his audience from mindless self-sacrifice, arguing that "one should not relinquish one's life for someone whose disposition to compassion is not as pure [as one's own]" (5.87, p. 41). For further discussion of the ideal of self-sacrifice in Buddhist literature see Ohnuma 1997.

[17] A number of *jātaka* tales are referred to in this context in the *Rāṣṭrapāla-paripṛcchā-sūtra*, though these do not appear in the earliest

Given the immensely long duration of the path to Buddhahood and the quite literal self-sacrifice it entails, what could have prompted certain members of the Buddhist community to forego the possibility of the immediate attainment of Arhatship in favor of such a prolonged and arduous path? Virtually all discussions of the bodhisattva path found in modern scholarly literature focus on a single factor as the cause: the bodhisattva's compassionate concern for others. The choice to pursue this path, in other words, is seen as the result of the bodhisattva's acute awareness of the suffering of others and his desire to remain in *saṁsāra* to be of help. The *Ugra*, however, calls this portrait into question, for here the ideal bodhisattva is portrayed as avoiding all nonessential contact with others. Though the beginning bodhisattva may be of service by giving to beggars (§§11, 15), for example, or by urging others in his community along the path (§8), the more advanced renunciant bodhisattva is urged to avoid all human contact in order to cultivate the qualities in himself that will eventually result in Buddhahood. The overall portrait of the bodhisattva in the *Ugra*, then, is not that of a "social activist," but of a loner engaged in solitary practice in the wilderness in rigorous preparation for his future Buddhahood.[18]

This brings us to another seeming anomaly in the *Ugra*'s description of the bodhisattva, for though the term "compassion" (*karuṇā*) does appear in the text, its use is rather restricted. Only once does it seem to be recommended as an attitude that should be cultivated toward all beings (§4A);[19] in all other contexts it is directed

---

recension of the text (see de Jong 1953 and more recently Boucher 1999). The story of the *ṛṣi* Kṣāntivādin referred to above is mentioned explicitly in the *Vajracchedikā-prajñāpāramitā-sūtra* at §14e (though, following certain manuscripts in which *kalirāja* "an evil king" has become *kaliṅga-rāja* "the king of Kaliṅga," Conze apparently did not recognize it as such), and the *jātaka* of the hungry tigress comprises an entire chapter in the *Suvarṇaprabhāsa-sūtra* (Chapter 18 of the Sanskrit version). Once we begin to be alert to their presence, substantial numbers of references to specific *jātaka* tales can probably be identified in Mahāyāna sūtras.

18 Once again there are distinct echoes of this stance in Śāntideva's *Bodhicaryāvatāra*, where it is argued that the perfection of giving, for example—arguably one of the most interactive of the *pāramitās*—is simply "the mental attitude itself" of relinquishing all that one has to others, and does not require actual giving of physical objects (5.10; Crosby and Skilton 1996, p. 34).

19 Also §7A (only in R and Tib), §27F (but "compassion" seems out of

not toward beings in general, but toward a particular individual who has violated the precepts or committed some other offense.[20] Though the standard translation of this term as "compassion" has been retained in the translation presented here, it clearly carries overtones of "pity" here.[21] In sum, *karuṇā* is not portrayed here as a generalized attitude to be cultivated toward all living beings, but only as a sentiment to be directed toward those who are spiritually inferior to onself.

Another one of the four *brahma-vihāra*s, however—"loving-kindness" or *maitrī*—is recommended by the *Ugra*'s authors for such general cultivation, and indeed it is this sentiment, and not *karuṇā*, that the bodhisattva is urged to direct toward sentient beings as a whole.[22] Unlike *karuṇā*, *maitrī* carries no hierarchical connotations—that is, it assumes no superiority or inferiority in the being toward whom it is directed—and thus it is ideally suited as an attitude to be diffused throughout the world. And it is this same *maitrī* (Pāli *mettā*) that is widely practiced as a form of meditation in the Theravāda world. The evidence contained in the *Ugra* suggests that in the early period of development of ideas about the bodhisattva path it may have been primarily *maitrī* that was cultivated, only gradually being eclipsed by the focus on *karuṇā*.

But if *karuṇā* had not yet become a central organizing concept in the *Ugra*'s presentation of the bodhisattva path, what could have prompted some members of the Buddhist community to embark upon such a grueling and time-consuming career? In addition to a general concern for other beings that may have emerged from *maitrī* practice, the *Ugra* provides us with clear evidence for another—rarely acknowledged—stimulus to pursuing the bodhisattva path: the ambition of the practitioner himself. We might not expect this motive to be singled out for attention, yet it is clear that the goal of becoming the highest being in the universe—a world-redeeming Buddha—

---

place in this list, which begins with the empty and signless), and §32C (not in AY).

[20] See for example §§5D, 8B, 17A, 24B. The term *karuṇā* also appears in §18A in a list of all four *brahma-vihāra*s, as well as in §25B where it is paired with *maitrī*.

[21] "Pity" is also the sense of the term most commonly used to translate *karuṇā* into Chinese, *pei* 悲.

[22] See §§7A(1), 11E, 14C (two times), 16B, 19P, 25L(3). The term also occurs in §11F and G (a total of four times), where it is an attitude to be directed toward beggars, in §18A in the list of four *brahma-vihāra*s, and in §25B, where it is paired with *karuṇā*.

seemed a glorious prospect indeed. The bodhisattva is explicitly told that he should cultivate the thought that "I must attain the body of a Buddha, ornamented with the thirty-two marks of a Great Man (*mahāpuruṣa*)" (§3B), and when he enters a monastery and pays homage to the Tathāgata he should reflect that "I, too, should become one who is worthy of this kind of worship" (§20B). The renunciant bodhisattva is encouraged to embark upon a life of solitary wilderness-dwelling by reflecting on the fact that one who does so is "praised by the Buddhas" and "esteemed by the noble ones" (§25K). And the repeated reminders that the bodhisattva should not become conceited due to his higher vocation and look down on Buddhists pursuing the *śrāvaka* path (e.g., §§3D, 17A-C) make it clear that part of the appeal of the bodhisattva path was the glory of striving for the highest achievement that the Buddhist repertoire had to offer. It is thus to the mentality of such people as Olympic athletes ("going for the gold") or Marine Corps recruits ("the few, the proud, the brave") that we probably should look if we want to understand what propelled these pioneering bodhisattvas to take on such a gargantuan task.[23] It is equally clear that such a difficult career would never have appealed—and indeed, was never intended to appeal—to all members of the Buddhist community. The initial introduction of the bodhisattva path thus appears not as the *substitution* of the goal of Buddhahood for that of Arhatship but the *addition* of a new alternative for Buddhist practice, one that was viewed at least in the beginning as appropriate only for those "few good men" who would venture to take it on.

Bodhisattva Vows

While many of the practices carried out by bodhisattvas were identical with those of their *śrāvaka* correligionists, one that set them apart from those not pursuing the path to Buddhahood was the taking of special vows. A great variety of such vows can be found in Buddhist literature, ranging from Śākyamuni's initial vow to become a Buddha made in a previous lifetime under Dīpaṁkara, to the vows made by Amitābha when he was still a bodhisattva concerning the features of

---

[23] Once again Śāntideva's work is illuminating, for the *Bodhicaryāvatāra* actually advocates cultivating pride (Skt. *māna*) in one's bodhisattva vocation as a useful technique on the path (7.46-60; Crosby and Skilton 1996, pp. 71-72).

his future realm of Sukhāvatī, to the "four universal vows" used in many traditions of East Asian Buddhism today. In the *Ugra* various terms for "vow" (Skt. **praṇidhāna*, **praṇidhi*, **pratijñā*) and its synonym "armor" (Skt. *saṁnāha*) occur with some frequency in the first part of the sūtra, though it is noteworthy that no occurrence of either is found in the latter portion of the text, which deals with the practices of the renunciant bodhisattva.[24] This suggests, though it certainly does not prove, that the making of vows was associated in the minds of the *Ugra*'s authors primarily with the beginning stages of the bodhisattva path.

In addition to the fact that the *Ugra* mentions vows only in connection with the lay practitioner, two things are particularly noteworthy about its treatment of bodhisattva vows. First, the sūtra never explicitly equates *bodhicitta* with the initial resolution of the bodhisattva to strive for Buddhahood. Rather, this term is used in a number of contexts where it seems to stand less for a decision or vow than for a certain state of mind (which I have translated, following Robert Thurman, as "spirit of enlightenment") within which other practices should be carried out.[25] Second, though the *Ugra* never prescribes the making of vows as a practice the bodhisattva ought to do (hence the absence of any discussion of vows in the previous chapter), it does mention in passing one specific list of four vows:

> The unrescued I will rescue.
> The unliberated I will liberate.
> The uncomforted I will comfort.
> Those who have not yet reached *parinirvāṇa* I will cause to attain *parinirvāṇa*. (§2C)[26]

---

[24] Terms for "vow" and "armor" occur in Part I of the sūtra in §§2C (twice), 2D (in AY only), 7b(10), 8B, and 8C (three times). There are no further occurrences of these terms either in Part II (which continues the discussion of the lay bodhisattva's practices) or in Part III (which deals with the activities of the renunciant bodhisattva).

[25] While the lay section (Parts I and II) consistently uses the term *bodhicitta* (with the exception of §4C, where equivalents of *sarvajñacitta* occur in R and Tib only), the renunciant section (Part III) does the reverse, using the term *sarvajñacitta* in every case but one (§25K, where the statement that "living in the wilderness, one does not forget *bodhicitta*" may well be a quotation from another source). An additional.occurrence of *bodhicitta* in §30A belongs to the conclusion of the sūtra and is not part of the renunciant section *per se*.

[26] The last of these vows is a good example of why the term *parinirvāṇa* should not be interpreted automatically as "final nirvāṇa" in the sense of

These pronouncements are not at all unique to the *Ugra*, for the same list of four resolutions occurs in such sources as the *Avadānaśataka*, the *Perfection of Wisdom in Eight Thousand Lines* (in the Chinese translations by Lokakṣema and Chih Ch'ien), the *Lotus Sūtra* (in the Chinese translations of Dharmarakṣa and Kumārajīva), and (with a different version of the third item) the *Karuṇāpuṇḍarīka Sūtra.*[27]

Another version of these vows—with a small but significant difference in wording—is found in a second group of sources, including the Dīpaṁkara *jātaka*, the *Mahāvastu*, the *Perfection of Wisdom in Eight Thousand Lines* (in the extant Sanskrit version and in the Chinese translation of Kumārajīva), and the *Perfection of*

"death." (It would be strange indeed if the bodhisattva's vow were to cause the death of others!) More than half a century ago it had been pointed out that the use of the term *parinirvāṇa* is not restricted to the death of an enlightened being, but also occurs in reference to the attainment of nirvāṇa within this life (see Thomas 1947); a richly annotated discussion of the same issue has appeared more recently in Fujita 1988. The conclusions of these two scholars concerning the uses of the term in early Buddhist literature are widely supported in Mahāyāna texts as well, where one finds countless references to the idea that (as here) the bodhisattva, having attained *parinirvāṇa* himself, should then cause others to enter *parinirvāṇa*. (For an explicit example see the translation, §20B.)

In early Buddhist literature the distinction between nirvāṇa experienced in this life and the final release (i.e., death) of an enlightened being is generally expressed by the terms *saupādisesa* (Skt. *sopadhiśeṣa*, "with substratum," i.e., "with the skandhas") and *anupādisesa* (Skt. *anupadhiśeṣa = nirupadhiśeṣa*, "without substratum"), but even this distinction is not always maintained in Mahāyāna texts. In the *Vajracchedikā-prajñāpāramitā-sūtra*, for example, the Sanskrit reads *yāvantaḥ Subhūte sattvāḥ ... te ca mayā sarve 'nupadhiśeṣe nirvāṇa-dhātau parinirvāpayitavyāḥ* "however many beings there are, Subhūti, ... all those I should cause to enter *parinirvāṇa*, the realm of nirvāṇa without substratum" (§3). Once again, it seems unlikely that the bodhisattva is being urged to bring about the death of living beings. Rather, what we seem to have here is simply an instance of terminological inflation: a term once reserved for the final liberation from existence in *saṁsāra* is now extended to include the experience of nirvāṇa within this life. Such a blurring of distinctions was no doubt fostered by the growing tendency in some Mahāyāna circles to collapse the categories of nirvāṇa and *saṁsāra*, thus rendering the original notion of "final nirvāṇa" obsolete.

[27] Most of the examples given here are drawn from Kagawa 1989. Kagawa does not include the *Ugra*, however, or the (Pāli) Dīpaṁkara *jātaka* in his discussion.

Wisdom in Twenty-Five Thousand Lines (in the Chinese translations of Mokṣala, Kumārajīva, and Hsüan-tsang), as well as in some but not all Sanskrit manuscripts of the *Lotus Sūtra*:

> Having crossed over [myself], I will rescue [others] [lit., "cause them to cross over"].
> Liberated, I will liberate [others].
> Comforted, I will comfort [others].
> Having attained *parinirvāṇa*, I will cause [others] to attain *parinirvāṇa*.

Because some of these texts are extant in Sanskrit it is possible to see exactly how this shift could take place. Indeed, in one manuscript of the *Lotus Sūtra* cited by KAGAWA Takao we find a mixture of the two: *tīrṇas tārayāmi amukto maucayāmi anāśvastā āśvāsayāmi aparinirvṛtaḥ parinirvāpayāmi* "having crossed over, I cause [others] to cross over; the unliberated I liberate, the uncomforted I comfort, those who have not attained *parinirvāṇa* I cause to attain *parinirvaṇa*."[28] The widespread fluctuation between these two alternatives, even in various manuscripts (or various translations) of a single sūtra, makes it virtually certain that in India these two renditions were frequently confused.

It seems quite clear, however, which is the earlier form, for it is possible to identify clear antecedents of these vows in pre-Mahāyāna literature. Specifically, these four vows appear to have evolved from an earlier set of statements describing the teaching activity of the Buddha. Kagawa cites two identical occurrences of such statements in the early sūtra literature (found in the Pāli *Dīghanikāya* and *Majjhimanikāya*, respectively, as well as in the corresponding Chinese *āgama* translations):

> Awakened, the Blessed One teaches the Dhamma for the sake of awakening (*buddho so bhagavā bodhāya dhammaṁ deseti*).
> Disciplined, the Blessed One teaches the Dhamma for the sake of disciplining (*danto ... damathāya*).
> Calmed, the Blessed One teaches the Dhamma for the sake of calming (*santo ... samathāya*).
> Having crossed over, the Blessed One teaches the Dhamma for the sake of crossing over (*tiṇṇo ... taraṇāya*).

---

[28] Kagawa 1989, p. 296, citing the Kashgar manuscript published in Toda 1981, Part I, p. 63 (123b-124a).

> Having attained *parinirvāṇa*, the Blessed One teaches the Dhamma for the sake of *parinirvāṇa* (*parinibbuto ... parinibbānāya*).[29]

Much remains to be done in the study of the evolution of bodhisattva vows and their interpretations,[30] but for our purposes the essential point is this: the four vows mentioned in passing in the *Ugra* appear in a wide range of Buddhist literature, not all of it of "Mahāyāna" affiliation, and they have clear antecedents even in earlier texts. The fact that these bodhisattva vows appear to have grown out of a simple description of the activities of the Buddha suggests, once again, that the idea of the bodhisattva path did not constitute a radical break with earlier tradition, but was simply the result of the appropriation of the story of the Buddha's life (and former lives) not simply as an ideal to be admired but as a script to be followed to the letter, at least by an intrepid few.

Stages of the Path

Like the vast majority of Indian Buddhist scriptures, the *Ugra* assumes that enlightenment is the result of a gradual process of self-cultivation, a process which could at least theoretically be subdivided into discrete stages. The *Ugra* betrays no knowledge, however, of any of the elaborate systems of four, six, ten, or even fifty-two stages of the bodhisattva path that appear in other Buddhist texts.[31] Even the minimal "two-*bhūmi*" system found in some relatively early scriptures such as the *Aṣṭasāhasrikā-prajñāpāramitā-sūtra*—consisting of those who are unable to fall away from continued progress toward Buddhahood (*avaivartika* or *avinivartanīya*) versus those who are still subject to retrogression (sometimes labeled *ādikarmika* "beginning" or *navayāna-saṁprasthita* "newly set out in the vehicle")—is never

---

[29] From the *Cūḷa-saccaka-sutta* (MN III, pp. 54.27-55.2) and the *Udumbarika-sīhanāda-suttanta* (DN I, p. 235, ll. 30-35), quoted in Kagawa 1989, p. 295 (but note that the references to DN and MN are reversed in the published version). The corresponding Chinese passages cited by Kagawa are found in T 1, 1.49a26-28, and T 11, 1.226a4-7.

[30] On the topic of vows in Buddhist literature in general see most recently Nihon Bukkyō Gakkai 1995.

[31] For a convenient English summary of some of the most influential of these systems see Hirakawa 1963, pp. 65-69.

discussed in detail.[32] A handful of scattered references, however, make it clear that the authors of the *Ugra* had such a rudimentary system in mind.[33]

Moreover, when the term *bhūmi* does occur in the *Ugra* it is used in a quite different sense: rather than referring to discrete stages of one's progress toward enlightenment, it is used to designate the "levels" of the home-dwelling (*gṛhin*) and renunciant (*pravrajita*) bodhisattvas, respectively (e.g., §§2D, 20G). The use of the term in such a context reinforces what we have already seen elsewhere: that for the authors of the *Ugra* the level of the householder is qualitatively lower than that of the renunciant.[34]

For the authors of the *Ugra*, then, the bodhisattva path was not yet subdivided into a series of graded steps to Buddhahood but only into two fundamental categories: those who are, and those who are not, still subject to retrogression.

---

[32] Some Japanese scholars, among them Hirakawa, have argued that the *Aṣṭa* (among other texts) contains a "four-*bhūmi*" system, consisting of (1) first bringing forth bodhicitta (*prathama-cittotpāda*), (2) practicing the six perfections [Hirakawa gives no Sanskrit equivalent for this stage], (3) becoming irreversible from full enlightenment (*avinivartanīya*), and (4) being "anointed" (*abhiṣikta*) or having only one more lifetime remaining before enlightenment (*ekajātipratibaddha*); see for example Hirakawa 1963, p. 66 and n. 71. While such a system may well occur in other scriptures, I can see no justification for reading it into the *Aṣṭa*. In this text a clear differentiation is made between bodhisattvas who can fall back and those who cannot, but neither *prathamacittotpāda* (which is simply presented as the beginning of the "reversible" stage) nor *ekajātipratibaddha* (a term which, to the best of my knowledge, occurs only toward the end of the sūtra, in materials borrowed from another source [xxvi.435]) is ever treated in similar fashion. The term *abhiṣikta* does not seem to occur in the sūtra at all. The reference to Kumārajīva's translation of the *Aṣṭa* given in this connection in Hirakawa 1963, p. 66, n. 71 (T 227, 8.575b) does not contain any of these expressions.

[33] Our text contains one reference to being certain (Tib. *nges-par byas-pa*, Skt. **niścaya* or **niyama*) to attain full enlightenment (§1B), two less explicit references to having entered a state of certainty (**niyama*, §25B and §31A[3]), and one reference to not being subject to retrogression (Tib. *phyir mi-ldog-pa*, Skt. **avaivartika* or **avinivartanīya*, §4C.

[34] Cf. the *Aṣṭasāhasrikā-prajñāpāramitā-sūtra*, where the term *bhūmi* is used to refer to the levels of the *śrāvaka* and the *pratyekabuddha*, in contrast to the allegedly higher level of the bodhisattva. What the quite different uses of the term in the *Aṣṭa* and the *Ugra* have in common is that they both mark a perceived difference in hierarchical status.

The Six *Pāramitās*

As we have seen, the *Ugra* contends that the focus of one's life as a bodhisattva is, or should be, on the effort to replicate Śākyamuni Buddha's own experience as a bodhisattva, and thus eventually to become a Buddha oneself. A key part of this process, from the perspective of the *Ugra*'s authors, is the practice of the set of virtues known as the *pāramitās*.[35]

Unlike some texts dealing with the bodhisattva career, which contain unusual lists of *pāramitās* or do not refer to the six perfections at all,[36] the *Ugra* reflects a time (or perhaps better, a place or a particular community) in which the *pāramitās* had been codified into a fixed set of six. But even in texts like the *Ugra* that do contain this standard list, it is rare that equal attention is devoted to each. Indeed, most bodhisattva sūtras seem to fall into one of two basic categories: those (like the *Ugra*) that emphasize *dāna*, and those (like the sūtras belonging to the "perfection of wisdom" category) that emphasize *prajñā*. There are also, of course, many sūtras that do not emphasize the *pāramitās* at all, and it should not be assumed that all the authors of sūtras dealing with the bodhisattva path considered these to be a vital element of the bodhisattva's practice.

Be that as it may, the *Ugra*'s authors were clearly aware of the standard set of six perfections, though only *dāna* is singled out for

---

[35] The etymology of the term *pāramitā* was a matter of dispute already in India. One interpretation (later preserved in the standard Tibetan translation *pha-rol-tu phyin-pa* "gone to the other shore") saw the term as derived from *pāram* "other (side)" plus the past participle *ita* "gone." Others, however, held that this etymology was fallacious, and derived the term from *parama* "excellent, supreme." (For an example of a vigorous defense of the latter interpretation and an apparent attack on the former, see the commentary on the *Heart Sūtra* by Vimalamitra, translated in Lopez 1996, pp. 52-53 and n. 14.) Interestingly, in early Chinese translations the word *pāramitā* is frequently translated as *tu wu-chi* 度無極, meaning "crossed over" (*tu*) plus "limitless" (*wu-chi*). As Zürcher (1959, p. 336, n. 140 to Chapter 2) pointed out long ago, this is a "double translation" incorporating parts of both of these etymologies. On the phenomenon of "double translations" as such (quite common in the work of the Dharmarakṣa [fl. 265-309 CE], among others) see Boucher 1999, pp. 489-494.

[36] Texts which contain aberrant lists of *pāramitās* or use the term *pāramitā* to refer to virtues not normally contained within the standard list of six include the *Lalitavistara*, the larger *Sukhāvatīvyūha*, the *Vimalakīrtinirdeśa*, and the *Mahāvastu*.

special attention.[37] Complete lists of the six perfections, together with brief discussions of their practice, occur in both the home-dwelling and renunciant sections of the sūtra.[38] Thus it is clear that the *Ugra*'s authors did not view these practices as the exclusive domain of renunciant bodhisattvas. On the contrary, the only extended discussion of any of the six—the practice of giving—occurs in the first part of the sūtra, which deals with the life of the home-dwelling bodhisattva.[39]

For the *Ugra*, in sum, the *pāramitā*s appear as an accepted, indeed well-established, part of the script for the bodhisattva path. Any association of individual *pāramitā*s with particular stages on the path, however, was still quite unknown.

Tactical Skill

Like the six *pāramitā*s, the concept of skillful means, or more precisely "tactical skill" (*upāya-kauśalya*), eventually came to be considered a central element of the bodhisattva's practice. It would even be included as a seventh *pāramitā* when the list was extended to ten.[40] There is widespread agreement on the meaning of this expression as embodying "skillfulness" in the sense of adapting the presentation of the Dharma to suit the needs of others.[41] The practice

---

[37] It is important to note, however, that in the *Ugra*'s discussion of giving this practice is not generally referred to as a *pāramitā*. See the section on "The Practice of Giving" in the previous chapter, pp. 111-114.

[38] See §11G and §25L, respectively. A list of the six *pāramitā*s (without discussion) also occurs in §26C, while a mention of the six (without individual enumeration) is made in §25B. A particularly interesting reference occurs in §20E, where the *bodhisattva-piṭaka* holder is said to be someone from whom the bodhisattva could learn about the six *pāramitā*s and *upāya-kauśalya*. This suggests that the *Ugra*'s authors viewed this enigmatic text (or more likely, section of a canon) as containing discussions of the practice of these items.

[39] See §§10-11 and 15. For a discussion of Schuster's contention that in AY giving is central to the practice of the renunciant bodhisattva as well see the previous chapter, n. 17.

[40] See Dayal 1932, pp. 248-269.

[41] Such an interpretation is given by no less an authority than F. W. Edgerton, who defines it as "the Buddha's skill in devising means to impress and convert people" (BHSD 146b).

of *upāya* is thus seen as an interpersonal act, employed above all in the context of teaching.

This is indeed the way the term is understood in the *Lotus Sūtra*, as well as in a number of other Buddhist texts, but in some of the earliest sūtras dealing with the bodhisattva career this is most assuredly not the case. In the *Aṣṭasāhasrikā-prajñāpāramitā-sūtra*, for example, *upāya-kauśalya* refers to the skillful techniques employed by the bodhisattva while carrying out such practices as meditation (in particular, the four *dhyāna*s) and the transformation of merit. Above all, it means the ability to practice states of deep meditative absorption while staving off what would be their natural karmic result: rebirth in one of the *rūpa-dhātu* heavens, or worse, the attainment of enlightenment as an Arhat. These results, while eagerly sought by other Buddhists, would delay or permanently derail the bodhisattva from his goal of attaining full Buddhahood, and were thus to be avoided at all costs. The term *upāya-kauśalya* as used in the *Aṣṭa* thus refers to what might best be described as a "balancing act," a set of countering techniques employed to alter the normal karmic chain of events. In no case, we should note, does it involve interaction with others.[42]

The *Ugra*, it would appear, shares this understanding. In two cases the term appears without discussion (§§20E, 25B), so little can be said concerning its implications here. But in a third passage we have a context that corresponds precisely to the use of the term in the *Aṣṭa*. The bodhisattva is told to go alone into an empty room to practice the four *dhyāna* meditations and is urged to call upon his tactical skill when he does so (§31B[3]).[43] Brief as it is, this passage

---

[42] See especially *Aṣṭa* 20.370-371, which contains an explicit discussion of the need to counteract the normal results of meditation practice. In other passages the *Aṣṭa* equates *upāya-kauśalya* with bringing to mind the "sign" (*nimitta*) of merit (during the practice of the transformation of merit) without treating it as a sign (6.150), or with cognizing a sign while (in Conze's translation) "he surrenders himself completely to the Signless" (19.356). Michael Pye is partially correct in associating the use of the term *upāya-kauśalya* in the *Aṣṭa* with a certain way of seeing reality (Pye 1978, especially pp. 108-112), since it is regularly paired with *prajñāpāramitā* as one of two major requisites of the bodhisattva. In reducing its meaning to seeing that dharmas are void while not abandoning living beings (p. 107), however, he elides the *Aṣṭa*'s main concern: that the bodhisattva not fall into Arhatship or a heavenly rebirth.

[43] This passage does not occur in AY.

makes it clear that the *Ugra* shares the *Aṣṭa*'s undertanding of *upāya-kauśalya* as something to be practiced alone, and as a technique used by the bodhisattva to avoid being sidetracked from his trajectory to Buddhahood.

There are, then, at least two fundamentally different uses of the term *upāya-kauśalya* in bodhisattva sūtras. In texts like the *Lotus*, it is a technique practiced by the Buddha (and, it is important to note, not by bodhisattvas in the *Lotus*, with the exception of the late chapters dealing with Avalokiteśvara and other celestial bodhisattvas) to adapt the Dharma teachings to the needs and capacities of others. In texts like the *Aṣṭa*, by contrast, it is practiced by bodhisattvas—Buddhas, after all, no longer have any need for such techniques—and it is a solitary (rather than interpersonal) practice designed to keep the bodhisattva from accidentally suffering a heavenly rebirth or slipping into a lower form of enlightenment.

It might seem strange that a single expression could be used in such radically different ways, yet we should bear in mind that the word *upāya* did not originate as a Buddhist technical term. In its more generic (and more original) sense *upāya* means simply "expedient," "artifice," or "strategem," including prominently within its semantic range the use of dissembling tactics to trick one's enemies.[44]

As in this broader use, what the two quite different Buddhist uses of *upāya* have in common is a recognition that certain challenging situations require the use of countering tactics, without which one's enterprise (whatever that may be) will not succeed. Whether employed by the Buddha in teaching or by the bodhisattva in practicing the four *dhyāna*s, the use of the concept of *upāya-kauśalya* suggests that Buddhist practice requires not spiritual naïveté but a sophisticated (even shrewd) realization that in certain cases the end may justify—and in fact require—extraordinary means.

The Buddha and the Practitioner

It has often been suggested that "the Mahāyāna" emerged in response to the desire of the laity for a closer devotional relationship with the Buddha. As we have seen, the idea that the bodhisattva path first emerged in a lay-oriented context is no longer tenable, but the role of devotion to the Buddha is a separate issue. At this point we will turn

---

44 See MW 215b.

our attention to the nature of the relationship the *Ugra*'s authors envisioned between the Buddha and the practicing bodhisattva. In particular, we will investigate what the *Ugra* has to tell us about the place of worship and devotion in the life of a candidate for Buddhahood.

A serious obstacle to this inquiry, however, is posed by the fact that in our culture—and by this I mean primarily that of North America, though some of what follows will apply to certain European cultures as well—the vocabulary for "worship" and "devotion" has become severely impoverished. This might seem strange, especially in the case of the United States, which regularly ranks in surveys of the religiousness of its citizenry not with the relatively low scores of most postindustrial nations, but with the high scores of developing countries such as India and Brazil. But the relevant factor here is not how greatly religion as such is valued in a given culture, but *which* religion sets the terms of the conversation. In the English-speaking world—where the religious ethos has been shaped predominantly by Protestantism—the understanding of "worship" has, I would argue, been narrowed to a very small subset of its possible range of meanings. Favoring a silent, individual, and iconless communion with a single divine being, mainstream Protestantism simply lacks the vocabulary to describe many of the forms of religious expression found in other cultures. Viewed in this light, the reflexive reductionism inherent in the reaction of early Protestant missionaries to seeing a Hindu (for example) revering an image of Viṣṇu—nicely captured in the hymn that reads "the heathen in his blindness bows down to wood and stone"[45]—is fully understandable as the result of the inadequacy of the conceptual categories of the observer to capture the sophisticated perspective of the performer.

Before considering the ways in which the *Ugra* represents the interaction between a bodhisattva and a Buddha, therefore, we must pause to sketch briefly the range of forms of worship and devotion that appear (and do not appear) in Indian Buddhist sources. The following is certainly not meant to be a definitive discussion (though I hope that others will pursue this subject further in the future); our purpose here is simply to resolve the variety of activities and attitudes

---

45 See line 2 of Reginald Heber's (1783-1826) classic missionary composition "From Greenland's Icy Mountains," reprinted in *Favorite Hymns of Praise* (n.p.: Tabernacle Publishing, 1967), p. 443. I am grateful to Glenn Zuber for providing a precise reference to this item.

that have been lumped together in English-language sources under the heading of "devotion" or "worship" into a somewhat larger—and thus more usable—range of categories. At a minimum, I would suggest, we need to distinguish among the following:[46]

(1) **Paying homage** (*namas√kṛ*, *vandana*, *mānana*, and similar expressions): an act of salutation made toward a person (living or dead) or an object viewed as worthy of reverence. The act itself may be as simple as folding the hands and bowing slightly, or as elaborate as performing a full prostration or pronouncing flowery words of praise. At the margins, of course, such behavior shades off into simple politeness, as in the use of the greeting *namaste* (lit., "homage to you") by Hindi speakers today. In particular, it is important to note that making such a gesture does not necessarily entail the cultivation of any ongoing relationship with the object toward which it is directed; it does, however, place the devotee in a hierarchical relationship either with the object itself or with some larger entity (e.g., the Buddhist sangha) with which it is associated.

(2) **Making offerings** (*dāna*): the act of providing material goods to an object of reverence. It is noteworthy that in Buddhist sources this practice is often explicitly, and unapologetically, associated with the making of merit (*puṇya*); it is also important to note—and indeed, this seems to be a corollary of the preceding—that the recipients of such gifts are quite varied, and indeed in some cases appear to be virtually interchangeable.[47]

---

[46] By providing Sanskrit equivalents of these categories I do not mean to suggest that these terms are consistently or exclusively used (even in Buddhist texts) in the sense indicated here. Rather, these equivalents are intended simply to point toward some of the terminology used to describe these activities. On the noticeable slippage of some of this vocabulary in later Buddhist texts see Harrison 1992a, especially pp. 224-225.

[47] Examples abound in Buddhist sources, ranging from the exhortations of King Aśoka to his subjects to make offerings to both *brāhmaṇas* and *śramaṇas* (i.e., to non-Buddhist as well as Buddhist mendicants) to the vow of Amitābha that bodhisattvas born into Sukhāvatī will be able to travel to other Buddha-fields to "worship"—that is, to serve and make offerings to—the Buddhas there.

(3) **Service** (*upāsanā*, *sevā*, *upasthāna*, etc.): the act of attending and caring for a venerated person or object. In many Buddhist texts this category is hardly distinguished from the previous one, but in the *Ugra* the objects of these two activities are quite different, so they will be treated separately here.

(4) **Meditative remembrance** (*anusmṛti*): the act of bearing a respectworthy object in mind. In Buddhist texts such remembrance is directed mainly toward the so-called "three jewels" (i.e., the Buddha, Dharma, and Sangha), though in certain texts the list of worthy objects of remembrance is extended to six or even ten.[48]

(5) **Petitionary prayer** (*ākrandaṁ √kṛ*, *āyācana*, etc.): a forthright request for help in worldly matters such as conceiving a child, recovering from illness, or escaping from danger. In Buddhist sources such prayers are directed primarily to lower-level spirits such as *yakṣa*s and minor *devatā*s (in pre-Mahāyāna literature) or toward celestial bodhisattvas (in Mahāyāna texts).

(6) **Devotional surrender** (*bhakti*): an act of submission to a divine Other who is viewed as both unique and personal in form. In India this type of worship is widely associated with theistic forms of Hinduism, above all with Vaiṣṇavism (though the term *bhakti* does appear in some Buddhist sources, where a thorough study of its significance has yet to be made). A key requisite of this form of devotional activity is an emphasis on the separateness of the object and the devotee, without which such an intensely emotional relationship would be impossible.

Both for Aśoka (for whom the goal is a heavenly rebirth for himself and his subjects) and for the author of the larger *Sukhāvatīvyūha* (for whom what is at issue, in this particular vow, is that these bodhisattvas acquire the requisite merit to become Buddhas), it is the merit resulting from these offerings, and not the individual identity of their recipients, that is the primary concern.

[48] For a detailed discussion of the practice of *anusmṛti* (or more specifically, *buddhānusmṛti*) as represented in Indian Buddhist texts see Harrison 1978a and 1992a.

(7) **Mystical union** (*saṁyoga*, *advaita*): the identification between the devotee and Ultimate Reality (generally conceived of, in this form of religious practice, as impersonal rather than personal). This can take two forms: (a) achieving union with a Being from whom one was previously separate, or (b) recognizing one's pre-existing identity with that Being. Both forms require positing the existence of an eternal divine Reality, which serves as the object of this mystical assimilation; accordingly, this form of devotional practice is virtually unknown in the Buddhist tradition.[49]

The reader will note that the word *pūjā*—one of the terms most frequently translated into English as "worship"—has not been assigned a separate category above. This choice was deliberate, for *pūjā*, at least as used in the Buddhist sources I have examined, does not comprise an independent form of activity but simply incorporates elements from the first three (and sometimes from the fourth and/or fifth) categories described above.[50]

---

[49] The practice of "deity yoga" in tantric Buddhism, in which one identifies fully with a visualized divine being, only to then dissolve the entire experience—including the meditational object—into nothingness, differs in significant ways from this form of religious cultivation, and might best be viewed as a distinctive form of "meditative remembrance" (*anusmṛti*).

[50] The translation of *pūjā* as "worship" can in fact be misleading, for in some cases it seems to mean nothing more than "in honor of." See for example the Prakrit Taxila copper plate inscription from around the first half of the 1st century CE (Konow 1929, pp. 23-29), where an official's son establishes a relic of Śākyamuni and a monastery (*saṁghārāma*), "in honor of all Buddhas" (*sarvabudhana puyae*), honoring his mother and father (*matapitaraṁ puyayaṁt*[*o*] and honoring all his brothers and other relatives (again using the term *puyayaṁto*). Likewise in the Mathurā lion capital inscription (c. mid-1st century BCE; Konow 1929, pp. 30-49) a stūpa and a monastery are offered by a prominent Saka official and his extended family "in honor of all the Buddhas, in honor of the Dharma, in honor of the Sangha" (*sarvabudhana puya dhamasa puya saghasa puya*), as well as "in honor of the whole Saka nation" (*sarvasa Sak(r)astanasa puyae*). In all of these contexts the term "worship" would surely be misleading; a closer approximation, in North America at the beginning of the 21st century, might be the donation of an auditorium or concert hall "in honor of" (but certainly not "in order to worship"!) one's deceased parents, teacher, or spouse. For further references on the use of the term *pūjā* see the sources cited in Schopen 1997, p. 227, n. 36.

Given the wide range of possible expressions of worship or devotion outlined above, which of these—if any—do we actually find in the *Ugra*? To begin with, we may eliminate petitionary prayer, devotional surrender, and mystical union from consideration, for none of these occurs at any point within our text. And while the latter two, as noted above, would not be expected to occur, it is worth emphasizing that petitionary prayer is also absent.[51] Indeed, in the very circumstances in which petitionary prayer is recommended in other sūtras—for example, in the Avalokiteśvara chapter of the *Saddharmapuṇḍarīka*, where the devotee is urged to rely on that bodhisattva for rescue in situations of danger—the *Ugra* recommends the cultivation of insight instead.[52] Rather than turning to a more powerful being for solace or aid, in other words, the bodhisattva is told to rely on himself.

The first four items on the above list, by contrast, are all well attested in our text, appearing in roughly equal proportions in the lay and renunciant sections. Thus we should note at the outset that the *Ugra*'s authors clearly saw such activities as equally appropriate to the householder and the monk, thus offering us no grounds to posit any special association between devotional practice and the laity. What may be surprising, though, is the identity not of the agent but of the *object* of these devotional acts, for as we will see in the following discussion, the overwhelming majority of mentions of paying homage, making offerings, and so on are directed toward objects other than the Buddha. While the topic of worship in Indian Buddhism deserves a thorough study in itself,[53] here we will deal with just one aspect of this larger agenda by considering these four types of "devotional" activity in the specific context of the *Ugra*.

---

[51] The sole item that might be construed as an exception occurs in the section of the text dealing with the *triskandhaka* ritual, where the bodhisattva is instructed to "request all the Buddhas to turn the wheel of the Dharma" (§16B). Though this is technically an act of petitionary prayer, it clearly does not fall into the category described above, for it merely expresses a general sentiment (addressed, we should note, not to a particular figure but to "all the Buddhas") and is not linked to the individual benefit of the petitioner.

[52] See for example §25H, where the bodhisattva who experiences fear while living in the wilderness is told to reflect on the fact that fear arises only when one postulates the existence of a "self", or §25J, where he is told to remember that grasses, shrubs, and trees are free of fear because they lack this concept.

[53] For a study of devotion (though not of specific acts of worship) in the Buddhism of medieval Sri Lanka see Hallisey 1988.

Paying homage. The *Ugra* abounds in references to acts of veneration, reverence, and homage, both in the portion of the sūtra devoted to the practice of the lay bodhisattva and in the renunciant section of the text. While it is not always easy to determine the precise terminology used in the underlying Indic texts (and I will not attempt to do so here), it is clear that the authors of the *Ugra* saw such acts as part of the very fabric of Buddhist life.

What is noteworthy, however, is that such acts of reverence are not restricted to the Buddha alone. While the sūtra does refer to revering the Tathāgata (§§20B; 25E, 26A) or (in the passage dealing with the *triskandhaka* ritual) paying homage to all the Buddhas of the ten directions (§16A), these passages are the sole instances in the text in which anything that could be construed as worship of the Buddha is mentioned. Far more numerous are references to other objects of reverence: the Dharma itself (§3C), the *vihāra*, or monastic community (§§3D [three mentions] and 18A), and above all, the bodhisattva's own human teachers (§§4B, 6B, 26C-D, 33B, 33E). Indeed it is here that the text waxes most eloquent, when describing the degree of reverence owed to a teacher from whom one has received instruction on the bodhisattva path.[54]

While acts of reverence are thus not limited to the Buddha, neither are they (at the other extreme) generalized to extend to all living beings, or even to all members of the Buddhist community. We find here no equivalent of the practice espoused by the bodhisattva "Never Despised" (Sadāparibhūta) in the *Lotus Sūtra*, for example, who bowed to every Buddhist he met in acknowledgement of his or her future Buddhahood and received nothing but scorn in return.[55] On the contrary, the *Ugra*'s authors seem careful to separate those objects that are worthy of reverence from those (including Buddhist ones) that are not.[56]

---

[54] See especially §§26C-D, and cf. the discussion under "Service" below.

[55] For the story of Sadāparibhūta see Chapter 19 of the Sanskrit version of the *Saddharmapuṇḍarīka*. The name is in fact ambiguous; it can be read either as *sadā* + *aparibhūta* "never having despised [other people]" or as *sadā* + *paribhūta* "always despised [by others]." While Kumārajīva understands it in the former sense, Dharmarakṣa reads it in the latter (see his translation of the *Saddharmapuṇḍarīka-sūtra*, T 263, 9.122b). On this name cf. also Nakamura 1981, 1128a.

[56] Note, for example, that in its discussion of how important it is for a lay bodhisattva not to criticize a monk who has broken the precepts (§17A), the *Ugra* does *not* urge the bodhisattva to venerate such a monk; indeed, it goes on

In sum, the act of paying homage is portrayed in the *Ugra* as a selective practice, to be directed only toward those perceived as admirable, or—to put it another way—as superior to oneself. By venerating the Buddha (during or after his lifetime), the Dharma, and living members of the monastic community the bodhisattva thus situates himself within a network of hierarchical relationships and affirms his membership in a particular religious community. But even while doing so he affirms that he will eventually surpass his relatively low present status, for in the most striking reference to worship in the sūtra the lay bodhisattva is urged to look forward to the day when he will become an object of worship himself. After paying homage to the Tathāgata at the entrance to the *vihāra*, the bodhisattva is told to remind himself that "I, too, should become one who is worthy of this kind of worship" (§20B). Thus even his own act of paying homage is carried out in anticipation of a far more glorious future in which he will become a world-redeeming Buddha himself, a topic to which we will return below.

Making offerings. The giving of gifts is discussed at considerable length in the *Ugra* in both the lay and renunciant sections of the sūtra. But here again, we find that the majority of such activities are directed toward objects other than the Buddha. The case of material gifts offers perhaps the most striking divergence from what we might expect, for in the *Ugra* the most extensive discussions of the practice of *dāna* are not in reference to giving to the Buddhist sangha, much less to the Buddha himself, but to ordinary (i.e., non-religious) beggars. Indeed—to return to the main issue that concerns us here—there is not a single case in in the *Ugra* in which the bodhisattva either makes, or is exhorted to make, an offering to the Buddha himself.[57]

A tabulation of all the references to giving away one's goods that occur in the *Ugra* reveals instead a surprising but significant pattern. While there are no mentions of giving to the Buddha and but a single mention of gifts to the sangha (§20D), giving to ordinary beggars is the subject of two rather lengthy discussions (§§11 and 15). But in

---

to make a clear distinction between those who are worthy of respect (i.e., the Noble Ones who uphold the precepts) and those who, being guilty of an offense, deserve his pity (*karuṇā*) instead. For the use of *karuṇā* in this sense see above, pp. 145-146.

57 The sole passage that might seem to be an exception is a single generic description of the Buddha as one who receives (during his final lifetime as Śākyamuni) the worship and offerings of the whole world (§26A).

the vast majority of cases the identity of the recipient of the donation is not specified.[58] In these instances it is clear that it is the act of giving itself that counts, not the identity (or the worthiness) of the recipient.

This unexpected pattern is noteworthy, and we will return to a discussion of its significance below. First, however, we should note that there is a clear asymmetry in the number of passages dealing with the practice of giving in the section of the sūtra addressed to the householder (eleven or more, depending on how one tabulates them; some of these passages are quite lengthy and could be subdivided) and the section devoted to the monk (where only three such mentions occur, two when the six perfections are listed[59] and a third which does not occur at all in the earliest recension of the sūtra[60]). Though recent scholarship has pointed to the importance of donations made by monks and nuns,[61] for the authors of the *Ugra* it seems clear that giving was viewed primarily as an activity for the householder. Indeed, in one strongly worded passage we are told that even if the lay bodhisattva were to make offerings "numerous as the sands of the Ganges River" for many days, and were to give away all of his possessions, those actions would be surpassed by the mere thought of becoming a monk (§20A).

What are we to make, then, of the seemingly peculiar pattern of the *Ugra*'s discussions of *dāna*? Given the fact that the paradigmatic "fields of merit" (*puṇya-kṣetra*)—the Buddha and his community of monastics—are rarely (or, in the case of the Buddha, never) mentioned as objects of giving, it seems clear that the *Ugra*'s authors viewed the activity of *dāna* through a lens that did not involve the worthiness of the recipient. Indeed, one could hardly find a less worthy object of generosity (according to Indian social standards of the day) than an ordinary—and quite likely low-caste—beggar. How are we to understand the fact that beggars receive so much attention in this text, second only to generic (and unnamed) recipients?

In another context Lawrence A. Babb has argued that an analysis

[58] See §§4E, 7a(5), 8A, 10A-B, 12C (where *dāna* occurs at the head of a list of virtues), 20E (where *dāna* occurs as the first of the four *saṁgrahavastus*, or "means of attraction"), 20G, 25L, 26C, and 31B(1).

[59] See §§25L and 26C. In neither case does *dāna* receive more attention than any of the other five *pāramitās*.

[60] See §31B(1), where the lay bodhisattva is told (in the later recensions of the sūtra) how he can emulate the asceticism of the monk.

[61] See Schopen 1988-1989.

of the handling of food offerings in religious ritual can reveal significant aspects of the relationship between the object of worship and the devotee. In contrast to the practice of Hindu Vaiṣṇavas, for example, where food offered to Kṛṣṇa is consumed by his devotees as *prasāda*, the food offered to an image of the Jina is never returned to the worshippers, but is typically given to the non-Jain officiants (*pūjārī*) of the temple (Babb 1998). The cult of Śiva, Babb observes, is in many ways more closely aligned with Jain practice than with Vaiṣṇava ritual, for here too the worshipper does not consume the food he or she has given. Such distinctions in ritual practice, Babb suggests, reveal a contrast between "transactional" and "non-transactional" understandings of the devotee's relationship to the object of worship, with the absence of the Tirthaṅkara (who has transcended the limits of *saṁsāra* and can no longer be contacted by his devotees) contrasting sharply with the understanding of Kṛṣṇa as making himself fully present in his images.

By drawing attention to the "nontransactional" structure of Jain ritual Babb raises important questions about Buddhist practice as well.[62] For our present purposes, however, it is another aspect of Babb's discussion that is of greatest relevance: a distinction between "giving to" and "giving up." While Kṛṣṇa's devotees are emphatically making their offerings *to* him as a personal divine being and receiving those offerings from him as *prasāda* in return, Jain devotees, Babb contends, are not giving food *to* the Tirthaṅkara (who cannot, after all, either receive or consume it), but giving *up* their offerings in emulation of the ascetic behavior of the renunciant community, and indeed of the Jina himself.

No direct comparison can be made between the content of the *Ugra* and the scenario Babb describes, for as we have seen there is not a single instance in which the bodhisattva is portrayed as making an

---

[62] Above all, if the Buddha is indeed in some sense present in his images and relics—as recent work by Eckel, Schopen, and others would appear to suggest—how are we to understand the striking absence of any form of foodstuffs from the long lists of items named in sūtra and vinaya literature (flowers, lamps; incense, banners, etc.) as appropriate gifts to the Buddha? Clearly food offerings did become a part of Buddhist ritual at some point, but to what extent were these offerings coined in emulation of ancestor worship (in East Asia) or of Hindu *pūjā* (in Sri Laṅka and elsewhere)? Though Babb does not say so, the fact that it is non-Jain *pūjārī*s who receive the food offerings given to the Jina strongly suggests that this practice entered the Jain tradition not as a result of internal developments but from another (non-Jain) source.

offering to the Buddhist analogue of the Tirthaṅkara—that is, to the Buddha himself. But it does seem clear that in the *Ugra* we have an understanding of giving that is based less on giving *to* a particular recipient than on renunciation of the donated object itself. And if this is the case, the act of *dāna* does not require the participation of a meritorious (much less saintly) recipient for its success. Indeed, from this perspective an insistent beggar could be an ideal recipient, since he might press the bodhisattva to make a donation he would otherwise be reluctant to make.

Be that as it may, while in many Buddhist texts there is great concern with the worthiness of the object of giving, in the *Ugra* the recipient's identity seems virtually irrelevant, and the Buddha and other worthy "fields of merit" are conspicuous by their absence. But if what counts is the practice of renunciation (*tyāga*), or giving *up*, in itself, we need no longer wonder at the fact that in the *Ugra* the overwhelming majority of donations are made to seemingly unworthy (or even anonymous) recipients.

Service. The *Ugra* contains far fewer references to acts of service than it does to making offerings, but it is nonetheless clear that such actions are viewed as an integral part of the Buddhist path. Yet in contrast to the previous category, here we find that all but one of these occurrences are in the portion of the sūtra dealing with the practice of the renunciant bodhisattva. For the *Ugra*'s authors, it would seem, making offerings is predominantly a practice for the lay person, while service is primarily performed by monks.

There is another factor that clearly distinguishes service from giving in the mind of the *Ugra*'s authors, however, for here the identity of the recipient of one's service is clearly of major concern. In the sole reference to service that occurs in the portion of the text dealing with the householder, the lay bodhisattva is told that he should serve *brāhmaṇa*s and *śramaṇa*s "who keep the precepts" (§17A). While it is noteworthy that the sūtra does not restrict the act of service to Buddhist recipients—for all *brāhmaṇa*s, and presumably most *śramaṇa*s, would be affiliated with other religious groups—it does restrict such service to recipients who are worthy, as exemplified by their adherence to the moral rules.

In the section of the sūtra devoted to the renunciant bodhisattva, however, the identity of a proper object of service becomes quite clear. And, as in the category of "paying homage" discussed above, it is the dharma-teacher—specifically, the teacher who instructs the renunciant in the practive of the bodhisattva path—who is worthy of receiving such service. Even as the *Ugra* reminds the renunciant bodhisattva that he should not long for service from others (§26A-B), it exhorts him to offer service to his own teachers in the most extravagant terms. If he receives from his teacher a single four-line verse concerning the bodhisattva path, for example, he should honor and serve that teacher for as many eons as there are words, syllables, and letters in that verse (§26C). And even then, the text goes on to say, his duty to the teacher will not be fulfilled (§26D).

The Buddha too—at least during his own lifetime—is clearly a worthy object of service, for the *Ugra* reminds its audience that, though he was worthy of receiving service from all beings, he never required it (§26A), and goes on to say that Ugra himself will in the future serve all the Buddhas of this *bhadrakalpa* (§32B; this passage does not occur in AY). Finally, in yet another passage that does not occur in the earliest translation of the text, there is an additional reference to serving the living monastic community, including both the Buddha and his monks (§33D).

In sum, while the *Ugra*'s authors appear not to have discriminated among the objects of giving—placing greater emphasis on the act of renunciation itself—the act of service is restricted to those viewed as worthy of veneration. Though upright practitioners of non-Buddhist paths might be included, the paradigmatic recipients of service are the Buddha and the monastic community, and above all teachers of the bodhisattva path. Finally, we should note that the *Ugra* also appears to restrict the offering of service to the community of living individuals, for there is not a single reference to offering service to the Buddha or any other recipient after his death.

Meditative remembrance. The first mention of "bearing in mind" occurs near the beginning of the section devoted to the householder bodhisattva (§4D), where it is used in the expression *buddha-anusmṛti* (Ch. *nien-fo* 念佛) that was later to become so influential in East Asia. Here obtaining "remembrance of the Buddha" (*buddha-anusmṛti*) after seeing the Buddha (or, as the Tibetan may suggest, seeing an image of him) is equated with "going to the Buddha for refuge." One might well conclude, as did MOCHIZUKI Ryōkō in the study of the *Ugra* included in his book on the *Mahāparinirvāṇa-sūtra*,[63] that *buddha-anusmṛti* as a devotional act is

---

[63] See Mochizuki 1988, especially pp. 312, 327, and 330.

particularly important in our text. But nothing further is ever said about this practice in the *Ugra* (though there is considerable discussion of it in the commentary on the sūtra contained in the **Daśabhūmikavibhāṣā*, by which Mochizuki was apparently misled). And as a closer look at the context immediately shows, the practice of *anusmṛti* is by no means directed exclusively toward the Buddha. Instead, the sūtra goes on to apply the same language to the Dharma (where *dharma-anusmṛti* is equated with "going to the Dharma for refuge") and to the Sangha as well, where again the equation with going for refuge is invoked. In sum, the practice of *buddha-anusmṛti* is by no means identified with exclusive devotion to the Buddha, but is rather presented as part of a constellation of practices involving the remembrance of a worthy or edifying object.

The same is true in a second occurrence of the term *anusmṛti*, where the renunciant bodhisattva is told that he should be "mindful of the six kinds of mindfulness" (§25B). Though no further discussion of this practice is given here, it is clear that the authors are drawing on an even longer traditional list of objects of remembrance, that is, the Buddha, Dharma, Sangha, morality (*śīla*), renunciation (*tyāga*), and the gods (*deva*).[64] The only other reference to the practice of *anusmṛti* occurs in the distinctive section dealing with the *triskandhaka* ritual, and here the practice is directed toward the remembrance of the whole range of good actions and good qualities of all the Buddhas of the ten directions (§16A). In sum, while the Buddha (that is, Śākyamuni Buddha) is included within the list of objects of remembrance, he is far from the only such object mentioned in the *Ugra*, and indeed in purely numerical terms acts of remembrance directed toward him constitute only a minority.

Conclusions: Imitative vs. Relational Cultivation

What can we conclude, then, about the relationship between the Buddha and the practitioner as envisioned in the *Ugra*? It is clear that our text pays no special attention to the cultivation of a relationship between the Buddha and the aspiring bodhisattva, but should we necessarily conclude from this absence that its authors saw this relationship as of little importance? Here again, as in several previous

---

64 For further discussion and additional references see n. 89 to the translation (§4D).

instances, we are confronted with the challenge of "reading from absence." Could it be that the authors of the *Ugra* saw this relationship—and the cultivation of a devotional attitude on the part of the bodhisattva—as so self-evidently central that they did not bother to discuss it at all?

While this is a theoretical possibility, the *Ugra* contains two additional passages that bear directly on this question and portray the bodhisattva's relationship with the Buddha in a perhaps unexpected light. The first of these occurs in a passage dealing with the proper understanding of "going to the Buddha for refuge." Surely here, if anywhere, the *Ugra*'s authors had a golden opportunity to expound on the cultivation of an attitude of devotion. But they do not do so, focussing instead on how the bodhisattva should strive to become a Buddha himself. The Buddha says to Ugra:

> O Eminent Householder, how should the householder bodhisattva go to the Buddha for refuge? O Eminent Householder, by forming the thought "I must attain the body of a Buddha, ornamented with the thirty-two marks of a Great Man," and by exerting himself to acquire those roots-of-goodness by which the thirty-two marks of a Great Man will be obtained, in this way does the householder bodhisattva go to the Buddha for refuge. (§3B)

While nothing contained here is anything but traditional, it is striking that the *Ugra*'s authors say nothing at all about fostering a bond between the Buddha and the practitioner, urging the bodhisattva to imitate the Buddha instead.

This perspective emerges in even sharper relief in another passage, already cited above, in which the lay bodhisattva is told that as he pays homage to the Buddha he should reflect that "I, too, should become one who is worthy of this kind of worship" (§20B). Even as he himself offers reverence to the Buddha, in other words, the bodhisattva is reminded to focus on his own attainment of that glorious status in the future.

It seems clear, in light of these passages, that the *Ugra*'s authors were not concerned with fostering a personal relationship between the bodhisattva and the Buddha that could be described in any sense as "devotional." There is nothing here that remotely resembles the erotic language of devotional Vaiṣṇavism, nor the language of gratitude and reliance on the Buddha that would later be characterized as *tariki* 他力 "other-power" in the "True Pure Land" (*Jōdo shinshū* 淨土真宗)

Buddhism of Japan, nor even the intimate references to "my Buddha" found in medieval Sinhalese texts (Hallisey 1988). Rather, in precisely those contexts in which we might have expected the authors of the *Ugra* to urge the bodhisattva to cultivate a personal relationship with the Buddha, they exhort him to focus on his own self-development instead.

If we were to draw a continuum, then, from a primarily relational practice to a primarily imitative one, the *Ugra* would clearly fall very close to the imitative end of the scale. It is possible, of course, to engage in the two activities simultaneously, as for example in the practice of contemporary members of the Mormon church (the Latter-day Saints) for whom worship of God in the present will lead in the future—for male members at least—to becoming the God of another world oneself. In the end, however, participants in any religious system must make a choice between viewing their primary objective as cultivating a relationship with an ultimate Other or becoming that ultimate entity oneself. Early Buddhism, like its first cousin Jainism, quite clearly fell into the nonrelational camp, and once again the *Ugra* exhibits a notable continuity with its ancestry.

CHAPTER 7

Telling Absences: What Is Not in the *Ugra*

At the beginning of Chapter 2 we noted that the *Ugra* should not be referred to as a "Mahāyāna sūtra"—not, that is, without careful qualification. At this point it is time to examine just what some of those qualifications might be. All of them have to do with certain absences in the text: that is, the absence of items which we might expect to find in a "Mahāyāna sūtra," but which do not appear in this sūtra at all. As we shall see, what is *not* in the *Ugra* may have as much to tell us about the circumstances surrounding the emergence of the bodhisattva path in India as what is actually found in the text.

An absence, of course, is difficult to perceive directly. To be able to discern what a text is telling us by its silence we must perform two operations simultaneously: first, to have some idea of what we might expect to find in such a text, an idea formed by previous exposure to other literature from a similar time or place; and second, to be alert to ways in which the text at hand does or does not conform to these expectations. An absence can be seen, in other words, only through an explicit process of comparison.

This is not, of course, the way in which absences have traditionally been treated by Buddhist writers, nor (somewhat more surprisingly) by modern scholars of Buddhist texts. Far too often absent items are simply "read into" a text, either because we have seen them in similar literature or because generalizations about what the "Mahāyāna" is have led us to expect them. But if we are to understand the world out of which the *Ugra* emerged we must resist this temptation. In fact, one of the most important procedures in analyzing Buddhist literature of any period is to get a clear sense of what its author did, and did not, assume as background.

In addition to considering items that do not occur in the sūtra at all, a thorough comparative reading must also take note of items that do appear in the text but which are used in a quite different way than in other Buddhist scriptures. We have dealt in the previous chapter with two of the most prominent of these: the *Ugra*'s use of the term *bhūmi* to refer to the levels of the householder and the renunciant, rather than to the more familiar "ten stages" (*daśabhūmi*) of the bodhisattva path, and its use of the term *upāya-kauśalya* to refer not to the bodhisattva's adaptation of the teachings to suit the needs of his hearers, but to certain countertactics used in solitary meditation to avoid falling into Arhatship or a heavenly rebirth. Careful attention to such distinctive usages will not only enhance our understanding of the perspective contained in the *Ugra* itself, but will ultimately allow us to begin to speak of "textual families" that are more or less closely related to our text. In this chapter, however, our discussion will be limited to the most extreme form of difference: the total absence of certain elements that are widely considered to be central features of "the Mahāyāna."

The Term "Hīnayāna"

Given the fact that all extant versions of the *Ugra* freely use the term *mahāyāna*, it is noteworthy that the corresponding term *hīnayāna* ("low vehicle," "inferior vehicle") does not occur in any version of our text. In this respect the *Ugra* is quite typical of bodhisattva sūtras translated into Chinese during the latter Han dynasty, for as Paul Harrison has shown, terms that can be equated with the word *hīnayāna* appear only rarely, occurring a total of four times in the entire corpus of eleven such texts, which means that the majority do not contain it at all.[1] Considerably more frequent—though still not as numerous as the occurrences found in later sūtra translations—are terms that can be equated with either *bodhisattvayāna* or *mahāyāna*.[2]

The unequal distribution of the terms *hīnayāna* and *mahāyāna* in these early translations might seem odd, given their obvious terminological symmetry. But the symmetry is only apparent. While the two terms are grammatically parallel, conceptually—and chronologically, so the evidence strongly suggests—they are not. As Hubert Durt has pointed out, in the earliest literature the term *bodhisattvayāna* and other synonyms appear to predominate, while the term *mahāyāna* only gradually came to be accepted as standard.[3]

---

[1] See Harrison 1987, p. 72.

[2] By Harrison's count the term *mahāyāna*, whether transliterated or translated as "great Way," appears only about twenty times in these same texts (*loc. cit.*). From both Harrison's list of authentic 2nd-century translations and from the nearly identical list given in Zürcher 1991 we should probably delete T 630, the *Ch'eng-chü kuang-ming ting-i ching* 成具光明定意經 attributed to Chih Yao 支曜 (late 2nd century), which is almost certainly a later apocryphon.

[3] Durt 1994, p. 778.

And it was even later, so the evidence assembled by Harrison and others would seem to suggest, that the word *mahāyāna* came to be paralleled by the strongly pejorative term *hīnayāna*.[4]

What are we to make, then, of the fact that the term *hīnayāna* does not appear in our text? As we have seen, there are at least three possible explanations for the absence of a given concept or term: (1) that the authors had never heard of it, (2) that they knew it and took it for granted, considering it too obvious to require special mention; or (3) that they knew it and rejected it, choosing not to mention it because they viewed it as unworthy of consideration.[5]

Which of these possibilities offers the most likely explanation for the absence of the term *hīnayāna*? To decide among these options we must first ask several questions: (1) Is the understanding of the *śrāvaka* path embodied in the term *hīnayāna* required or implied by other things that are present in our text? (2) On the contrary, is that same understanding contradicted by the content of our text? And finally, (3) does our text contain anything that could be described as a less fully developed—that is, an earlier—version of that concept?

The first and second questions represent two mutually exclusive possibilities, and it is quite clear where the *Ugra* falls on this issue. For the notion of the *śrāvaka* path as a despised "inferior vehicle" is explicitly and emphatically contradicted by the contents of our text. The bodhisattva is repeatedly reminded that his duty as a candidate for Buddhahood is to prepare himself to teach others the *śrāvaka* path, and that members of the *śrāvaka* vehicle are worthy of respect even if they have broken the precepts. In sum, to use the term *hīnayāna* would violate a central tenet of our text: the ultimate worthiness of the *śrāvaka* path itself.

---

[4] It is important to point out that the term *hīnayāna* does not mean "small vehicle." The Indian epithet *hīna-*, from the root √*hā* "discard, shun; be deficient," carries a range of strongly negative associations, including "lower, weaker, inferior, deficient, defective, low, vile," and "mean" (see MW 1296b-c); the standard Tibetan equivalent *theg-pa dman-pa* "low vehicle" accurately captures this negative connotation, as does the expression *lieh-sheng* 劣乘 "inferior vehicle" used by Dharmarakṣa and some other early Chinese translators. In fact, the English expression "small vehicle" is not based on the Indian term at all, but on the Chinese expression *hsiao-sheng* 小乘 "little vehicle" used by Kumārajīva and others. It may well be that Kumārajīva (whose own background was originally Sarvāstivādin) deliberately chose a less offensive, though technically inaccurate, expression to translate *hīnayāna*.

[5] See above, Chapter 3, p. 69.

As noted in the previous chapter, it has sometimes been suggested that the use of the term *mahāyāna* marks the emergence of the bodhisattva "movement" as a separate institution or organization. As we have seen, however, the *Ugra* itself—which uses the term *mahāyāna* quite freely yet portrays bodhisattvas as living within the framework of the traditional monastic sangha—contains evidence that this is not the case. But the term *hīnayāna*, I would suggest, does indeed function as such a marker. While it is entirely possible (though not necessarily easy, as we have seen in Chapter 4) for practitioners of the traditional path to Arhatship to inhabit a religious community together with others who are pursuing a path to Buddhahood that is viewed as superior, it is unlikely that any semblance of harmony could be maintained within such a community if bodhisattvas were referring to the religious practice of their *śrāvaka* coreligionists as "low" or "debased." The fact that the *Ugra* is free of any occurrence of this pejorative and divisive term may thus be taken as yet another indication that it is the product of a community in which both the bodhisattva and the *śrāvaka* paths were still viewed as legitimate, indeed admirable, religious vocations.[6]

Bodhisattva Universalism

Given that the authors of the *Ugra* viewed the *śrāvaka* and bodhisattva vehicles as separate (though overlapping) paths leading to separate and quite unequal goals, it is hardly surprising that we find in this sūtra not a trace of the doctrine of "one vehicle" (*ekayāna*) that has been so widely influential in East Asia. But what is perhaps more

---

[6] It seems likely that the sequence of development of this terminology began with the straightforward expression *bodhisattvayāna*, which was then qualified with the epithet "great" (*mahāyāna*), and which finally led to the creation of the term *hīnayāna* as a back-formation (i.e., formed as the opposite of the already existing *mahāyāna*) as attitudes toward practitioners of a non-bodhisattva path became, at least in some circles, ever more critical. The term *bodhisattvayāna* would thus represent the emergence of the path to Buddhahood as a distinct vocational alternative, the term *mahāyāna* a mere expression of admiration for that path, and the term *hīnayāna* an expression of a derisive attitude toward non-bodhisattva practitioners. In other words, only the first and last terms in this sequence—and not the epithet *mahāyāna* itself—actually represent significant turning points in the development of the Mahāyāna tradition.

unexpected is the absence of an attitude that is widely regarded as a key element, even the defining feature, of "the Mahāyāna": an attitude which we might call "bodhisattva universalism." By this I mean simply the idea that the bodhisattva path is appropriate for all, and that all Buddhists either are, or should be, on that path.

This idea exists in two forms: a weak form, found in a wide range of Mahāyāna sūtras which admit that an Arhat really has been liberated from *saṁsāra* but contend that this is not an admirable goal, and a strong form best known from its appearance in the *Lotus Sūtra*, where it is argued that all Buddhists (knowingly or unknowingly) are on the path to Buddhahood, and that the supposed nirvāṇa of the Arhat is only an illusion. The strong form of bodhisattva universalism may thus be equated with the doctrine of *ekayāna*, according to which only one path (and one goal) really exists, while the weak form retains the traditional scenario of the "three vehicles." What both positions have in common is the idea that only Buddhahood is a desirable destination, and thus only the bodhisattva vehicle is a respectworthy path.

As I have argued elsewhere, however, bodhisattva universalism is far from universal in Mahāyāna Buddhist texts.[7] Indeed, a substantial number of sūtras—texts like the *Akṣobhyavyūha*, the *Aṣṭasāhasrikā-prajñāpāramitā-sūtra*, and even the early recensions of the larger *Sukhāvatīvyūha*—clearly accept the validity, indeed the desirability, of Arhatship as a spiritual goal. Though they share with the "weak form" of bodhisattva universalism the idea that Arhatship is a real, final, and admittedly lower spiritual destination, they stop short of urging all beings to become bodhisattvas. On the contrary, they recognize that not all beings have the capacity to become Buddhas, and that the *śrāvaka* and not the bodhisattva path is appropriate for some. Thus even as they instruct the bodhisattva on the specifics of his or her chosen path—for in some of these scriptures bodhisatvas may also be women[8]—they also treat the path of the *śrāvaka* as entirely legitimate. A careful reading of the surviving texts classified as "Mahāyāna sūtras" (preserved, for the most part, only in Chinese and/or Tibetan) shows that this nonuniversalist position was actually quite widespread, especially in the early stages of the production of Mahāyāna literature.

---

[7] See Nattier 1999.
[8] See Harrison 1987 and 1998.

The *Ugra*, quite clearly, belongs to this more conservative—that is, nonuniversalist—camp. Though it clearly treats Buddhahood as more exalted than Arhatship and urges bodhisattvas (and, in one passage, other advanced practitioners not yet irreversible from Arhatship)[9] to strive to attain it, the *Ugra* still treats Buddhahood as appropriate for, and attainable by, only the few. Thus the "default" option, or the usual outcome of Buddhist practice, remains the attainment of Arhatship, and this is viewed as entirely legitimate. Once again, the *Ugra* (like other nonuniversalist bodhisattva sūtras) exhibits a striking continuity with earlier Buddhism, for these scriptures hold that the job description of a Buddha is to help others attain Arhatship, just as it was in the time of Śākyamuni Buddha.[10]

The Supermundane Buddha

What bodhisattvas are trying to become, according to the *Ugra*, is indeed glorious: a world-redeeming Buddha, ornamented with the thirty-two marks of greatness and endowed with a level of insight (labeled *sarvajña*, "omniscience") that far exceeds that of Arhats and Pratyekabuddhas. And yet it is important to point out that this goal, glorious as it is, lacks many of the features of Buddhahood regularly expounded in other Mahāyāna (and even non-Mahāyāna) scriptures.

We do not see, for example, any trace of the doctrine of the "three bodies of the Buddha" (*trikāya*), according to which the earthly Buddha Śākyamuni is a mere manifestation of an eternal and unchanging "dharma-body" (*dharmakāya*). Nor do we see even the earlier "two-body" system, distinguishing between a "dharma-body" (here understood as "body of the teachings") and a "form-body" (*rūpakāya*, understood as the physical body of the Buddha and, after his death, his relics).[11] What both of these multibody systems do, in effect, is to reduce the importance of the Buddha's physical presence, subordinating it to his teachings in the two-body system or to a

[9] See §4C, where the lay bodhisattva is told to think that "those who have [not yet] definitively entered into the Śrāvaka Vehicle he should lead to the spirit of Omniscience."

[10] We may recall, for example, the passage in which the bodhisattva who is tempted to look down on his *śrāvaka* coreligionists is reminded that when he becomes a Buddha, he too will head a sangha of *śrāvaka*s (§3D). For further discussion see above, pp. 84-89.

[11] See Harrison 1992d.

transcendent, almost Brahman-like, force in the *trikāya* scheme. For the *Ugra*, however, the glorious body of a Buddha—"ornamented with the thirty-two marks of a Great Man (*mahāpuruṣa*)" as the text explicitly puts it (§3B)—is precisely what the bodhisattva is striving to attain. Rather than subordinate this objective to another construct, the *Ugra*'s authors simply urge the bodhisattva to pay homage to the marks of the Buddha and to strive to attain those same marks for himself.

Yet despite the fact that the attainment of these marks clearly sets a Buddha apart from other human beings, the *Ugra* does not go on to make the docetic move characteristic of the Lokottaravādin Mahāsaṁghika school and of some (but certainly not all) Mahāyāna scriptures. Nowhere does it refer to the Buddha as a supermundane (*lokottara*) being who does not need to eat or sleep but does so merely to conform to the expectations of the world (*lokānu-vartana*).[12] On the contrary, the Buddha is presented not as an otherworldly being but as the pinnacle of possible human attainment, and thus as something that the bodhisattva himself can become.[13]

Not surprisingly, then, the *Ugra* also lacks any reference to the Buddha's lifespan as infinite, or even (as in the *Lotus Sūtra* and the larger *Sukhāvatīvyūha*) as limitless (*amita*) or immeasurable (*aprameya*). While the sūtra takes quite literally the idea that billions of years are required to assemble all the qualities of a Buddha, this does not translate, for the authors of the *Ugra*, into the assumption that one's own future lifetime as a Buddha will last for an equally unfathomable length of time. On the contrary, once again the *Ugra* takes a quite traditional stance, assuming that eons of rigorous and

---

[12] See Harrison 1982.

[13] It is noteworthy that the understanding of the Buddha as supermundane most often occurs in contexts in which Buddhists are not being encouraged to emulate him. Indeed, such an image of the Buddha makes it difficult to conceive of becoming such a being oneself. It seems likely—though to confirm or deny such a thesis would require extensive research that cannot be undertaken here—that the *lokottara* perspective evolved not in a context of active bodhisattva practice, but in an atmosphere of competition with Hindu and other cults of transcendent beings. To put it another way, such a supermundane concept of the Buddha can be very helpful in a context in which what is expected is worship of the Buddha (especially if the Buddha is, in this capacity, in competition with other deities); it can be distinctly unhelpful in a context in which people are being urged to become bodhisattvas, and thus to strive for Buddhahood, themselves.

ascetic practice as a bodhisattva will lead to one glorious lifetime—but a lifetime of normal duration—as a Buddha.[14]

It is worth noting, incidentally, that references to unusually long lifespans seem to emerge, in Buddhist literature, in two quite distinct contexts: in reference to Buddhas of the distant past, on the one hand, and to Buddhas presently living in other world-systems, on the other. These two instances, I would suggest, are responses to quite different kinds of forces. The long lifespans of past Buddhas may be simply the result of the assumption that the human lifespan has been shrinking over the course of eons, and that as a corollary any Buddha living in a previous eon would have had a longer lifespan than our own. (The fact that the future Buddha Maitreya is regularly assigned a lifespan of 80,000 years is a part of this same system, since he is to appear in our world at the peak of the next cycle, at which time the human lifespan will have returned to its maximum extent.)[15] The lifespans of Buddhas such as Akṣobhya and Amitābha, by contrast, transcend even the maximum numbers allowed within this standard cosmological system, and are in all probability a response to a different set of concerns. Since their role is to provide an optimal place of rebirth for Buddhists from other worlds, it is vital that their lifespans be immeasurably long. It would be sad indeed if one fulfilled in this Sahā world all the prerequisites for rebirth in Abhirati or Sukhāvatī, only to find, upon arriving there, that the Buddha in question had passed away!

In sum, while the *Ugra* clearly portrays the Buddha as a glorious being, it exhibits no awareness of any of the substantial innovations in buddhology that would characterize a number of later Mahāyāna sūtras. On the contrary, the portrait of the Buddha that we see here is profoundly continuous with the earlier tradition, offering nothing that would be out of place in a Sarvāstivādin, Theravāda, or Dharmaguptaka text. Since the *Ugra* neither assumes nor argues against such innovations, we may conclude that its authors were entirely unaware of these developments, if indeed they had yet taken place at all.

---

[14] The *Ugra* does not discuss this issue explicitly, but here I believe we are entitled to take the sūtra's silence as an indication that it did not hold any unusual views concerning the duration of a Buddha's life.

[15] On the human lifespan in the time of Maitreya and of the various Buddhas of the past see Nattier 1991, pp. 19-26.

The Rhetoric of Emptiness

Of the many items that are absent from the *Ugra* one of the most striking, from the point of view of what is generally taken as essential to the "Mahāyāna," is the absence of the rhetoric of absence itself. That is to say, the *Ugra* lacks anything that could be construed as a "philosophy of emptiness." Granted, the word *śūnyatā* (or its simple adjectival form *śūnya*) does appear in the sūtra a handful of times, but a careful examination of these occurrences reveals a clear and rather unexpected pattern: when the term "empty" is not simply being used in its everyday, nontechnical sense (e.g., in references to an "empty city" or an "empty house"),[16] it appears simply as one of the members of the traditional list of the three doors to liberation (*vimokṣa*), that is, the empty (*śūnya*), the signless (*animitta*), and the wishless (*apraṇihita*).[17] The word "emptiness" shows no sign either of having been singled out for special attention vis-à-vis these two associated ideas or of having received the kind of philosophical development that would culminate in the dialectical subtleties of the Mādhyamika. In short, the *Ugra* is clearly not a sūtra based on the idea of *śūnyatā*.

The negative discourse that is so prominent in many Mahāyāna scriptures need not proceed, of course, solely on the basis of this term. In one of the earliest scriptures of the Prajñāpāramitā group, the *Perfection of Wisdom in Eight Thousand Lines* (*Aṣṭasāhasrikā-prajñāpāramitā-sūtra*), for example, the term *śūnyatā* appears only rarely in the early chapters, and in the *Diamond Sūtra* (*Vajra-*

---

[16] The two examples of this usage in the Tibetan text are in §27D, where the sense organs and their objects (the twelve *āyatanas*) are described using the metaphor of an "empty city," and in §31B(3), where the householder bodhisattva is told that he should go to an "empty house" to meditate (this passage is not found in the earliest translation).

[17] This usage occurs in §§18A, 25B, and 25G. A similar instance occurs in §27F, where "emptiness" is followed by the "signless," but then (perhaps through an error in transmission) the list shifts to other matters. A reference to emptiness alone (without the other two elements) occurs in §25I, but with precisely the same vocabulary that has been used in an earlier section in reference to all three doors to liberation (§25G). Finally, the sole reference in the sūtra to what might be construed as emptiness in the developed philosophical sense is probably simply another example of everyday usage: "Living at home one fashions things according to one's own way of thinking, but they are devoid of essential reality (*ngo-bo-nyid-[kyis] stong-pa*), like the makeup of a performer" (§9D).

cchedikā) it is never used at all. Yet the rhetoric of negation is nonetheless carried on with great intensity through the use of other terminology.[18] But in the *Ugra* such antiessentialist and antireifying arguments are conspicuous by their absence. While the text takes a quite traditional stance in denying the existence of a "self" (e.g., §25 H and J; note that these discussions take place only in the renunciant section of the sūtra), it does not go on to apply such negative rhetoric to Arhatship, Buddhahood, or the path. Indeed the *Ugra*'s authors appear to take a quite literal and affirmative view of these entities, and the text abounds in terms like "procure," "attain," and "achieve"—all freely used without any philosophical qualification—in its discussions of the bodhisattva's task of acquiring all the qualities that constitute a Buddha.

A comparison of the *Ugra* with other early Mahāyāna sūtras shows that it is not unique in this regard. The *Akṣobhyavyūha*, for example, is also quite unselfconscious in urging both *śrāvaka*s and bodhisattvas to hasten their progress toward their respective goals by seeking rebirth in Akṣobhya's (apparently quite real) paradise.[19]

---

[18] The authors of the *Aṣṭa* favor the use of experiential terminology such as "is not found" (*na saṁvidyate*), "is not obtained" (*nopalabhyate*), etc., and Śāriputra is ridiculed by Subhūti when he makes inquiries about the ontological status of things; the authors of the *Vajracchedikā*, by contrast, are quite willing to make explicit ontological statements using positive or negative forms of the verb "to be" (*asti*, *na asti*). This is only one of many reasons to suspect that the *Vajracchedikā* is the product of an environment quite separate from the ones that produced most of the other *prajñāpāramitā* texts.

[19] The sole passage that could be construed as an exception appears toward the end of Chapter 4, when the narrative suddenly shifts from a dialogue between Śāriputra and the Buddha to a conversation between Ānanda and Subhūti. When Ānanda expresses the desire to see Akṣobhya's buddha-land Subhūti tells him to look upwards, but Ānanda sees nothing but empty space. Subhūti then tells him that the Buddha Akṣobhya, his disciples, and his buddha-field are "just like this," and goes on to assert that because of the sameness of all dharmas, there is no difference between the bodhisattvas of that world and those bodhisattvas in this world whose attainment of Buddhahood has been predicted (for the Chinese versions see T 313, 11.760b9-18, and T 310[6], 11.108c15-109a5; for the Tibetan see the Stog Palace reprint edition, 11[6], vol. 36, 128.7-130.2).

This brief passage, however, seems quite out of place with respect to what is found elsewhere in the sūtra, and indeed it bears all the hallmarks of an interpolation. The sudden appearance of Ānanda (who has only made one brief appearance earlier in the sūtra) and of Subhūti (who is never mentioned

Likewise the larger *Sukhāvatīvyūha* seems unconcerned about any possible hazards of reification, and simply devotes its energy to encouraging both bodhisattvas and *śrāvaka*s to seek rebirth in Amitābha's realm. Even the *Lotus Sūtra*—widely read through the lens of "emptiness" philosophy by both traditional East Asian Buddhists and modern readers—only rarely uses the term *śūnyatā*,[20] and in general seems more concerned with urging its listeners to have faith in their own future Buddhahood than in encouraging them to "deconstruct" their concepts.

In contrast to texts like the *Aṣṭa* and the *Vajracchedikā*, then—which rarely exhort the budding bodhisattva to undertake any practice without the immediate caution that he should not conceptualize himself as a "bodhisattva" or others as "beings to be rescued"—the *Ugra* offers no such caveats. Instead it is

---

anywhere else in the text) is paralleled by their equally sudden disappearance at the end of this exchange and the resumption of the conversation-in-progress between the Buddha and Śāriputra. Interestingly, these lines are reminiscent of an exchange between Ānanda and the Buddha that takes place in the *Aṣṭa* (a text in which Subhūti, of course, plays a major role, though he is not a speaker in this passage). In this case the Buddha enables Ānanda to gain a vision of Akṣobhya's world, which then disappears as suddenly as it came (xxviii.464-465). Here too the ensuing discussion has to do with the nature of "all dharmas" (465-466), which in the context of this *prajñāpāramitā* text seems quite natural.

It would be too much to claim that this anomalous passage in the *Akṣobhyavyūha* is a borrowing from the *Aṣṭa* as we have it, for the passages are far from identical; in particular, while in the *Aṣṭa* Ānanda receives a brief vision of Akṣobhya's world, in the *Akṣobhyavyūha* he never sees it at all. Nonetheless, given the striking parallels between the two accounts we may infer that a pericope featuring Ānanda's desire for a vision of Akṣobhya's world was circulating in some form (oral or written), and that it was adopted—without disguising the telltale cut-and-paste marks—by an author or editor of the *Akṣobhyavyūha*. The scene in the *Vimalakīrtinirdeśa* in which the Buddha passes the audience's request to see Akṣobhya's world on to Vimalakīrti, who proceeds to use a radically different technique to make that world manifest—reducing it in size and physically transporting it into the Sahā world, thus arousing panic among some of Abhirati's inhabitants—could be viewed as a parody of the same motif.

20 A computer search of Kumārajīva's version of the *Lotus Sūtra* (T 262) turned up only about a dozen occurences of the term "empty" (*k'ung* 空) in the entire sūtra in contexts where the word does not mean simply "sky," "empty" in the nontechnical sense (e.g., an empty wasteland), or one of the traditional (pre-Mahāyāna) "three doors to liberation" (*śūnyatā-animitta-apraṇihīta*).

straightforward in its enthusiasm for the practice of the bodhisattva path and apparently unconcerned with the dangers of conceptualization. Thus the authors of the *Ugra* appear to be engaged in the preliminary work of establishing the guidelines for the bodhisattva path and not yet concerned with refining (or critiquing wrong ways of understanding) the practice of that path.

It is tempting, therefore—and it may well be correct—to view the *Ugra* as representing a preliminary stage in the emergence of the bodhisattva vehicle, a phase centered on the project of "constructing" ideas about the practices of the bodhisattva that preceded a later "deconstructionist"—or better, dereifying—move. Yet it is clear that the move from affirmation to antireification did not proceed in one-way fashion. On the contrary, what we see in later literature is more like a series of zigzag developments, with each new idea about the bodhisattva path first asserted in positive (or "constructionist") fashion, and then negated in subsequent texts.

The Cult of the Stūpa

There would be no reason even to bring up the issue of the "cult of the stūpa" in our analysis of the *Ugra* were it not for the strong tendency in Japanese scholarship, and the growing tendency in Western-language scholarship, to associate the origins of the Mahāyāna with the worship of stūpas. HIRAKAWA Akira, as is well known, has held for several decades the position that the Mahāyāna emerged outside the Buddhist monastic community, among lay-centered groups that assembled at stūpas.[21] More recently a back-formation of Hirakawa's theory has appeared in the work of SHIMODA Masahiro, who argues that the Mahāyāna emerged not from the affirmation but from the rejection of the stūpa cult.[22] While Shimoda is clearly correct in noting that in a number of Mahāyāna sūtras the cult of the stūpa is portrayed as less worthy than other Buddhist practices, it is less clear that this was true in the early stages of development of the bodhisattva path. Indeed, the most likely scenario is that the cult of the stūpa—already accepted as a central

---

21 See above, Chapter 4, pp. 89-93.

22 See Shimoda 1997, and (in English) the review by SASAKI Shizuka (Sasaki 1999).

part of Buddhist practice centuries before the emergence of the "Mahāyāna"—had nothing to do with Mahāyāna origins at all.[23]

In any event, it is clear that the cult of the stūpa plays no role whatsoever in the *Ugra*. The word does not even appear in the earliest extant recension of the sūtra,[24] and there is no argument either for or against the stūpa cult at any point in the text. Even in its latest recensions the *Ugra* mentions stūpa worship only once, in a formulaic passage in which the Buddha tells Ānanda that it is far better to receive and recite this sūtra (i.e., the *Ugra*) than to worship the stūpas of the Buddhas of the past and to serve the present Buddha and his saṁgha of *śrāvaka*s (§33D).[25] The fact that this statement appears only in the conclusion of the text (which, like the opening *nidāna*, is generally one of the most fluid parts of Indian sūtra texts), and that the entirety of this passage (not just the mention of the stūpa) is missing from the earliest Chinese translation, strongly suggests that even this tangential reference was absent from the original text.

What, then, are we to make of this absence? There is clearly nothing in the *Ugra* that conflicts with the cult of the stūpa; bodhisattvas are urged to emulate the Buddha in every respect, indeed to strive to attain a body exactly like his, and there is never any suggestion in the sūtra that the physical body whose relics would be

---

23 It is well known, for example, that the practice of constructing and paying homage to stūpas was already well established in the time of King Aśoka, who refers in one of his inscriptions to refurbishing the stūpa of a former Buddha, Kanakamuni (Prakrit *Konākamana*; see Bloch 1950, p. 158.2). Indeed, aside from the Aśokan inscriptions, stūpas are the oldest surviving Buddhist remains in India, dating back to at least the 2nd century BCE (Huntington 1985, Chapter 5, especially pp. 61-74). And the fact that donative inscriptions found at these sites mention a variety of Buddhist ordination lineages (*nikāya*), but are silent (until the 5th or 6th century CE) about anything that can be identified as the "Mahāyāna" (Schopen 1979), makes it clear that interest in and sponsorship of stūpas had no necessary connection with the practice of the bodhisattva path. On the contrary, going on pilgrimage and paying homage to stūpa sites appears to have been part and parcel of Buddhist practice virtually from the beginning. Cf. Snellgrove 1973, especially pp. 409-411.

24 See above, Chapter 4, pp. 90-93 and n. 26.

25 Not in AY or Dh. Another mention of the stūpa has been interpolated into the sūtra by Sakurabe, who reads "[the bodhisattva] should do homage to the stūpa which is the symbol of the Tathāgata" (1974, p. 277; cf. the translation below, §20B). The Tibetan text itself, however, states only that the bodhisattva "should do homage to the marks of the Tathāgata" (*de-bzhin-gshegs-pa'i mtshan-ma-la phyag bya'o*).

enshrined within the stūpa is not worthy of extreme respect. On the other hand, given the fact that stūpa worship was so widespread in early Buddhism, the silence of the *Ugra* on this score speaks quite loudly indeed. There is every reason to conclude, in sum, that the authors of the *Ugra* simply took the cult of the stūpa for granted, not as a distinctive "Mahāyāna" practice (for if this were so it would surely have received at least a passing endorsement), much less as the source of the bodhisattva vehicle itself, but as one of the givens of Buddhist life in India around the beginning of the Common Era.

The Cult of the Book

It has now been more than a quarter of a century since Gregory Schopen first drew the attention of western readers to the centrality, in a number of Mahāyāna scriptures, of what he referred to as "the cult of the book."[26] Observing that a number of well-known sūtras promise substantial amounts of merit to those who read and recite (sometimes copying is mentioned as well) the text within which such an exhortation occurs, Schopen argued that "adherence to Mahāyāna meant primarily adherence to special texts in addition to those recognized by the established orthodoxy," and that the sites where such texts were taught (or, when taken down in written form, were stored) "may well have formed one of the 'institutional bases' (consciously leaving room for the very likely possibility of there having been more than one) out of which early Mahāyāna arose" (Schopen 1975, p. 181). As a corollary, Schopen went on to suggest that the early Mahāyāna, far from being a single identifiable group, "was in the beginning a loose federation of a number of distinct though related cults, all of the same pattern, but each associated with its specific text" (*loc. cit.*).

By focusing on a practice that is actually prescribed in Mahāyāna scriptures (and which distinguishes them from earlier texts), Schopen's work provided a much-needed corrective to Hirakawa's inspired but speculative notion that the cult of the stūpa (which, as Shimoda [1997] has shown, is actually demoted rather than promoted in many Mahāyāna texts) was a distinctive feature of the early Mahāyāna. In an interesting twist on the idea of the book cult,

---

[26] Schopen 1975; see also the references to a handful of earlier mentions of the book cult cited by Schopen on p. 168, n. 38.

Richard Gombrich has even suggested that "the rise of the Mahāyāna is due to the use of writing" (1990, p. 21). More specifically, Gombrich argues that it was the introduction of writing that allowed Mahāyāna scriptures to be preserved, while in an earlier period such deviant texts would not have survived (*loc. cit.*).

There is no doubt that the reading, reciting, and copying of particular Mahāyāna scriptures played an important cultic role in Indian Buddhism, and moreover that the communities that formed around such texts were multiple, for as Schopen rightly contends "each text placed itself at the center of its own cult" (1975, p. 181). It is also certain that, as Gombrich's work suggests, the introduction of writing introduced important new dynamics into the practice of Buddhist scriptural transmission. Yet it is far less clear that, as both writers suggest, the cult of the book (or, according to Gombrich, the production of the *written* book) played a role in the initial emergence of the Mahāyāna. For though references to reading and reciting a particular scripture as a central source of merit are quite common in Mahāyāna literature, a number of early Mahāyāna scriptures seem not to know of such a practice. And the *Ugra*, in fact, is one such text.

The *Ugra* provides a particularly interesting lens through which to view the emergence of the book cult, for while references to gargantuan amounts of merit obtainable by adherence to the text are absent from its earliest extant recension, such claims do occur in later versions of the text. What we seem to see here, in other words, is the production of a distinctive Mahāyāna sūtra *followed by* the addition of new passages—whether a year or several centuries later we may never know—advertising its efficacy. To what extent the introduction of this new material was a response to contending claims emanating from other sūtra-cults is an intriguing question, but one for which we will probably never be able to offer a satisfactory answer.

Be that as it may, the early *Ugra*—or rather, our oldest (2nd century CE) extant exemplar—appears to have set forth instructions for the practice of the bodhisattva path in relatively straightforward fashion, without offering its audience any special merits for preserving the text itself. In later editions, by contrast, we encounter precisely the same sūtra-centered rhetoric that is well known from other book-cult texts.

If the emergence of the Mahāyāna, then, does not begin with the cult of the book, but rather culminates in it at a certain point, how are we to understand the sequence of development in the understanding of this new form of Buddhist practice? That is, if our very earliest

Mahāyāna scriptures already take the bodhisattva path for granted, and a book-centered cult is added at a slightly later stage, how can we account for the emergence of such a new (and from a certain point of view, quite revolutionary) form of Buddhist practice?

One possible solution, I would suggest, has been right under our noses for many decades, and we have been prevented from seeing it only by our propensity to treat only self-proclaimed "Mahāyāna sūtras" as relevant data in this case. But if Mahāyāna sūtras are the precipitate, and not the initial cause, of bodhisattva practice, we must look to earlier traditions (not all of them codified in written or even oral scriptures) as possible sources of inspiration. And the obvious source, in my view—and one frequently alluded to or even cited directly in Mahāyāna sūtras—is the collection of stories of Śākyamuni Buddha's former lives. While such tales can of course inspire devotional reverence for the Buddha, they can easily inspire active imitation as well.[27] Indeed, it seems likely that early references to a *bodhisattvapiṭaka*, over which so much scholarly ink has been spilled, refer to tales of previous lives of the Buddha, which those who chose to become bodhisattvas could endeavor to put into practice.[28] To put it another way, a single text could be either a Mahāyāna scripture or a non-Mahāyāna scripture, depending upon the use to which it was put.

It is thus to the transitional literature of the *jātaka* tales (widely represented in sculpture and inscriptions from an early date, and often quoted or alluded to in explicitly Mahāyāna texts), as well as to the closely related *avadāna* literature, that we should probably turn if we wish to gain a glimpse of the Mahāyāna in its formative stage.[29]

---

27 So suggested, for example, in Lamotte 1954, pp. 378-379 (though Lamotte goes on to connect the imitation of the Buddha's previous lives with the concerns of the laity, a position which no longer appears tenable).

28 For a sampling of western-language studies on this topic, together with a number of canonical references to the term, see Pagel 1995, pp. 7-36.

29 An excellent example of such a transitional text is the *Liu-tu chi ching* 六度集經 (T 152 , **Ṣaṭ-pāramitā-saṃgraha*), translated into Chinese by K'ang Seng-hui 康僧會 in the middle of the 3rd century CE (see the French translation in Chavannes 1910, pp. 5-346). Here we see a collection of tales of Śākyamuni's former lives arranged according to which of the six perfections they are thought to exemplify, sprinkled here and there with elements generally considered peculiar to the Mahāyāna (e.g., the appearance of the celestial bodhisattva Mañjuśrī in tale no. 13). There has been some controversy concerning the provenance of the text, dating from Chavannes' own statement

Devotion to Celestial Buddhas

One of the great innovations found in certain Mahāyāna sūtras is the exhortation to seek rebirth in a world other than our own, where one can look forward to living in the presence of a "celestial Buddha." By far the best known of such Buddhas is Amitābha, who presides over the distant western realm of Sukhāvatī, where countless millions of devotees in East Asia (and a considerably smaller number in other Buddhist countries) have hoped to be reborn. But there are many other such figures as well, beginning with Akṣobhya in the East (who appears to have been the earliest "celestial Buddha" to appear in Buddhist sources) and eventually expanding to include lesser-known figures in "Buddha-fields" (*buddha-kṣetra*) throughout the ten directions.[30] The term "celestial Buddha" is not without difficulties, but I will use it here to refer to those Buddhas who preside over worlds other than our own, worlds which—not coincidentally—are uniformly described as paradiselike in form. Indeed, these realms are explicitly modeled on preexisting Buddhist understandings of heaven, as the *Akṣobhyavyūha* and the larger *Sukhāvatīvyūha* make clear when they compare the worlds of Akṣobhya and Amitābha to the Trayastriṁśa and Paranirmitavaśavartin heavens, respectively. Yet these Buddha-fields are not in fact heavens, but entire world-systems containing heavens of their own, systems that are shorn only of the most unattractive features of our own world-system, including the possibility of rebirth as a hell-being, animal, or ghost (*preta*).

Such figures were to become major objects of devotion in certain Mahāyāna circles, and references to Akṣobhya, Amitābha, and other celestial Buddhas appear widely even in scriptures not centrally concerned with their cults.[31] Akṣobhya, for example, is the object of considerable discussion in the *Aṣṭasāhasrikā-prajñāpāramitā-sūtra*

---

that the collection may be either a translation of an Indian original or a compilation produced by K'ang Seng-hui himself (p. iii). Yet regardless of where this text was assembled, the fact remains that it consists of materials that are for the most part quite traditional, set within what appears to be a Mahāyāna framework (that is, employing the schemata of the six *pāramitās*) yet without explicitly inviting its audience to imitate the actions described. We can only speculate on the uses to which this collection (whether in India or China) was actually put.

[30] For a discussion of the apparent chronological priority of Akṣobhya see Nattier 2000a.

[31] See Schopen 1977.

and the *Vimalakīrti-nirdeśa*, while Amitābha makes an appearance in the *Pratyutpanna-buddha-saṁmukha-avasthita-samādhi-sūtra*, the *Kāraṇḍavyūha*, the *Bhaiṣajyaguru-sūtra*, and a host of other texts.[32]

In the *Ugra*, however, we find not a trace of such beliefs. Granted, there is a reference to the "Buddhas of the ten directions" in even the earliest version of the sūtra, but none of these Buddhas are singled out for particular attention—nor even, for that matter, are they named. Moreover, the fact that this reference occurs in a portion of the sūtra which is in certain respects anomalous—the section dealing with the *triskandhaka* ritual—raises the possibility that this notion was simply incorporated into the *Ugra* along with the discussion of the ritual itself.

Likewise there is no evidence that the *Ugra*'s authors sought to encourage bodhisattvas to seek rebirth in Abhirati, Sukhāvatī, or any other such realm. All explicit discussions of the bodhisattva's eons-long trajectory through *saṁsāra* appear to refer only to our own world-system, again in all probability simply taking their cue from the *jātaka* tales of Śākyamuni's former lives.

There is every reason to conclude, therefore, that the *Ugra* (though not the *triskandhaka* section which has been incorporated into the text) was composed in a community which presupposed only a single world-system, and which accepted the fact that a bodhisattva's entire career could successfully be carried out within this realm. The fact that the *Ugra* makes no reference to any possible way to shorten the duration of the path by being reborn in the presence of a Buddha in another world-system makes it virtually certain that its authors did not envision such a possibility.

Devotion to Celestial Bodhisattvas

The term "celestial bodhisattva," like its counterpart "celestial Buddha," must be defined carefully if we are to avoid confusion. There seems to be no Sanskrit (or for that matter, Chinese or Tibetan) equivalent of this term, and this fact alone should give us pause. Yet it is clear that there is a distinct category of named bodhisattvas—characters such as Avalokiteśvara (Tib. *Spyan-ras-gzigs*, Ch. *Kuan-yin* 觀音, Jpn. *Kannon*), Kṣitigarbha (Ch. *Ti-tsang* 地藏, Jpn. *Jizō*), Tārā (Tib. *Sgrol-ma*), and others—to whom a Buddhist practitioner in

32 For further references see Schopen 1977.

distress may turn for help. Like Catholic saints, such figures are seen as endowed with a surplus of religious merit which can be used for the benefit of their supplicants in facing worldly calamities such as famine, sickness, warfare, attacks by robbers and wild animals, and so on. Though Avalokiteśvara is by far the most popular, a great many such figures have served as objects of devotion for practitioners, both lay and monastic, across the Buddhist world.

Interestingly, these bodhisattvas—unlike the celestial Buddhas discussed in the previous section—seem not to be tied to a single geographical location. Though Mañjuśrī is associated with Wu-t'ai shan 五台山 in China, and Avalokiteśvara with the Potala in Tibet, these figures appear to be far more mobile—in India, at any rate—than their celestial Buddha counterparts. Far from being located in a realm in the distant East or West, celestial bodhisattvas seem to hover at an approachable distance within our own world-system, ever ready to assist devotees in distress.[33]

Once again, however, we find in the *Ugra* not a trace of this concept, though the names of some of these figures (Mañjuśrī, Apāyajaha, and Avalokiteśvara) appear in the introductory *nidāna* even in the earliest translation of the text. Yet they never reappear after being placed in the audience, and once again we may suspect—given the well-known fluidity of *nidāna*s in general—that their names were added at some point after the intial composition of the text. Be that as it may, they play no role whatsoever in the body of the sūtra,[34] and just as bodhisattvas are never urged to seek rebirth in the presence of a celestial Buddha, so they are never urged to appeal to celestial bodhisattvas for aid. Indeed, as we have already seen, in precisely those situations of crisis in which other sūtras recommend

---

[33] An important (but perhaps anomalous) exception is the larger *Sukhāvatīvyūha*, in which Avalokiteśvara and Mahāsthamaprāpta are said to dwell with Amitābha in Sukhāvatī. Indeed, in the two earliest Chinese versions of the sūtra (T 362 and 361, respectively, for which see Harrison 1998, pp. 556-557 and Harrison et al. 2002), these two bodhisattvas are said to succeed to Buddhahood in sequence after Amitābha's death (Nattier 1999).

[34] The cameo appearance of Maitreya (who, together with an unknown bodhisattva named *Sarvacaryāviśuddha, is asked by the Buddha to ordain Ugra and his friends) is not an exception to this statement, for Maitreya does not belong to the category of celestial bodhisattvas. For a discussion of his role see Nattier 1988.

petitionary prayer to a celestial bodhisattva, the *Ugra* recommends self-reliance and insight instead.[35]

Conclusions: The Significance of Absence

The *Ugra* is clearly a Mahāyāna text, in the sense that its entire *raison d'être* is to instruct bodhisattvas in the practice of their chosen path. Yet there are a whole range of elements usually thought of as central to the Mahāyāna—ranging from the philosophy of emptiness to belief in a transcendent Buddha—that are absent from our text. And indeed it is these absences that tell us most about where to place the *Ugra* in the history of the Mahāyāna. For while Indian Buddhism would eventually see acrimonious disputes between bodhisattvas and *śrāvaka*s, distinct philosophical schools associated with the practice of the bodhisattva path, and even freestanding Mahāyāna institutions, the *Ugra* was clearly composed at a time when none of this had taken place. Likewise, as we have seen in the previous chapter, the *Ugra* either lacks or contains unusual interpretations of many other items that are widely taken as "signature" features of the Mahāyāna. Does this mean, then, that in reading the *Ugra* we are encountering the Mahāyāna in its very earliest phase?

Unfortunately it does not, for there is yet another absence in the text that tells us we are not in the presence of the initial formation of the practice of the bodhisattva path. The *Ugra* never explicitly advocates, much less argues in favor of, the legitimacy of this practice. On the contrary, it simply takes the possibility of becoming a Buddha for granted and goes on to describe the practices that are viewed as leading to that goal. We see here no trace of the astonishment—or at least the surprise—that must have greeted the first proponents of this novel idea.[36]

But the *Ugra* is not alone in this regard, for I would suggest that in *no extant* Mahāyāna scripture—at least, in no such scripture that I have encountered to date, nor in any of those that have been

---

[35] See above, Chapter 6, pp. 168-170.

[36] It is possible, of course, that even this description of the inception of the Mahāyāna vocation is exaggerated, and that in its own time this innovation was viewed in at least some circles as emerging naturally from the descriptions of the Buddha's former lives found in the *jātaka* tales. If this is the case, the *Ugra* might be placed even earlier in the history of the Mahāyāna than I have suggested.

discussed in detail by scholars of Buddhism thus far—do we see such a reaction, for the initial stage in the formation of the idea of the bodhisattva vocation clearly took place off-camera. Even in scriptures like the *Ugra* that lack most of the characteristic features of later Mahāyāna texts, and thus arguably comprise the earliest explicitly Mahāyāna literature available, we see evidence that the bodhisattva vocation was already taken for granted within at least a subset of the larger Buddhist community. In the *Ugra*, indeed, we even have several passing mentions of the existence of other scriptures devoted to the bodhisattva path.[37]

It is true that reports of hostility toward bodhisattvas can be found in many bodhisattva texts, but it would be a profound misinterpretation to see these as a rejection of the "Mahāyāna"—and thus as an initial reaction to the propagation of the bodhisattva path—as such. In the *Lotus Sūtra* (*Saddharmapuṇḍarīka*), for example, the hostility expressed toward bodhisattvas is not directed toward their practice of the bodhisattva path as such, but toward their insistence that all Buddhists—whether they know it or not—are also on that path. In the *Aṣṭa* bodhisattvas are likewise criticized, but this time for their assertion that the Prajñāpāramitā literature is *buddhavacana*. And criticisms of monastic laxity in texts like the *Rāṣṭrapāla-paripṛcchā*, which have often been misinterpreted as criticisms of the entire sangha of *śrāvaka*s by a competing Mahāyāna group, should rather be viewed as expressions of a conservative vision of the ideal monastic life that was widely shared by *śrāvaka*s and bodhisattvas alike. In sum, none of these scriptures can offer us an *entrée* into the formative stages of the bodhisattva practice, for Mahāyāna scriptures are the precipitate—and not the cause—of this development.

What Mahāyāna scriptures do provide, however, is a kaleidoscopic assortment of combinations of the presence and absence of elements that until now have been widely—but wrongly—grouped together as essential components of the "Mahāyāna." Thus we find one scripture (the *Akṣobhyavyūha*) that advocates both *śrāvaka* and bodhisattva practices, propounds the possibility of rebirth in a pure land, and enthusiastically recommends the cult of the book, yet seems to know nothing of emptiness theory, the ten *bhūmi*s, or the *trikāya*,

---

[37] See §20C, where a *bodhisattva-piṭaka* is mentioned in addition to the usual three, and §26C, where the bodhisattva is told that he should offer service to a teacher who provides him with even a single four-line verse concerning the bodhisattva path for as many eons as there are words, syllables, and letters in that verse.

while another (the *P'u-sa pen-yeh ching* 菩薩本業經) propounds the ten *bhūmis* and focuses exclusively on the path of the bodhisattva, but never discusses the *pāramitās*.[38] A Mādhyamika treatise (Nāgārjuna's *Mūlamādhyamika-kārikās*) may enthusiastically deploy the rhetoric of emptiness without ever mentioning the bodhisattva path, while a Yogācāra treatise (Vasubandhu's *Madhyānta-vibhāga-bhāṣya*) may delve into the particulars of the *trikāya* doctrine while eschewing the doctrine of *ekayāna*. We must be prepared, in other words, to encounter a multiplicity of Mahāyānas flourishing even in India, not to mention those that developed in East Asia and Tibet.

The fact that the *Ugra* contains one of the most minimalist assortments of so-called "Mahāyāna" elements strongly suggests that it is one of the earliest Mahāyāna scriptures available to us, but once again we must bear in mind that it grows out of a period in which the bodhisattva path was already well established, and thus does not reflect the very dawn of the Mahāyāna itself. Barring the discovery of an entirely new body of sources—or perhaps, a sweeping scholarly reinterpretation of the *jātaka* and *avadāna* literature—it seems likely that this first stage will remain forever hidden from view.

---

[38] T 281, 10.446-450. The word *pāramitā* does appear twice in the text (10.447b11, 諸度無極 and 447c21 , 慧度無極) but no number, list of items or discussion is given. This intriguing little text is, in my view, the core out of which the voluminous *Avataṁsaka* sūtra eventually grew. I hope to publish a study and translation of this important work in the future; in the meantime, see the M.A. thesis done at the University of Hawaii by SHI Chikai (= Ching-mei Shyu), which contains a very useful study of the style and vocabulary used by Chih Ch'ien in this text and in T 225, the *Ta ming-tu ching* 大明度經 (Shi 2000).

CHAPTER 8

The Mahāyāna in the Mirror of the *Ugra*

What, then, can we say about the nature of the Mahāyāna after an encounter with a text like the *Ugra*? The sūtra freely uses the term "Mahāyāna," yet as we have seen in the previous chapter, it fails to conform—in a significant number of respects—to features modern scholars have generally considered essential to this form of Buddhism. What can we learn from the *Ugra* about the way the Mahāyāna was perceived in India around the beginning of the Common Era?

It is evident that to understand what the *Ugra*'s authors meant by "Mahāyāna" we will have to give up many of the categories regularly applied to this entity by English-speaking scholars—words like "school," "sect," and even "movement." The *Ugra* offers us no grounds, first of all, for describing the Mahāyāna as a new philosophical or doctrinal school, for it contains nothing in this regard that is not continuous with the Buddhism of its past. It offers no new ontology based on the concept of "emptiness," nor does it expand the categories of abhidharma analysis (as the Yogācāra school would later do) or reject the value of abhidharma altogether (as Mādhyamika thinkers would do). It offers no reinterpretation of the nature of a "Buddha," whether in docetic terms (as in Lokottaravādin and certain Mahāyāna scriptures) or in terms of the *trikāya* theory (subsequently elaborated in a great many Mahāyāna texts). It offers no vision of rebirth in a "pure land," nor does it promise the believer access to a "transfer of merit" from a celestial Buddha or bodhisattva. It does not even hold out the hope of special benefits—in its earliest recension, at least—if a believer recites and remembers the text of the *Ugra* itself. There is, in short, nothing at all here that can be described as a new doctrine, unless we wish to consider the idea of emulating Śākyamuni Buddha in every detail—following his example so precisely that one becomes a Buddha rather than an Arhat—to be such a teaching. In sum, the *Ugra* offers no evidence that Mahāyānists saw themselves—or were seen by others—as members of a new doctrinal school.

Nor can the "Mahāyāna," as reflected in the *Ugra*, be described as a sect in the sociological sense—that is, as a protest group that has broken off from a dominant "church" because it views the latter as in need of reform.[1] Granted, the Mahāyāna is frequently described in this way in western (and even Japanese) scholarly literature, but the *Ugra* offers us no grounds for subscribing to this interpretation. On the contrary, it portrays practitioners of the Mahāyāna as located solidly within the traditional monastic community, or as lay associates who aspire to that status. Far from describing the Mahāyāna as a form of protest against those pursuing the traditional path to Arhatship, the *Ugra* urges its audience to maintain harmony within the Buddhist community by honoring one's *śrāvaka* coreligionists. There is, in sum, not a shred of evidence that the *Ugra*'s authors considered the *śrāvaka* path illegitimate—far from it, for they remind the bodhisattva that when he becomes a Buddha, he will lead a community of *śrāvaka*s himself.

What, then, of another term favored in recent buddhological literature—the idea of the Mahāyāna as a new "movement"? This term has no exact sociological meaning, nor has it been precisely defined (so far as I am aware) by any of the scholars writing on early Mahāyāna. Yet it suggests, in standard English usage, the coalescence of a group of like-minded individuals who join forces to accomplish a certain goal. But what goal would that be, and what sort of "group" might we envision, from the perspective articulated in the *Ugra*? Eventually, of course, bodhisattvas within a given monastery (and even lay people on the outside) did form special subgroups, as the use of terms such as *bodhisattva-gaṇa* (which might be translated as "bodhisattva interest-group") attests. But in the *Ugra* we see no evidence of such a subcommunity. On the contrary, as we have seen, there is no mention at all of bodhisattvas (whether lay or monastic) gathering together in any kind of horizontal or egalitarian association; instead, the *Ugra* portrays strictly individual (and explicitly hierarchical) relations between a bodhisattva and his teachers. Likewise the goal, too, appears to be an individual one: the attainment of buddhahood oneself. If the most extreme example of such individualism and isolation is that of the renunciant bodhisattva practicing alone in the wilderness, the theme of solitude and

---

[1] So defined, for example, in Stark and Bainbridge (1985), Chapter 2. For the *locus classicus* of the category of "sect" in western sociology of religion—articulated exclusively with respect to Christianity, however—see Troeltsch 1960 (translation of Troeltsch 1911), vol. 1, pp. 331-349.

withdrawal from all fraternization—I would argue—pervades the *Ugra*'s perception of the bodhisattva path as a whole.[2]

If the Mahāyāna as reflected in the *Ugra* thus fails to conform to any of the three major categories—a new doctrinal school, a reformist sect, or simply a "movement"—to which it has been assigned in buddhological literature to date, how then was this term used by the *Ugra*'s authors? Somewhat surprisingly, perhaps—given the volume of ink that has been spilled in an attempt to define the "Mahāyāna" in recent years—the *Ugra* offers us a very simple and straightforward answer. For the authors of this sūtra, the Mahāyāna is nothing more, and nothing less, than a synonym of the "bodhisattva path." For the *Ugra*, in other words, the Mahāyāna is not a school, a sect, or a movement, but a particular spiritual *vocation*, to be pursued within the existing Buddhist community. To be a "Mahāyānist"—that is, to be a bodhisattva—thus does not mean to adhere to some new kind of "Buddhism," but simply to practice Buddhism in its most rigorous and demanding form.

Other accretions of meaning, of course, would subsequently adhere to the word "Mahāyāna," and recent scholarship has drawn attention to the difficulty of constructing a useful and universally applicable definition of the term.[3] Yet its original referent—the

---

[2] We should not let our fear of reading modern western individualism into earlier sources prevent us from seeing the fact that the *Ugra* envisions the bodhisattva path as a profoundly individual and solitary enterprise. Indeed, I suspect that this was true of many (perhaps most) of the *śramaṇa* movements in India during and after the Buddha's time. An examination of this issue by a scholar better versed in the comparative study of individualism and identity construction than I would no doubt yield rewarding results.

[3] See for example Richard Cohen (1995), who claims that "in the end, there is no Mahāyāna/Hīnayāna distinction: there are many" (p. 21). Cohen is right to draw our attention to the variety of uses of these terms in different contexts, yet by simply arguing against existing scholarly distinctions rather than offering clearly contextualized alternatives his discussion leaves the waters muddier than before. His claim that the donor of Cave 22 at Ajaṇṭā, for example, "can be a [*sic*] both a 'Mahāyānist' and a 'Hīnayānist,' albeit not within the same taxonomic moment" (*loc. cit.*) is quite misleading, for it continues a modern scholarly error in equating the term "Hīnayānist" with "member of a Nikāya lineage," thus using this terminology in a way that Buddhists of the time and place in question did not do. Just as the term Mahāyāna refers consistently—but not always exclusively—to the practice of the bodhisattva path, so the term Hīnayāna (as used by Indian Buddhists) refers consistently to those who do *not* practice that path. To say that a single individual could be both of these—

vocation of the bodhisattva—is never lost. Thus while it is always safe to interpret the term Mahāyāna as referring to "the bodhisattva vehicle," the addition of other layers of meaning must be justified in each instance, based on what we actually find in a given source.

If the *Ugra* cannot (as we have seen in the previous chapter) offer us a glimpse into the very dawn of the bodhisattva enterprise, it nonetheless remains a valuable witness to one of the earliest stages in the development of that path. It portrays a Buddhist community in which the path of the bodhisattva was viewed as an optional vocation suited only for the few; where tensions between bodhisattvas and *śrāvaka*s were evident, but had not yet led to institutional fission generating a separate Mahāyāna community; and where texts containing instructions for bodhisattva practice were known and transmitted by specialists within the larger monastic *saṁgha*. It emphatically does *not* convey a picture of the Mahāyāna as a "greater vehicle" in the sense of a more inclusive option, for the bodhisattva vehicle is portrayed as a supremely difficult enterprise, suited only (to borrow the recruiting slogan of the U.S. Marine Corps) for "a few good men." And while the *Ugra* reflects an environment in which lay men were beginning to participate in such practices, there is no evidence that its authors even considered the possibility that women (whether lay or monastic) might do so as well.

Having considered in detail what this once highly influential scripture reveals about an early stage in the development of the bodhisattva vocation, we may now move on to the study of other scriptures that can tell us how this path was understood in other times and places. Though most of these sources have been lost in their

---

whatever "taxonomic moment" one might wish to invoke—simply creates confusion by prolonging this erroneous scholarly usage. (An interesting project remains to be done in tracking the extent to which this error has its roots in medieval East Asian and/or Tibetan misunderstandings of the Indian situation; in any event, it seems clear that the equation of "Hīnayāna" with "Nikāya" is not based on Indian usage.)

Cohen misrepresents my own stance on this issue, incidentally, by giving only a partial citation of a footnote (Nattier 1991, p. 9, n. 1; cf. Cohen, p. 8) in which I propose to use the term "Nikāya Buddhism" in reference to the so-called Eighteen Schools, "in place of the pejorative (and inaccurate) 'Hīnayāna.' " Omitting the qualifying phrase "and inaccurate," Cohen goes on to assert that I treat the terms *nikāya* and *hīnayāna* as synonymous, which is precisely the opposite of what this note was intended to say.

original Indic-language versions, the Chinese canon (and to a lesser extent, the Tibetan) contains a treasure trove of texts that promise to cast light on a whole range of other understandings of the Mahāyāna. For those few who embark on the sometimes daunting vocation of the buddhologist, there is much that remains to be done.

PART TWO

TRANSLATION

Translation Techniques and Conventions

This section contains a complete English translation of *The Inquiry of Ugra*, designed to make this widely influential text available to readers in its entirety for the first time. Yet to translate this Buddhist scripture into English is no straightforward matter. Since this study is intended primarily as a contribution to our understanding of the history of Buddhism in India, the natural choice would have been to translate an Indic-language version of the text. But, as is the case with most Mahāyāna sūtras, no Sanskrit or Prakrit version of this scripture has survived. We are thus dependent—with the exception of the passages cited in Śāntideva's Sanskrit *Śikṣāsamuccaya*—on versions of the sūtra preserved in other Asian languages, three in Chinese and one in Tibetan.[1] At the outset, therefore, we are faced with the task of working from versions of the text which are already at a considerable cultural and linguistic remove from the underlying Indic original.

Our task is further complicated by the fact that, even in India, there was never a single "original." Many different versions of the *Ugra* were once in circulation, and the four translations preserved in Chinese and Tibetan represent four quite different Indian recensions. In a sense we are fortunate to have so many versions at our disposal, but this raises the question of which one should be given priority by the translator. Should we choose the earliest version (that of An Hsüan and Yen Fo-t'iao) on the grounds of its historical priority? Or the version contained in the Chinese *Ratnakūṭa* section, because it is the most used in East Asia today? Or the Tibetan version, because it contains the fullest version of the text and is by far the easiest to interpret? (It would be difficult to defend the choice to translate from Dharmarakṣa's Chinese rendition, since of the four extant versions it is the most riddled with errors.)

Even after selecting one (or more) of these versions as the base-text, the translator must then decide which reading of the Chinese or Tibetan text she will adopt. Will she attempt to represent the scripture as it would be read by a Chinese or Tibetan audience today, for example, or should she try to convey the way in which it might have been heard by a Chinese or Tibetan audience at the time of its initial

---

[1] For details see above, Chapter 2.

translation? Or yet again, will she choose to read *through* a Chinese or Tibetan version to recover the content of the lost Indian original?

Clearly no one of these choices will be optimal in all cases, for the resulting products will have different purposes and are appropriate for different audiences. Indeed it should be acknowledged at the outset that there is no such thing as "the perfect translation." Every translation is also a creation, a scholarly artifact which is no less the culturally shaped product of a particular time and place than is the ancient or medieval version from which the translator chooses to work. Precisely because of this, the translator's responsibility—in my view—includes an attempt to articulate the intention behind her choices as clearly as possible, and thus to provide the reader with a clear sense of the decisions that have led to the production of the work she is about to read.[2] It is this task that I will attempt to carry out in the following brief discussion.

Which Text?

Since one of the objectives of this study is to provide the reader with a sense of how a particular Buddhist scripture (in this case, the *Ugra*) has changed and expanded over time, it is important to provide access not just to one version of the sūtra but, on some level at least, to all four. Ideally this might mean translating all of the extant versions, yet—however interesting the *Ugra* might be—most scholars would agree that it would not be the best use of the translator's efforts (or of the reader's time) to prepare complete English translations of all four Chinese and Tibetan texts. On the other hand, to take a minimalist approach—simply ignoring three of these four versions and translating from one recension alone—would render this process of growth and change invisible to all who do not have access to the scripture in its Chinese and Tibetan versions. Fortunately, however, a middle path between these two extremes is easily identifiable: to use the longest and latest version (i.e., the Tibetan) as the base text, but to include annotations documenting all significant variants in any of the three Chinese versions. This procedure has two advantages. First, it is far easier to establish with some degree of certainty the Indic terminology underlying the Tibetan text than that of any of the Chinese versions, for translation terminology was regularized and standardized in Tibet to a degree that was unknown in China. Second,

[2] I have explored these issues with respect to several recent translations of the *Vimalakīrtinirdeśa* in Nattier 2000b.

because the Tibetan text is the most recent, portions of the sūtra that are absent from earlier versions can simply be printed in smaller type.

This would be a quite straightforward process if the four extant versions were linear descendants of one another, but it is important to emphasize that they are not.[3] In some cases (e.g., at the end of §1B) a line occurs only in the earliest version (AY) and not in the later ones; in others, only the second version (Dh) contains extra material (e.g., §13F'). In some cases the third version (R) lacks material that is present in all three of the other versions (e.g., §23D), while in still others the earliest and latest versions (AY and Tib) agree with one another against the testimony of the other two witnesses (e.g., §20F [n. 451] and §32D [n. 760]). The evidence available to us, in sum, does not allow the construction of a straightforward stemma of these texts, which may imply that active use of the sūtra in India had resulted in multiple instances of cross-lineage contamination.

The fact that there are significant divergences at every level of transmission means that simply indicating earlier and later portions of the text by using larger and smaller type sizes is not sufficient to convey a sense of the diversity of these texts. For this reason I have also discussed any significant variants (i.e., passages in one or more of the Chinese versions that differ from the reading found in the Tibetan) in the footnotes. "Significance" is of course in the eye of the beholder; thus while some readers may find the text overannotated, others may wish that still other divergences had been documented. What must be emphasized here, however, is simply the fact that not every difference in wording could be noted. I will leave it to the reader to decide whether my intended "middle path" has been achieved.

In sum, the following English translation provided here is itself designed to serve as a "critical edition" of sorts, making transparent even to readers who do not have access to the primary languages the most significant variations in the text over time. In selecting this method I am following in the footsteps of such scholars as Konstanty Régamey and Étienne Lamotte, who have used such a multitext approach to good advantage.[4] I am explicitly *not* following the

[3] For details see the discussion in Chapter 2, pp. 14-15.

[4] See for example Régamey 1938 and Lamotte 1976. Lamotte includes actual variant readings (those of Hsüan-tsang) within his translated text, while Régamey consigns these to the footnotes. By choosing the latest version as my base text, and thus needing to note only omissions (in the earlier versions) and variant readings, I will be able to follow Régamey's approach, which should

practice advocated by, for example, Edward Conze (e.g., 1975, pp. ix-x), who felt free to mix readings from more than one original text in a single translation, to alter the textual sequence and/or chapter divisions of the originals, and even to omit substantial material that might be "off-putting" to the modern reader.[5]

Which Reading?

Since this study is devoted primarily to expanding our knowledge of Indian Buddhism, I have eliminated from consideration at the outset a number of readings that other translators might have chosen. A translator primarily concerned with the initial reception of Buddhism in China, for example, might have chosen to read the earliest Chinese version (AY) as it might have been received by a Chinese audience in the late 2nd century CE—that is, to read the Chinese as Chinese (bracketing any awareness of the underlying Sanskrit or Prakrit terms, since these would have remained opaque to virtually all Chinese readers) and to deal extensively with the overtones of certain vocabulary choices in terms of their resonance with other Chinese texts circulating at that date.[6] Another translator might choose to treat the Tibetan as the base text and to translate it as a contemporary Tibetan audience might understand it.[7] Yet another might have chosen to read the sūtra the way a contemporary Japanese audience would understand it, choosing the version that has been treated as

---

keep the main text considerably more readable.

[5] As his own writings make clear, Conze was more concerned with conveying the "essential teachings" of Buddhism than with adhering faithfully to the content of any given text as it has come down to us. As valuable as his pioneering contributions to the western study of Buddhism have been, it is my firm conviction that it is the scholar's responsibility *not* to create, in the course of translation, a hybrid text that has never before existed, but rather to make transparent one version of the text just as it has come down to us, with references to other versions clearly labeled as such.

[6] The opening of the sūtra, using this approach, would state that the Mass of Blessings (眾祐, for *bhagavan*) was sojourning in the Hear-Things country (聞物國, for Śrāvastī), together with a great assembly of 1,250 famine-discarders (除饉, for *bhikṣu*).

[7] In such a case the Tibetan word for Arhat (*dgra-bcom-pa*) would necessarily be rendered "one who has subdued the enemies" (in contrast to its earlier and linguistically more solidly grounded interpretation as "worthy one"), while nirvāṇa (Tib. *mya-ngan-las 'das*) would be rendered as "having passed beyond suffering."

"standard" in recent centuries in East Asia (R) and reading the Buddhist technical terms in light of their contemporary Japanese meanings.[8] The choice of whose reception of the text one wishes to represent in English, in other words, will result in widely differing translations.

What I have chosen to do here, therefore, is to ignore (in most cases) the overtones that the text might have to a Chinese or Tibetan audience and to concentrate on conveying the meaning of the underlying Indic-language text. Since no such text is extant, the success of this project rests largely on the viability of my suggestions for the reconstruction of its terminology. Happily the context makes this a straightforward matter in many cases, but there are some passages in which other possibilities exist as well. The reader should therefore view this translation as an educated guess as to how the lost Indian text would have read, based primarily on the canonical Tibetan version.

Symbols and Conventions

A number of procedures—some of them standard, some not—have been used to try to accomplish the objectives outlined above. In brief, they are the following:

9 pt — small type indicates sentences, phrases, or words found in later translation(s) but missing from at least one early version of the text (and thus presumably an interpolation);

{9 pt} — small type in braces indicates words found in one or more of the early versions but absent from later ones, and which may either have dropped out in the course of transmission or may be a peripheral development in one branch of the textual family tree;

11 pt — full-size type indicates portions of the text that are found in all extant versions of the text; where variants in wording

---

[8] To some degree the Japanese version found in Nagai 1932 could also be described as such a translation, though the language used there is far from colloquial. Sakurabe's Japanese translation offers a mixed case, employing the Tibetan version as its basis but reading some of what is found in that version in light of modern Japanese understandings.

occur in one or more versions, these are indicated in the notes.

Abbreviations used to refer to the Chinese and Tibetan translations in the notes are the following:

Chinese translations

AY = An Hsüan and Yen Fo-t'iao, 181 CE (T 322)
Dh = Dharmârakṣa, 265-309 CE (T 323)
R = *Ratnakūṭa* edition (translator uncertain; early 5th century CE or after) (T 310[19])

Tibetan translation (= Tib)

D = Derge xylograph edition (1978 Delhi reprint edition)
L = London manuscript edition (British Library)
N = Narthang xylograph edition (Harvard-Yenching Library)
P = Peking xylograph edition, 2nd printing, dated to 1720 (1955 Ōtani reprint edition)
S = Stog Palace manuscript Kanjur (1979 Leh reprint edition)

In Sanskrit, [this text is called] ***Ārya-ugra-paripṛcchā-nāma-mahāyāna-sūtra.***

In Tibetan, [it is called] ***The Noble Mahāyāna Sūtra entitled "The Inquiry of Ugra."***[1]

[PRACTICES OF THE LAY BODHISATTVA][2]

Section one.[3]

[§0. OPENING SALUTATION]

Homage to all the Buddhas and bodhisattvas.[4]

{Chapter 1: The Superior Man}[5]

[§1. THE SETTING]

[1A] Thus have I heard at one time.[6] The Blessed One was staying at Śrāvastī, at the pleasure garden of Anāthapiṇḍada, in the

---

[1] On the variety of names given to this sūtra in its Sanskrit, Chinese, and Tibetan versions see Chapter 2, pp. 26-31.

[2] This and all other section titles and numbers given in brackets have been added by the translator for convenience of reference and are not found in the Chinese or Tibetan originals. Of the three Chinese versions, only Dh has added chapter numbers and titles; where these occur, they will be given (like all other material that occurs in one or more of the earlier versions but not in the Tibetan) in braces.

[3] Tib only. The antecedents of the term *bam-po* "section" in Tibetan have yet to be fully elucidated, but a connection with Ch. *chüan* 卷 "fascicle" seems inevitable. It is probably significant that while the titles of chapters (Tib. *le'u*) are given at the end of the sections in question, *bam-po* numbers appear at the *beginning* of the materials to which they refer, as is of course the case with *chüan* numbers in Chinese texts (though the latter generally appear at the end of the section in question as well). No equivalent of the term *bam-po* has been identified in Sanskrit Buddhist texts.

[4] Tib only. On the apparently late introduction of these opening formulas see Chapter 2, pp. 26-27 and n. 34.

[5] Dh only.

[6] On this phrase see Brough 1950, Silk 1989, and Harrison 1990, p. 5, n. 3. For a more extended bibliography see the sources cited in Bongard-Levin, Boucher, Fukita, and Wille 1996, p. 90, n. 1.

Jeta grove, with a great *bhikṣu-saṁgha* of 1,250 *bhikṣus*, and with five thousand[7] bodhisattvas: the bodhisattva-mahāsattvas Maitreya, Mañjuśrī, Apāyajaha, Avalokiteśvara, Mahāsthāmaprāpta,[8] and so on. At that time the Blessed One, surrounded and attended by an assembly of many hundreds of thousands, was teaching the Dharma.[9] And he fully and thoroughly taught [the Dharma which is] pure conduct, good at the beginning, good in the middle, good at the end, good in meaning, good in letter, uncontaminated, complete, pure, and spotless.[10]

[1B] {At that time in the city of Śrāvasti there was an Eminent Householder named Ugra.}[11] Then Ugra the Eminent Householder[12] together with five hundred attendants[13] set out from the great city of Śrāvastī and went to where the Blessed One was, at the pleasure garden of

---

7 AY "five hundred." An increase in the number of members of the audience from earlier to later versions is a common development in Mahāyāna sūtra literature.

8 Not in AY or Dh. For a synoptic list of these names in Chinese and Tibetan see Appendix 2.

9 AY "was expounding the sūtras for them" (*wei shuo ching* 為說經). The translation of the Indian word *dharma* as *ching* 經 "classic" (which became the standard equivalent of "sūtra" in Buddhist Chinese) is frequent in pre-5th century Chinese translations, and demonstrates the extent to which the Buddhist teachings were identified, in the Chinese cultural context, with the texts in which they were recorded.

10 Tib only. This list of epithets of the Dharma (for which see *Mvy*. 1280-1289, under the heading *dharmaparyāya*) is a standard enumeration, known also in the Pāli sources (e.g., *Vinaya*, *Mahāvagga*, I.11.1). The expression "pure conduct" (Tib. *tshangs-par spyod-pa*, Skt. *brahmacarya*) of course implies not only purity in a general sense but complete abstinence from any sexual activity.

11 Only in AY and Dh.

12 "Eminent Householder" translates Tib. *khyim-bdag*, the regular equivalent of Skt. *gṛhapati* (Pāli *gahapati*; lit. "house-lord"). While Dh and R use the standard equivalent of *chang-che* 長者, AY has *li-chia* 理家 "household manager," a term which also occurs ias a translation of *gṛhapati* in the translations of K'ang Seng-hui 康僧會 (mid-3rd century CE; cf. T 152, 3.13c25, 14a26, 15a16, and *passim*). For a discussion of the term *gṛhapati* and its social and economic implications see Chapter 2, pp. 22-24.

13 Tib. *g.yog* "servant, attendant," Skt. *parivāra* (*Mvy*. 3829). R (and later in this passage, Dh) uses *chüan-shu* 眷屬 "household, dependents," while AY reads simply *chung* 眾 "assembly." Sakurabe translates *hanryo* 伴侶 "companions, partners" (p. 234), but this is far too horizontal a term to convey the hierarchical nature of this expression. Those to whom this term is applied are clearly Ugra's subordinates, not his equals.

Anāthapiṇḍada, in the Jeta grove. And having arrived there, they bowed their heads at the Blessed One's feet, circumambulated the Blessed One three times,[14] and sat down to one side.[15] And in the same way other eminent householders as well—named Eminent Householder *Sukhakāma, Eminent Householder Yaśaskāma, Eminent Householder Sudatta, Eminent Householder *Nandaka, Eminent Householder Yaśodatta, Eminent Householder Sudhana, Eminent Householder *Guptika, Eminent Householder Anāthapiṇḍada, Eminent Householder *Nāgaśrī, and Eminent Householder *Satyarati[16]—these and a great many other such eminent householders, each with five hundred attendants, set out from the great city of Śrāvastī and[17] went to where the Blessed One was, at the pleasure garden of Anāthapiṇḍada, in the Jeta grove. And having assembled there,[18] they bowed their heads at the feet of the Blessed One, circumambulated the Blessed One three times,[19] and sat down to one side.[20] All those eminent householders, together with their numerous attendants,[21] had set out in the Great Vehicle,[22] had planted the roots-

---

[14] Not in AY.

[15] Not in AY. Here and below AY makes no attempt to represent the culturally specific practice of triple circumambulation and of sitting to one side of an eminent person rather than directly in front of him.

[16] The names of those who accompany Ugra on his visit to the Buddha vary slightly from one version of the sūtra to another. Names prececeded by an asterisk are less than certain reconstructions.

[17] Not in AY.

[18] Not in AY or Dh.

[19] Not in AY.

[20] Not in AY.

[21] Not in Dh or, at this point, in AY, which however attributes the two following attainments to the attendants as well as their masters.

[22] Though the Tibetan renders what was certainly the standard expression *mahāyāna-saṁprasthita* as "having entered into" (*yang-dag-par zhugs-pa*) the Great Vehicle, AY reads "had begun to seek" the Great Vehicle, while Dh and R have "were directed toward" and "had turned toward" the Great Vehicle, respectively. The Sanskrit verb *sam-pra-√sthā* generally means "to set out for" (a goal), not to enter into something; so the renderings found in Dh and R are somewhat more expected than is the Tibetan. AY's "seek" could be explained as the result of a confusion between (*sam*)*prasthita* "having set out for" and *prārthita* "having desired, wished for," a confusion documented in Karashima 1992, p. 61 (73a11); cf. BHSD 393a-b, s.v. *prārthanā*. In light of Karashima's findings on the confusion between *jñāna* and *yāna* as reflected both in the extant Indic texts and in their Chinese translations and his provocative suggestion that the notion of *yāna* itself may be founded on an incorrect back-formation of the

of-goodness, and were assured of Supreme Perfect Enlightenment.[23] {Only Anāthapiṇḍada had not.}[24]

[§2. UGRA'S INQUIRY]

[2A] Then Ugra the Eminent Householder, knowing that the great assembly of eminent householders had gathered, by the power of the Blessed One[25] rose from his seat, arranged his outer robe on one shoulder, pressed his right knee to the ground,[26] made the gesture of *añjali*[27]

Middle Indic word for "knowledge" in the process of Sanskritization (Karashima 1993), it seems worth considering the possibility that the expression *mahāyāna-saṁprasthita* was originally understood, in a Prakrit form, as **mahājñāna-saṁprasthita*, "having set out for the Great Knowledge," that is, for Buddhahood. On the confusion between *jñāna* and *yāna* see Karashima 1993; on the term *mahāyāna-saṁprasthita* see Salomon 1999 and 2002.

23 That is, they were irreversible from the attainment of Buddhahood (Tib. *bla-na-med-pa yang-dag-par rdzogs-pa'i byang-chub-tu nges-par byas-pa*, Skt. **anuttarasamyaksambodhi-niyāma*; the Chinese translations all use *chüeh* 決 [AY, Dh] or *chüeh-ting* 決定 [R] "fixed, set").

24 This strange sentence occurs only in AY. It is difficult to avoid the suspicion that this phrase is the result of contamination by the standard exemption clause following the enumeration of Arhats in the audience of Mahāyāna sūtras: "with the exception only of Ānanda" (in this case, the exception being the fact that of all the Buddha's leading disciples, only Ānanda had not yet attained enlightenment at the time of the Buddha's death).

25 Not in AY. This phrase (in Sanskrit usually *buddhānubhāvena*) is one of those "inflationary flourishes" that appear to multiply in later recensions of Mahāyāna sūtras as the Buddha's level of influence increases and the importance of the follower's initiative is reduced. An illuminating instance of the multiplication of uses of this expression is found in the opening section of the *Aṣṭasāhasrikā-prajñāpāramitā-sūtra*, where Subhūti reads Śāriputra's mind under his own power according to all the translations done during the 5th century CE or before (T 224, 225, 226, and 227, as well as one of the 7th-century translations by Hsüan-tsang, T 220[5]) but through the Buddha's *anubhāva* according to all later versions (T 228, the Sanskrit, and the Tibetan, as well as Hsüan-tsang's other translation, T 220[4]). In the following exchange Subhūti requires this *anubhāva* even to address the Buddha according to the Sanskrit and the Tibetan, though none of the Chinese translations contains this statement.

26 Tib only.

27 That is, saluted the Buddha by placing his palms together. This is of course a culturally specific gesture; Chinese translators often used terminology (as AY does here) that reflects not Indian conventions of politeness, but their own.

toward the Blessed One, and spoke to the Blessed One as follows: "If, for the sake of receiving an explanation in response to my question, the Blessed One[28] grants me the opportunity, I would like to ask the Blessed One, the Tathāgata, the Arhat, the Samyaksaṁbuddha,[29] about a certain

---

[28] While AY, R, and Tib have terms that clearly go back to an underlying *bhagavan*, Dh alone reads *t'ien-chung t'ien* 天中天 "god among gods." Schuster (1976, pp. 68-70, n. 217) claims that Dharmarakṣa must have been using an Indian text that read *devātideva*, and goes on to assert that "the manuscript used by Dharmarakṣa does demonstrate, by the use of terms such as this, the probable influence of the culture of the Kuṣāṇas" (p. 69). There are several problems, however, with such an assertion. First of all, though the Kushans did use titles of a similar pattern on their coins—viz., "king of kings," in Bactrian ραονανο ραο [*shaonano shao*] and in Prakrit *rajadiraja*—these titles are applied exclusively to rulers, not to the Buddha or other religious figures. It is of course possible that the Kushans extended this political terminology into the religious realm, but we have no direct evidence of such use. Second, even if (as seems likely) the term "king of kings" did serve as the basis for the Buddhist expression "god of gods," this does not necessarily point to the Kushans as its source. Prior to the Kushan period the expression appears (in both Greek and Prakrit) on the coins of the Sakas, an Iranian-speaking people who ruled in the northwestern portions of the subcontinent prior to the Kushans (see Mitchiner 1975-1976, vol. 6). The Sakas, in turn, are thought to have adopted this terminology from the Parthians, who had inherited it from Achaemenid Persian terminology (see Wolski 1990). Third, it is not necessary to assume (as Schuster does) that where Dharmarakṣa has *t'ien-chung t'ien* the Indic manuscript he was using read *devātideva*. In fact, as Boucher has demonstrated (1996, pp. 210-214), Dharmarakṣa uses this epithet in a wide range of contexts, and where an Indic text is available for comparison, Dh's *t'ien-chung t'ien* generally does not correspond to *devātideva* but to another epithet of the Buddha. In the translations of Lokakṣema (late 2nd century CE), where this epithet first appears, *t'ien-chung t'ien* is used with special frequency in direct address to the Buddha, where the corresponding Sanskrit has the vocative *bhagavan* (see Iwamatsu 1985).

In sum, the presence of the epithet *t'ien-chung t'ien* in a Chinese translation cannot be taken as evidence that the underlying Indic text read *devātideva*, nor should this epithet be associated exclusively with the Kushans. On the contrary, expressions such as "king of kings" and "god of gods" seem to have enjoyed broad currency in the Iranian-speaking world and its environs, creating a situation in which certain early Chinese translators used *t'ien-chung t'ien* as the equivalent of a variety of words for "Buddha," whether for reasons of stylistic preference, literary variation, or the requirements of meter.

[29] Not in AY or Dh.

matter." When he had spoken thus,[30] the Blessed One spoke to Ugra the Eminent Householder as follows: "O Eminent Householder, the Tathāgata will always grant you an opportunity. O Eminent Householder, ask the Tathāgata, {the Arhat, the Samyaksaṁbuddha}[31] whatever things you like, and I will gladden your mind by means of an answer to those questions."[32]

[2B] When the Buddha had spoken those words, Ugra the Eminent Householder spoke as follows to the Blessed One: "O Blessed One, those gentlemen or ladies[33] who arouse their thoughts toward Supreme Perfect Enlightenment; who are devoted to the Great Vehicle; who stand firm in the Great Vehicle; who desire to attain the Great Vehicle; who desire to enter into the Great Vehicle; who pledge themselves to the Great Vehicle;[34]

---

30 Not in AY or Dh.

31 Only in AY.

32 This exchange, expressed in highly formulaic and standardized language, occurs in a great many Mahāyāna sūtras. For an example in an extant Sanskrit text see the *Suvikrāntavikrāmi-paripṛcchā-prajñāpāramitā-sūtra*, §3a (Hikata 1958, p. 3):

> *"Pṛccheyam ahaṁ Bhagavantaṁ tathāgatam arhantaṁ samyaksambuddhaṁ kaṁcid eva pradeśaṁ, saced Bhagavān avakāśaṁ kuryāt pṛṣṭaś ca praśnavyākaraṇāya." Evam ukte Bhagavān Suvikrāntavikrāmiṇaṁ bodhisatvaṁ mahāsatvam etad avocat: "Pṛccha tvaṁ Suvikrānta-vikrāmiṁ-s-Tathāgatam arhantam samyaksambuddhaṁ, yad yad ev'-ākāṁkṣasy, ahaṁ te tasya tasyâiva praśna-vyākaraṇena cittam ārādhayiṣyāmi."*

For the first part of this formula cf. *Mvy*. 6310. The wording is slightly different, but also quite formulaic, in the Chinese versions.

33 "Gentlemen or ladies" translates the plural forms of *kulaputra* (Tib. *rigs-kyi bu*, "son of lineage") and *kuladuhitṛ* (Tib. *rigs-kyi bu-mo*, "daughter of lineage"), respectively. I have eschewed the well-established Buddhist Hybrid English expressions "son of good family" and "daughter of good family" both because they are needlessly wooden and because they fail to capture the nuance of the underlying Indian terms. As used in Buddhist texts, at least—I have not made a comparative study of their use in other Indian literature—these are simply polite expressions referring to the person in question as of "good birth" in a formulaic way. Since "gentleman" and "lady" are not used in the singular as forms of direct address in English (except in a rather pejorative usage of the latter), when these terms occur in the vocative singular I have translated them as "sir" and "madam," respectively.

34 The wording of this list varies slightly in the Chinese versions.

[2C] "Who, in order to take care of, comfort, and protect all beings, seek the armor[35] [of the bodhisattva]; who for the benefit of all beings take on the great burden,[36] vowing:

The unrescued I will rescue.
The unliberated I will liberate.
The uncomforted I will comfort.
Those who have not yet reached *parinirvāṇa*
I will cause to attain *parinirvāṇa*,[37]

and who are established in this great exalted vow;[38] who, having heard of

---

[35] The motif of girding on the armor (Skt. *saṁnāha*, Tib. *go-cha*) is widely used in Mahāyāna sūtras in connection with the career of the bodhisattva. Its referents are unstable (or perhaps better, are multiple): in some cases it is equated with the bodhisattva's vow to rescue all beings, in others with his exertion (*vīrya*), and in still others with his practice of endurance (*kṣānti*, for which see below, §11G(3), n. 240). Of these the meaning "vow" is the most widespread; so well established is this equivalence that the term *saṁnāha* is sometimes translated into Chinese (as here and below [12.17b3, 5, and 8] by AY) simply as "vow" (*shih* 誓). For this equivalence in a Sanskrit text see the *Aṣṭasāhasrikāprajñāpāramitāsūtra* (Vaidya 1960, p. 220.14-15), *sattvān parinirvāpayiṣyāma iti saṁnāhaṁ saṁnahyante* "they arm themselves with the armor [of the vow that] 'we shall cause beings to attain *parinirvāṇa*.'"

[36] The image of the bodhisattva as one who "carries the burden" (**bhārahārin*) is a commonplace in Mahāyāna sūtras. The burden in question is that of the five *skandha*s: the bodhisattva is portrayed as willing to endure continued existence in *saṁsāra* (and thus in embodied form) far longer than would have been necessary if he were a candidate for the nirvāṇa of the Arhat. It seems likely that a direct contrast was intended between the bodhisattva, who voluntarily carries such a burden throughout countless eons until all the qualities of a Buddha have been attained, and the Arhat, who has "put it down" (*apahṛtabhāra*, one of the standard list of *śrāvaka-guṇa*s; see *Mvy.* no. 1084).

The idea of the five *skandha*s as a burden is an old one in Buddhist literature. One of the best known occurrences is in the *Saṁyutta-nikāya*, which contains an entire sūtra devoted to this idea (see the *Bhārasutta*, SN XXII, §22). The image apparently led to some difficulties for Buddhist theorists, however, as the idea of a burden suggests the existence of a bearer, i.e., a self (see *Abhidharmakośa* IX, 257 and Conze 1962, pp. 124-125).

[37] On these four vows see Chapter 6, pp. 148-151.

[38] The Tibetan reads, more literally, "who are established in the great exalted *entrance*" (*'jug-pa rlabs-po-che chen-po-la rab-tu gnas-pa*), a phrase whose meaning is difficult to construe. I am sorely tempted to take the word *'jug-pa* here as a nonstandard rendering of Skt. *praṇidhāna* that was overlooked in the course of the 9th-century revision of this translation. The term *praṇidhāna* usually means "vow" in Buddhist usage (and in this sense is

the infinite knowledge of the Buddha, seek the armor in order to attain that knowledge;[39] who, though aware of the many defects of saṃsāra, with unwearied mind circle for countless kalpas without becoming dejected—as to those, O Blessed One, among those gentlemen and ladies who belong to the bodhisattva vehicle there are those who leave the household and acquire the qualities conducive to enlightenment[40] while not living at home, and there are those who acquire the qualities conducive to enlightenment while[41] living at home.[42] O Blessed One, out of kindness toward the world with its gods, humans, and asuras,[43] in order to maintain this Great Vehicle, in order to ensure that the lineage of the three jewels is not cut off,[44] and in order to make

---

ordinarily translated into Tibetan as *smon-lam*), but its general—that is, not specifically Buddhist—meaning is "access, entrance" (see MW 660a). The term I have translated as "exalted" (Tib. *rlabs-po-che*) is a standard equivalent of Skt. *udāra* (*Mvy.* no. 2688), which in turn is a common epithet of the bodhisattva's vow. See for example the longer *Sukhāvatīvyūha* (Müller 1881), p. 56.1 (*udārasaṁnāhasaṁnaddhāḥ*, "armed with the exalted armor") and p. 10.14 (*udātaraṁ ca praṇidhānam akārṣīt* "and [Dharmākara] made the most exalted vow"). Finally, it is significant that AY reads "vow" (*shih* 誓), not "entrance," at this point.

[39] Not in AY or Dh.

[40] Tib. *byang-chub-kyi phyogs-kyi chos-rnams*, Skt. *bodhipakṣa-dharma*. This traditional list of qualities conducive to enlightenment includes the four *smṛtyupasthānas*, the four *samyakpradhānas*, the four *ṛddhipādas*, the five *indriyas*, the five *balas*, the seven *bodhyaṅgas*, and the eightfold path. For a comprehensive discussion of these items see Gethin 1992.

[41] Not in AY.

[42] R adds "without going forth from the household."

[43] Not in AY; Dh reads only "with its gods and humans."

[44] The expression "lineage of the three jewels" (Tib. *dkon-mchog gsum-gyi rigs*, Skt. **triratna-vaṁśa*) carries a great deal more weight than at first meets the eye. What is at issue here is not merely the preservation of the teachings of Śākyamuni (for which the simple term *saddharma* would more commonly be used), but the possibility of the rediscovery of the same truths in the future by others who will replicate his career. The underlying idea is, in essence, that if no one in the Buddhist community chooses to become a bodhisattva rather than to strive for Arhatship, there will be no possibility of the appearance of another Buddha in the future, and the lineage to which Śākyamuni himself belonged (as described, for example, in the Pāli *Buddhavaṁsa*) will become extinct.

In a number of bodhisattva-vehicle texts a sharp distinction is drawn between those who belong to this lineage—that is, bodhisattvas who will themselves become Buddhas in the future—and other Buddhists, even enlightened ones, who do not. In the *Kāśyapaparivarta* (§82), for example, we

the omniscience [of the Buddhas] long endure,[45] I ask the Blessed One to explain the particular qualities in which householder bodhisattvas should train themselves.

[2D] "How should the householder bodhisattva, while dwelling at the household stage,[46] act in accordance with the Tathāgata's word, not damage or fall away from the qualities conducive to enlightenment,[47] be free of blameworthy deeds in this lifetime, and be distinguished in future lives? O Blessed One, the bodhisattvas who

---

find a forceful statement of the idea that only bodhisattvas—not ordinary *śrāvakas*—are true "sons of the Tathāgata" (*kiṁ cāpi tathāgato koṭīśatasahasra-parivāraḥ śrāvaker na cātra kaścid bodhisatvo bhavati na tatra tathāgatasya putrasaṁjñotpadyate*). The text goes on to say that even a bodhisattva in whom *bodhicitta* has just arisen for the first time should be viewed as superior to Arhats who have attained the eight *vimokṣas*, because it is the bodhisattva, not the Arhats, who "will not cut off the lineage of the Buddhas" (*buddhavaṁśasyānupacchedāya sthāsyati*, §83).

The word *vaṁśa* itself originally meant "bamboo" but by extension "race, family, lineage" and even "tradition." It is interesting to note that AY renders the term as *tien-chi* 典藉 "books, record," thus echoing another meaning of the term in Buddhist usage—that is, as the name of a genre of literature, the "chronicle" in the sense of a record of the lineage of Buddhas of the past (e.g., the *Buddhavaṁsa*) or of the ongoing tradition of Buddhism in the present age (e.g., the *Mahāvaṁsa* and *Dīpavaṁsa*, though neither of these had yet been written in AY's time). Once again AY reveals the Chinese propensity to view Buddhism primarily through the lens of its scriptural texts.

45 The term "omniscience" (Skt. *sarvajña* ~ *sarvajña-jñāna* ~ *sarvajñatā*, Tib. *thams-cad mkhyen-pa* ~ *thams-cad mkhyen-pa'i ye-shes* ~ *thams-cad-mkhyen-pa-nyid*) occurs frequently in sūtras dealing with the career of the bodhisattva. Like the term *anuttarasamyaksambodhi*, it is reserved for the insight attained by a Buddha, in contrast to the presumably lesser degree of awakening experienced by an Arhat or Pratyekabuddha. There seems to be little or no difference in meaning between the various forms of *sarvajña* (all of which occur in, for example, the *Aṣṭasāhasrikā-prajñāpāramitā-sūtra*); rather, the longer forms appear to be simply another manifestation of the tendency toward "terminological inflation" that is so ubiquitous in Indian Mahāyāna literature.

46 Tib. *sa*, Skt. *bhūmi*. This is a clear instance of a nontechnical use of the term *bhūmi*, in contrast to the systematic uses to which it would be subsequently put in the various *daśabhūmi* systems. See Chapter 6, pp. 151-152. AY and Dh have no reference to "stage" or *bhūmi* here.

47 AY alone adds a reference to not damaging "what he originally vowed (*ch'i pen so yüan* 其本所願), that is, [to attain] *anuttarasamyaksambodhi*." Cf. below, §6B, where AY alone appears to interpolate the following two phrases.

go forth from the home, abandoning what is dear and not dear,[48] cutting off their hair and beard, putting on the saffron robe, and with true faith going forth from the household to the houseless state[49]—please explain how they practice the Dharma and practice virtue through both teaching and instruction. How should the householder bodhisattva and the renunciant bodhisattva live, and how should they practice?"[50]

[2E] When Ugra the Eminent Householder had spoken those words,[51] the Blessed One spoke to him as follows: "Good, good, O Eminent Householder! It is appropriate that you have thought to ask me about this matter.[52] Therefore, listen carefully and take this to heart, and I will explain to you how the householder and renunciant bodhisattvas should dwell in excellent conduct while taking on the qualities to be cultivated, and how they should practice." Saying "So be it, O Blessed One,"[53] Ugra the Eminent Householder listened as the Blessed One had instructed him, and the Blessed One spoke to him as follows.

[§3. GOING FOR REFUGE]

[3A] "O Eminent Householder, a householder bodhisattva, while living at home, should go to the Buddha for refuge, go to the Dharma for refuge, and go to the Sangha for refuge. And the root-of-goodness produced by that act of going for refuge to those three jewels[54] he should transform into Supreme Perfect Enlightenment.[55]

---

[48] Dh and R refer only to abandoning what is beloved or precious, but AY and Tib agree in stating that a renunciant gives up the objects of both like and dislike. Since the latter is a common pairing (Skt. *priyāpriya*, Pāli *piyāppiya*) it is presumably the original reading.

[49] R alone omits "cutting off their hair and beard, putting on the saffron robe, and with true faith going forth from the household to the houseless state," while AY introduces a statement not found in any other version of the text: "the home-dweller has faith; the one who has left home practices the Way" (*tsai-chia yu hsin, li-chia wei tao* 在家有信離家為道). This neat pair of four-character phrases has all the earmarks of an internal Chinese emendation.

[50] R is quite abbreviated here, omitting (among other things) any reference to the householder bodhisattva.

[51] Tib only.

[52] AY "about the conduct (*shih-hsing* 施行) of the householder and renunciant bodhisattvas." On the meaning of this term see Chapter 5, p. 111, n. 17.

[53] Not in AY or Dh.

[54] Not in AY or Dh; Tib omits the word "jewels."

[55] A detailed discussion of the practice of transforming merit—that is,

[3B] "O Eminent Householder, how should the householder bodhisattva go to the Buddha for refuge?[56] O Eminent Householder, by forming the thought 'I must attain the body of a Buddha, ornamented with the thirty-two marks of a Great Man,'[57] and by exerting himself to acquire those roots-of-goodness by which the thirty-two marks of a Great Man will be obtained, in this way does the householder bodhisattva go to the Buddha for refuge.

[3C] "O Eminent Householder, how should the householder bodhisattva go to the Dharma for refuge? O Eminent Householder, with reverence and respect for the Dharma, having the Dharma as his objective,[58] desiring the Dharma, rejoicing and delighting in the pleasure of the Dharma, being intent upon the Dharma, inclined toward the Dharma, with a propensity for the Dharma, protecting the Dharma, abiding in the preservation of the Dharma, dwelling in the

---

directing it toward a specific goal—is found in the *Aṣṭasāhasrikā-prajñā-pāramitā-sūtra* (Vaidya 1960, p. 40.23-27, and cf. Conze's English translation [1973], pp. 111-112). It is important to note that what is at issue here is not the redirecting of one's own merit toward others, but an almost alchemical transformation of the content of the merit itself, so that it will lead to one's full enlightenment as a Buddha rather than than to other, lesser rewards. On the distinction between these two types of *pariṇāmanā* (viz., "transfer" and "transformation" of merits) see above, Chapter 5, pp. 114-115.

56 AY asks about all three types of refuge-taking here. The Tibetan introduces each of these questions with the expression *zhe-na* "if one asks," which I have omitted in translation.

57 The thirty-two marks (*lakṣaṇa*) of the Great Man (*mahāpuruṣa*) are considered to be physical signs of personal greatness, and are possessed in their entirety by only two figures according to Buddhist tradition: an enlightened Buddha (not an Arhat or Pratyekabuddha) and a world-ruling *cakravartin*. An entire sutta in the Pāli canon is devoted to a discussion of these marks and the actions in Śākyamuni's previous lives that brought them about; see *Dīghanikāya*, sutta no. 30 (*Lakkhaṇa-sutta*). For an extensive and technical discussion of the elements of this list and their terminological variants, see BHSD 458a-460a; cf. de Jong 1954. The fact that one of these marks (a "sheathed" or "retractable" male organ) is an exclusively masculine attribute is no doubt one of the factors that contributed to the virtually universal consensus that Buddhahood—unlike Arhatship—is inaccessible to women.

58 AY "seeking the Dharma," Dh "clarifying the Dharma's marvelous meaning," R "expounding the Dharma." What has certainly happened here is that the Chinese and Tibetan translators interpreted an underlying word *artha*—which means "objective, aim" as well as "meaning"—in a variety of ways.

accomplishment[59] and practice of the Dharma, mastering the Dharma, seeking the Dharma, having the power of the Dharma, having the sword [which is] the gift of the Dharma,[60] doing what is to be done with respect to the Dharma, and by having those qualities, bearing in mind the thought "When I have awakened to Supreme Perfect Enlightenment,[61] I must rightly share the Dharma[62] with the world with its gods, humans, and asuras'[63]—O Eminent Householder,[64] this is how a householder bodhisattva goes to the Dharma for refuge.

[3D] "O Eminent Householder,[65] how should the householder bodhisattva go to the Sangha for refuge? O Eminent Householder,[66] as to the householder bodhisattva going to the Sangha for refuge,[67] if he sees monks who are[68] stream-enterers, or once-returners, or non-returners, or Arhats, or ordinary persons (*pṛthagjana*), who are[69] members of the Śrāvaka Vehicle, the Pratyekabuddha Vehicle, or the Great Vehicle,[70] with

---

59 The Tibetan reads *grags* "fame," but a comparison with the corresponding Chinese versions strongly suggests that the underlying Sanskrit term was *prasiddha* (one of several possible antecedents of *grags* according to LC 378b), which means "adornment, accomplishment, attainment" as well as "celebrity, renown." Note in particular that the corresponding term in AY is *shu* 術 "art, skill, method."

60 R reads "giving Dharma-weapons" (*shih fa ch'i-chang* 施法器仗), thus echoing Tib's reference to a "sword," but AY and Dh refer only to "Dharma-wealth" or "Dharma-treasure," respectively. Was there a confusion between *dhana* "wealth" and *dāna* "gift," which was then further compounded by the association of the gift of the Dharma with the sword of wisdom?

61 Not in AY.

62 Or more literally, "I must share the Dharma by means of the Dharma."

63 Not in AY or Dh.

64 Not in AY or Dh.

65 Not in AY or Dh.

66 Not in AY or Dh.

67 Tib only.

68 The word "monk" appears in Tib only, but given the context it is almost certainly implied in the other versions as well.

69 For "who are" R and Tib read "or." AY and Dh, where all of the previously mentioned categories are subsumed under the heading of "members of the Śrāvaka Vehicle," probably represent the original (and more logical) reading.

70 Not in AY or R; Dh reads "the Pratyekabuddha Vehicle" but does not mention the Mahāyāna. The original reading is probably the one preserved in AY and R, since what is at issue here is the necessity of avoiding showing any disrespect toward those Buddhists who are not on the bodhisattva path.

reverence and respect toward them he exerts himself to stand up, speaks to them pleasantly,[71] and treats them with propriety.[72] Showing reverence toward those he meets with and encounters, he bears in mind the thought 'When I have awakened to Supreme Perfect Enlightenment, I will teach the Dharma which brings about[73] [in others] the qualities of a Śrāvaka or a Pratyekabuddha[74] in just this way.' Thus having reverence and respect for them, he does not cause them any trouble.[75] That is how a householder bodhisattva goes to the Sangha for refuge.

[§4. THE REFUGES, REPEATED]

[4A] "And again, O Eminent Householder, if a householder bodhisattva has four things,[76] he is one who 'goes to the Buddha for

---

[71] Not in AY or Dh; R omits the reference to "speaking to them pleasantly."

[72] The wording varies slightly in AY and Dh, but in all versions the idea is that the householder bodhisattva should act with reverence and respect toward members of the Śrāvaka Vehicle.

[73] Reading with S which, alone of the Tibetan versions consulted, conforms to the sense represented in all three Chinese translations. The addition of the word *phyir* "in order to" in P, D, and N (resulting in a phrase meaning "I will teach the Dharma *in order to* cultivate the qualities") appears to be an intra-Tibetan emendation.

[74] Tib only.

[75] AY "he does not envy them," Dh "he does not disrespect them," R "his heart does not dwell among them" (*hsin pu chu chung* 心不住中). The quite divergent wording given in R bears a strong resemblance to a passage that occurs in the *Aṣṭasāhasrikā-prajñāpāramitā-sūtra*, also in the context of a discussion of how the bodhisattva should relate to *śrāvaka*s: *ye 'pi Subhūte śrāvakagūṇāḥ tān api sa jānāti, na tatrāvatiṣṭhate* (p. 433; cf. Conze 1973, p. 253), "He knows the [good] qualities of the *śrāvaka*s, but he does not dwell among them." The reading found in R is almost certainly the result of a memorization error, elicited by the "trigger-word" *śrāvakagūṇa*. Note that R again diverges from the other versions below (§4C), again reading "his heart does not dwell among them" (with identical wording in the Chinese) following another mention of the *śrāvakaguṇa*s. For a detailed discussion of memorization errors of this sort see above, Chapter 3, pp. 52-55.

[76] Tib. *chos* "dharma." This is clearly an instance of the use of the word "dharma" in the non-technical sense, that is, simply in the sense of "thing" or "item." (Note that in at least one instance [12.23c13] Dh has *shih-fa* 事法 "thing-dharma" in place of the simple *fa* 法 found in the other two translations.) AY and R agree in reading "if the bodhisattva *carries out* four things" (*hsiu-chih* 修治 and *ch'eng-chiu* 成就, i.e., "cultivate" and "accomplish"), whereas the

refuge.' What are the four? (1) he does not abandon the spirit of enlightenment;[77] (2) he does not break his promise;[78] (3) he does not forsake great compassion; and (4) he does not concern himself with the other vehicles. O Eminent Householder, if a householder bodhisattva has these four things, he is one who 'goes to the Buddha for refuge.'[79]

[4B] "And again, O Eminent Householder, if a householder bodhisattva has four things, he is one who 'goes to the Dharma for refuge.' What are the four? (1) he relies on and associates with those people who are preachers of the Dharma,[80] and having revered and done homage to them, he listens to the Dharma; (2) having heard the

---

Tibetan version and Dh read simply "if the bodhisattva *has* four things." This tetradic formulation is extremely common in early Mahāyāna texts (in which this literature follows formulas set by its Mainstream predecessors, e.g., the *Aṅguttara-nikāya*); for countless examples in Mahāyāna texts see among others the **Jagatīṁdhara-sūtra* (T 481 and 482, and Peking 841), the *Sumati-dārikā-paripṛcchā-sūtra* (T 310[30], 334, 335, and 336, and Peking 760[30]), and the *Kāśyapa-parivarta* (T 310[43], 350, 351, 352, and Peking 760[43]).

77 Skt. *bodhicitta*, Tib. *byang-chub-kyi sems*. I have adopted Robert Thurman's felicitous rendering of this term in place of the more common "thought of enlightenment," since the latter suggests a (primarily) rational, verbal, and reflective commitment to enlightenment, which is not always the case in the texts I have examined. Indeed there are instances in which *bodhicitta*, rather than being "thought about" (or consciously summoned up) by the practitioner, seems to be a mood or an attitude that arises in him unsolicited. The question of whether *bodhicitta* was originally expected to arise as the result of a conscious decision, or was understood as something that simply arises unbidden in some people (and not in others)—after which an explicit vow or resolution may be made—is an extremely important one for understanding the early development of the practice of the bodhisattva path. To put it another way: if *bodhicitta* is understood primarily as an act of conscious resolution (as is certainly the case in later Mahāyāna literature), then the bodhisattva path is theoretically open to all; if it is envisioned, on the other hand, as a specific "calling" which can be experienced but not deliberately produced, then the bodhisattva vocation is necessarily restricted to those individuals fortunate enough to have this experience.

78 Tib. *dam-bcas-pa*, Skt. **pratijñā*. The promise (or "pledge") in question is to attain Supreme Perfect Enlightenment, i.e., Buddhahood. Cf. below, §6B and n. 124.

79 As in §3B above, "going to the Buddha for refuge" is presented here in terms of replicating what the Buddha has accomplished rather than establishing a relationship with him.

80 Tib. *chos smra-ba*, Skt. **dharmabhāṇaka*.

Dharma, he thoroughly reflects upon it; (3) just as he has heard and absorbed it himself, he teaches and explains those Dharmas[81] to others; and (4) he transforms that root-of-goodness which has sprung from his gift of the Dharma into Supreme Perfect Enlightenment.[82] O Eminent Householder, the householder bodhisattva who has these four things may be said to be 'going to the Dharma for refuge.'

[4C] "And again, O Eminent Householder, if a householder bodhisattva has four things, he may be said to be one who 'goes to the Sangha for refuge.' What are the four? (1) those who have [not yet] definitively entered[83] into the Śrāvaka Vehicle[84] he should lead to the spirit of Omniscience;[85] (2) those who are drawn to material things he causes to be drawn to the Dharma; (3) he relies on the irreversible bodhisattva[86] Sangha, not on the Sangha of the Śrāvakas; and (4) he strives for the good qualities of the Śrāvakas, but does not delight in their form of liberation.[87] O Eminent Householder, if a

---

[81] The Tibetan is explicitly plural.

[82] Not in AY. Other (more minor) differences in this list among the extant versions of the sūtra will not be noted here.

[83] Tib. *skyon med-pa-la zhugs-pa-rnams* "those who have entered into the faultless," but the underlying Sanskrit was surely *niyāma-(~nyāma)-avakrānta* "having entered into a fixed/established state" (for this equivalence see *Mvy.* 6503, and cf. BHSD 314b, where the erroneousness of this Tibetan translation is discussed). The statement that the bodhisattva should persuade those who have definitively entered into the Śrāvakayāna (that is, whose course in that vehicle is set) does not appear logical, since it would seem that such persons would not be suitable candidates for Buddhahood. AY and R, as well as the citation preserved in the *Dbhv.*, suggest that the original reading was "who have *not yet* definitively entered the Śrāvakayāna"—that is, those whose course is not yet fixed and who might be persuaded to transfer to the bodhisattva vehicle instead. In view of the evidence provided by these other witnesses, I have emended the text accordingly.

[84] Dh adds "or Pratyekabuddha Vehicle."

[85] Skt. **sarvajñacitta*, here used as the equivalent of *bodhicitta* in the sense of the aspiration for Buddhahood.

[86] Not in AY or Dh. On the "irreversible Sangha" in general cf. the *Druma-kinnara-rāja-paripṛcchā-sūtra*, Chapter 9 (Harrison 1992b, p. 190, line 2). It is interesting that the citation preserved in the *Dbhv.* refers not to the "irreversible sangha" but to "the sangha of those who have attained the four fruits"—that is, from stream-enterer to Arhat (26.55a9). These four persons are, of course, also "irreversible," though in this case it is the enlightenment of an Arhat for which they are irrevocably destined.

[87] Once again, R (or his Indic source)—apparently prompted by the trigger-

householder bodhisattva has these four things, he may be said to be 'going to the Sangha for refuge.'

[4D] "And again, O Eminent Householder, if the householder bodhisattva, having seen the form of[88] the Tathāgata, obtains remembrance of the Buddha,[89] that is 'going to the Buddha for refuge.' If, having heard the Dharma, he obtains remembrance of the Dharma, that is 'going to the Dharma for refuge.' If, having seen the Tathāgata's Sangha of Śrāvakas,[90] he remembers the spirit of enlightenment, that is 'going to the Sangha for refuge.'[91]

[4E] "And again, O Eminent Householder, if a householder bodhisattva gives a gift because he wishes to associate with the Buddha[s],[92] that is 'going to the Buddha for refuge.' If he gives a gift in order to protect the True Dharma, that is 'going to the Dharma

---

word *śrāvakagūṇa*—has emended the text to read "his heart does not dwell among them" (*hsin pu chu chung* 心不住中). Cf. above, §3D and n. 75.

88 Or "body" (Tib. *sku-gzugs*; cf. *Dbhv.* 形像 which could also mean "body, form" or even "image"). Not in AY or Dh.

89 Tib. *sangs-rgyas rjes-su dran-pa*, Skt. *buddhānusmṛti*. On this important term see Harrison 1992c. It is important to point out that—the comments of some Japanese and western interpreters notwithstanding—the *Ugra* does not single out "remembrance of the Buddha" for special attention; rather, the Buddha is simply included as one of the standard list of three jewels, all three of which are treated as valid objects of remembrance. The extension of the practice of remembrance to objects other than the Buddha is not unusual; cf. the *Druma-kinnara-rāja-paripṛcchā-sūtra*, Chapter 9 (Harrison 1992b, pp. 189-190), where the objects of *anusmṛti* include the Buddha, the Dharma, the Sangha, the precepts (*śīla*), renunciation (*tyāga*), and the devas. This is a standard list (see for example *Mvy.* nos. 1148-1154), and it seems certain that the "six remembrances" (Tib. *rjes-su dran-pa drug*) mentioned—but not elaborated upon—in the *Vimalakīrtanirdeśa* (Peking 843, Ōtani ed. vol. 34, 83.3.7; cf. Thurman 1976, p. 40) are to be understood as referring to these same six items. In the Theravāda tradition the list of six was eventually expanded to ten; for references to both lists see PTSD 45a, s.v. *anussati*.

90 Both AY and Dh seem to have been working from manuscripts that read *āryasaṁgha*, while R and the Tibetan are translating *śrāvakasaṁgha*. For a similar instance cf. below, §16A and n. 332.

91 Note the contrast, even tension, between seeing the community of Śrāvakas (who are presumably not on the bodhisattva path) and bearing one's own *bodhicitta* in mind. For a similar substitution see §4E below and cf. *Pratyutpanna*, §4C.

92 For "because he wishes to associate with the Buddha[s]" Dh substitutes "desiring to fulfill his vow."

for refuge.' If he transforms that gift into Supreme Perfect Enlightenment, that is 'going to the Sangha for refuge.'

[§5. GOOD DEEDS]

[5A] "And again, O Eminent Householder, the householder bodhisattva who lives at home should do the deeds of a good man, not of a lowly man.[93] O Eminent Householder, what deeds are those of a good man and not a lowly one?[94] O Eminent Householder, the householder bodhisattva seeks wealth according to the Dharma; he does not seek it according to what is non-Dharmic. He seeks it fairly, not unfairly. He pursues right livelihood, not wrong livelihood. He does not cause harm to others by means of the wealth he has rightly attained. Building up his cultivation of the idea of its impermanence, he obtains the very substance of wealth.[95] Thus he pays respect to his

---

[93] The term *satpuruṣa* "good man" is frequently met with in Mahāyāna literature, where it is generally applied to male lay disciples of the Buddha, and in particular to those of high social standing. In some sūtras—for example, the *Pratyutpanna-buddha-saṁmukha-avasthita-samādhi-sūtra* and the *Lotus Sūtra*—we find a fixed list of eight or sixteen such persons, headed by the lay bodhisattva Bhadrapāla (see Harrison 1990, pp. 6-8, n. 7, and BHSD 554a). While *satpuruṣa* comes to be used as a technical term in this sense, its negative counterpart *kāpuruṣa* "lowly man" does not; its presence here may indicate that both terms are being used in an early (that is, pretechnical) sense. On the *sappurisa* (in its Pāli spelling), and in particular on his wealth and gift-giving, see *Aṅguttara-nikāya* iii.46-47, iii.172-173, and iv.244-245; I am grateful to Paul Harrison for providing these references. Cf. also suttas 110 and 113 of the *Majjhimanikāya*, where the opposite of *sappurisa* is not *kāpurisa* (which does however occur elsewhere in Pāli), but *asappurisa*.

[94] The following lines are cited in *Śikṣ* 267.12-13:

iha gṛhapate gṛhī bodhisatvo [*sic*] *dharmeṇa bhogān*
paryeṣate na adharmeṇa | *samena na viṣameṇa* |
samyagājīvo bhavati na viṣamājīva iti ||

[95] That is, precisely because he is not attached to wealth for its own sake, he is able to attain wealth and to make the most use of it. The Tibetan reads simply "he obtains the essence" (*snying-po len-to*), where *snying-po* is almost certainly a translation of Skt. *sāra*, a term meaning "essence, marrow, substance" but also "riches, wealth" (see MW 1208a). I have given an overtranslation of the term ("the very substance of wealth") in order to convey this multivalence. Cf. below, §6B, n. 120.

parents;[96] he duly bestows wealth upon his children, his wife,[97] his male and female slaves,[98] hired hands, and wage-earners; and he honors and esteems his friends, companions, kinsfolk, and relatives, and by leading them into the Dharma he increases his liberality.[99]

[5B] "And again, O Eminent Householder, the householder bodhisattva[100] exerts himself in order to carry the burden he has taken on, by carrying the burden of the five *skandhas*[101] for all beings.[102] And he does so in this way: not rejecting [those who are in] the Śrāvaka and

---

96 The following lines are cited in *Śikṣ* 144.5-6:

> *putra-bhāryā-dāṃsī*[sic]*-dāsa-karmakara-pauruṣeyāṇaṃ samyak-paribhogeneti* |

This is a standard list of dependents, occurring elsewhere in Indian Buddhist literature and often (as here) in conjunction with mention of parents, on the one hand, and friends and companions (*mitra-āmātya*) on the other. See (for example) the *Siṅgālovāda-suttanta* (*Dīgha-nikāya*, sutta no. 31), §27:

> *Cha imā, gahapati-putta, disā veditabbā. Puratthimā disā mātā-pitaro veditabbā. Dakkhiṇā disā ācariyā veditabbā. Pacchimā disā putta-dārā veditabbā. Uttarā disā mittâmaccā veditabbā. Heṭṭhimā disā dāsa-kamma-kara-porisā veditabbā.*

(DN iii.188-189; cf. the English translation in Walshe 1987, p. 466).

97 Not in AY.

98 Or "servants" (depending upon one's interpretation of the terms *dāsī* and *dāsa*).

99 Tib only.

100 Not in AY or Dh.

101 Not in AY.

102 AY, while obscure at certain points, offers a fairly good parallel to the Tibetan here. Dh, by contrast, has an entirely different reading, stating that the bodhisattva renounces all burdens (!) and relieves all beings of the burden of the five *skandhas*. Dh goes on to say that by being constantly energetic in his determination the bodhisattva causes the various burdens not to arise (!). Clearly Dh has misunderstood the meaning of "burden" (for which cf. n. 36 to §2C above) in this context.

The Tibetan text reads "the burden of the five *skandhas of* all beings" (*sems-can thams-cad-kyi phung-po lnga'i khur*), but this is almost certainly a misinterpretation of an underlying Sanskrit genitive used in the dative sense, signifying "for the benefit of," not "belonging to." The idea here is not that the bodhisattva somehow manages to carry the weight of other beings' *skandhas*, but rather that he is willing to continue to bear the burden of his own so that he can become a Buddha for their benefit. On the idea of the "burden" as such see above, §2C, n. 36.

the Pratyekabuddha vehicles,[103] he exerts himself to carry the burden he has taken on. He is not wearied by the beings who are to be matured; not desiring happiness for himself, he causes all beings to attain happiness.[104] Unmoved by profit or loss, fame or infamy, praise or blame, happiness or suffering, he transcends worldly things.[105] He does not become arrogant because of amassing profit and wealth, nor is he discouraged by the absence of profit, fame, or praise. He acts thoughtfully and guards his attainments. He does not rejoice in wrong conduct; with a mind not dwelling on it, he simply sees its arising. Not having a mind like cotton,[106] he fulfills what he has promised.[107]

[5C] "He does what is to be done for others; he renounces what is to be done for himself.[108] He does not expect to be repaid for what he has done for others; he does not repay the harm done to him by others.[109] He is grateful and thankful [for what others have done for him]. He does good deeds: he distributes wealth to the poor, subdues pride in the powerful, and comforts the fearful with fearlessness. For those who are afflicted with sorrow, he removes the arrow of sorrow.[110] He is patient and

---

[103] The Chinese versions offer different readings here. AY states that not taking on the burden (重任, lit., "heavy responsibility") is what is referred to as matters associated with "the wisdom of the disciples and pratyekabuddhas" (弟子各佛智之事). Dh, by contrast, states that the bodhisattva will cause (others) not to train themselves in these two vehicles. Note the apparent confusion here, incidentally, between *yāna* (reflected in Dh, R, and Tib) and *jñāna* (reflected in AY); on this issue and its implications see Karashima 1993.

[104] For "happiness" Dh reads "tranquillity," and adds a reference to bearing in mind the idea of impermanence.

[105] Tib. *'jig-rten-gyi chos-rnams*. These four pairs of opposites are traditionally referred to as the eight "worldly things" (Skt. *lokadharma*, Pāli *lokadhamma*), that is, things of concern only to those whose primary orientation is toward enjoying life in this world.

[106] Cited in *Śikṣ*. 180.14: *apagata-tūlapicūpamatācittasya*. The implication here is that the bodhisattva's mind is not "light as a feather" (and thus easily swayed). The phrase is missing from the Chinese editions.

[107] AY, like the Tibetan, states that the bodhisattva will achieve what he has vowed; Dh, by contrast, interprets what was probably an underlying *praṇidhāna* as "wish" rather than "vow," and states that the bodhisattva will obtain his desires and will cause others to have their own desires fulfilled as well.

[108] Cited in *Śikṣ*. 145.10: *parakṛtyakāritaḥ* [ms: *-tā*] *svakārya-parityaga*.

[109] Tib only.

[110] The Tibetan reads only *mya-ngan-gyi zug-rngu*, "the pain of sorrow,"

accepting of those who are weak.[111] He abandons pride and conceit; he is respectful toward teachers, adheres to those who are learned, and makes inquiries of those who are wise. His views are upright, and he conducts himself with consistency.[112] Without deception or artifice, he never tires of searching for what is lovable and virtuous in all beings. He is never satisfied with how much he has learned.

[5D] "With respect to his undertakings, he is firm in his sense of obligation. He associates with noble people; toward people who are not noble, he is exceedingly compassionate.[113] He is a steadfast friend, and he is even-minded toward those who are his friends and those who are not. With respect to all the Buddha-Dharmas, he does not have the closed fist of the teacher.[114] He teaches the Dharmas just as he has heard them, and he reflects on the meaning of what he has heard.

[§6. THE BODHISATTVA'S PERSPECTIVE]

[6A] "He considers all enjoyment of and delight in the objects of desire to be impermanent. He considers his body as not worthy of concern,[115] his life to be like a drop of dew, and his wealth to be like

---

but *zug-rngu* also serves as a translation of Skt. *śalya* "arrow, thorn" (see LC 1852a). Hence the underlying Indian text surely contained the well-known phrase "remove the arrow of sorrow" (cf. PTSD 724a, *sokasalla* "the dart or sting of sorrow"), as confirmed by R, which reads "he removes others' arrows of grief."

[111] For "weak" AY reads "powerless," while Dh and R reflect instead the sense of "lowly." Dh seems to say that the bodhisattva should teach the lowly ones to be patient, while the other versions imply that it is the bodhisattva himself who should be patient with their weakness.

[112] Not in AY or Dh. R reads "his conduct is unconditioned" (*wu-wei* 無為, here perhaps invoking the native Chinese sense of "inaction").

[113] Not in AY.

[114] Not in AY or Dh (though Dh does refer to even-mindedness in general). The meaning of the phrase "closed fist of the teacher" (made explicit in R) is that he shares the teachings freely rather than keeping them to himself or parceling them out in a stingy fashion.

[115] Tib. *mi-lta-ba*, Skt. *nirapekṣa* (LC 1797b). Here D exhibits one of a number of interesting editorial emendations, reading *lus-la mi-gtsang-bar 'du-shes-pa*, "conceiving of the body as impure." In all of these instances what the Derge editors have done is to regularize the reading, offering a more standard term. The same phenomenon can be observed in other Kanjur texts; see for example the opening lines of the *Diamond Sūtra*, where the Peking and Stog Palace editions read *de-nas ... chos-gos gsol-te*, while D replaces the honorific (but potentially ambiguous) *gsol-te* with the more standard *bgos-te*.

an illusion or a mirage.[116] {He considers his household dependents to be enemies.}[117] He considers his wife and children to be denizens of the Avīci hell. He considers the administration of houses and fields and the acquisition of various sorts of clothing to be being afflicted by misfortune. He considers seeking [belongings] to be the destruction of his roots-of-goodness. He considers his dwelling-place to be like a murderer; he considers his friends, companions, kinsfolk and relatives to be the guardians of hell.[118] Day and night he calculates [as follows]:[119]

[6B] "He thinks in terms of extracting the substance from his insubstantial body, extracting the substance from his insubstantial life, and extracting the substance from his insubstantial wealth.[120] What is

---

[116] The image of a "drop of dew" suggests that his life is precarious and transitory.

[117] Only in AY and Dh; AY reads "dependents and guests."

[118] There are minor differences among the three Chinese versions, but all agree with the general theme: possessions are causes of suffering, and other people (especially family and friends) are obstacles to the path.

[119] Sakurabe translates "he has the thought [of] reflecting 'what difference is there between day and night?' " So in fact the Tibetan appears to read, but something seems to have gone awry in translation. AY, Dh, and R read "day and night he has the same thoughts," thus suggesting that the underlying Indian text had something like "without distinguishing day from night." Because the Tibetan makes no sense as it stands, I have translated in light of the three Chinese versions.

[120] The idea of "extracting the substance" from these three items—viz., body (*kāya*), life (*jīva*), and wealth (*bhoga*)—while at the same time maintaining a view of them as insubstantial is a well-established trope in Mahāyāna sūtras. These three items occur together, though without a detailed discussion, in the *Vimalakīrtinirdeśa*; see Peking 843, Ōtani ed. vol. 34, 83.3.6, *snying-po med-pa-las snying-po len-pas ... lus dang | srog dang | longs-spyod rnyed-pa* "extracting the substance from the insubstantial, one obtains body and life and wealth" and 82.3.7-8, *lus dang | srog dang | longs-spyod-rnams-las snying-po blangs-pa* "having extracted the substance from body, life, and wealth." (In light of these sources the suggestion made by Thurman [1976, p. 122, n. 34] that the "body, health and wealth" mentioned here refer to the "true body of the Buddha" can now be set aside.) In other instances individual items from this group of three may appear alone; "wealth" alone has already appeared above (see §5A and n. 95), while "body" alone is likewise mentioned in this connection in the *Ratnarāśi-sūtra*, for which passage we happily have a Sanskrit citation preserved in the *Śikṣāsamuccaya* (*Ratnarāśi* §V,17: *snying-po med-pa'i lus-las snying-po blangs-par 'gyur-ba* [text in Silk 1994a, p. 471]; cf. *Śikṣ*. 200.17,

'thinking in terms of extracting the substance from one's insubstantial body'? It is taking pleasure in doing all that is to be done for others; speaking respectfully to one's teachers, doing homage to them, rising up, pressing one's palms together, and bowing to them—this is 'thinking in terms of extracting the substance from one's insubstantial body.' And what is 'thinking in terms of extracting the substance from one's insubstantial life'? It is not damaging the roots-of-goodness that one has previously planted, but causing them to increase—this is 'thinking in terms of extracting the substance from one's insubstantial life.' And what is 'thinking in terms of extracting the substance from one's insubstantial wealth'? It is restraining the spirit of stinginess, causing the spirit of great liberality to increase, and distributing gifts—this is 'thinking in terms of extracting the substance from one's insubstantial wealth.' O Eminent Householder, in these ways a householder bodhisattva does the deeds of a good man, not those of a lowly one.[121] If he does so, he will not be declared at fault by the Tathāgatas,[122] but will be declared to be one who speaks appropriately and one who speaks [in accord with] the Dharma.[123] Thus one will not abandon or forsake one's previous promise[124] to attain Supreme Perfect Enlightenment, {and will be faultless in conduct in this life, and in future lives will follow a distinguished path.}[125]

'sārāt kāyāt sāram ādattaṁ bhaviṣyati). See also the discussion and additional references in Silk, *op. cit.*, pp. 353-354, n. 1.

121 Not in AY.

122 Dh reads "he does not violate the precepts of the Tathāgata, the Arhat, the Perfectly Enlightened Buddha."

123 The Tibetan has *chos smra-ba*, which often serves as a translation of Skt. *dharmabhāṇaka*, but in the present context I suspect that the underlying Indian term is *dharmavādin* (which would agree with the reading given in R). For the latter equivalence see LC 744b.

124 Tib. *dam-bcas-pa*, Skt. *pratijñā*. Reference to a vow is also explicit in R; AY and Dh state only that such a bodhisattva will not turn away from Supreme Perfect Enlightenment. Cf. above, §4A.

125 Only in AY. This apparent interpolation recapitulates material that appeared above (§2D) in the same context—that is, following a remark about not abandoning or falling away from one's vow to attain Buddhahood.

{Chapter 2: Precepts}[126]

[§7. THE ELEVEN PRECEPTS]

[7A] "And again, O Eminent Householder, the householder bodhisattva upholds all[127] the precepts, as follows. Having accepted the five precepts,[128]

(1) "He should abstain from[129] the taking of life. Relinquishing the sword and the staff, having a sense of shame and being compassionate, being by nature one who does not do harm[130] to any living things, and even-minded toward all beings, he should constantly dwell in loving-kindness.[131]

(2) "He should abstain from taking what is not given.[132] Contented with his own wealth, not longing for the wealth of others, being devoid of passion and covetousness,[133] and not desiring the property of others,[134] he should not take

---

[126] Dh only.

[127] Tib only.

[128] Here our text actually goes on to discuss not five but eleven precepts, a total resulting from the merger of the list of five *śikṣāpada*s with that of the ten *kuśala-karmapatha*s. (Since all of the former except the fifth—the prohibition against alcohol—are found in the latter list, the resulting total is eleven.) For a discussion of this distinctive list (which occurs in a number of other sources besides the *Ugra*) see Chapter 5, pp. 107-111 and Nattier 2002.

[129] Where Tib reads "should abstain from" (*spang-bar bya*) each of the first five offenses, AY and Dh state that the bodhisattva should "not delight in" them (AY *pu hao* 不好, Dh *pu yao* 不樂). R also begins with a comparable expression (*yao pu* 樂不, "delights in not doing"), but then shifts to other expressions meaning "avoids, abstains from." The translation "not delight in" seems to be a literalistic interpretation of an underlying *vi√ram* "abstain from," interpreted etymologically as consisting of "separate from" (*vi-*) + "rejoice, delight in" (*√ram*). In the citations preserved in the *Śikṣāsamuccaya* the Sanskrit term is *prativirata* (see below, nn. 137 and 148).

[130] Not in AY or Dh.

[131] Not in AY.

[132] The Chinese versions are more direct: R reads "He should not steal," AY and Dh "He should not steal other people's goods."

[133] Not in AY; Dh substitutes "rejecting flattery" (presumably as a means of talking people out of their belongings).

[134] Not in AY.

even a blade of grass or a leaf[135] that has not been given to him.[136]

(3)[137] "He should abstain from wrong conduct with regard to desire. Being satisfied with his own wive(s)[138] and without desire for the wive(s) of others, looking with a dispassionate eye, he should think to himself 'Agitation[139] and desires[140] are indeed painful,' and make efforts to establish a dispassionate state of mind. And when the notion of desire arises toward his own wife, because it is due to the influence of the defilements,[141] at that time he should look upon his own wife

---

135 Dh adds "or a grain of rice."

136 Not in AY.

137 The following lines are cited in the *Śikṣ.*78.7-13:

> *tena kāmamithyācārāt prativiratena bhavitavyaṁ svadāra-saṁtuṣṭena paradārānabhi-lāṣiṇāraktanetraprekṣiṇā nirviṇa-manasā | ekāntaduṣkhāḥ kāmā ityabhīkṣṇaṁ manasikāra-prayuktena | yadāpyasya svadāreṣu kāmavitarka utpadyeta | tadāpi tena svadāreṣv-aśubhānudarśinā uttrastamanasā | kleśavaśatayā kāmāḥ pratisevitavyāḥ | na tv adhyavasāna vinibaddhena nityamanityānātmāśucisaṁjñinā | evaṁ cānena smṛtirūpa-sthāpyā | tathāhaṁ kāriṣyāmi yathā saṁkalpair api kāmān na paribhokṣye | kaḥ punar vādo dvīndriyasamāpattyā vānaṅgavijñaptyā veti ||*

138 Though the Chinese and Tibetan translations give no indication of number, in the Sanskrit citation the bodhisattva's wives are explicitly referred to in the plural (see the previous note). The fact that the *Ugra* has nothing whatsoever to say about the relations between the bodhisattva and her husband reinforces the contention we have made in the introduction that this text is addressed primarily (if not exclusively) to the male aspirant for Buddhahood (see Harrison 1987, p. 75).

139 Tib. *yid byung-ba'i yid*, Skt. *udvigna-manas*, an epithet of the god Kāma.

140 Or "pleasures" (Tib. *'dod-pa-dag*, Skt. **kāmāni*). The Tibetan is explicitly plural.

141 Tib. *nyon-mongs-pa*, Skt. *kleśa*. As Edgerton points out (BHSD 198a) the term *kleśa* is very common in Buddhist literature, but its meaning is vague. The *Dharmasaṁgraha* (§67) gives a list of six *kleśas* (*rāga*, *pratigha*, *māna*, *avidyā*, *kudṛṣṭi*, and *vicikitsā*), while in the *Abhidharmakośa* (V, §1c-d) the same six items are given, but under the name *anuśaya* (which is, according to La Vallée Poussin, a synonym of *kleśa* for the Sarvāstivādins).

as impure[142] and attend to his desire with a fearful mind. Conceiving of her as not the sort of being who should be grasped because of passion—that is, as characterized by impermanence, suffering, absence of self, and impurity[143]—he should think to himself 'I should not act on my desires even by inclining my mind toward them; how much less should I enter into the actual conjunction of the two sexes or into erotic love?[144] No, I should not do so.'

(4) "He should abstain from false speech. Speaking truly and correctly, acting in accordance with his words,[145] not deceiving [others], and being thoughtful, mindful, and aware, he should speak in accordance with what he sees and hears.[146] As one who protects the Dharma, he should not say anything he knows to be false, even to save his own life.[147]

(5)[148] "He should abstain from intoxicating drinks such as liquor or alcohol.[149] He does not get drunk, or crazy,

---

[142] Tib. *mi-sdug-pa*, Skt. *aśubha* (*Mvy.* 1155). Note that this is the same word that is used for for the traditional practice of meditation on a corpse (*aśubha-bhāvanā*) as a means of countering sensual desire.

[143] Tib only. These are the four marks that were to be inverted in later Mahāyāna literature (most notably in the Mahāyāna *Mahāparinirvāṇa-sūtra*) in the famous formulation of "permanence, bliss, [true] self, and purity" (*nityatā, sukha, ātman, śuddhi*) as epithets of *nirvāṇa* or the Buddha-nature. The *Ugra* falls quite clearly within the traditionalist camp here.

[144] Tib. *yan-lag ma-yin-pa = anaṅga* "limbless, bodiless," an epithet of Kāma, which also occurs in the titles of literary works as a synonym for "love, erotics" (MW 24b). The same passage is repeated in §31B below, and is also cited (perhaps drawing on the *Ugra* itself) in *Pratyutpanna* §16M. The phrase in small type occurs only in the Tibetan.

[145] Not in AY.

[146] Or "has seen and heard." There is no indication of tense in the Tibetan text.

[147] Literally, "even for the sake of body (*kāya*) and life (*jīva*)."

[148] The following lines are cited in *Śikṣ*. 120.3-5:

> *tena surā-maireya-madyapramādasthānāt prativiratena bhavitavyam amattena-anunmattena-acapalena-acañcalena-asaṃbhrāntena-amukhareṇa-anunnaḍena-anuddhatenopasthiti smṛti-saṃprajanyena*

[149] Tib. *'bru'i chang* (Skt. *surā* "liquor, wine") and *sbyar-ba'i chang* (Skt. *maireya*, "a kind of alcoholic drink"). Neither is included in the list of types of *chang* in Jä. 154a; presumably both were coined as translation terms.

or befuddled, or foolish in his speech, or agitated, or wild, or giddy,[150] but remains mindful and maintains his consciousness. Then, when the spirit[151] of giving away all his property enters [into him] and he thinks to himself, 'I should give food to those who desire food, and drink to those who desire drink,'[152] he even gives alcohol to others.[153] And he does so reflecting in this way:[154] 'Now is the time for the perfection of giving. The time has come for giving to others whatever they may desire. And so I should act in this way: having given alcohol in this way to various people, I should induce mindfulness and awareness in those who are steady in conduct.' And why is this? To fulfill all their desires is to carry out in full the bodhisattva's perfection of giving. And so, O Eminent Householder, even if the householder bodhisattva gives alcohol to others, he will not be found at fault by the Tathāgatas.[155]

"O Eminent Householder, that householder bodhisattva should transform the roots-of-goodness which result from his upholding of the five precepts[156] into Supreme Perfect Enlightenment. And he should carefully maintain those five precepts.

[7B] (6) "And in addition, he should not slander others, but should reconcile those who are at odds.[157]

---

150 Not in AY or Dh.

151 Literally, "mind" (Tib. *blo*, Skt. **mati*).

152 AY adds "vehicles" and "clothing" to the list.

153 On the issue of whether it is acceptable for a bodhisattva to give alcohol to others cf. *Pratyutpanna-buddha-saṁmukha-avasthita-samādhi-sūtra*, §11B, which argues—*contra* our text—that it is not.

154 The following lines are cited in *Śikṣ*. 271.9-11:

dāna-pāramitā-kālo 'yaṃ yasya yenārthas tasya
tat pradāna-kālaḥ | api tu tathāhaṃ kāriṣyāmi |
madyapebhya eva madya-pānaṃ dāsyāmi | tāṃs
tān smṛtisaṃprajanye samādāpayiṣyāmi

155 Not in AY; Dh reads "with respect to the Dharma."

156 Not in AY; Dh omits only the number "five."

157 Note that in all versions of the sūtra the sixth and seventh precepts are reversed (vs.the standard list given in *Mvy*. nos. 1685-1698).

(7) "Nor should he speak harsh words; rather, he should speak the truth[158] with smooth speech and gentle words.

(8) "He should not indulge in idle chatter, but rather say what is timely, what is true,[159] what is meaningful,[160] what is associated with the Dharma, what is appropriate, and what is useful for disciplining.[161] He should answer questions well, and act in accordance with what he has said.[162]

(9) "He should not have covetous thoughts, but should think of the advantage and welfare of all beings.[163]

(10) "He should not have thoughts of malice, but should constantly gird himself with the armor of the power of endurance.[164]

(11) "He should see things as they truly are,[165] and be devoid of all warped and wrong views. Adhering to the thought of the Buddha as his god, he should not embrace other gods.[166]

{Chapter 3: The Physician}[167]

[§8. THE BODHISATTVA IN SOCIETY]

[8A] "Moreover, O Eminent Householder, in whatever village, town, city, kingdom,[168] or capital[169] the bodhisattva may dwell, there

---

158 Not in AY.

159 Not in AY.

160 R "what is beneficial to others." Presumably this difference is the result of divergent interpretations of an underlying **artha*, "benefit, objective, meaning."

161 Not in AY or Dh.

162 Not in AY.

163 Dh appears to have skipped this item.

164 Tib. *bzod-pa'i stobs*, Skt. *kṣānti-bala*.

165 All three Chinese versions read "he should have right views."

166 AY "He should only bow to the Buddhas, the Blessed Ones, and not to other gods and spirits." Cf. *Aṣṭa* (Vaidya 1960, 161.14-15), where it is stated that the irreversible bodhisattva does not pay homage to, make offerings to, or take refuge with other gods. There, as here, the term is *anyadeva* (rather idiosyncratically translated by Conze [1973, p. 200] as "strange Gods"); cf. BHSD 20a, s.v. *ananyadeva*. The same injunction occurs in *Pratyutpanna* §§11B, 12B, and 12C(2). Dh offers a completely different reading, whose source is unclear: "What he gives is not inconsistent."

167 Dh only.

168 The Tibetan term *ljongs* actually means "(large) valley, cultivated area,"

he should pronounce a Dharma-talk,[170] and those who have no faith he should induce to have faith. Those beings who are devoid of respect and who do not recognize father and mother, *śramaṇas* and *brāhmaṇas*,[171] who do not honor their superiors,[172] and who act without propriety and go beyond the bounds of custom—those he should induce to have respect for teachers and to practice the Dharma. Those beings who are ignorant he should cause to associate with those who are knowledgeable.[173] The greedy he should induce to renunciation; those who are weak in morality to the observance of morality; those who are hostile he should cause to be patient and good-natured; those who are lazy, to make efforts to exert themselves; those who are confused to mindfulness and awareness; and those who are weak in insight, to insight.[174] Upon the poor, one should bestow wealth;[175] to the sick one should give medicine. One should be a protector to those who have no protector, a refuge for those who are without a refuge, an asylum for those who have no asylum.[176] In whatever way is

---

and thus by extension "district, region, realm." The word is used here, however, to translate Skt. *rāṣṭra* "kingdom, dominion, realm" (as attested by the form of this standard list of locations in the *Śikṣāsamuccaya* 199.14). Elsewhere, however, *ljongs* is used to translate Skt. *janapada* (e.g., *Mvy.* no. 5508), which means simply "country" with no implications as to its political structure.

169 Tib. *ljongs-kyi phyogs*, an expression not found in the *Mahāvyutpatti* but serving here as a translation of Skt. *rājadhānī* (more commonly translated into Tibetan as *rgyal-po'i pho-brang*; see *Mvy.* no. 5510).

170 Not in AY or Dh; rather than suggesting that a lay bodhisattva should preach the Dharma, these versions exhort him to support and protect it.

171 The reference to *śramaṇas* and *brāhmaṇas* occurs only in R and Tib.

172 Tib. *rigs-kyi gtso-bo*, literally, "clan-leader," but corresponding Sanskrit terms include *kulajyeṣṭha*, *pramukha*, *sreṣṭha*, etc. (see Rerikh 7.177b). Dh and R both interpret this as a reference to their "seniors" (i.e., their elders). The same list given here occurs in the *Dīghanikāya* (III.145; cf. Walshe 1987, p. 442); there the Pāli term is *kulajeṭṭha* "clan-head," which would support a reconstruction of an underlying Sanskrit *kulajyeṣṭha* here. The passage as a whole is not included in AY.

173 Not in AY.

174 Note that what we have here is an aberrant list of the *pāramitās*, in which *dāna* is replaced by *tyāga* "renunciation," *sauratya* "good-natured" added following *kṣānti*, and *dhyāna* replaced by *smṛti* "mindfulness" and *saṃprajāna* "attentiveness."

175 This sentence is omitted (presumably inadvertently) in Dh.

176 Dh, who has "he rescues (*chiu* 救) those who are without rescue," may have read an underlying **parāyaṇa* "resort, asylum" (the term that would be expected here) as **tārāyaṇa* "cause of salvation."

appropriate for all those kingdoms and capitals, in that way he should protect [them] by means of the Dharma, so that not even one being will fall to a bad rebirth.[177]

[8B] "O Eminent Householder, if—despite a bodhisattva's attempts to establish beings in good qualities by instructing them one, or two, or three, or up to seven[178] times—they do not[179] abide in any suitable qualities whatsoever, O Eminent Householder, at that time that householder bodhisattva should bring forth great compassion toward them.[180] And girding himself with the firm armor of Omniscience, he should pronounce the following words: 'Until I succeed in bringing to full maturity[181] those wild and unruly beings, I will not attain Supreme Perfect Enlightenment.'

[8C] " 'And why? It is for their sake that I have put on the armor, not for the sake of beings who are upright, unwavering, free from illusion, and endowed with good conduct, nor have I put on the armor for the sake of those who are already endowed with good qualities.[182] {It is only because I want the former ones to hear the Dharma and be

---

177 Not in AY. Tib. *log-par ltung-ba*, Skt. *vinipātayati* (BHSD 489b); Conze (*MDPPL*, p. 356) suggests the translation "experience great distress." In any event, the ruin or distress in question is generally understood as that of falling to one of the unfortunate rebirths (*durgati*), viz. the animal realm, the preta realm, and the hells; see *Mvy.* no. 4748, where the sole listing of *log-par ltung-ba* is included in the section dealing with the *durgatis*. The same usage is found in Pāli; see PTSD 624b.

178 AY and Dh read "one hundred." Presumably this discrepancy is the result of a confusion between *śata* "hundred" and *sapta* "seven," which would have been virtually identical (*sata* vs. *satta*) in some Prakrits.

179 The negative is omitted in AY and Dh.

180 Note that once again the term "compassion" (*karuṇā*) is being reserved for those who are viewed as defective in some way.

181 The Chinese versions offer varying nuances: AY has the bodhisattva say that he will not attain Buddhahood "until [those beings] become accomplished" (*te ch'eng-chiu* 得成就) while R reads "for as long as I haven't disciplined [them]" (*t'iao* 調), and Dh has the bodhisattva say that he will first save them (*tu-t'o* 度脱) and then attain Buddhahood himself.

182 The term is *yon-tan* (Skt. *guṇa*), which is frequently used in Buddhist texts to refer not just to "qualities" in general, but to positive attributes. The epithets given in this sentence vary slightly in the Chinese translations, but all versions agree that it is the underachievers to whom the bodhisattva should devote his attention.

transformed that I do this, making a vow by means of this vow.}[183] So I should by all means see to it that my efforts are not in vain, so that as soon as beings see me they will attain happiness and faith. This should I accomplish, and thus should I apply my efforts.' Thus he should think.[184]

[8D] "O Eminent Householder, in whatever village, town, city, kingdom, or capital a bodhisattva may dwell, if he does not admonish [those who live there] and cause them to be mindful,[185] when those beings fall into any of the evil rebirths as a result, that bodhisattva will be blamed by the Tathāgatas.[186] O Eminent Householder, it is like this: for example, if in a certain village, town, city, kingdom, or capital there lives a skillful doctor, but he is unable to cure the poison of even a single being,[187] then when that being dies the doctor will be blamed by many people. O Eminent Householder, in the same way, if there is a bodhisattva living in a village, town, city, kingdom, or capital, if he fails to admonish even a single being and does not cause him to be mindful, if he is born into any evil rebirth whatsoever, that bodhisattva will be blamed by the Tathāgatas.[188] O Eminent Householder, this being the case, a bodhisattva living in a village, town, city, kingdom, or capital should by all means gird himself with the armor of this thought: 'I should see to it that not a single being falls into a bad rebirth.[189] This I should accomplish, and thus should I apply my efforts.'[190]

---

[183] AY only. The word "vow" is a translation of the term *saṁnāha*, translated in this section and elsewhere as "armor" in other versions.

[184] Tib only.

[185] Tib only.

[186] So according to Dh, R, and Tib; AY states only that "it will be the bodhisattva's fault." Cf. above, §7A(5), where the active role of the Tathāgata(s) also appears only in later versions of the text.

[187] The literal meaning of the Tibetan is unambiguous, but the sense is less than clear. AY reads "[if even a single being] dies before his time," Dh "dies of unnatural causes," and R "falls ill and dies." No other version of the sūtra contains any reference to poison.

[188] Here all versions are unanimous in saying that the Buddha(s) will hold that bodhisattva to be at fault.

[189] This sentence (missing from Dh and R due to an inadvertent omission in their common Indian ancestory?) is found only in AY and Tib.

[190] Tib only.

{Chapter 4: The Filthy Home}[191]

[§9. THE FAULTS OF THE HOUSEHOLD LIFE]

[9A] "Moreover, O Eminent Householder, the householder bodhisattva should be knowledgeable about the faults[192] of living at home. He should train himself to think as follows:[193] '"Home" is something that destroys the roots-of-goodness, crushes their sprouts, and causes their stems to fall.[194] Therefore it is called "home." "Living at home" is the place of all the corruptions. It is the place of mental fabrication due to the roots of evil. It is the place of foolish ordinary people, the undisciplined, and the unguarded. It is the place of those who do what is not virtuous. It is the place where evil people gather. Therefore it is called "living." "Living at home" is declared to be the place of all painful things. It is the place where the roots of goodness that one has previously cultivated are impaired. Therefore it is called "living at home."[195]

[9B] "'As to what is called "home," living there one acts improperly with respect to one's obligations. Living there, one becomes disrespectful toward father and mother, *śramaṇas* and *brāhmaṇas*.[196] Therefore it is called "home." As to what is called "home," because one takes pleasure in the clinging vine of[197] desire,[198] sorrow and lamentation and suffering and unhappiness will arise. Therefore it is called "home."

---

191 Dh only.

192 AY reads *e* 惡 "evils, bad [points]" while Dh has *hui* 穢 "vileness, filthiness." R (or its underlying Indian source) simply elides the term altogether.

193 Not in AY.

194 Tib only.

195 There is considerable variety among the various versions of this section, but all offer various critiques of living at home. In the underlying Indic text there was surely a series of plays on the word *gṛha* "home" and *āvāsa* "dwelling" here, but its exact wording is less than transparent in any of the translated versions.

196 AY and Dh add additional items to this list, including "respectworthy elders and sages" in AY and "respectworthy elders and Blessed Ones" as well as "Taoists" (sic! *tao-shih* 道士) in Dh.

197 Tib only.

198 P and D read *srid-pa* (which would correspond to Skt. *bhava*) "existence," clearly an internal Tibetan divergence from the nearly identical-looking *sred-pa* (Skt. *tṛṣṇā*) "craving, thirst, desire" found in S and N. Sakurabe (p. 251), following P alone (and adding some explanatory words which have no counterpart in the Tibetan), reads "because one loves the creeping vine of illusory existence" (*mayoi no sonzai no tsurukusa*).

As to what is called "home," the activities[199] of killing, binding, striking, threatening, injuring, insulting, reviling, maligning, and harmful speech come together there. Therefore it is called "home." As to what is called "home," one will not plant the roots-of-goodness that have not yet been produced, and the roots-of-goodness that have already been produced will be destroyed. One will be criticized by those who are wise,[200] by the Buddhas, and by the Buddha's disciples. Living there, one will be reborn in the lower rebirths.[201] Living there, one will become devoid of a refuge due to[202] desire. One will become devoid of a refuge due to[203] hatred, fear, and delusion. Therefore it is called "home." Here one does not guard the *śīla-skandha*, casts aside the *samādhi-skandha*, does not enter into the *prajñā-skandha*, does not obtain the *vimukti-skandha*, and does not generate the *vimukti-jñāna-darśana-skandha*.[204]

[9C] " 'Living [at home] one desires to hold onto one's parents, children, wife, male and female slaves, workers, wage-earners, friends, companions, kinsfolk, relatives, and attendants.[205] Living at home is like the ocean which can never be filled, no matter how many streams enter it.[206] Living at home is like a fire that can never consume enough wood to be satisfied. Living at home is to have unsteady thoughts, as changeable as the wind. Living at home is destruction, like the destruction of a city made of sand.[207] Living at home is contaminated,

---

199 Literally "roads" or "paths" (Tib. *lam*, Skt. *patha*). The resulting image of the home as a "crossroads" of all pathways of evil action (*akuśalakarma-patha*) cannot be conveyed directly in English.

200 Tib. *mkhas-pa*, Skt. *paṇḍita*.

201 Not in AY.

202 Not in AY.

203 Not in AY.

204 This set of five "pure *skandhas*" consists of a core of three (*śīla*, *samādhi*, and *prajñā*, comprising the three segments of the eightfold path) plus two additional components (*vimukti* and *vimukti-jñāna-darśana*), the latter two added in all probability in imitation of the format of the earlier set of five *skandhas* in the sense of the components of the human being. For the three and five "pure *skandhas*" (as well as an intermediate set of four) see PTSD 233a, *Mvy.* nos. 103-108, and *Abhidharmakośa*, I, §27. Cf. below, §17A.

205 AY gives a shorter list of dependents and associates, but adds "brothers and sisters"; Dh also adds "brothers" (only).

206 I have given a very free translation here and in the following sentences in the interests of readability. The Tibetan text actually reads "it is difficult to fill, like stream[s] into the ocean." The terseness of these expressions in the original text suggests that they would have been too well known to the intended audience to need explanation.

207 Tib only.

like good food that has been tainted by poison. Living at home there is constant suffering, because of being at odds [with those one lives with], like an enemy.

[9D] " 'Living at home causes obstacles to the accomplishment of the noble qualities.[208] Living at home there is mutually caused fighting. Living at home there is constant discord due to animosity toward one another. Living at home there is much harm due to being involved in both good and bad deeds. Living at home one constantly exerts oneself, because no matter what one does, it is never enough. Living at home is impermanent, because what one has collected over a long time consists of perishable things.[209] Living at home is suffering, because of searching for things and [then] having to protect them.[210] Living at home is constant fear, because of being unfriendly to one another, like an enemy. Living at home is heedlessness, because of being in the grip of error. Living at home one fashions things according to one's own way of thinking, but they are devoid of essential reality, like the makeup of a performer. Living at home people quickly become alienated from one another, and will ultimately go to destruction.[211]

[9E] " 'Living at home is like looking at an illusion, because since people come together adventitiously, they are always devoid of essential reality. Living at home is like a dream, because all one's possessions will finally go to destruction. Living at home is like a drop of dew, because it quickly dissipates. Living at home is like a drop of honey, because the desirable flavor only goes a little way.[212] Living at home is like a net of thorns, because one is tormented by forms, sounds, smells, tastes, touch-objects, and mind-objects. Living at home is like a stinging insect, because one does not tire of thinking about unvirtuous things.

[9F] " 'Living at home life is destroyed, because of deceiving one another.[213] Living at home there is constant fighting, because of one's mind being troubled. Living at home one's property is held in

---

[208] Tib. *'phags-pa'i chos*, Skt. *ārya-dharma*. Note that AY and Dh have interpreted the word *dharma* here as "scriptures" and "teaching," respectively.

[209] The term used here is *dharma*, but it is not necessary to interpret this in a technical abhidharmic sense. More commonly—when not used in the sense of "Buddhist teachings"—the word simply means a "thing" or "item," as here.

[210] Not in AY or Dh.

[211] Not in AY. Substantial portions of this paragraph are also missing from Dh.

[212] For this sentence Dh substitutes "Living at home is like [being] a father and mother, for pleasure is minimal and grief is abundant."

[213] Not in Dh.

common,[214] because it is taken over by kings and robbers, fire and water, and fate.[215] Living at home offers little enjoyment, because one has many troubles.' O Eminent Householder, in that way should the householder bodhisattva who lives at home be knowledgeable about the faults of living at home.

{Chapter 5: Giving}[216]

[§10. THE BENEFITS OF GIVING]

[10A] "Moreover, O Eminent Householder, by living at home, the householder bodhisattva should accomplish a great deal of giving, discipline, self-restraint, and gentleness of character.[217] He should reflect as follows: 'What I give away is mine; what I keep at home is not mine. What I give away has substance; what I keep at home has no substance. What I give away will bring pleasure at another [i.e., future][218] time; what I keep at home will [only] bring pleasure right now.[219] What I give away does not need to be protected; what I keep at home must be protected. [My] desire for what I give away will

---

214 That is, it is not "one's own."

215 Not in AY or Dh.

216 Dh only.

217 Not in AY or Dh. Here we have a clearcut example of an interpolation in the text: AY has only *dāna*, while Dh has expanded that term to the full list of the six *pāramitās*. In the text that served as the basis for Tib, on the other hand, *dāna* has been used as the basis for expansion into a different list beginning with the same word, viz. *dāna*, *dama*, *saṁyama*, and *sauratya* (an expanded version of which appears in §12C below). R appears to reflect the latter list as well, though in a somewhat different sequence, while the citation preserved in *Dbhv.* mentions only *dāna* and *śīla*. For a discussion of various categories of interpolations in Buddhist texts and the use of "trigger words" (such as the word *dāna* in the present case) as their basis see the Chapter 2, pp. 53-55.

218 Confirmed by Dh and R. Here the sequence (and some of the content) of the various versions begins to diverge, though the overall purport is the same.

219 The following lines are cited in *Śikṣ.* 19.1-3:

> *yad dattaṁ tan na bhūyo rakṣitavyaṁ | yad gṛhe tad rakṣitavyaṁ | yad dattaṁ tat tṛṣṇākṣayāya | yad gṛhe tat tṛṣṇāvarddhanaṁ | yad dattaṁ tad aparigrahaṁ yad gṛhe tat saparigrahaṁ | yad dattaṁ tad abhayaṁ yad gṛhe tat sabhayam | yad dattaṁ tad bodhimārgopastambhāya | yad gṛhe tan māropastambhāya |*

[eventually] be exhausted; [my] desire for what I keep at home increases. What I give away I do not think of as "mine"; what I keep at home I think of as "mine." What I give away is no longer an object of grasping; what I keep at home is an object of grasping. What I give away is not a source of fear; what I keep at home causes fear. What I give away supports the path to *bodhi*; what I keep at home supports the party of Māra.

[10B][220] " 'What I give away knows no exhaustion; what I keep at home is exhausted. What I give away is pleasurable; what I keep at home is painful, because it must be protected. What I give away leads to the abandoning of the corruptions; what I keep at home will cause the corruptions to increase. What I give away will yield great enjoyment; what I keep at home will not yield great enjoyment.[221] Giving things away is the deed of a good man; keeping things at home is the deed of a lowly man. What I give away is praised by all the Buddhas; what I keep at home is praised by foolish people.' Thus he should reflect. O Eminent Householder, in that way the bodhisattva should 'extract the substance' [from the insubstantial].[222]

[§11. THOUGHTS WHEN ENCOUNTERING BEGGARS]

[11A] "Moreover, O Eminent Householder, when the householder bodhisattva sees a beggar,[223] he should bring forth three

---

[220] The following lines are cited in *Śikṣ.* 19.3-7:

> *yad dattaṁ tad akṣayam* I *yad gṛhe tat kṣayi* I *yad dattaṁ tataḥ sukham yad gṛhe tadārabhya duṣkhaṁ* I *yad dattaṁ tat kleśotsargāya* I *yad gṛhe tat kleśavarddhanam* I *yad dattaṁ tan mahābhogatāyai* I *yad gṛhe na tan mahābhogatāyai* I *yad dattaṁ tat satpuruṣakarma* I *yad gṛhe tat kāpuruṣkarma* I {*yad dattaṁ tat satpuruṣacitta-grahaṇāya* I *yad gṛhe tat kāpuruṣacittagrahaṇāya* I} *yad dattaṁ tat sarvabuddha-praśastaṁ* I *yad gṛhe tad bālajanapraśastam* II

The portion of the text enclosed in braces has no equivalent in the Tibetan.

[221] The Tibetan and Sanskrit terms (*longs-spyod* and *bhoga*, respectively) could also be interpreted as "wealth" (as does AY, where this sentence occurs earlier at 17c28-29).

[222] Cf. above, §6B, n. 120. In the present instance the object from which the substance is to be extracted is material wealth, the third of the three items in the traditional list.

[223] Note that the references to giving in this section are not to Buddhist monks or other religious mendicants but to ordinary beggars (Tib. *slong-ba*, Skt. *yācanaka*; cf. below, §15B, for which a Sanskrit citation is preserved in the *Śikṣāsamuccaya*), a fact that has considerable implications for the institutional

thoughts. And what are the three? (1) the thought of [the beggar] as his *kalyāṇamitra*; (2) the thought that he will become wealthy in his next life; and (3) the thought that [giving to the beggar] supports the path to *bodhi*.[224] O Eminent Householder, when the householder bodhisattva sees a beggar, he should bring forth those three thoughts.

[11B] "Moreover, O Eminent Householder, when the householder bodhisattva sees a beggar, he should bring forth three thoughts. And what are the three? (1) the thought of suppressing one's greed; (2) the thought of giving everything away; and (3) the thought of the vision of Omniscience.[225] O Eminent Householder, when the householder bodhisattva sees a beggar, he should bring forth those three thoughts.[226]

[11C] "Moreover, O Eminent Householder, when the householder bodhisattva sees a beggar,[227] he should bring forth three thoughts. And what are the three? (1) the thought of what is to be done according to the word of the Buddha; (2) the thought of restraining Māra; and (3) the thought of not[228] expecting any reward. O Eminent Householder, when the householder bodhisattva sees a beggar, he should bring forth those three thoughts.[229]

[11D] "Moreover, O Eminent Householder, when the householder bodhisattva sees a beggar, he should bring forth three thoughts. And what are the three? (1) the thought of the beggar as his attendant; (2) the thought of not abandoning the means of attraction;[230] and (3) the thought that what is unreal arises from grasping. O Eminent

---

and economic impact of these prescriptions. Here and throughout this section, AY refers simply to "a person who comes to ask for things.

224 Although S is the sole witness for the reading *nye-bar rton-pa*—the other Tibetan versions have *nye-bar ston-pa*, which would correspond to Skt. *upa√diś*—I have chosen this reading because it is supported by all three Chinese versions (explicitly by AY and R, implicitly by Dh). Sakurabe, following P alone, reads "the thought that this person [i.e., the beggar] is a person who will teach him the path to awakening" (p. 254). Cf. also §10A above, where the same phrase occurs verbatim, in this case with *nye-bar rton-pa* in all the Tibetan versions but Derge (which again has *ston*). The confusion between *rton* and *ston* is extremely common in Kanjur texts.

225 Tib. *thams-cad mkhyen-pa'i ye-shes-la lta-ba*, Skt. **sarvajña-jñāna-darśana*. Dh has "the concept of not abandoning Omniscience."

226 The whole of §11B has no parallel in AY or R. In addition, Dh omits the second occurrence of the phrase "O Eminent Householder, when the householder bodhisattva sees a beggar."

227 Tib only.

228 R (or his Indic source) has dropped the negative here.

229 Not in AY or R; Dh has simply "These are the three things."

230 Skt. *saṃgrahavastu*. These items (amusingly translated by Har Dayal as "the four requisites of propaganda," by La Vallée Poussin as "moyens de

Householder, when the householder bodhisattva sees a beggar, he should bring forth those three thoughts.[231]

[11E] "Moreover, O Eminent Householder, when the householder bodhisattva sees a beggar, he should bring forth three thoughts. And what are the three? (1) the thought of being separated from greed; (2) the thought of cultivating loving-kindness;[232] and (3) the thought of not entering into delusion. O Eminent Householder, when the householder bodhisattva sees a beggar, he should bring forth those three thoughts.[233]

[11F] "And why is this? O Eminent Householder, in this way, whenever the householder bodhisattva sees a beggar, [his] greed, hatred, and delusion will grow weaker. O Eminent Householder,[234] if one asks 'How do greed, hatred, and delusion grow weaker when the householder bodhisattva sees a beggar?',[235] [it works as follows]: When one thinks of his goods with equanimity and gives them up, his greed becomes weaker. When one calls to mind loving-kindness toward beggars,[236] his hatred grows weaker. And when one who has given things transforms [the resulting merit] into Supreme Perfect Enlightenment, his delusion grows weaker. O Eminent Householder, in that way, whenever the householder bodhisattva sees a beggar, his greed, hatred, and delusion will grow weaker.[237]

---

séduction," and by H. Kern as "articles of sociability"; for these and other such attempts see Dayal 1932, pp. 251-252) are: (1) giving (*dāna*), (2) pleasant speech (*priyavāditā* and variants), (3) promoting the interests of others (*arthacaryā*, var. *arthakriyā*), and (4) sharing the concerns of others (*samanārthatā*). For a discussion of these four items and variations in their interpretation in traditional texts see Dayal, *op. cit.*, pp. 251-259. These items are not peculiar to the Mahāyāna; see for example the section on "Fours" in the *Aṅguttara-nikāya*, ii.32 (sutta #32). I am grateful to Thanissaro Bhikkhu for calling my attention to this reference.

231 The whole of §11D has no parallel in AY.

232 Here "loving-kindness" (Tib. *byams-pa*, Skt. *maitrī*) is presented as an antidote to hatred or animosity (Skt. *dveṣa*), the second of the three poisons; in fact, Dh and R both read simply "getting rid of hatred," with no mention of loving-kindness. This list consists, in other words, of thoughts concerned with countering or providing antidotes for these three basic faults of unenlightened existence.

233 The whole of §11E has no parallel in AY.

234 Not in AY.

235 Not in AY.

236 Once again Dh does not mention loving-kindness, but simply refers to "not having angry thoughts" toward the beggar.

237 Not in AY or Dh.

[11G] "Moreover, O Eminent Householder, when the householder bodhisattva sees a beggar, he will fulfill the cultivation of the six perfections.

(1) "O Eminent Householder, if as soon as the householder bodhisattva is asked for any object whatsoever, his mind no longer grasps at that object, in that way his cultivation of the perfection of giving will be fulfilled.

(2) "If he gives while relying upon the spirit of enlightenment,[238] in that way his cultivation of the perfection of morality will be fulfilled.

(3) "If he gives while bringing to mind loving-kindness toward those beggars[239] and not producing anger or hostility toward them, in that way his cultivation of the perfection of endurance[240] will be fulfilled.

(4) "If he is not depressed due to a wavering mind that thinks 'If I give this away, what will become of me?'[241] in that way his perfection of exertion will be fulfilled.

(5) If one gives to a beggar and, after having given, is free

---

[238] Dh "his heart not grieving [at] the Buddha-Way"!

[239] Tib only.

[240] The third perfection (Skt. *kṣānti*) is most commonly translated into English as "patience," but in my view this is far too mild a word to convey the sense of the term in Sanskrit Buddhist sources. Nor do the renditions of Conze ("patient acceptance," *MDPPL*, p. 159) or Edgerton ("intellectual receptivity," BHSD 199b) capture the necessary range of meanings. The word is used in early bodhisattva sūtras in two distinct contexts: on the one hand, to describe the optimal reaction of a bodhisattva when he is insulted, injured, or otherwise impinged upon by others (a context in which the emphasis is generally upon the bodhisattva's ability to avoid becoming angry with those who are his tormentors); and on the other, to describe the bodhisattva's reaction to certain cognitive propositions, e.g., the fact that all things are unoriginated (*anutpattikadharmakṣānti*). In both cases the optimal response is much more than "patience," but requires the ability to endure torment without responding with anger (in the former case) or fear and disorientation (in the latter). For a different (but also quite plausible) interpretation of the term see the discussion of its use in the Gilgit manuscript of the *Vajracchedikā-prajñāpāramitā-sūtra* by Gregory Schopen, who contends that the basic meaning of the term in Buddhist sources is "unaffected (by)" and suggests that it be translated as "composure" (Schopen 1989, p. 139, n. 20).

[241] More literally, "if it has been given, what will [I] do?" Cf. R, which reads "If, at the time of giving, he does not arouse egotistical thoughts of scarcity" (11.474c25-26).

of sorrow and regret,[242] and moreover he gives [these things] up from the standpoint of the spirit of enlightenment[243] and is delighted and joyful, happy, and pleased,[244] in that way his cultivation of the perfection of meditation will be fulfilled.

(6) And if, when he has given, he does not imagine the dharmas [produced by his giving][245] and does not hope for their maturation, and just as the wise do not settle down in [their belief in] any dharmas, just so he does not settle down [in them], and so he transforms them into Supreme Perfect Enlightenment[246]—in that way his cultivation of the perfection of insight will be fulfilled.

"O Eminent Householder, in that way when the householder bodhisattva sees a beggar he will fulfill the cultivation of the six perfections."

---

242 Cf. *Śikṣ.* 147.20: *dattvā ca na vipratisāracittamutpādayitavyam.*

243 Tib only.

244 Not in AY.

245 Not in AY; Dh reads "he is not attached to any thing (*dharma*)," while R has "he does not obtain"—or "grasp at"? (*te* 得)—any *dharma*. Note the increasingly abhidharmic tone of this passage over time.

246 Not in AY or Dh.

Section two.[247]

[§12. DETACHMENT FROM PEOPLE AND THINGS]

[12A][248] "Moreover, O Eminent Householder, the householder bodhisattva who lives at home, by being free of attachment and aversion, should attain equanimity with respect to the eight worldly things.[249] If he succeeds in obtaining wealth, or a wife,[250] or children, or valuables, or produce,[251] he should not become proud or overjoyed. And if he fails to obtain all these things, he should not be downcast or distressed. Rather, he should reflect as follows: 'All conditioned things are illusory[252] and are marked by involvement in fabrication.[253] Thus my father and mother, children, wife, male and female slaves, hired hands, wage earners, friends, companions, kinsfolk, and relatives—all are the result of the ripening of actions.[254] Thus they are not "mine," and I am not "theirs."

---

[247] On the term *bam-po* "part, section, fascicle" see above, n. 2. Nothing corresponding to this division appears here in any extant Chinese version.

[248] The following lines are cited in *Śikṣ.* 180.1-6:

> *punar aparam gṛhapate gṛhiṇā bodhisattvenānunayaprati-ghāpagatena bhavitavyam aṣṭalokadharmānanuliptena | tena bhogalābhena vā bhāryāputralābhena vā dhanadhānya-vittalābhena vā nonnamitavyaṃ na praharṣitavyaṃ | sarvavipattiṣu cānena nāvanamitavyaṃ | na durmanasā bhavitavyaṃ evaṃ cānena pratyavekṣitavyaṃ | māyākṛtam sarvasaṃskṛtaṃ viṭhapanapratyupasthānalakṣaṇaṃ | karma-vipāka-nirvṛttā hy ete | yad idaṃ mātāpitṛputrabhāryādāsī-dāsakarmakarapauruṣeya-mitrāmātyajñāti-sālohitā | naite mamasvakāḥ | nāham eteṣāṃ iti ||*

[249] See above, §5B and n. 105.

[250] Not in AY.

[251] Tib. *'bru*, Skt. *phala* ("fruit") or *dhānya* ("grain"), a reference to the fruits of the harvest in general. The image here is clearly that of abundance within an agricultural economy; note the inclusion of the bodhisattva's children (and in the three later versions, his wife) in the midst of this list of possessions!

[252] Tib. *sgyu-ma byas-pa*, Skt. *māyākṛta*. This expression means not just illusory in a neutral sense, but actively deceptive (cf. PTSD 529b, s.v. *māyākata*); note that the related agent-noun *māyākāra* means "conjurer, magician" (BHSD 430a).

[253] Tib. *rnam-par bsgrubs-pas so-sor nye-bar gnas-pa'i mtshan-nyid-do*, Skt. **viṭhapana-pratyupasthānalakṣaṇaṃ* (cf. *Mvy.* nos. 185 and 7233). For an extended discussion of this phrase see BHSD 486b.

[254] Tib only. This entire sentence and the following one are missing (probably due to a copying error) in Dh.

[12B] " 'And why? Because my father, mother, and so on are not my protector,[255] refuge, resort, place of rest,[256] island, self, or what belongs to the self. If even my own perishable *skandhas*, sense fields, and sense organs and their objects are not "me" or "mine," how much less are my father, mother, and so on "me" or "mine," or I "theirs"? And why? Because I am subject to my actions and heir to my actions, I will inherit [the results of] whatever I have done, whether good deeds or bad. I will taste the fruit of every one of them and will experience the ripening of every one. And because these people are also subject to their actions and heir to their actions, they too will inherit [the results of] whatever they have done, whether good deeds or bad. They will experience the ripening of every one of them and will taste the fruit of every one.[257]

[12C] " 'It is not my business to accumulate unvirtuous deeds for their sake. All of them are a source of pleasure now, but they will not be a source of pleasure later on. Instead, I should devote myself to what is really mine: that is, to the virtues of giving, discipline, self-restraint, endurance, good character, exertion, vigilance,[258] and the accumulation and production of the factors of enlightenment.[259] That is what is actually mine. Wherever I may go, these qualities will go with me.' Thinking in this way, he does not accumulate offenses, even for the sake of his own life or for the sake of his wife and son.[260]

[§13. CULTIVATING AVERSION FOR ONE'S WIFE][261]

[13A] "O Eminent Householder, the householder bodhisattva who lives at home should bring forth three thoughts toward his own wife. And what are the three? The thought of her impermanence, the

---

255 This and the following items occur in a list of "refuges" in *Mvy.* (nos. 1740-1752).

256 Tib. *gnas*, literally just "place," but the term also serves as a translation of Skt. *layanam* "place of rest" (*Mvy.* no. 1747).

257 Not in AY or Dh.

258 For a parallel to some of the items in this list (Skt. *dāna*, *dama*, *saṁyama*, *kṣānti*, *sauratya*, *vīrya*, and *apramāda*) cf. above, §10A. AY offers a close match (apparently reflecting an underlying *dāna*, *dama*, *śama*, and *saṁyama*), while Dh has a quite different list (*dāna*, *śīla*, *prajñā*, and *vīrya*). Presumably both lists were generated by the same "trigger-word," i.e., *dāna*.

259 That is, the seven factors of mindfulness (*smṛti*), the investigation of things (*dharma-pravicaya*), exertion (*vīrya*), joy (*prīti*), serenity (*praśrabdhi*), meditative absorption (*samādhi*), and equanimity (*upekṣa*). For details see Dayal 1932, pp. 149-155.

260 R includes a parallel only to the first sentence of §12C.

261 This section clearly includes a number of late additions to the Indian text, as most of it (§§13J through 13GG) is missing from the two earliest translations (AY and Dh). As usual R offers the closest match to the Tibetan, though

thought of her unreliability, and the thought of her changeableness. O Eminent Householder, the householder bodhisattva who lives at home should bring forth those three thoughts toward his own wife.[262]

[13B] "O Eminent Householder,[263] the householder bodhisattva who lives at home should bring forth three thoughts toward his own wife. And what are the three? The thoughts that 'she is my companion in happiness and enjoyment, but not my companion in the next world'; that 'she is my companion in eating and drinking, but not my companion in experiencing the ripening of actions'; and that 'she is my companion in pleasure, but not my companion in suffering.' O Eminent Householder, the householder bodhisattva who lives at home should bring fortth those three thoughts toward his own wife.[264]

[13C] "O Eminent Householder, the householder bodhisattva who lives at home should bring forth three thoughts toward his own wife. And what are the three? The

---

even here not all that is found in the Tibetan text has a parallel. It is interesting to note that there are also occasional items in one or another Chinese version of the text that have no parallel in the Tibetan. The isolatedness of most of these examples (that is, they occur in only one of the three Chinese texts) suggests that they are the result of further interpolations taking place in individual manuscript copies of the text, and not that their absence from the Tibetan is evidence for a scribal omission. The content of §§13 and 14 is echoed in *Pratyutpanna*, §2H(109) and (110).

262 There are minor differences in the various Chinese versions; the mildest rendition is that of AY, which says that the householder should think of his wife's impermanence, the fact that she will not be with him for long, and of their eventual separation.

263 The following lines are cited in *Śikṣ.* 78.14-16:

> *bodhisatvena svabhāryāyā antike tisraḥ saṃjñā utpādayitavyāḥ | katamāstisraḥ | ratikrīḍāsahāyikaiṣā naiṣā paralokasahāyikā | annapānasahāyikaiṣā naiṣā karmavipākaanubhavanasahāyikā | sukhasahāyikaiṣā naiṣā duṣkha*[sic]-*sahāyikā* ||

264 Not in AY; Dh reads simply "these are the three thoughts." AY and Dh are noticeably different from the Tibetan here. According to the former, the householder's pleasure with his wife in this life will elicit suffering in the next; his enjoyment of food and drink with her will elicit disastrous offenses, and in general his pleasures with her will elicit suffering. According to Dh, although she is his companion in enjoyment in the present, she will not be his companion in future lives; that the practice of mindfulness is as good a companion as she is; and that although she may be with him in times of comfort, she is not a companion in suffering.

thought of [her][265] as impure, the thought of her as stinking, and the thought of her as disagreeable.[266]

[13D] "O Eminent Householder, the householder bodhisattva who lives at home should bring forth three thoughts toward his own wife. And what are the three? The thought of her as an enemy; the thought of her as an executioner; and the thought of her as an antagonist.[267]

[13E] "O Eminent Householder, the householder bodhisattva who lives at home should bring forth three thoughts toward his own wife. And what are the three? The thought of her as an ogre, the thought of her as a demon, and the thought of her as a hag.

[13F] "O Eminent Householder, the householder bodhisattva who lives at home should bring forth three thoughts toward his own wife. And what are the three? The thought of her as difficult to satisfy, the thought of her as depraved, and the thought of her as ungrateful.[268]

[13F'] "{And again there are three. And what are the three? First, the thought [of her] as a bad friend. Second, the thought of her as covetous and grasping. Third, the thought of her as interfering with the purity of his *brahmacarya*. These are the three.}[269]

[13G][270] "O Eminent Householder, the householder bodhisattva who lives at home should bring forth three thoughts toward his own wife. And what are the three? The thought of her as destined for [rebirth as] a hell-being,[271] the thought of her as destined for the animal realm, and the thought of her as destined for the world of Yama.[272]

---

265 The female pronoun is not used explicitly here or in any of the following statements, but it is clearly implied throughout.

266 Not in AY.

267 Not in AY or Dh.

268 Dh and Tib only.

269 Dh only.

270 §13G has no equivalent in R.

271 Dharmarakṣa seems to have understood these statements not as a reference to the wife's own destiny, but to her dragging others into these unfortunate rebirths. AY, however, agrees with the Tibetan. There is no equivalent of §13G in R.

272 On Yama (the traditional "king of the dead" in Indian mythology) see Wayman 1959. The fact that Yama is considered the king of the *pretas* (see *Abhidharmakośa* III, §59c-d) explains the frequent appearance of the expression "Yama's world" (*yamaloka*) where one would expect a reference to the *preta* realm.

[13H][273] "O Eminent Householder, the householder bodhisattva who lives at home should bring forth three thoughts toward his own wife. And what are the three? The thought of her as a burden, the thought of her as an obligation,[274] and the thought of her as an obligation he has taken on.

[13I] "O Eminent Householder, the householder bodhisattva who lives at home should bring forth three thoughts toward his own wife. And what are the three? The thought of her as 'not mine,' the thought of her as someone who cannot be possessed, and the thought of her as borrowed.

[13J] "O Eminent Householder, the householder bodhisattva who lives at home should bring forth three thoughts toward his own wife. And what are the three? The thought of her as an occasion[275] for committing sins of the body, the thought of her as an occasion for committing sins of speech, and the thought of her as an occasion for committing sins of the mind.[276]

[13K] "O Eminent Householder, the householder bodhisattva who lives at home should bring forth three thoughts toward his own wife. And what are the three? The thought of her as an occasion for the construction of lustful thoughts, the thought of her as an occasion for the construction of malicious thoughts, and the thought of her as an occasion for the construction of hostile thoughts.[277]

[13L] "O Eminent Householder, the householder bodhisattva who lives at home should bring forth three thoughts toward his own wife. And what are the three? The thought of her as a prison, the thought of her as killing, and the thought of her as binding.[278]

[13M] "O Eminent Householder, the householder bodhisattva who lives at home should bring forth three thoughts toward his own wife. And what are the three?[279] The

---

273 §13H has no equivalent in R.

274 Tib. *srid-pa*, usually a translation of Skt. *bhava* "becoming," but this meaning seems irrelevant here. The Tibetan can also mean "obligation," however (Jä. 582a), and I have followed this interpretation.

275 Tib. *gnas*, "place." Though my translation is based on the assumption that she is an "occasion of sin" for the bodhisattva himself, it is also possible to read these lines as referring to the wife as herself the agent of their commission.

276 Not in AY or Dh.

277 Not in AY or Dh.

278 Not in AY or Dh.

279 The following lines are cited in *Śikṣ*. 78.17:

śīlāntarāyasaṁjñā dhyānāntarāyasaṁjñā prajñāntarāya-saṁjñā ||

thought of her as an obstacle to morality, the thought of her as an obstacle to meditative absorption,[280] and the thought of her as an obstacle to insight.[281]

[13N] "O Eminent Householder, the householder bodhisattva who lives at home should bring forth three thoughts toward his own wife. And what are the three? The thought of her as a trap, the thought of her as a snare, and the thought of her as a net.[282]

[13O] "O Eminent Householder, the householder bodhisattva who lives at home should bring forth three thoughts toward his own wife. And what are the three? The thought of her as a plague, the thought of her as an injury, and the thought of her as an infectious disease.[283]

[13P] "O Eminent Householder, the householder bodhisattva who lives at home should bring forth three thoughts toward his own wife. And what are the three? The thought of her as a dispute, the thought of her as a mishap, and the thought of her as a hailstorm.[284]

[13Q] "O Eminent Householder, the householder bodhisattva who lives at home should bring forth three thoughts toward his own wife. And what are the three? The thought of her as sickness, the thought of her as old age, and the thought of her as death.[285]

[13R] "O Eminent Householder, the householder bodhisattva who lives at home should bring forth three thoughts toward his own wife. And what are the three? The thought of her as Māra,[286] the thought of her as a retainer of Māra, and the thought of her as Bhairava.[287]

[13S] "O Eminent Householder, the householder bodhisattva who lives at home should bring forth three thoughts toward his own wife. And what are the three? The thought of her as sorrow, the thought of her as grieving, and the thought of her as suffering, depression, and distress.[288]

[13T] "O Eminent Householder, the householder bodhisattva who lives at home

---

280 Both Tib and R point to an underlying *samādhi* (rather than *dhyāna*) for this item, as indeed one would expect in this list of the three components of the eightfold path, viz., *śīla*, *samādhi*, and *prajñā*.

281 Not in AY or Dh.

282 Not in AY or Dh.

283 Not in AY or Dh.

284 Not in AY or Dh.

285 Not in AY or Dh.

286 On Māra see Wayman 1959.

287 Not in AY or Dh. The name "Bhairava" ("frightful, horrible") has a variety of referents, *inter alia* a jackal, a *yakṣa*, and a form of Śiva (MW 767a).

288 Not in AY or Dh. This section is unusual in that it contains five rather than the usual three items. The only available parallel (found in R) has only three (or perhaps four, if the last two characters in the series are read separately) of these items. Apparently what has happened here is that the list (which

should bring forth three thoughts toward his own wife. And what are the three? The thought of her as a huge wolf, the thought of her as a huge sea monster, and the thought of her as a huge cat.[289]

[13U] "O Eminent Householder, the householder bodhisattva who lives at home should bring forth three thoughts toward his own wife. And what are the three? The thought of her as a black snake, the thought of her as a crocodile, and the thought of her as a demon causing epilepsy.[290]

[13V] "O Eminent Householder, the householder bodhisattva who lives at home should bring forth three thoughts toward his own wife. And what are the three? The thought of her as without a protector, the thought of her as without a refuge, and the thought of her as without a place of rest.[291]

[13W] "O Eminent Householder, the householder bodhisattva who lives at home should bring forth three thoughts toward his own wife. And what are the three? The thought of her as swollen, the thought of her as shriveled up, and the thought of her as diseased.[292]

[13W'] "{And again he should bring forth three thoughts: the thought of her as his mother, as his elder sister, and as his younger sister.}[293]

[13X] "O Eminent Householder, the householder bodhisattva who lives at home should bring forth three thoughts toward his own wife. And what are the three?[294] The thought of her as a robber, the thought of her as a prison guard,[295] and the thought of

---

presumably originally consisted only of three items) has been expanded to include all of the terms for suffering and lamentation traditionally given at the end of the twelve-fold chain of causation, viz., *śoka-parideva-duḥkha-daurmanasya-upāyāsā.*

289 Not in AY or Dh.

290 Not in AY or Dh. For the last item in the list the Tibetan has *mdangs 'phrog-ma*, Skt. **apasmāra* (for which see BHSD 46a).

291 Not in AY or Dh. Presumably the idea being expressed in this section is not that the bodhisattva should pity his wife for being in this sad state, but rather that he will never be able to attain any of these things (and indeed may lose them) as a result of his association with her.

292 Tib only.

293 R only.

294 The following lines are cited in *Śikṣ.* 78.17-18:

corasaṁjñā badhakasaṁjñā narakapālasaṁjñā iti ||

295 R (which offers the only Chinese parallel here) reads "killer," as does the translation of the word *badhaka* in the *Śikṣ.* by Bendall and Rouse, for reasons that are not clear to me. Perhaps the latter were influenced by the (mistaken?) equation of *badhaka* with *gsod-pa* "killing, killer" given in *Mvy.* no. 3838. The Tibetan, however--which clearly reads "prison guard" (*btson-srungs*)—suggests that the Sanskrit term in the text from which the Tibetans were working was *bandhanika* "jailer" (MW 721a), not *badhaka*.

her as a guardian of hell.[296]

[13Y] "O Eminent Householder, the householder bodhisattva who lives at home should bring forth three thoughts toward his own wife. And what are the three? The thought of her as a flood,[297] the thought of her as an intersection, and the thought of her as a knot.[298]

[13Z] "O Eminent Householder, the householder bodhisattva who lives at home should bring forth three thoughts toward his own wife. And what are the three? The thought of her as a swamp, the thought of her as a chasm, and the thought of her as a whirlpool.[299]

[13AA] "O Eminent Householder, the householder bodhisattva who lives at home should bring forth three thoughts toward his own wife. And what are the three? The thought of her as a rope, the thought of her as a fetter, and the thought of her as a snare.[300]

[13BB] "O Eminent Householder, the householder bodhisattva who lives at home should bring forth three thoughts toward his own wife. And what are the three? The thought of her as like a fire pit, the thought of her as like a grass-fire lamp, and the thought of her as like a razor.[301]

[13CC] "O Eminent Householder, the householder bodhisattva who lives at home should bring forth three thoughts toward his own wife. And what are the three? The thought of her as useless, the thought of her as a thorn, and the thought of her as poison.[302]

[13DD] "O Eminent Householder, the householder bodhisattva who lives at home should bring forth three thoughts toward his own wife. And what are the three? The thought of her as a extremely vain, the thought of her as obsessed with clothing, and the thought of her as clinging.[303]

---

296 Not in AY or Dh.

297 The Tibetan reads *chu-bo* (Skt. *ogha*, LC 704b). The term *ogha* has longstanding negative connotations in Buddhist literature; for examples of this usage cf. PTSD 164a-165b.

298 Not in AY or Dh. The logic of the list given in the Tibetan version is less than obvious; R (which offers the only parallel) maintains the water imagery throughout.

299 Not in AY or Dh.

300 Not in AY or Dh.

301 Not in AY or Dh. All of the items in this list are intriguingly similar to the names of Buddhist hells, but only the first (Tib. *me-ma-mur*, Skt. *kukkula*) offers an exact parallel (see *Mvy.* no. 4937). R (which offers the sole Chinese parallel) reads "fire pit, knife pit, and grass torch."

302 Not in AY or Dh.

303 Tib only. My translations of all three of these items (for which no

[13EE] "O Eminent Householder, the householder bodhisattva who lives at home should bring forth three thoughts toward his own wife. And what are the three? The thought of her as a jailer,[304] the thought of her as inflicting punishment, and the thought of her as wielding a sword.[305]

[13FF] "O Eminent Householder, the householder bodhisattva who lives at home should bring forth three thoughts toward his own wife. And what are the three? The thought of her as quarreling, the thought of her as contentious, and the thought of her as fault-finding.[306]

[13GG] "O Eminent Householder, the householder bodhisattva who lives at home should bring forth three thoughts toward his own wife. And what are the three? The thought of being with what one dislikes, the thought of being separated from what one likes, and the thought of what is painful.[307]

[13HH] "In short: he should bring forth the thought of her as the impurity of fighting, the thought of her as the tumult of fighting, the thought of her as the cause of all harm, and the thought of her as the root of all bad actions. O Eminent Householder, the householder bodhisattva who lives at home should

---

Chinese parallel is available, and whose Sanskrit counterparts are less than certain) are extremely tentative.

304 Tib. *shar-gnyer*, an expression not registered in existing dictionaries, with the exception of LC 2343a, which gives the rather unhelpful equivalent of Skt. *muka* "the smell of cow dung"! Interpreting *shar* as a form of *sha* "flesh, meat," Sakurabe translates the phrase as "flesh-seeker" (*niku o motomeru mono*, p. 264). Fortunately, the term appears in the *Rāṣṭrapāla-paripṛcchā-sūtra* (94.10), where the Sanskrit equivalent is *vaira* "enemy." (I am grateful to Paul Harrison for providing this reference.) This meaning fits well in the context in which the word is used below (§19S), but in the present instance one more interpretive step is required. Given the fact that R here reads "prisoner" (and that the word "jailer" would fit the context quite well), I suspect that what has happened is a confusion between some form of *vārika* "guard, superintendent" and *vairika* "enemy" (for which see BHSD 477b and 511b, respectively), or between *vāraka* "restrainer" and *vārakin* "opposer, enemy" (both at MW 944a). In other words, an underlying *vārika* or *vāraka* "[prison] guard, restrainer" has been understood by the Tibetan translator as *vairika* or *vārakin* "enemy," and translated accordingly as *shar-gnyer*. My translation as "jailer" is thus based directly on the (postulated) underlying Sanskrit form, and is not intended as an equivalent of *shar-gnyer* itself.

305 Not in AY or Dh.

306 Not in AY or Dh. For the last item in this list R has "restrictive."

307 Not in AY or Dh. These three items correspond to three of the forms of *duḥkha* registered in *Mvy.* nos. 2237-2238 and 2229, respectively.

regard his own wife with such thoughts as these in mind {and not desire her}.[308]

[§14. CULTIVATING DETACHMENT FROM ONE'S SON]

[14A] "Moreover, O Eminent Householder, the householder bodhisattva should not bring forth the thought of excessive affection toward his son. O Eminent Householder,[309] if he brings forth the thought of excessive affection toward his son, while not doing so toward other beings, he should reproach himself[310] with three reproaches. And what are the three? '*Bodhi* belongs to the bodhisattva whose mind is impartial, not to the one whose mind is partial;[311] *bodhi* belongs to the bodhisattva who strives rightly, not to the one who strives wrongly; and *bodhi* belongs to the bodhisattva who does not make distinctions, not to the one who makes distinctions.' Thus having reproached himself with these three reproaches, he should

---

[308] Dh only.

[309] The following lines are cited in *Śikṣ.* 19.8-14:

> *yāvat sacet punar asya putre 'tiriktaraṃ premot-padyate* [*na*] *tathā 'nyeṣu satveṣu tena tisṛbhiḥ paribhāṣaṇābhiḥ svacittaṃ paribhāṣitavyaṃ* | *katmābhis tisṛbhiḥ* | *samyak*[*pra*]*yuktasya sama-cittasya bodhisatvasya bodhir na viṣama-cittasya bodhir na mithyāprayuktasya* | *anānātvacāriṇo bodhisatvasya bodhir na nānātvacāriṇaḥ* | *ābhis tisṛbhiḥ paribhāṣaṇābhiḥ svacittam paribhāṣya-nyatre* [sic] *'mitrasaṃjñotpāda-yitavyā 'mitraṃ hy etan mama* | *na maitraṃ* [sic] | *yo 'ham asyārthāya buddhaprajñaptāḥ* [sic] *śikṣāyā udvuratād* [sic] *gatvā 'smin putre 'tiriktataraṃ premotpādayāmi* | *na tathā 'nyeṣu satveṣu* |

The Sanskrit text is quite corrupt; cf. the discussion of various elements in this passage in Mochizuki 1988, notes to p. 248.

[310] Literally (here and below) "reproach his own mind."

[311] Throughout this section the Indian author has availed himself of the multiple meanings of certain Sanskrit expressions—in particular, the terms *sama* and *viṣama*—in ways that cannot be replicated directly in English. In the present case "impartial" translates an underlying *sama* (which means "same, even, smooth," but by extension "good, just, fair"), while "partial" is a translation of *viṣama* (which means "unequal, uneven," but also "bad, unjust, unfair"). Thus the contrast here is not just between partiality and impartiality, but between good and bad conduct on the bodhisattva's part. For another play on these expressions see below, n. 319.

bring forth the idea of 'enemy'[312] toward his son, thinking 'He is an enemy, and is not dear to my heart. If for his sake I bring forth excessive affection toward that son of mine while not doing the same toward other beings I will be deviating from the training prescribed by the Buddha.[313]

[14B] " 'For his sake I have damaged my roots-of-goodness and have heedlessly endangered my own life; therefore he is harmful to me. For his sake I have followed a path that is not in accord with the path of *bodhi*; therefore he is my opponent.' Thinking in this way, he should bring forth those three thoughts.[314]

[14C] "Taking his son as the cause,[315] just as he feels fondness toward his son, he ought to bring forth the spirit of loving-kindness toward all beings; and just as he feels loving concern for himself, so he should bring forth loving-kindness toward them. And he should carefully reflect as follows: 'Just as he has come from elsewhere, so I too have come from elsewhere. All living beings have once been my sons, and I have been the son of all beings. Thus in him there is no being who belongs to me, or to another, or to anyone at all.[316]

[14D] " 'And why? Due to partiality one goes from being a friend to being an enemy throughout the five realms,[317] so I should

---

[312] Tib. *mi-sdug-pa*, most commonly used as a translation of Skt. *apriya* "not loved, unpleasant," and so on, but here the quotation preserved in the *Śikṣāsamuccaya* gives the corresponding Sanskrit form as *amitra* "non-friend" or, more usually, "enemy."

[313] Not in AY.

[314] There is considerable variety in wording among the three Chinese versions, though not in their overall purport.

[315] The following lines are cited in *Śikṣ*. 19.14-17:

> *tena tathā tathā cittam utpādayitavyaṃ yathā*
> *yathāsya sarvasatveṣu putra-premānugatā maitry*
> *utpadyate* | *ātmakṣemānu*[*gatā*] *maitry utpadyate* |
> *evaṃ cānena yoniśaḥ pratyavekṣitavyam* | *anyata eṣa*
> *āgata* | *anyato 'haṃ* | *sarvasatvā api mama putrā*
> *abhūvan* | *ahaṃ ca sarvasatvānām putro 'bhūvan* |
> *neha saṃvidyate kaścit kasya ci*[*d ahaṁ vā*] *paro vā* |

The letters in brackets are supplied by Mochizuki 1988 (p. 248 and n. 70).

[316] Not in AY.

[317] R "six realms"; no number is given in AY or Dh. The *asura* realm was accepted by some, but not all, Indian Buddhists as constituting a distinctive sixth realm of rebirth (*gati*); for the Sarvāstivāda school's objection to the creation of this category see the *Mahāvibhāṣā*, T 1545, 27.868b1ff. In some Mahāyāna texts (e.g., the *Saddharmapuṇḍarīka-sūtra*) references to both five

act in such a way as to be a friend or an enemy to no one. And why? When one considers someone an enemy, no matter what he does, it is displeasing. When one considers someone a friend, no matter what he does, it is pleasing. Thus one cannot awaken to the the sameness of [all] things[318] by means of the two mental states of "affection" and "antipathy."

[14E] " 'And why? Bad behavior leads to a bad rebirth; good behavior leads to a good rebirth.[319] Thus I should not do bad deeds. Acting impartially toward all beings, I will awaken to Omniscience.' O Eminent Householder,[320] in that way the householder bodhisattva should not take any thing whatsoever as 'mine.' He should not be attached to it, or swayed by it, or desirous of it.

[§15. HOW TO INTERACT WITH BEGGARS]

[15A][321] "O Eminent Householder, when a beggar approaches a householder bodhisattva and asks for a certain thing, if he has not already given that thing away, he should reflect as follows:[322]

---

and six *gatis* occur. Clearly the transition from the shorter to the longer list was a gradual (and at times, hotly contested) one.

318 Tib. *chos*, Skt. *dharma*, but the term is not necessarily to be understood in a technical sense here.

319 Again the Indian author seems to have been indulging in a play on the words *sama* and *viṣama*: good (i.e., impartial, *sama*) conduct leads to a good (*sama*) rebirth, while conduct that is bad (i.e., showing favoritism, *viṣama*) results in a bad (*viṣama*) rebirth.

320 This sentence and the next are cited in *Śikṣ*. 19.17-19:

> *yāvad evaṃ hi gṛhapate | gṛhiṇā bodhisatvena na kasmiṃś cid vastuni mamatvaṃ parigraho vā kartavyaḥ | nādhyavasānaṃ | na niyatiḥ na tṛṣṇānuśayaḥ kartavyaḥ |*

321 Cited in *Śikṣ*. 19.19-20.3:

> *sacet punar gṛhapate gṛhiṇaṃ bodhisatvaṃ yācanaka upasaṃkramya kiñcid eva vastu yāceta | saced asya vastv aparityaktaṃ bhavet | naivaṃ* [sic] *cittaṃ nidhyāpayitavyaṃ | yady aham etad vastu parityajeyaṃ yadi vā na parityajeyam avaśyaṃ mamaitena vastunā vinābhāvo bhaviṣyati | akāmakena maraṇam upagantavyaṃ bhaviṣyati | etac ca vastu māṃ tyakṣyati ahaṃ cainaṃ tyakṣyāmi | etac ca vastu parityajyāhaṃ āttasāraḥ kālaṃ kariṣyāmi etac ca parityaktaṃ na me maraṇakāle cittaṃ paryādāya sthāsyati | etac ca me mara-ṇakāle prītiṃ prāmodyam avipratisāritāṃ ca janayiṣyati |*

322 The text cited in the *Śikṣ*. differs significantly from the Tibetan here

'Whether I give this thing away or not, I will surely be separated from it in the future. Though I may not want to, I will die and this thing will abandon me, and I will abandon it. But if I give this thing up now, I will die with a joyous mind,[323] having "extracted the substance"[324] from it. So if I give this thing up, at the time of my death it will not continue to haunt me, but on the contrary, at the time of my death this thing will be the cause of happiness, rejoicing, delight, and freedom from regret.'[325]

[15B][326] "But if, having thought in that way, he is still unable to give that object away,[327] he should explain to the beggar by means of three[328] explanations: 'At this point my strength is meager and my roots-of-goodness are immature. I am only a beginner in the Great

---

and below (see §15B, n. 327). In the present case, the Sanskrit reads *naivaṁ cittaṁ nidhyāpayitavyaṁ*, translated by Bendall and Rouse as "he must not allow himself to reason in such wise as this" (p. 22). Needless to say, the introduction of the negative *na* yields a significant difference in meaning. Since the reading found in the Tibetan is supported by all three Chinese versions (none of which contains a negative here), it seems likely that the word *na* is a relatively late corruption in the Sanskrit.

323 Not in AY.

324 For this concept see above, §6B, n. 120.

325 Not in AY.

326 Cited in *Śikṣ.* 20.3-9:

> *sacet punar evam api samanvāharan 'śaknuyāt tad vastu parityaktum | tena sa yācanakaś catasṛbhiḥ saṃjñaptibhiḥ saṃjñapayitavyaḥ | katamābhiś catasṛbhiḥ | durbalas tāvad asmy aparipakva-kuśalamūlaḥ | ādikarmiko mahāyāne | na cittasya vaśī parityāgāya | sopādānadṛṣṭiko 'smi | ahaṃkāra mamakāra-sthitaḥ | kṣamasva satpuruṣa | mā pari-tāpsīs tathāhaṃ kariṣyāmi tathā pratipatsye | tathā vīryam ārapsye | yathainaṃ ca tavābhiprāyaṃ paripūrayiṣyāmi sarvasatvānāṃ ceti | evaṃ khalu gṛhapate | tena yācanakaḥ saṃjñapayitavyaḥ |*

327 Again the Sanskrit citation in the *Śikṣ.* differs noticeably from the Tibetan, reading *sacet punar evam api samanvāharan śaknuyāt tad vastu parityaktum*, translated by Bendall and Rouse as "If it be only such considerations as these that enable him to give up the object" (p. 22). The Tibetan is again supported by all three Chinese versions, which agree in reading "if he is unable to give."

328 All three Chinese versions, as well as the Sanskrit citation preserved in the *Śikṣ.*, refer explicitly to "four explanations." It is not at all clear in the Tibetan text where the three explanations are to be divided.

Vehicle. I am subject to thoughts of not giving. I still have the perspective of grasping, and am stuck in taking things as "me" and "mine." And so, good sir,[329] I beg you to forgive me and not to be upset. [In the future] I will act, accomplish, and exert myself so as to fulfill your desires and those of all beings.' O Eminent Householder, thus should the householder bodhisattva explain to the beggar by means of three explanations.

[§16. THE *TRISKANDHAKA* RITUAL]

[16A] "Moreover, O Eminent Householder, the householder bodhisattva who lives at home should be skilled in constant and continual transformation.[330] If he has access to the word of the departed Teacher,[331] but there is no arising of a Buddha,, there is no Dharma teacher, and he does not meet with the Sangha of the Noble Ones,[332] he should do homage to all the Buddhas of the ten directions, and should bring to mind and rejoice in all their previous actions,[333] good actions, virtuous actions, their resolutions and intense resolve, and their attainment of all the Buddha-qualities of those who have attained *bodhi*.

[16B] "And he should also do as follows: Three times in the daytime and three times at night, with bodily deeds, vocal deeds, and mental deeds purified and cleansed, with pure resolve, skilled in the cultivation of loving-kindness, wearing clean clothes, and adorning himself with modesty and shame, having accumulated the stock of merit comprised by the roots of goodness, beautiful,[334]

---

[329] Tib. *skyes-bu dam-pa*, Skt. *satpuruṣa*. Note the extremely polite language the bodhisattva is being enjoined to use in addressing someone who would have been at the very bottom of the Indian social scale.

[330] Tib only. The meaning of this phrase is less than transparent. The term rendered here as "transformation" (Tib. *yongs-su bsngo-ba*) is the standard equivalent of Skt. *pariṇāmana* (for which cf. above, §3A, n. 55), but the transfer or transformation of merit does not seem to be the topic of discussion here.

[331] AY "if he is without the instruction of a teacher," Dh "if he is without the Blessed One's teaching."

[332] Skt. **Ārya-saṃgha*, ordinarily not used in reference to the Sangha as a whole, but only to those members who have attained one of the degrees of liberation up to and including Arhatship. It seems likely, however, that our text is using the term in a somewhat looser sense, and in particular, that it is to be understood as including bodhisattvas.

[333] Tib. *sngon-gyi spyod-pa*, Skt. *purvacarya*, referring in particular to their actions in previous lives that led to their attainment of Buddhahood.

[334] Tib. *mdzes-pa*, Skt. *prāsādika* etc. (for numerous possible equivalents

delighting in the spirit of enlightenment, gentle in character, pleasant to associate with, a doer of good deeds, respectful, pleasant in speech, and cutting off egotism, arrogance, and pride, he should confess all the bad deeds he has committed and restrain himself from then on. Rejoicing in all the merits [of others] and fully accumulating the marks,[335] he should request all the Buddhas to turn the wheel of the Dharma and should uphold all the Dharmas. And in order to preserve his life in countless Buddha-fields, he should recite the *Triskandhaka* dharma-text.[336]

---

see LC 1991A). The significance of this word here (which means "beautiful, attractive, lovely," etc.) is unclear, and there is no counterpart in any Chinese version of the text. Sakurabe attempts to salvage the situation by supplying an interpretive gloss, viz. "beautiful in spirit" (*kokorobae utsukushiku*, p. 270).

335 Tib. *mtshan*, Skt. *lakṣaṇa*, i.e., the thirty-two marks of the "great man" (see above, §3B, n. 57).

336 This paragraph (which in the Tibetan consists of a string of twenty-four short phrases, each connected to the next by the word *dang* "and") offers the translator no grammatical guardrails whatsoever. Accordingly, the translation offered here is extremely tentative. The last sentence is quoted in *Śikṣ.* 315.14-15, though with a significant difference from the Tibetan: *dharmagrāhyatām upādāyāprameyāsaṁkhyeyeṣu buddhakṣetresvāyuḥ parirakṣanāya*, translated by Bendall and Rouse as ""in order to comprehend the Law for guarding one's life in numberless and infinite fields of the Buddha" (1922, p. 282).

The majority of the text in §16B does not appear in AY (as indicated by the smaller type), nor for that matter does it appear in the same wording in the other Chinese versions. Since the differences among the various recensions are so great, I will provide a translation of each of the Chinese versions here. In chronological order, they read as follows:

AY: Then, three times in the day and three times at night, he should recite the three-part (**triskandhaka*) dharma. He should confess to and repent of all the evil he has done in former lives, making amends for the past and cultivating [good deeds in] the future, and should seek the indulgence of all the Buddhas. For the sake of the Dharma he should grieve and be remorseful about it; for the sake of the measureless and unlimited Dharma he should grieve and be remorseful about it.

Dh: Three times each day and night, having purified body, speech, and mind, he should practice equal (*teng* 等) loving-kindness and bring to mind all good roots and distance himself from his present state [lit. "from what he has"]. With shame and modesty he should adorn himself with the roots-of-goodness. His heart having become pure, he will cause people to rejoice. Delighting in the Buddha-Way with a faithful mind, he will be free of confusion. Being calm and respectful in what he does, and he cuts off all arrogance and pride. He should recite the three-part (**triskandhaka*) dharma, abandon all evil conduct, and repent of the eighty things. With concentrated mind he should

[§17. WHEN MONKS VIOLATE THE PRECEPTS]

[17A] "Moreover, O Eminent Householder, the householder bodhisattva who lives at home should undertake the eight-fold abstinence.[337] He should wait upon, serve, and honor those *brāhmaṇas* and

---

rejoice [lit. "exhort and encourage," but the characters *ch'üan-chu* 勸助 are regularly used to translate Skt. *anumodanā* "rejoicing"] in the possession of the major and minor marks of merit (**puṇya-lakṣaṇa*). He should turn the Dharma-wheel of the Buddhas [*sic*!] and rejoice in the Buddhas' turning of the wheel. Through such limitless conduct, he himself will receive a [Buddha]-field where the span of life cannot be measured.

R: Thus three times every day and night he should purify the deeds of body, speech, and mind. And purified with loving-kindness and goodness, with modesty and shame and [wearing] clean clothes, with the spirit of enlightenment he should rejoice in all the good roots that have been accumulated. Gentle, pleasant, and good, being respectful and cutting off arrogance, he should practice the three divisions and chant the three-division (**triskandhaka*) dharma. Singlemindedly repenting of all his bad deeds and [resolving] not to do them again, he rejoices in all fortune-producing deeds. He gathers together all of the major and minor marks and entreats the Buddhas to turn the Dharma-wheel, receiving and upholding all the Dharmas that they teach. He desires that the Buddhas live long, "and by accumulating deep roots of goodness, may my own Buddha-world be thus."

Hirakawa (1989, vol. I, p. 115) makes much of the fact that the word *ching* 經 (the standard Chinese translation of "sūtra") is used here in AY (though not, it should be noted, in R, nor does any word that could be construed as a translation of "sūtra" appear in the Tibetan). On this basis Hirakawa concludes that "there was at an early time the practice of reciting the *Triskandhaka-sūtra*, revering the Buddhas of the ten directions, and repenting" (*loc. cit.*). What he ignores, however, is the fact that the term *ching* is frequently used by AY (e.g., §§1A, 3D) as a translation not of "sūtra" but of "dharma," and that Dh also uses the word *ching* (or more frequently, the compound *ching-fa* 經法) when the underlying Indian text surely had only "dharma." There is, in other words, no solid evidence—and indeed, there is considerable counterevidence provided by R and Tib—that the underlying Indian text referred to a "sūtra" named *Triskandhaka*.

[337] AY "should understand the conduct of the *śramaṇa*," R "should receive the eight precepts and practice the conduct of a *śramaṇa*." The Tibetan has *bsnyen-gnas* (Skt. *upavāsa*), that is, the eight precepts voluntarily taken on by some lay Buddhists on the *poṣadha* (Pāli *uposatha*) day, viz., to abstain from taking life, taking what is not given, sexual misconduct (on *poṣadha* days interpreted as complete avoidance of any sexual activity), drinking alcohol,

śramaṇas who keep the precepts, possess good qualities, and possess virtuous attributes. And while waiting upon them, serving them, and honoring them faithfully, he should recognize his own offenses.[338] And if he sees a monk who has fallen away from the conduct of a *śramaṇa*, he should not disrespect him even in the slightest. Rather, he should think to himself: 'The reddish-brown robe of the Blessed One, the Tathāgata, the Arhat, the Samyaksaṁbuddha—who is without stain and who is free from any stain of the defilements—is permeated by morality; it is permeated by meditative absorption, wisdom, liberation, and the vision of the cognition of liberation.[339] This being the case, it is the banner-of-sages[340] of the Noble Ones.' And having brought forth respect toward them,[341] he should bring forth great compassion[342] toward that monk.

---

eating after midday, wearing adornments or watching entertainment, and sleeping in a high bed. These are virtually the same as the ten rules for a novice monk or nun; the latter list simply divides "wearing adornments" and "watching entertainment" into two rules rather than one, and adds a tenth rule requiring that the novice not handle money.

Despite the prominence given to this topic in some secondary works (e.g., Hirakawa 1990b, pp. 117-120 and, to a lesser extent, Mochizuki 1988, p. 314), these items are not even enumerated, let alone discussed in detail, in any version of the sūtra. Moreover, they are not even mentioned in the oldest extant recension (AY). Thus they can hardly be described as one of the central organizing concepts of the *Ugra*; on the contrary, they are likely to be an interpolation that entered the text only in the middle period of its development.

338 Not in AY.

339 Cf. above, §9B, n. 204. The same wording is applied in other sources not to the monastic robe, but to the physical relics of the Buddha; see Schopen 1987, pp. 204-205.

340 Tib. *drang-srong-gi rgyal-mtshan*, Skt. **ṛṣi-dhvaja*, Pāli **isi-dhaja*. The expression "banner of the sages" appears already in the Pali canon (e.g., *Saṁyutta-nikāya* II, 280; *Aṅguttara-nikāya* II, 24, 51; and *Vinaya* IV, 15, 22), though in these instances the expression refers to the Dhamma itself and not to the monastic robe. The idea of the robe as a banner, however, is common in early Mahāyāna sūtras; see for example the *Ratnarāśi*, translated in Silk 1994a, pp. 276-278.

341 I.e., toward the "noble ones" (*ārya*), the most advanced members of the Buddhist community. Sakurabe reads "toward the robe," but the object of respect in the Tibetan is explicitly plural.

342 Once again "great compassion" (Tib. *snying-rje chen-po*, Skt. *mahākaruṇā*) is to be applied not to sentient beings in general, but only to those who are seen as one's inferiors.

[17B] "And he should think, 'This sinful conduct is not good. This defiled conduct is not good. That monk wears the banner-of-sages of the Blessed One, the Tathāgata, the Arhat, the Samyaksaṁbuddha—who is disciplined, calmed, restrained, and well bred[343]—but he himself is not purified, not calmed, not restrained, not disciplined, and he acts in a way that is not well bred. Since the Blessed One has said, "Do not despise the unlearned,"[344] it is not he who has committed the offense; rather, it is whatever defilements there are in him that have manifested this unvirtuousness. Since he has access to the teaching of the Buddhas, the Blessed Ones, if he fully comprehends whatever defilements he has and examines them carefully, he will be able to obtain the first fruit,[345] and he will attain the status of one who is assured of Supreme Perfect Enlightenment.'[346]

[17C] "And why? Thinking about the fact that defilements are removed by knowledge,[347] and the Blessed One has also said 'One

---

343 Tib. *cang shes-pa* "all-knowing," an old translation error (canonized in *Mvy.* no. 1080 and elsewhere) for Skt. *ājāneya* "well bred." The Tibetan translators took this term as a derivative of √*jñā* "know" rather than of √*jan* "generate, beget." For a discussion of the Sanskrit term and its variants see BHSD 90a (s.v. *ājanya*).

344 Tib. *ma-bslabs-pa-la ma-brnyas-shig.* This was evidently a well-known saying; it is also quoted in the *Vimalakīrtinirdeśa* (Peking 843, Ōtani ed. vol. 34, p. 94.1.4), where the Tibetan text reads *ma-bslabs-pa-la brnyas-par mi-bya'o.* Lamotte (1976, p. 206) translates the latter "Has not the Tathāgata said that *aśaikṣa* should not be despised?" The term *aśaikṣa*, however, means "those for whom there is no further study" (Tib. *mi-slob-pa*, *Mvy.* no. 1734), not "the unlearned" (Tib. *ma-bslabs-pa*, Skt. **aśikṣita*). Here Thurman's translation (1976, p. 79) is to be preferred: "Those who are unlearned should not be despised."

345 Interpreted quite plausibly by Sakurabe as a reference to attaining the fruit of the stream-enterer (*śrotāpanna*), the first of four levels of attainment in Mainstream Buddhism. (Precisely this definition of the expression "attain the first fruit" is given in T 1521, 26.25c24, for example.) Dharmarakṣa, however, took this expression as a reference to the first moment of *bodhicitta* (*ti-i tao-i* 第一道意). The corresponding phrase in AY, *ti-i te* 第一德 ("first virtue" or "first quality") makes little sense until we realize that *te* 德 "virtue" is a common error for *te* 得 "attainment." With this emendation AY reads "first attainment," which corresponds well to the other versions.

346 Only in R and Tib. No equivalent in AY; Dh reads "he will be able to attain the production of impartial endurance" (*p'ing-teng jen* 平等忍).

347 Tib. *ye-shes*, Skt. *jñāna*. On the removal of defilements (or more specifically, *rāga* "passion") by knowledge see *Abhidharmakośa*, VI, 76c.

person should not evaluate another, for if one person evaluates another, harm will result,'[348] and since 'the Tathāgata knows, and I do not,'[349] he should bring forth no ill will, hatred, anger, or animosity toward that *bhikṣu*.

{Chapter 6: Worshipping the Stūpa}[350]

[§18. WHEN VISITING A MONASTERY]

[18A] "O Eminent Householder, if the householder bodhisattva wishes to go inside a monastery,[351] he should remain at the monastery door with a well-bred mind, with a gentle mind, with reverence, respect, faith, and veneration,[352] and should prostrate himself toward the monastery. Only then should he go inside the monastery. And he should reflect to himself as follows: 'This is a place for dwelling in emptiness.[353] This is a place for dwelling in the signless. This is a place for dwelling in the wishless.[354] It is a place for dwelling in loving-kindness,

---

[348] This was evidently a well-known saying; cf. *Śikṣ*. 92.2-4 (quoting from the *Śūraṅgamasamādhi-sūtra*, with the Buddha speaking to Kāśyapa): *mā bhikṣavaḥ pudgalena pudgalaṁ pravicetavyam | yacchrīgram kṣaṇyati* [sic] *hi bhikṣavaḥ pudgalaḥ pudgalaṁ pravicinvan | ahaṁ vā pudgalaṁ pramiṇuyām yo vā syān mādṛṣaḥ |*

[349] This was also apparently a common saying; see for example the *Kāśyapaparivarta* (von Staël-Holstein 1926, §6: *tathāgata eva jānāti nāham* [*jānāmi*]), AN iii.347-351, *Śikṣ*. 55.3, etc.

[350] Dh only. Note that Dharmarakṣa here adds a reference to the stūpa which does not occur in the text itself.

[351] Tib. *gtsug-lag khang*, Skt. *vihāra*.

[352] Tib only.

[353] Tib. *stong-pa-nyid-la gnas-pa'i gnas*, Skt. **śūnyatā-vihārāvāsa*. Although no Sanskrit citation of this passage has come down to us, the use of the term *miao* 廟 "temple, monastery" in AY makes it clear that the Indian author was indulging in a play on the word *vihāra* "monastery," which in ordinary (nontechnical) usage means simply "dwelling place." The word play in question may have been elicited not by this reference to the three doors of liberation (for which see the following note) but by the subsequent reference to the four "sublime states," known in Sanskrit as the four *brahma-vihāra*s (see below, n. 355).

[354] Not in AY. On the empty, signless, and wishless as the "three doors to liberation" cf. the *Visuddhimagga*, p. 367. It is worth noting that emptiness in this sense appears fairly frequently in early Buddhist literature, and does not in itself signify the presence of distinctively Mahāyāna ideas.

compassion, sympathetic joy, and equanimity.[355] This is a place of practitioners of meditation,[356] a place for those who have cut off all places.[357] This is the place of those who have truly gone forth[358] and have truly entered the path.[359] When will I be able to go forth from the dusty place,[360] the household place, and conduct myself in this way? And when will I be able to take part in[361] the activities of the Sangha, the activities of the *poṣadha* ceremony,[362] the activities of the *pravāraṇa* ceremony,[363] and the activities of paying respects?'[364] And so thinking, he should rejoice in the thought of going forth as a monk.

[18B] "For no bodhisattva who lives at home has ever attained Supreme Perfect Enlightenment.[365] Those who have done so have all

---

[355] I.e., the four *brahma-vihāras* or "divine abodes" (viz., *maitrī*, *karuṇā*, *muditā*, and *upekṣā*). R attempts to make this identification explicit by labeling the entire group *fan-hsing* 梵行 ("brahma-conduct," which however is more properly the equivalent of *brahmacarya*), while AY and Dh simply list the four items. For further references see Lamotte 1976, p. 18, n. 66.

[356] Not in AY. The Tibetan term for "meditation" is *bsam-gtan* (Skt. *dhyāna*). It seems likely, given the context, that this is a reference to the eight meditational states corresponding to the *rūpa* and *arūpa* realms of Buddhist cosmology (known more widely by the Pāli term *jhāna*).

[357] Tib only.

[358] Sakurabe reads "who have left behind worldly desires," but this does not seem to be supported by the Tibetan.

[359] So also Sakurabe. The general meaning is confirmed by the Chinese, but the sentence as it stands remains unsatisfyingly vague.

[360] The image of the household (in contrast to the open air of the renunciant's sphere of action) as "dusty" (in Pāli, *rajāpatho*) is an ancient motif in Buddhist literature; see for example DN I.63, MN I.179, I.240, I.267, I.344, and so on.

[361] More literally, "to dwell in, pass time." Continuing the word play observed above, I strongly suspect that the underlying Sanskrit text had a form of the verb *vi√hṛ*.

[362] The communal recitation of monastic rules, performed on full- and new-moon days.

[363] A ritual performed by monks and nuns at the close of the rainy season, signifying a return from the settled to the wandering lifestyle.

[364] Tib. *'dud-pa*, Skt. *sāmīcī*. Judging by the uses of this term in the Pāli texts (e.g., *Vinaya* II, 22, 162, 255 and III, 246; AN I, 123 and II, 180; and DN III, 83) it refers not to a formal ceremony like the *poṣadha* and the *pravāraṇa* services but to a variety of acts of respect made to monks.

[365] This scripture's categorical denial of the possibility of a lay person attaining Buddhahood is discussed in detail in Chapter 5, p. 122.

gone forth from the household, and having done so, they have thought of the wilderness; they have had the wilderness as their goal.[366] And having gone to the wilderness,[367] there they have awakened to Supreme Perfect Enlightenment. And it is there that they have acquired the equipment [of *bodhi*]."[368] {As to the disparaging of home-dwelling, to leave home is praised by the wise.}[369]

[§19. CONTRASTS BETWEEN HOUSEHOLD AND RENUNCIANT LIFE][370]

[19A] "Household life is harmful and dusty; the renunciant life is praised by the Buddhas and their disciples.[371] Household life abounds in faults and bad qualities;[372] the renunciant life abounds in good qualities. Household life is constricted; the renunciant life is spacious.[373] Household life is defiled by ownership;

---

366 Tib only.

367 AY "mountains and swamps," Dh "mountains" (though the word "wilderness-dweller" follows immediately after), R "empty wilderness-land." AY and Dh clearly reflect Chinese notions of the proper habitat of a renunciant sage, while R adheres more closely to what must have been the wording of the Indian text.

368 Tib only. The equipment (Skt. *saṁbhāra*, Tib. *tshogs*) in question is merit (*puṇya*) and knowledge (*jñāna*); see BHSD 580a.

369 AY only.

370 Here begins a voluminous list of contrasts between the household life (Tib. *khyim-na gnas-pa*, Skt. **gṛhāvāsa*) and the renunciant life (Tib. *rab-tu byung-ba*, Skt. *pravrajyā*), all to the detriment of the former. There are 97 such contrasts in R, and an even longer list of 105 in Tib. The fact that the entire list, however—with the exception of the first item—has no parallel in AY or Dh makes it clear that the bulk of this section is a relatively late interpolation. Cf. below, §20, n. 417.

371 AY "As to the disparaging of home-dwelling, to leave home is praised by the wise"; Dh "And why? Dwelling at home is filthy dwelling; going forth from the home is praised by the wise." R has no reference to praise by the Buddhas or other wise ones, reading simply "living at home is very dusty; going forth from the home is marvelous."

372 Tib. *nyes-pa'i skyon-chags-pa*, Skt. **duṣṭadoṣa*. The term *doṣa* "fault, bad quality" is frequently contrasted with *guṇa* "good quality"; see MW 498C.

373 Though this translation may seem unexpected, the reading found in R seems to confirm its accuracy. Tib. *nyam-nga-ba* would normally be translated as "anxious, fearful," but it is also given as the equivalent of Skt. *sambādha* "cramped space, crowded place" in *Mvy.* no. 6468, while the Tibetan phrase used in the second part of this pair, *bag yangs-pa*, can mean "open space" as well as the more common "fearless." R has *tsai-chia chü fo* 在家具縛, "at home one is entirely bound" vs. *ch'u-chia wu-ai* 出家無礙 "leaving home is without obstruction" (11.476a24-25), surely an attempt to translate a version of the classic

the renunciant life is liberation from ownership.[374] Household life is the basis of bad conduct; the renunciant life is the basis of good conduct.[375]

[19B] "Household life is dwelling in the dust; the renunciant life is not dwelling in the dust. Household life is sinking into the mud of desire; the renunciant life is escaping from the mud of desire. Household life is the arena of the foolish; the renunciant life is the arena of the wise. In the household life it is difficult to purify one's livelihood; in the renunciant life it is easy to purify one's livelihood. In the household life one has many rivals; in the renunciant life one is free of rivals.[376]

[19C] "Household life abounds in poverty; the renunciant life is free of poverty.[377] Household life is the place of suffering; the renunciant life is happiness. Household life is a stairway to the bad rebirths; the renunciant life is a stairway to the heights. Household life is bondage; the renunciant life is liberation. Household life is fearful; the renunciant life is fearless.[378]

[19D] "In the household life one acts under the compulsion of punishment; in the renunciant life one acts without punishment. Household life is involved with the use of weapons; in the renunciant life, one does not make use of weapons.[379] In the household life one experiences upsetting things; the renunciant life is devoid of upsetting things. Household life is suffering, due to seeking; the renunciant life is happy because of being devoid of seeking. Household life is wild; the renunciant life is pacified.[380]

---

classic phrase "household life is cramped; going forth is [like] open air" (in Pāli *sambādho gharavāso abbhokāso pabbajjā*; e.g., DN I.63). Translating from the Tibetan alone, Sakurabe reads "being at home is anxious; leaving home is fearless" (p. 273).

374 Tib. *yongs-su 'dzin-pa*, Skt. *parigraha* "upholding, acquisition" (also "property" according to BHSD 321c). According to my reading the emphasis is on possession itself, hence my translation of the term as "ownership." R reads simply "at home there is much defilement; leaving home, one abandons [it] and separates oneself [from it]" (11.476a25-26)

375 Not in AY or Dh.

376 Not in AY or Dh. R reads "at home it is very dirty" (*kou* 垢, a character already used above in §19A); "leaving home is free of dirt" (*wu kou* 無垢, a phrase used elsewhere to translation Skt. *vimala*). Presumably the translator of R misread Skt. *sapala* "having rivals" as *samala* and understood the latter as "filthy, dirty," and also misread its opposite *asapala* "without rival" in the same way (cf. DES p. 694b, s.v. "rival").

377 Rather than "poverty," R reads "decline," though perhaps the sense is the same.

378 Not in AY or Dh.

379 R, for reasons that escape me, reads instead "much distress" (*huan* 患) instead of "without distress."

380 Not in AY or Dh. R reads "in the household life one is in motion; leaving home, one is without motion."

[19E] "Household life is characterized by greed; the renunciant life is without greed. In the household life one is weak; in the renunciant life, one is not weak. Household life is ignoble; the renunciant life is noble.[381] Household life is a blazing flame; the renunciant life stills the flame. In the household life one benefits others; in the renunciant life one benefits both others and oneself.[382]

[19F] "Household life is of small benefit; the renunciant life is of great benefit. Household life is small in splendor; the renunciant life is great in splendor. Household life is subject to suffering due to defilement; the renunciant life is characterized by happiness due to leaving the world. Household life brings forth thorns; the renunciant life eliminates thorns. In the household life one possesses a small Dharma; in the renunciant life, one possesses a great Dharma.[383]

[19G] "In the household life one acts contrary to the Vinaya; in the renunciant life, one carries out the Vinaya. In the household life one has regrets; in the renunciant life, one has no regrets.[384] In the household life the ocean of tears, milk, and blood[385] expands; in the renunciant life, the ocean of tears, milk, and blood dries up. Household life is criticized by the Buddhas, Pratyekabuddhas, and *śrāvaka*s; the renunciant life is praised by the Buddhas, Pratyekabuddhas, and *śrāvaka*s. In the household life one is never satisfied; in the renunciant life, one knows satisfaction.[386]

[19H] "Household life causes Māra[387] to rejoice; the renunciant life causes Māra to suffer. Household life leads to great troubles; the renunciant life leads to the quieting of

---

381 The terms used, in both Tib and R, have to do with class status and not with moral character.

382 Not in AY or Dh. For the second part of this sentence R (seconded by *Dbhv.*) has only "leaving home benefits oneself." My suspicion is the version found in the Tibetan reflects a "sanitizing" of what was seen as an unacceptably self-oriented statement. It would be more difficult to explain an emendation in the other direction.

383 Not in AY or Dh. For "possesses" (Tib. *dang-ldan-pa*) R reads "actualizes, accomplishes" (*ch'eng* 成); presumably the underlying Indian term was some form of *sampanna* "possessed of, having completed." I do not know what "large" and "small" Dharma are intended to imply here, unless the simple contrast between the duties (*dharma*) of a householder and the pursuit of religion (*dharma*) on the part of the renunciant is meant.

384 R has no exact equivalent of this pair. For this and the previous sentence, R reads instead "At home one does not control [oneself]; leaving home one controls and subdues [oneself]. At home one diverges from the precepts; leaving home, one follows [lit. "protects"] the precepts."

385 This is a standard image in Buddhist literature, which is intended to evoke a sense of the unimaginable number of lifetimes every living being has endured.

386 Not in AY or Dh.

387 Or perhaps "the Māras," though neither Tib nor R is explicitly plural.

all troubles. In the household life one is untamed; in the renunciant life, one is tamed. In the household life one does the work of a servant; in the renunciant life, one is the master. Household life has saṁsāra as its end; the renunciant life has nirvāṇa as its end.[388]

[19I] "Household life is a precipice; in the renunciant life, one has passed beyond the precipice. Household life is darkness; the renunciant life is light. In the household life one does not have lordship over the senses;[389] in the renunciant life, one has lordship over the senses. Household life gives rise to pride;[390] the renunciant life subdues pride. Household life gives rise to what is not genuine;[391] the renunciant life gives rise to what is genuine.[392]

[19J] "Household life gives rise to the lower rebirths; the renunciant life gives rise to the fortunate rebirths. Household life is not worthy of regard; the renunciant life is worthy of regard. In household life one has many undertakings; in the renunciant life, undertakings are few. The fruit[393] of the household life is small; the fruit of the renunciant life is great. Household life is crooked; the renunciant life is straight.[394]

[19K] "In the household life there is much dejection; in the renunciant life, there is much joy. Household life abounds in the arrows [of suffering];[395] in the renunciant life, the arrows are removed. In the household life one suffers from illness; the renunciant life cures one of illness. Household life brings about the exhaustion of the Dharma; the renunciant life causes the Dharma to spread. Household life makes one heedless; the renunciant life makes one attentive.[396]

[19L] "Household life evokes lack of insight;[397] the renunciant life causes insight to increase. The household life is an obstacle to insight; the renunciant life enlivens one's insight. In the household life one is exposed to entrapment; in the renunciant life one is not exposed to entrapment. In household life there are many activities; in the

---

388 Not in AY or Dh.

389 Judging from the wording of the Tibetan (and perhaps also of R), the underlying Indian text must have read "one is not an Indra [i.e., a lord] with respect to the *indriyas* [sense organs]," a play on words that is impossible to convey directly in English.

390 R "wild excess."

391 Tib. *dam-pa ma-yin-pa*, Skt. **asat*; R reads "what is not appropriate" (*pu hsiang-ying* 不相應).

392 Not in A Y or Dh.

393 R reads "strength, power" (*li* 力), presumably the result of an aural confusion between *bala* "power" and *phala* "fruit."

394 Not in AY or Dh.

395 For this image see above, §5C and n. 110.

396 Not in AY or Dh.

397 Or alternatively, "faulty perspective" (Tib. *'chal-pa'i shes-rab*, Skt. *dauṣprajña*).

renunciant life, activities are few. Household life is like a drink containing poison; the renunciant life is like a drink containing ambrosia.[398]

[19M] "Household life is harmful; the renunciant life is devoid of harm. Household life is contaminated; the renunciant life is uncontaminated. Household life is like the fruit of the *kiṁpāka* plant;[399] the renunciant life is like an ambrosia-fruit. Household life causes one to come into contact with what is unpleasant; the renunciant life causes one to be separated from what is unpleasant. Household life causes one to be separated from what is pleasant; the renunciant life causes one to come into contact with what is pleasant.[400]

[19N] "Household life is weighed down by delusion; the renunciant life is lightened by knowledge. Household life destroys one's yogic practice;[401] the renunciant life purifies one's yogic practice. Household life destroys one's resolve;[402] the renunciant life purifies one's resolve. Household life destroys one's firm determination;[403] the renunciant life purifies one's firm determination.[404]

[19O] "Household life causes one to be without a resort; the renunciant life provides a resort. Household life causes one to be without a protector; the renunciant life provides a protector. Household life causes one to be without a place of rest; the renunciant life provides a place of rest. Household life causes one to be without a refuge; the renunciant life provides a refuge.[405]

[19P] "In the household life malice abounds; in the renunciant life, loving-kindness abounds. In the household life one carries a burden; in the renunciant life, one puts it down. Household life causes instability; the renunciant life causes all activities to attain their ends. In the household life one possesses blameworthy deeds; in the renunciant life, one is free of blameworthy deeds. In the household life one will be tormented; in the renunciant life, one will not be tormented. Household life possesses defilements; the renunciant life is free of defilements. In the household life one possesses worldly goods; the renunciant life is devoid of worldly goods.[406]

---

398 Not in AY or Dh. Tib. *bdud-rtsi*, Skt. *amṛta*.

399 The *kiṁpāka* is "a cucurbitaceous plant (of very bad taste)" according to Monier-Williams (283b).

400 Not in AY or Dh.

401 In place of "yogic practice" (Tib. *sbyor-ba*, Skt. **yoga*), R reads *fang-pien* 方便, usually a translation of Skt. *upāya* "skillful means" but used by a number of early translators, including An Shih-kao and Chih Ch'ien, to translate *vyāyāma* "effort, exertion."

402 Tib. *bsam-pa*, Skt. *āśaya*.

403 Tib. *lhag-pa'i bsam-pa*, Skt. *adhyāśaya*.

404 Not in AY or Dh.

405 Not in AY or Dh.

406 Not in AY or Dh.

[19Q] "Household life is characterized by arrogance; the renunciant life is free of arrogance. In the household life, one makes wealth the essence; in the renunciant life, one makes good qualities the essence. Household life is a plague; the renunciant life assuages the plague. Household life contracts; the renunciant life expands. Household life is easy to find; the renunciant life is difficult to find even once in a hundred thousand eons.[407]

[19R] "The duties of the household life are easy; the duties of the renunciant life are difficult. In the household life one goes with the current; in the renunciant life one goes against the current. Household life is a flood [of passion];[408] the renunciant life is a ship [to cross to the other shore]. Household life is a flood of defilements; the renunciant life is a bridge [to the other side]. Household life is the hither shore; the renunciant life is the other shore.[409]

[19S] "In the household life one is subject to the control [of others]; in the renunciant life one is free of being controlled.[410] Household life is characterized by enmity; in the renunciant life enmity is alleviated.[411] In the household life one acts according to the orders of the king; in the renunciant life, one acts according to the religion of the Buddha.[412] In the household life one suffers from torment; in the renunciant life, one is free of torment. In the household life suffering arises; in the renunciant life, happiness arises.[413]

[19T] "Household life is puffed up; the renunciant life is profound. In the household life companions are numerous; in the renunciant life, companions are few. In the household life one associates with one's wife; in the renunciant life, one associates with earnest cultivation.[414] Household life is like [being caught in] a net; in the renunciant life, one tears open the net. In the household life one assiduously calculates how to cause harm to others; in the renunciant life, one assiduously calculates how to benefit others.[415]

[19U] "In the household life one highly esteems material giving; in the renunciant life, one highly esteems giving the Dharma. In the household life one upholds the banner of Māra; in the renunciant life, one upholds the banner of the Buddha. Household life is the foundation of suffering; the renunciant life destroys the foundation of suffering. In

---

[407] Not in AY or Dh.

[408] Or "river" (Tib. *chu-bo*, Skt. **ogha*). For this image see above, §13Y, n. 297.

[409] Not in AY or Dh.

[410] Cf. R, which reads "bound" instead of "free of bonds."

[411] Tib. *shar gnyer-ba* (for a discussion of this term see above, §13EE, n. 304). R has "At home [one feels] antagonism; leaving home calms antagonism."

[412] The underlying text must have contained a play on the word *śāsana*, which means both "order, command" and (in Buddhist usage) "religion."

[413] Not in AY or Dh.

[414] Tib. *mos-pa*, Skt. **adhimukti*. R reads instead "leaving home, one associates with the heart" (or "mind," *hsin* 心).

[415] Not in AY or Dh.

the household life the *skandhas* expand; in the renunciant life, one discards all the *skandhas*. Household life is darkness; in the renunciant life, one is liberated from darkness. O Eminent Householder, in that way should the householder bodhisattva apply himself to the renunciant life.[416]

[§20. WHEN VISITING A MONASTERY, CONT'D.][417]

[20A] "And he should think as follows: 'If I make offerings as numerous as the sands of the Ganges River for many days,[418] and give away all my possessions,[419] those actions will be surpassed by the mere thought of becoming a renunciant in the well-taught Dharma and Vinaya,[420] {which will cause my mind to rejoice}.'[421] And why? O Eminent Householder, material giving is inferior, since even unbelievers, ingrates, robbers, outcastes,[422] mercenaries of the king, and henchmen of his ministers[423] give gifts. O Eminent Householder, the householder bodhisattva should think, 'I should not be satisfied with the substance of giving. Therefore, I ought to make morality, learning, and pure conduct[424] my substance.'[425]

[20B] "When he comes to a monastery, he should do homage to the marks of the Tathāgata.[426] And having done homage to them, he should bring forth three thoughts. And what are the three?

---

416 Not in AY or Dh.

417 Note that this section resumes where §18 left off: there we left our home-dwelling bodhisattva at the entrance to the monastery, and now he is being given instructions on what to do when he actually goes inside. This serves to underscore the identity of the intervening material as an interpolation.

418 AY "all day long."

419 Not in AY.

420 Not in AY or Dh; R "in the well-disciplining Dharma" (*sic*!).

421 Dh only.

422 Tib. *gdol-pa*, Skt. *caṇḍāla*.

423 Tib. *blon-po'i ya-nga-ba*. The term *ya-nga-ba* means "frightening, fearful" (Rerikh 8.224a), but what the phrase as a whole means I am not sure. Only AY includes kings themselves in this list; the skirting of direct references to the ruler and his immediate associates in later versions of the sūtra may have been the result of a deliberate attempt to avoid arousing the ire of the authorities.

424 Tib only (*tshangs-par spyod-pa*, Skt. *brahmacarya*, i.e., the observance of celibacy).

425 In the underlying Indian text there was surely a play on the word *sāra*, which means both "substance, essence" and "wealth, riches." For a discussion of this term see above, §5A, n. 95 and §6B, n 120.

426 In an egregious example of overtranslation, Sakurabe reads "he should

(1) I, too, should become one who is worthy of this kind of worship.
(2) 'Out of pity for living beings, I should bestow my own body.[427]
(3) 'I should train and make efforts in whatever way will cause me to quickly attain Supreme Perfect Enlightenment and to do the deeds of a Buddha, and by having experienced the *parinirvāṇa* of a Tathāgata, to cause others to attain *parinirvāṇa*.'

Thus he should think.[428]

[20C][429] "And when he goes inside the monastery, he should reflect on all the activities of the community of monks as follows:

---

do homage to the stūpa which is the symbol of the Tathāgata" (p. 277)! Presumably Sakurabe was taking his cue here not from the Tibetan text itself but from R, which does have a reference to "the stūpa of the Tathāgata" (*ju-lai t'a* 如來塔) at this point. But no word that could be construed as meaning "stūpa" appears here in any other version of the text, and there is every reason to suspect that the word *t'a* 塔 was added as an interpretive gloss by the the translator of R. The cult of the stūpa is, in fact, conspicuous by its absence from the *Ugra*; for a discussion of this issue and its implications for the institutional context of early Mahāyāna practice see Chapter 7, pp. 182-184.

427 Tib. *byin-gyis brlabs-pa*, Skt. **adhi√sthā*. It is not entirely clear what this is intended to mean, but note that the term *adhiṣṭhāna* also occurs in the *Saddharmapuṇḍarīka-sūtra* in the context of a donation of the body—in this case, when a bodhisattva is about to burn his body in order to honor the sūtra. The text reads *svakam adhiṣṭhānam akarot* (407.6), which Edgerton (BHSD 15b) takes as "made his resolve," but it seems to me more likely that the phrase should be read as a double accusative, i.e., "he made himself (*svaka*) a bestowal (*adhiṣṭhāna*)"; note that in the following phrase *svam* rather than *svakam* is used when the intended meaning is "his." The word *adhiṣṭhāna* is surely one of the most complex and multivalent terms in the Buddhist lexicon; among other things, it can be used to mean "blessing," "empowerment," "designation/setting aside" (of something for a specific purpose) and, if Edgerton is correct, "resolve." R reads "I should leave behind my body" (or perhaps "relics"; the Chinese reads *she-li* 舍利, but the underlying *śarīra* could be taken in either sense). There is no equivalent in AY; Dh has "not begrudging his body and life."

428 Not in AY; Dh has only item (3), which reads in his translation "I should cause those who have not attained *parinirvāṇa* to attain *parinirvāṇa*." The final sentence ("Thus he should think") occurs only in Tib.

429 For a synoptic chart of the monastic specialties listed in this section according to all versions of the *Ugra* and its citations in the *Daśabhūmika-vibhāṣā* see Appendix 3. See also the considerably shorter list (shorter, that is, in all versions except the Tibetan) that occurs immediately below, §20E.

'Which monk is a learned one? Which monk is a Dharma-preacher? Which monk is a Vinaya-holder? Which monk is a Mātṛkā-holder? Which monk is a Bodhisattva-piṭaka-holder?[430] Which monk is a wilderness-dweller?[431] Which monk lives on almsfood? Which monk dresses in rags from the dust heap,[432] has few desires,[433] is satisfied [with what he has], and lives in seclusion?[434] Which monk does yogic practice? Which monk practices meditation? Which monk belongs to the Bodhisattva Vehicle?[435] Which monk is in charge of repairs?[436] Which monk is the administrator? Which monk is the overseer?'[437] Thus should he reflect on all the activities of the community of monks. And having reflected on their activities, in order to conform to them all, he should dwell in

---

[430] Note that we have listed here the upholders of four sections of a Buddhist canon: the Dharma- (= Sūtra), Vinaya-, Abhidharma-, and Bodhisattva-piṭakas. (Sakurabe [p. 278] interprets the third term as a reference to the Vinaya- rather than the Abhidharma-mātṛkā, though he does not provide any justification for this reading; cf. §20E, n. 445 below.) The Bodhisattva-piṭaka has been discussed most recently (though not without some serious problems in interpretation) in Pagel 1995. It is also worth noting that a distinction is drawn here between the *dharmabhāṇaka* (if that indeed is the underlying term) and the holder of the *bodhisattvapiṭaka*, implying that the former is understood as a specialist in the recitation of Mainstream, not Mahāyāna, sūtras. For further details see Appendix 3.

[431] This and the next two items—living in the wilderness, eating only almsfood, and dressing in dust-heap rags—form part of the list of the twelve (sometimes thirteen) ascetic practices known as *dhūtaguṇa*s. For a useful overview of these items as described in Sanskrit sources see Dayal 1932, pp. 134-140, and more recently Ray 1994, pp. 293-318. For a discussion including a wider range of literature (including texts preserved only in Chinese) see Miyamoto 1954, pp. 302-310, especially the chart on p. 304 tabulating differences in the sequence of these items in various texts. (I am grateful to Paul Harrison and Jonathan Silk for bringing Miyamoto's work to my attention.) It is perhaps significant that the three items from this list which are singled out for attention here are also emphasized in the *Ratnarāśi* (and given in the same sequence), where a separate chapter is devoted to each. See Silk 1994, p. 70 and his translation of Chapters 5-7 of the sūtra on pp. 338-385.

[432] Not in AY.

[433] Not in AY or Dh.

[434] Not in AY.

[435] Omitted in R and *Dbhv*.

[436] AY and Tib only (*sic*!).

[437] Not in AY or Dh.

conformity with them. And he should display no other actions in the presence of others.[438]

[20D] "And why? What goes on within the monastery is hidden from the village; what goes on within the village is hidden from the monastery[439] He whose activities of speech are well controlled should not speak of monastic affairs in the village, nor of village affairs in the monastery. {He supports and serves the one who is learned, who will correct his learning. He supports and serves the one who explicates the sūtras, who will explain the exegesis of the sūtras for him. He supports and serves the one who upholds the Vinaya, who will explain to him how to overcome his faults. He supports and serves the bodhisattva who upholds the profound *piṭaka*, who will explicate matters having to do with the six perfections and tactical skill.}[440] To the monk who is in need of a robe, a bowl, or medicines and supplies for illness, he should give them to him in such a way that others will not speak ill of him or become angry. And why? Because the attachments of gods and humans are characterized by envy and greed; therefore it is the ordinary person who needs to be protected, and not the Arhat. And why? Faults arise in ordinary beings, while in the Arhat they do not.

[20E][441] "Therefore, through relying[442] on one who is

---

[438] There is considerable variety in the renderings of this sentence: AY "and he should not turn them to mutual jealousy," Dh "all of [the monks] he should equally satisfy and give to, and he should not practice with any other state of mind," and R "he should not bring about scolding."

[439] AY and R correspond fairly well to Tib here, but Dh's version seems garbled.

[440] This material, which occurs here in AY only, is given in §20E in the other versions.

[441] Most of the items in this section are missing from the three Chinese translations, though they occur above in §20C. While all three Chinese versions include references to the learned monk (*bahuśruta*), the *dharmabhāṇaka* or sūtra specialist, the *vinaya-dhara*, and the upholder of the *bodhisattva-piṭaka*, all other items on this list are omitted in AY and Dh. R alone adds a mention of the wilderness-dwelling monk (*āraṇyaka*).

[442] The Tibetan texts offer two divergent readings throughout this passage, viz., *brten* "rely on" in S and N and *bsten* "serve" in P and D (a not uncommon alternation in Kanjur texts). Both terms, however, can also serve as translations of Skt. *avaṣṭhamba* "approach" (see *Mvy.* nos. 4089 and 4093), a sense that would agree with the reading given in R and perhaps also Dh; AY, however, reads "serve." In any event the basic meaning is clear: by frequenting (and perhaps by offering specific service to) each of these members of the monastic community, the lay bodhisattva will be able to make progress in their respective areas of expertise.

learned,[443] he should exert himself to strive for learning. Relying on the Dharma-preacher, he should exert himself in learning the exegetical sayings.[444] Relying on the Vinaya-holder, he should exert himself to subdue his faults and defilements. Relying on the Mātṛkā-holder, he should exert himself in the obligations of body, speech, and mind.[445] Relying on the Bodhisattva-piṭaka-holder, he should exert himself in the six perfections and in skill-in-means. Relying on the wilderness-dweller, he should exert himself to cultivate seclusion.[446] Relying on the one who lives on alms, he should exert himself to be unmoved by profit or loss, fame or infamy, praise or blame, happiness or suffering. Relying on the one who dresses in dust-heap rags, he should exert himself not to delight in wearing monastic robes or in ornamentation. Relying on the one whose desires are few, he should exert himself to have few desires. Relying on the one who is satisfied, he should exert himself to experience satisfaction. Relying on the one who lives in seclusion, he should exert himself to cultivate seclusion. Relying on the *yogācāra* practitioner, he should exert himself in solitary meditation,[447] paying attention to the *śamatha* and *vipaśyanā* of the inner mind. Relying on the *dhyāna* practitioner, he should exert himself to eliminate the defilements. Relying on the member of the Bodhisattva Vehicle, he should exert himself in the four means of attraction: giving, pleasant speech, promoting the interests of others, and sharing their concerns.[448] Relying on the superintendent of repairs, he should exert himself to be energetic in renouncing all objects. Relying on the monastery administrator, he should exert himself in carrying out his duties. Relying on the overseer he should cause his mind to be unwearying. O Eminent Householder, thus should the householder bodhisattva who lives at home conform to those activities just as they are.[449]

---

443 Dh specifies that the learned one is a *bhikṣu*.

444 Tib. *rnam-par nges-pa'i gtam*, Skt. **viniścayakathā*.

445 Tib only. Note the interesting association of the *mātṛkā* (i.e., the proto-abhidharma) with obligations or vows (Tib. *sdom-pa*, Skt. *saṁvara*). Perhaps on this basis, Sakurabe interprets "Mātṛkā-holder" both here and above in §20C as a reference to the *Vinaya-mātṛkā* (Sakurabe 1974, pp. 278 and 279), though he does not discuss or defend this interpretation. Unfortunately the Chinese versions cannot be called upon to adjudicate, since this sentence is missing from all three.

446 Not in AY. Dh has "to cultivate the practice of *dhyāna*," while R agrees with the Tibetan.

447 Tib. *nang-du yang-dag 'jog*, Skt. **pratisaṁlayana* (*Mvy.* no. 1488).

448 For these items cf. above, §11D, n. 230.

449 Tib only.

[20F] "If he furnishes a monk whose course is not yet certain[450] with a robe and bowl, he should induce that monk to [strive for] Supreme Perfect Enlightenment. And why? Because material furnishings provide an occasion for Dharma-furnishing. O Eminent Householder, in that way should the householder bodhisattva become knowledgeable about the conduct of the *śramana*. Moreover, he should reconcile those *śramaṇa*s who are in a state of discord with one another. At the time when the True Dharma is disappearing[451] he should uphold the True Dharma even at the cost of his own life. O Eminent Householder, if a householder bodhisattva sees a sick monk he should cure him of that sickness, even by means of his own flesh and blood.

[20G] "Moreover, O Eminent Householder, by giving up [his possessions] the householder bodhisattva also incites others to do so.[452] And having given, he does not bring forth thoughts of regret, for at the forefront of all his roots-of-goodness should be the spirit of enlightenment. O Eminent Householder, in that way a householder bodhisattva who dwells at the household stage[453] acts in accordance with the Tathāgata's word, does not fall away from the qualities conducive to enlightenment, is free of blameworthy deeds in this lifetime, and will be distinguished in future lives." [454]

---

450 Presumably this refers to the fact that the monk in question is not yet irreversible from either Arhatship or Buddhahood. For the underlying Sanskrit term and its (faulty) Tibetan translation see above, §4C and n. 83.

451 Tib. *dam-pa'i chos rab-tu rnam-par 'jig-pa*, Skt. **saddharma-vipralopa*. For a discussion of this expression and associated concepts see Nattier 1991. AY agrees with the Tibetan, reading "when the True Dharma is about to decline and disappear" (*jo cheng-fa yü shu-wei-che* 若正法欲衰微者 not, as per Schuster (1985, p. 231), "If there are some who wish to deprecate the True Dharma." Dh, by contrast, seems to have read *vipralāpa* "dispute" rather than *vipralopa* "extinction," which he translated "if there is quarreling concerning the Dharma" (*jo i fa cheng* 若以法諍). R has no exact parallel, but it does contain an additional reference to "contention" which may be a vestige of this line.

452 Not in Dh.

453 Tib. *sa*, Skt. *bhūmi*. Cf. above, §2D and n. 46.

454 Not in AY or Dh. Cf. above, §2D, where precisely the same wording occurs.

[§21. THE ORDINATION OF UGRA AND HIS FRIENDS (version 1)][455]

[21A] Then with one voice Ugra and the other eminent householders praised the words of the Blessed One, and spoke to the Blessed One as follows: "It is amazing, O Blessed One, how the Blessed One has spoken so well about the faults, obligations, and activities of the household life, and about the advantages of the good qualities of the renunciant. O Blessed One, now that it has become clear to us the extent of the faults and bad qualities of the household life and the endless advantages of [456] the qualities of the renunciant, O Blessed One, please let us go forth and receive full ordination in the well-taught Dharma and Vinaya taught by the Well-Gone One." When they had spoken thus, the Blessed One replied, "O Eminent Householders, the renunciant life is difficult; one must keep one's conduct perfectly pure." When he had spoken those words, the eminent householders replied, "O Blessed One, it may be true that the renunciant life is difficult, but we ask the Blessed One to allow us to go forth. We ask to be allowed to exert ourselves in the Blessed One's teachings." And the Blessed One allowed them to go forth.[457]

[21B] Then the Blessed One said to the bodhisattva Maitreya and the bodhisattva *Sarvacaryāviśuddha,[458] "Good men, cause these eminent householders to go forth and ordain them!"[459] When the Blessed One had spoken, the bodhisattva Maitreya presided over the going forth of nine thousand[460] eminent householders, while the bodhisattva *Sarvacaryāviśuddha presided over the going forth of seven thousand[461] eminent householders.[462]

[21C] And upon the teaching of this Dharma-text concerning the course of training of householder bodhisattvas, a thousand[463] living

---

455 In AY Ugra and his friends receive ordination at the end of the sūtra (§30b), not here. For a discussion of this editorial emendation in the later versions see Chapter 3, pp. 62-63.

456 One of the Tibetan versions (D) has been emended to read "and" rather than "of" (though this emendation is not made in the same phrase immediately above).

457 Not in AY (but cf. below, §30b).

458 This bodhisattva (whose name means "pure in all his conduct") appears to be quite unknown.

459 The term used is *bsnyen-par rdzogs-par byed-pa* (Skt. *upasaṁpadā*), the technical term for full ordination as a *bhikṣu*. This expression is regularly preceded, as here, by some form of the verb *pra√vraj* (see BHSD 143a).

460 Dh "twelve hundred."

461 Dh "twelve hundred." R does not mention this second bodhisattva, stating only that "Maitreya and others" ordained nine thousand eminent householders.

462 Not in AY (but cf. below, §30b).

463 Dh "twelve hundred."

creatures[464] brought forth the spirit of Supreme Perfect Enlightenment. {Two thousand five hundred bodhisattvas attained echo-endurance,[465] and four thousand gods and humans attained receptive dharma-endurance.}[466] {And two thousand gods and humans there arose the dust-free and undefiled eye of the dharmas.}[467]

---

464 Tib. *srog-chags*, Skt. **prāṇin*. This is an interesting choice of terms to describe the audience, since the species and *gati* of the listeners are not specified. AY and Dh, however, specify that humans (*jen* 人) are meant, while R has "eminent householders and others" (*chang-che teng* 長者等).

465 This strange term (*yin-hsiang jen* 音響忍 appears almost exclusively in translations by Dharmarakṣa (e.g., T 291, 10.614b21 and 23; T 398, 13.448a18 and 449b19), but it also occurs once in the version of the *Larger Sukhāvatī-vyūha* attributed to Saṁghavarman (T 360, 12.271a14), where it is translated by Gómez as "serene acceptance of the word" (Gómez 1996, p. 181). Unfortunately this is a portion of the text that does not have a parallel in Sanskrit, so we cannot use this occurrence to establish what—if anything—the corresponding Indic term might be. In at least some of these texts *yin-hsiang jen* appears, as it does here, as one of a number of different *kṣāntis* (ten in T 291, three in T 360) that the bodhisattva might obtain. The following expression, *jou shun fa-jen* 柔順法忍 "submissive dharma-endurance," occurs quite frequently in Dharmarakṣa's work, where it may reflect an underlying *anulomika-dharma-kṣānti* (cf. Karashima 1998, p. 353).

466 Dh only.

467 AY only (but cf. below, §30, in the other versions). The plural of "dharmas" is explicit.

[PRACTICES OF THE MONASTIC BODHISATTVA]

Section three.[468]

{Chapter 7: Satisfaction}[469]

[§22. THE RENUNCIANT BODHISATTVA'S PRACTICES]

[22A] Then Ugra the Eminent Householder spoke to the Blessed One as follows: "The Blessed One[470] has explained the householder bodhisattvas' household stage and the {good and}[471] bad points of living at home, {as well as the practice of giving, morality, endurance, exertion, concentration, and insight—in other words, the practice of the Mahāyāna.}[472] But would the Blessed One please explain the renunciants' accomplishments, morality, learning, ascetic qualities, austerities,[473] the conduct and way of acting possessed by those who are counted as[474] renunciant bodhisattvas?[475] O Blessed One, how can the bodhisattva who has gone forth in the well-taught Dharma and Vinaya ensure that the actions of welcoming, salutation, rising to one's feet, making the gesture of *añjali*, and acts of respect are not in vain?"[476]

---

[468] Tib only. On the term *bam-po* "part, section, fascicle" see above, §1, n. 2.

[469] Dh only.

[470] Dh "the Tathāgata, the Arhat, the Samyaksaṁbuddha."

[471] AY and Dh only.

[472] AY and Dh only. Note that while these early Chinese versions mention some positive aspects of the household life, R and Tib do not.

[473] Not in AY. Dh reflects a version that read "morality, exertion, insight, and the ascetic qualities (*dhutaguṇa*)," with the latter strangely translated as *chih-tsu chih te* 止足之德 "qualities of satisfaction," presumably as the result of a confusion between *dhuta* and some Prakrit form of *tuṣṭa* "satisfied, contented" such as **tuṭṭha* (cf. PTSD 304b). An even more grievous misinterpretation below (see §25K, n. 644) makes it clear that Dharmarakṣa was entirely unfamiliar with this expression. R has *chieh-wen kung-te* 戒聞功德 "precept-listening qualities" (is he confusing *dhuta* with Pkt. *suta* "heard"?). On the *dhutaguṇas* themselves see Chapter 5, p. 130 and n. 50. "Austerities" translates Tib. *yo-byad bsnyungs-pa* (lit., "reduced possessions"), a regular equivalent of Skt. *saṁlekha*.

[474] Only in Tib.

[475] Dh adds "who have cut off their beard and hair." Here and throughout this section, AY renders "renunciant" (*pravrajita*) as *ch'ü-chia hsiu-tao-che* 去家修道者 "one who has left home to pursue the Way."

[476] Not in AY; Dh substitutes "What is it to cut off one's beard and hair and undertake the practice of the Dharma and Vinaya? What is going forth from the household?—His mind is without deviation, his conduct is unswerving.

[22B] When he had spoken thus,[477] the Blessed One addressed Ugra the Eminent Householder as follows: "O Eminent Householder, it is good, it is good[478] that you have asked the Tathāgata about the renunciants' accomplishments, morality, learning, ascetic qualities, austerities, conduct, and[479] way of acting possessed by those who are counted as[480] renunciant bodhisattvas.[481] Therefore, O Eminent Householder, listen well and[482] bear this in mind, and I will explain to you how those who are counted as[483] renunciant bodhisattvas should dwell and what they should accomplish." Ugra the Eminent Householder said "Good, O Blessed One," and[484] listened as the Blessed One had instructed him.

[22C] And the Blessed One spoke to him as follows. "O Eminent Householder, pondering to himself 'for whose sake have I gone forth from home into

---

And he does not seek welcoming, greetings, ceremonial conduct, or the gesture of *añjali*." (The negative "does not seek" does not appear in any other version and may well be Dh's own addition.) R, apparently not recognizing the underlying technical terms, produced a rendition which veers off into several typically Chinese paired expressions: "What is it for the bodhisattva to discipline himself in the good and wondrous Dharma, to go forth from the home, to worship, and to rise and stand, go and come, proceed and stop?" All of the items in the list found in Tib are included in section §XCVIII of the *Mahāvyutpatti*, titled *Mānanā-paryāyāḥ*, "Expressions of Respect," viz., *abhivādanam* (*gus-par smra-ba*, no. 1786), *vandanam* (*phyag 'tshal-ba*, no. 1754), [*praty*]*utthanam* ([*mngon-par*] *ldang-ba*, no. 1767), *añjali-karma* (*thal-mo sbyar-ba*, no. 1766), and *sāmīcī* (*'dud-pa*, no. 1768). All of these are stylized expressions of politeness that would be exchanged within the monastic community and made toward monks in general by outsiders.

477 Tib only.

478 Not in AY.

479 Tib only.

480 Tib only.

481 Dh again adds "who have cut off their beard and hair." R omits this entire sentence.

482 Not in AY or R. The Tibetan text requires the interpretation "listen well and bear this in mind," but the underlying Indic text almost certainly read "listen and bear this well and carefully in mind" (*śṛṇu sādhu ca suṣṭhu ca manasikuru*; cf. *Vajracchedikā*, §2), where both adverbs modify the second verb. (AY alone gets the adverbial placement right, reading "think about this diligently and well.") The standard counterpart of this formula in Pāli is even simpler, viz., *suṇahi* (var. *suṇohi*), *sādhukaṁ manasikarohi*, "listen and bear this well in mind."

483 Tib only.

484 Not in AY.

homelessness?'[485] the renunciant bodhisattva should exert himself in the pursuit of knowledge as if his head and clothes[486] were on fire.[487] And having reflected on that, first of all he should dwell in the four[488] noble traditions, taking delight in the ascetic practices and the austerities.[489]

[§23. THE FOUR NOBLE TRADITIONS]

[23A] "O Eminent Householder,[490] how should the renunciant bodhisattva dwell in the four noble traditions?[491] O Eminent Householder, the renunciant bodhisattva is content with any old robe.[492] He praises being content with any old robe,[493] and he does not make any inappropriate efforts[494] for the sake of [obtaining] a robe. If he does not manage to obtain a robe, he is not disturbed or upset. And if he does obtain a robe, he does not become attached to it, infatuated with it, delighted by it, or attracted to it. Having seen the fault [of such attraction] and having become clearly conscious of its arising, he

---

485 Not in AY; Dh reads "for what reason" instead of "for whose sake."

486 Tib only.

487 This is a common image in Buddhist literature for the sense of urgency that should be felt by the practitioner in pursuit of enlightenment. It occurs, for example, in the *Kāśyapaparivarta* at §2; the Sanskrit text is lost at this point, but cf. the citation from the *Akṣayamatinirdeśa* in the *Śikṣāsamuccaya*, 191.8-9: *ādīptaśiraścailopamatā jñānaparyeṣṭvā*. For additional examples (including similar wording in Pāli) see BHSD 94b.

488 Not in AY or Dh.

489 Not in AY or Dh; R omits "and the austerities."

490 Not in AY or Dh.

491 Tib. *'phags-pa'i rigs*, Skt. *āryavaṁśa*. For an extended discussion of this term and the practices to which it refers see Chapter 5, pp. 127-130. Though all three Chinese versions include a list of these four items, virtually all of the detail and repetition within this section is absent from AY and Dh.

492 The underlying Sanskrit expression was surely *itaretareṇa cīvareṇa* "with this or that robe, with any robe." The Tibetan epithet *ngan-ngon* is more strongly negative, and could be translated as "mean, inferior, poor." Maurice Walshe's "any old [robe, etc.]" seems an inspired choice for the Pāli equivalent *itarītara*, and I have adopted his wording here. Here and throughout AY reads "[he is satisfied with] one robe, one meal," and so on.

493 Sakurabe (p. 284) interprets this line as meaning praising someone else who is content with his own inferior robe, but the Pāli antecedents support the reading given here. Dh seems to say that the bodhisattva will be renowned (*ming wen* 名聞) for his contentment with each of these items.

494 R "does not speak falsely."

acts with non-attachment. And the one who is content with any old robe does not praise himself or blame others.[495]

[23B] "Moreover, O Eminent Householder, the renunciant bodhisattva[496] is content with any old almsfood.[497] Praising the act of being content with any old almsfood, he does not make inappropriate efforts to obtain almsfood. If he does not obtain almsfood, he is not disturbed or upset. And if he does obtain almsfood, he does not become attached to it, infatuated with it, delighted by it, or attracted to it. Having seen the fault [of such attraction] and having become clearly conscious of its arising, he acts with non-attachment. And the one who is content with any old almsfood does not praise himself or blame others.[498]

[23C] "Moreover, O Eminent Householder, the renunciant bodhisattva is content with any old lodging.[499] He praises being content with any old lodging, and does not make any inappropriate efforts for the sake of [obtaining] lodging. If he does not manage to obtain lodging, he is not disturbed or upset. And if he does obtain lodging, he does not become attached to it, infatuated with it, delighted by it, or attracted to it. Having seen the fault [of such attraction] and having become clearly conscious of its arising, he acts with non-attachment. And the one who is content with any old lodging does not praise himself or blame others.[500]

[23D] "Moreover, O Eminent Householder, the renunciant bodhisattva is content with any old medicines and requisites for illness.[501] He praises being content with any old medicines and requisites for illness, and does not make any inappropriate efforts for the sake of [obtaining] medicines and requisites for illness. If he does not manage to obtain medicines and requisites for illness, he is not disturbed or upset. And if he does obtain medicines and requisites for illness, he does not become attached to them, infatuated with them, delighted by them, or attracted to them. Having

---

495 Not in AY or Dh. Dh replaces this entire paragraph with "Thus he knows satisfaction, and knowing satisfaction, he is renowned."

496 Not in AY or Dh.

497 Dh adds "and being content with almsfood, he is renowned."

498 Not in AY or Dh.

499 Dh adds "and being content with bedding, he is renowned." The underlying term is *śayanāsana* (for which the Tibetan text reads *mal-cha* "bedding," though the *Mahāvyutpatti* [no. 2375] prescribes *mal-stan* "bed and seat" and AY and Dh read *ch'uang* 床 and *ch'uang-wo* 床臥 "bed, couch," respectively). The term *śayana* itself means "bed," while *āsana* of course is "seat," but by extension the compound expression came to mean "lodging" as well (for which see PTSD 723a, s.v. *senāsana*). In R §§23B and C are combined.

500 Not in AY or Dh; R omits this entire paragraph (see previous note).

501 Dh adds "and being content with medicines for illness, he is renowned."

seen the fault [of such attraction] and having become clearly conscious of its arising, he acts with non-attachment. And the one who is content with any old medicines and requisites for illness does not praise himself or blame others.[502]

[23E] "He delights and takes pleasure in abandonment [of negative qualities],[503] and finding joy in abandonment he makes efforts associated with delight in abandonment. He becomes happy through abandoning bad and unvirtuous things; he does not do so by not abandoning them. Delighting in the cultivation [of good qualities],[504] he makes efforts connected with delight in cultivation. He becomes happy by cultivating virtuous things; he does not do so by not cultivating them. And the one who delights in abandonment, finds joy in abandonment, and makes efforts associated with abandonment, and who delights in cultivation, finds joy in cultivation, and makes efforts associated with delight in cultivation does not praise himself or blame others. O Eminent Householder, in this way does the renunciant bodhisattva dwell in the four noble traditions.[505] And why are they called "noble traditions"? Because all the qualities conducive to enlightenment[506] reside within them. Therefore they are called "noble traditions."[507]

[§24. THE NOBLE TRADITIONS AND OTHER ASCETIC PRACTICES][508]

[24A] "Moreover, O Eminent Householder,[509] the renunciant

---

502 Not in AY or Dh; R also omits this entire paragraph, treating the following item ("delighting in abandonment and cultivation") as the fourth of the noble traditions.

503 Tib. *spong-ba*, Skt. *prahāṇa* (for this equivalence see *Mvy.* nos. 959, 967-970, 7027, and 7606). For the Sanskrit term (which in other contexts, though not here, can mean "exertion") cf. BHSD 389b-390a and Gómez and Silk 1989, p. 87, n. 44. For Pāli parallels to this passage see Chapter 5, pp. 128-129, n. 47.

504 Tib. *bsgom-pa*, Skt. *bhāvanā*.

505 Not in AY or Dh.

506 Skt. *bodhipakṣa-dharmas*. Here, as above (§2C), Dh reads *fo-fa* 佛法 "buddha-dharmas."

507 R alone omits the last three sentences in this paragraph, presumably via a scribal error due to repetition.

508 The content of this section appears rather jumbled: it begins with a recapitulation of the first two of the items of contentment discussed above (viz., the monastic robe and alms-food), but in §24C—which has no counterpart in AY or R and appears later in Dh, following §25E—the discussion shifts to the fourth object of contentment (in one of the *āryavaṁśa* lists), viz., medicine. At this point, instead of discussing the third object of contentment (the monk's bed or dwelling place, Skt. *śayanāsana*), the text extols the virtues of wilderness-dwelling (Skt. **āraṇyavāsa*) instead.

509 Not in AY.

bodhisattva wears the monastic robe because of delight[510] in its ten benefits. And what are the ten?[511] They are as follows:[512] one wraps it around oneself because of modesty and shame; as a shield against mosquitoes, gnats, wind, sun, and snakes; because it displays the form[513] of the *śramaṇa*[514] and the insignia of the *śramaṇa*;[515] because it is

---

[510] Tib. *dga'-ba*. The Indic text undoubtedly had some form of **tuṣṭa* "delight, satisfaction"; AY and Dh both read "satisfaction."

[511] In the Tibetan text the items are not numbered, and there are several possibilities for dividing this account into ten segments. Following the original, I have not attempted to do so here (though Dh, whose list varies slightly from the one given in the Tibetan, does—as is his usual style—number the items).

[512] The following lines are cited in *Śikṣ*. 136.1-7:

> *hrīrapatrāpyakaupīnaḥ pracchādanārthaṁ śramaṇa-liṅgasaṁdarśanārtham imāni ca kaṣāyāṇi* [sic] *deva-mānuṣāsurasya lokasya caityam iti | caityārthaṁ samyag-dhāritavyāni | nirvṛtivirāgaraktāni etāni | na rāgaraktāni | upaśamānukūlāny etāni | na saṁkleśasaṁdhukṣaṇānu-kūlāni | ebhiś ca kāṣāyair vivṛtapāpā bhaviṣyāmaḥ | sukṛtakarmakāriṇo na cīvaramaṇḍanānuyogam anuyuktāḥ | etāni ca kāṣāyāṇy āryamārga-saṁbhārānukūlānīti kṛtvā tathā kariṣyāmo yathā naikakṣaṇam api sakaṣāyāḥ kāye kāṣāyāṇi dhārayiṣyāma iti ||*

There are some considerable differences between the Sanskrit citation and the content of the extant versions of the *Ugra*. For a translation of the *Śikṣ*. citation see Silk 1994a, p. 82.

On the basis of versions of the *Śikṣ*. extant in the Chinese and Tibetan, Bendall (p. 136, n. 1) suggests that several items against which the robe provides protection (viz., mosquitoes, gnats, wind, and in the Tibetan version also sun and snakes) have dropped out of the Sanskrit *Śikṣ*. In this regard Mochizuki 1988 offers a useful citation from the *Sabbāsava-sutta* of the *Majjhima-nikāya* (I, 10) where the same list occurs:

> *katame ca bhikkhave āsavā paṭisevanā pahātabbā: idha bhikkhave bhikkhu paṭisaṅkhā yoniso cīvaraṁ paṭisevati, yāvad eva sītassa paṭighātāya uṇhassa paṭighātāya ḍaṁsa-makasa vātātane-siriṁsapasamphassānaṁ paṭighātāya, yāvad eva hirikopīna paṭicchādanattaṁ*

Once again what is at issue here (and in the following portion of the text) is the proper use of the four requisites of the renunciant contained in one of the *āryavaṁśa* lists (viz., robe, almsbowl, lodging, and medicinal supplies).

[513] The Tibetan reads *kha-dog* "color," but this is a mistranslation of Skt. *rūpa* (as confirmed by AY, which reads *hsing-chuang* 形狀 "appearance, form, shape"). R has *chieh-hsiang* 戒相 "precept-mark" where *chieh* 戒 is presumably

said of those reddish-brown robes that they are a *caitya*[516] for the world with its gods, humans, and asuras,[517] and since they are a *caitya*, one ought to wear them properly;[518] because they are dyed without agitation or passion, not dyed with passion;[519] because they are suitable for peaceful calm, not suitable for the igniting of the defilements; because having wrapped and covered oneself with these reddish-brown robes, one will turn away from doing evil deeds and toward doing good deeds, and will not attempt to use the robe as an ornament; and because, realizing that these reddish-brown robes are

---

a copying error for *hsing* 形 "form, appearance"; Dh reads simply "clothing" (*fu* 服). No equivalent of this expression appears in the Sanskrit citation preserved in *Śikṣ*.

514 While Dh and R transliterate this term, AY translates it as *hsi-hsin* 息心 "one whose heart is calmed," following an old etymology that derives the term *śramaṇa* not from √*śram* "to exert oneself, become tired" but from √*śam* "to become calm, quiet." Or more accurately, this is an etymology that must have been formulated in a Prakrit language in which these two roots would have fallen together as √*sam*. Such an etymology is in fact known in Pāli sources; see *Dhammapada* §265 and its commentary in DhA III.84. The corresponding verse in the Gāndhārī *Dharmapada* (§189) shows the difficulties this etymology caused when Buddhist texts were transposed into languages in which these two roots diverged in spelling. In Gāndhārī the usual spelling of Skt. *śramaṇa* is *ṣamaṇa* (following the standard pattern of *śr* > *ṣ*), but this form could not easily be associated with Gāndhārī √*śam* "calm," and as a result the usual Gāndhārī *ṣamaṇa* was eschewed in favor of the Sanskritic *śramaṇa*, which was apparently perceived as more closely approximating the root √*śam* upon which this etymological explanation depends. For further discussion see Brough 1962, p. 240, note to §189.

515 Not in AY or Dh. The term "insignia" translates Tib. *rtags*, Skt. *liṅga*.

516 Tib. *mchod-rten*, which can stand for either *caitya* or *stūpa* but surely represents the former here. AY reads *shen* 神 "spirit" and Dh *fu* 福 "good fortune." Could both of these be editorial emendations of (or errors for) an earlier *tz'u* 祠 "shrine, temple"?

517 Not in AY (who for "the world with its gods" reads "the gods of the ten directions"). Dh omits "asuras" (as previously in §2C) but here reads, oddly, *t'ien shih jen* 天世人 "people [of] the heavenly world(s)."

518 On the monastic robe as a *caitya* cf. the *Ratnarāśi*, I.8 (for which see Silk 1995, p. 280). The same image occurs in the *Lalitavistara* 226.12.

519 Or, to translate the underlying Indian term *rāga* in another way, "they are not dyed with dye" (cf. PTSD 567b, where *rāga* is defined as "colour, hue, dye" and only secondarily as "passion"). According to Silk 1994 (p. 82, n. 2), the pun is on the word *rāga* in the specific sense of the color "red," though this is not a meaning of the term registered in PTSD or BHSD.

in harmony with the equipment[520] of the Noble Path, he thinks 'We ought to wear the reddish-brown robes while not being associated with impurities even for a moment.'[521] O Eminent Householder, delighting in those ten benefits the renunciant bodhisattva should wear the dharma-robe.

[24B] "O Eminent Householder, having seen its ten benefits, the renunciant bodhisattva should not abandon begging for alms[522] for as long as he lives. And what are the ten? [He thinks to himself:] 'I should live by my own power, not in dependence upon another; if certain beings desire to give me alms when I want them, I should establish those alms-givers in the three jewels, and only afterwards accept their alms; if some people do not give alms to me when I want them, I should generate great compassion toward them;[523] and having done so, I should make efforts to induce them to renunciation;[524] doing what is to be done, one eats his almsfood; I will become one who has acted in accordance with the word of the Tathāgata; I will produce the cause of being full to the brim and easy to nourish;[525] I will apply myself to breaking my pride; I will accumulate the virtuous roots [necessary to attain] the invisible crown of the head;[526] having seen me, beings

---

520 Tib. *tshogs*, Skt. *sambhāra*. AY, here and below (§24B), reads "heavy burden" (*chung-jen* 重任), apparently understanding *sambhāra* as a form of *bhāra* "burden."

521 Here again we find a play on words, this time between the virtually identical *kaṣāya* "impurity" and *kāṣāya* "monastic robe." The two terms are often confused in manuscripts.

522 AY, strangely, reads "lives in the *araṇya* so as not to practice begging" (and repeats the same statement at the end of §24B). Could *hsing* 行 "practice" be a hypercorrection from an earlier character meaning "abandon, cease," or did AY simply misunderstand?

523 Note that once again "great compassion" (*mahākaruṇā*) is being applied not toward beings in general, but toward those who are guilty of a particular shortcoming.

524 Not in AY or Dh.

525 The Chinese versions all seem to refer to bringing about the cause of contentment.

526 The "invisible crown of the head" (Tib. *spyi-gtsug bltar mi-mthong-ba*, Skt. *anavalokita-mūrdhatā*) is not included on the oldest lists of the thirty-two major and eighty minor marks (nor, for that matter, in the lists of marks given in the *Mahāvyutpatti*), but it does appear as one of the minor marks (*anuvyañjana*) in a substantial number of Mahāyāna sources; for copious references see Lamotte 1944-1980, vol. 3, p. 1346, n. 1. On the origins of this

will practice accordingly,[527] but I will not rely on any man, woman, boy, or girl;[528] and even when I am practicing the acceptance of alms, I will be even-minded toward all beings, and thus I will become equipped with the knowledge of Omniscience.'[529] O Eminent Householder, having seen these ten advantages, the renunciant bodhisattva will not abandon begging for alms for as long as he lives.[530] And if someone invites him [for a meal] he should go, in order to arouse that person's resolve, confidence, and serene faith. And in so doing there is no deception or hypocrisy.[531] For whoever, when receiving almsfood, is able to bring about the benefit of both self and other, I allow that bodhisattva to go in response to an invitation.

[24C] "Moreover, O Eminent Householder, the renunciant bodhisattva, seeing ten benefits, should be content with [meager] medicinal preparations[532] for as long as he lives. And what are the ten? [He thinks to himself:] 'I will enter into the teaching of the Tathāgata; I will not look another in the face; I will retain the concept of the disagreeable; I will establish a concept which does not involve a "self"; I will get rid of the attachment to good tastes without difficulty; all the common people will have confidence in me; I will need less food; I will not suffer from the poverty of seeking for medicine; my mind will not be harmed by the sickness of the defilements; and having entered [into this practice], I will quickly attain freedom from the sickness of the defilements.' O Eminent Householder,

---

mark see Durt 1967. This same mark is singled out for special attention in the *Pratyutpanna*; see Harrison 1990, §8A, p. 68 and n. 1.

527 R omits "having seen me, beings will practice accordingly."

528 Not in AY; for this entire list R reads simply "toward all beings."

529 The underlying term is presumably **sarvajña-jñāna-sambhāra*. As above, AY again reads "heavy burden" (see §24A, n. 520). R has the rather unexpected reading *chuang-yen* 莊嚴, interpreted by Schuster as a translation of *alaṁkāra* "adornment" (1976, p. 247) but in the present context certainly an equivalent, albeit a rather uncommon one, of *sambhāra* (see BCSD, 1015b). The reading found in Dh ("concentrating my will and arriving at the attainment of Omniscience") diverges from the other versions.

530 The following lines are cited in *Śikṣ.* 131.10-12:

yasyāścāntike piṇḍapātaṁ paribhujya na śaknotyātmanaḥ
parasya cārthaṁ paripūrayitum anujānāmy ahaṁ tasya
piṇḍacāriksya bodhisatvasya nimantraṇam

531 AY, in a reading that diverges both from the other Chinese versions and from the Tibetan, has the Buddha say "I do *not* permit this." Cf. the *Śikṣāsamuccaya*, which also has a negative here (cited in previous note).

532 This is probably a reference to fermented cow urine (Pāli *pūtimutta-bhesajja*, Skt. *pūtimuktabhaiṣajya*), a medication allowable even for renunciants (see Zysk 1991, p. 39ff.).

seeing these ten benefits, the renunciant bodhisattva will be content with [meager] medicinal preparations for as long as he lives.[533]

[24D] "Moreover, O Eminent Householder, the renunciant bodhisattva, having seen ten advantages, will not abandon wilderness-dwelling for as long as he lives. And what are the ten? [He will see that] 'With a happy mind, I will go there under my own power; being without the idea of "mine," I will become free of grasping; lodging will be given to me in abundance; I will not be devoid of delight in living in the wilderness; with respect to dwelling-places, I will have few objectives and little to do; casting off my dependents,[534] I will have no regard for body and life; being happy alone, I will abandon noisy gatherings; I will give up the goal of [attaining] qualities produced by actions; in accord with [the practice of] *samādhi*, my mind will become one-pointed; and my attention will be wide open[535] and without defilement.'[536] O Eminent Householder, having seen these ten advantages, the renunciant bodhisattva will not abandon wilderness-dwelling so long as he lives.[537]

[24E][538] "O Eminent Householder, if the wilderness-dwelling

---

[533] This entire paragraph has no counterpart in AY or R, and it is out of sequence (with respect to the Tibetan) in Dh, where it follows §24E. Dh diverges from the Tibetan in several particulars, but the overall sense is the same.

[534] Tib only.

[535] Lit., "without a cover" (Tib. *bla-gab med-pa*), a term not registered in existing dictionaries or in the *Mahāvyutpatti*. The same expression occurs, however, in Chapter 3 of the *Aṣṭasāhasrikā-prajñāpāramitā-sūtra* (Peking. 734; Ōtani ed. vol. 21, 70.2.3), where the corresponding Sanskrit text has *abhyavakāśa* "open space" (Vaidya 1960, 25.20), a term whose meaning fits well here. In light of this equivalence, we may take AY's *wu-i* 無益 "without profit" as a copyist's hypercorrection of *wu-kai* 無蓋 "without a cover."

[536] Tib only. There are some minor variants in the contents of this list in the Chinese versions.

[537] R and Tib only.

[538] The following lines are cited in *Śikṣ*. 200.7-11:

> *sacet punar gṛhapate āraṇyako bodhisatvo dharma-śravaṇārthika ācāryopādhyāya-darśanārthiko vā glāna-paripṛcchako vā grāmāntikaṁ śayanāsanam āgacchet tena sāyam āgamanāya prakramaṇāya ca cittam utpādayi-tavyaṁ | sacet punar asya parapratibaddha uddeśāḥ svādhyāyo vā tena vihāre prativasatā 'raṇya pravaṇa-cittena bhavitavyaṁ | eṣa eva ṭasyāraṇyavāso yat sarva-vastuṣu araṇya saṁjñā dharmaparyeṣṭyā cātṛptatā*

bodhisattva, in order to listen to the Dharma[539] or to see his teacher or preceptor, or to ask about an illness,[540] goes to a village area,[541] in order to go back [to the wilderness] he should arouse the thought of going.[542] If he relies on another for teaching or recitation, even while he is staying in the monastery, with a mind that remains in the wilderness he should think of all things as 'wilderness,' and [think to himself] 'never tiring of seeking the Dharma—that indeed is wilderness-dwelling.'[543]

---

[539] AY reads "to study the *ching* 經 or to recite the *ching*," where *ching* is, as is so often the case with the earliest Chinese translators, a translation of "Dharma" rather than "sūtra" (though the two terms are used interchangeably in Indian texts on occasion). R has "to listen to the Dharma," while Dh reads simply "if he goes to a Dharma-assembly."

[540] Not in AY. "To ask about an illness" presumably refers to having an illness of his own diagnosed or treated, not (as per Bendall and Rouse, Schuster, and Sakurabe) to visit or inquire about someone else who is sick. For a wilderness-dwelling bodhisattva to be worrying about a sick friend would be completely out of keeping with the isolationist and frankly antisocial way of life that is being advocated here.

[541] AY and Dh both refer to a monastery (AY *miao* 廟, Dh *ching-she* 精舍), while R and Tib read simply "village." For a wilderness-dwelling monk, however, to go to the village effectively means to go to the *vihāra*; thus the difference is merely one of wording and not of sense. On the various terms for "monastery" and their meanings in this text see above, Chapter 4, pp. 90-93.

[542] AY "he should dwell there with his mind turned toward the wilderness," Dh "he should concentrate on the wilderness," R "he should bring forth the thought 'Tonight I will return.'"

[543] There seem to have been significant differences in the texts used by the various translators here. Where Tib and *Śikṣ.* state that the bodhisattva should think of all things (*sarvavastu*) as "wilderness," the texts used by AY and Dh seem to have read "non-self "(**anātman*) rather than "wilderness" (*araṇya*). In both cases—and in a degree of agreement between these two versions that is rather unusual—AY and Dh go on to say that he should regard all things as belonging to others. R offers yet a third reading: "With respect to all things, he does not have the concept of quarreling; with respect to all things he does not have the concept of obstruction, and he is without repulsion concerning the collocated dharmas."

{Chapter 8: Leisurely Dwelling}[544]

[§25. THE VIRTUES OF WILDERNESS-DWELLING]

[25A][545] "Moreover, O Eminent Householder, the renunciant bodhisattva who lives in the wilderness should reflect as follows: 'For what reason do I live in the wilderness? Wilderness-dwelling alone does not make one a *śramaṇa*. There are many living here who are not purified, not guarded,[546] not calmed, not tamed, and are devoid of exertion and efforts, such as deer, monkeys, flocks of birds, robbers, and outcastes.[547] They do not have the qualities of a *śramaṇa*. So why do I live in the wilderness? It is for this [reason]: I should fulfill the aim of the *śramaṇa*.'

[25B] "O Eminent Householder, if one asks what is the renunciant bodhisattva's *śramaṇa*-aim, it is the following: it is mindfulness and clear consciousness,[548] being undistracted, attaining the *dhāraṇīs*,[549] {not being satisfied with what he has learned, having attained

---

[544] Dh only. The overtones of the Chinese term *hsien-chü* 閑居 "leisurely dwelling," which suggest the country retreat of a cultured gentleman, are radically at odds with the ascetic tone of the underlying Indian text.

[545] The following lines are cited in *Śikṣ*. 198.1-6:

> *punar aparaṁ gṛhapate pravrajitena bodhisatvenāraṇye pratīvasatā evam upaparīkṣitavyaṁ | kim artham aham araṇye prativasāmi | na kevalam araṇyavāsena śramaṇo bhavati | bahavo 'py atrādāntā avinītā ayuktā anabhiyuktāḥ prativasanti | tad yathā | mṛgavānarapakṣisaṁghacauracaṇḍālāḥ prativasanti | na ca te śramaṇaguṇasamanvāgatā bhavanti | api tu khalu punar ahaṁ yasyārthāyāraṇye prativasāmi sa mayā 'rthaḥ paripūrayitavyo yad uta śrāmaṇyārthaḥ* [sic] ||

[546] The Tibetan actually reads *ma-sbas-pa* "not hidden, not secret," but a comparison with AY (which reads *pu-shou* 不守 "not protected") and *Dbhv*. (which has *pu hu* 不護, *id.*) suggests that there may have been a confusion in the underlying text between √*rakṣ* "protect, guard" and √*rah* "separate, withdraw into privacy, be secret." Unfortunately the extant Sanskrit text is somewhat distant from both the Tibetan and the Chinese versions, and thus does not help to resolve the issue.

[547] Tib. *gdol-ba*, Skt. *caṇḍāla*. The list of attributes and of animals and humans varies slightly in the different translations of the text.

[548] Tib only.

[549] The word *dhāraṇī* is surely one of the most misunderstood terms in the Buddhist lexicon. It is often treated as virtually synonymous with *mantra* (in the sense of "spell, magic charm"), especially in the field of East Asian

eloquence[550] in speech,}[551] relying on loving-kindness and compassion,

---

Buddhism, where the two terms are often not distinguished. There are, however, important differences between them in the Indian context. First and foremost is their range of usage: while *mantra* is a pan-Indian term, originally used in reference to the verses of the Vedas but eventually adopted by virtually every religious tradition on the subcontinent, the word *dhāraṇī* is used exclusively by Buddhists, and only by Mahāyāna Buddhists at that (cf. BHSD 284b, where Edgerton notes that the term occurs only in Buddhist Hybrid Sanskrit texts, and the *Ta chih-tu lun*, T 25.269b ff. [translated in Lamotte 1944-1980, vol. 4, pp. 1876-1877], where the author takes it for granted that *dhāraṇīs* are used only in Mahāyāna circles and proceeds to discuss why they should be unknown to the *śrāvakas*). Second, while both of these terms can be used in Buddhist writings to mean "magic formula" (the sole definition of *dhāraṇī* given in BHSD, *loc. cit.*), the word *dhāraṇī* has another—and in all probability more original—meaning, viz., "mnemonic device."

The use of the word *dhāraṇī* to refer to a list of concepts to be fixed in memory via the use of the *arapacana* syllabary (which appears to be simply the ordinary syllabic sequence of the Kharoṣṭhī script; cf. Salomon 1990) may well be the earliest instance of the term in Buddhist literature (see for example the *Pañcaviṁśatisāhasrikā-prajñāpāramitā-sūtra* translated by Edward Conze [1975], pp. 160-162, and the Sanskrit text in Dutt 1934, pp. 212-214). While the use of an alphabet (or rather, a syllabary) as a mnemonic device is virtually unknown in India—a culture in which the sophistication of other memorization techniques would have made such a simple approach seem quite childish—it is a fundamental element in the religious cultures of the Semitic and Mesopotamian worlds. Compare for example the mystical significance of the letters of the Hebrew alphabet in the Jewish system of the Kabbalah (e.g., Scholem 1974, pp. 23-26 and *passim.*) or the construction of Manichaean Parthian hymns so that each line begins with a sequential letter of the alphabet (Boyce 1952). The use of an alphabetic sequence to order Manichaean religious texts was apparently quite widespread; the claim of the 10th-/11th-century Arab scholar al-Bīrūnī that Mani's "Living Gospel" was organized into twenty-two chapters corresponding to the letters of the Aramaic alphabet (Sachau 1879, p. 190), for example, has now been confirmed by a list of section headings, based on the twenty-two letters of the Aramaic alphabet, preserved in a fragmentary Coptic commentary on that text (Mirecki 1994, pp. 199-200). (I would like to thank Jason BeDuhn for providing references to these Manichaean materials.) The fact that the use of the word *dhāraṇī* in Buddhist scriptures appears early (and perhaps originally) in conjunction with a Semitic script—specifically, the Aramaic-based Kharoṣṭhī script—may take on added significance in this context.

550 AY *pien-tz'u* 辯辭, Dh *kao-ming* 高明, Skt. **pratibhāna*. The terminology is not Dharmarakṣa's usual; was he reading *pratibhāsa* "appearance, illumination" rather than *pratibhāna*? (For *ming* 明 as the equivalent of

having mastery of the paranormal powers,[552] fulfilling the cultivation of the six perfections, not abandoning the spirit of Omniscience,[553] cultivating the knowledge of skillful means, maturing sentient beings,[554] not abandoning the four means of attraction,[555] being mindful of the six kinds of remembrance,[556] not discarding learning and exertion, properly analyzing the dharmas, exerting oneself in order to attain right liberation,[557] knowing the attainments of the fruit,[558] dwelling in the state of having entered into a fixed course,[559] and protecting the True Dharma.

[25C] "It is having right view, by having confidence in the maturing of deeds; having right intention, which consists in the cutting off of all discursive and divisive thought;[560] having right speech, which consists of teaching the Dharma in accordance with the receptivity [of others]; having right action, by completely annihilating action; having right livelihood, by overcoming the residue of attachments;[561] having right effort, by awakening to

---

pratibhāsa see BCSD, p. 596a.) For an insightful study of the notion of "eloquence" in Buddhist scriptures see MacQueen 1981 and 1982.

551 AY and Dh only. Dh seems to understand that the bodhisattva *is* satisfied with what he has heard.

552 Tib. *mngon-par shes-pa*, Skt. *abhijñā*. For the five (sometimes six) paranormal powers that are said to result from ascetic practice see Dayal 1932, pp. 106-121.

553 Tib. *thams-cad mkhyen-pa-nyid-kyi sems*, Skt. *sarvajñatācitta*, a synonym of "spirit of enlightenment" (*bodhicitta*). Cf. above, §2C, n. 45.

554 For this phrase AY substitutes "gathering people together by his gift of the Dharma."

555 Cf. above, §11D, n. 230.

556 Cf. above, §4D, n. 89.

557 Tib. *yang-dag-par rnam-par grol-ba*, Skt. **samyagvimokṣa*.

558 Not in AY or Dh.

559 Tib. *skyon med-pa-la 'jug-pa*, Skt. **niyāma-avakrānta*. The Tibetan literally means "having entered into the faultless," but this is an old error (canonized in *Mvy.* 6502 and 6503) based on the interpretation of *niyāma* "fixed, certain" as consisting of *ni* + *āma* "without fault"! (see BHSD 34b, s.v. *nyāma*). The same term appears below, §31B(3). The Chinese versions read differently: AY refers to not entering into matters having to do with the correct Way (*cheng-tao* 正道), while Dh has "not departing from a place of calm collectedness" (*pu-li chi-ting chih ch'u* 不離寂定之處). R has no equivalent.

560 Tib. *rtog-pa* (Skt. *kalpa*) and *rnam-par rtog-pa* (*vikalpa*).

561 Tib. *bag-chags-kyi mtshams sbyor-ba*; Skt. **vāsana-sambandha*?

sambodhi;[562] having right mindfulness, by constant non-forgetfulness; and having right absorption, by fully attaining the knowledge of Omniscience.

[25D] "It is not being frightened by emptiness, not being intimidated by the signless, and not being overpowered by the wishless, and being able through one's knowledge to be reborn at will.[563] It is relying on the meaning, not on the letter; relying on knowledge, not on discursive consciousness; relying on the Dharma, not on the person; and relying on the definitive sūtras, not on the sūtras that must be interpreted.[564] In accord with the primordially non-arising and non-ceasing nature of things, it is not mentally constructing an essence of things[565]—that, O Eminent Householder, is what is called the *śramaṇa*-aim of the renunciant bodhisattva.'

[25E] "Moreover, O Eminent Householder,[566] the renunciant bodhisattva should not be in close contact with many people.[567] He should think to himself as follows: 'I should not bring forth the roots-of-goodness for just one being; rather, I should bring forth the roots-of-goodness for all beings.'[568] Nonetheless, O Eminent Householder, the

---

562 R reads *ting* 定, apparently reflecting an underlying "samādhi" rather than *sambodhi*.

563 Tib only. The same statement, however, appears in *Dbhv.* 26.112b23-24.

564 For an accessible discussion of these four criteria for interpretation see Lamotte 1988b. Note that these items do not occur in their standard sequence in Tib or R, though in AY and *Dbhv.* they do (cf. *Mvy.* nos. 1545-1549). The text given in Dh is completely garbled.

565 Tib only. "Essence" translates Tib. *ngo-bo-nyid*, Skt. *svabhāva*. I agree with José Cabezón (1992) and Jay Garfield (1995, p. 89, n. 4) that the term "essence" better conveys to Western readers the implications of the underlying Sanskrit than do such literalistic alternatives as "own-being," "self-nature," and so on.

566 Not in AY or Dh.

567 More literally, "should greatly be in non-contact." The meaning is confirmed by all three Chinese versions. On the tactical isolationism of the renunciant bodhisattva see Chapter 5, pp. 132-135.

568 The Tibetan reads "of just one being" and "of all beings," but this is clearly another misunderstanding of the Sanskrit genitive used in a dative sense (cf. above, §5B, n. 102), as confirmed by AY and Dh, which have "for the sake of all beings." The first part of this sentence, together with a portion of the previous one, is cited in *Śikṣ.* 196.7-8 and does indeed contain such an expression (*satvasaṁsargo me na kartavyo na hi mayaikasatvasya kuśalamūlāni saṁjanayitavyāni*). Oddly, Śāntideva does not go on to quote the second half of

Tathāgata has allowed the following four [kinds of] association for the renunciant bodhisattva.[569] And what are the four? To associate with others in order to listen to the Dharma; to associate with others in order to mature beings; to associate with others in order to worship and revere the Tathāgata; and to associate with those whose spirit of Omniscience is uncontaminated. O Eminent Householder, the renunciant bodhisattva is allowed these four [kinds of] association by the Tathāgata. O Eminent Householder, this being the case, the renunciant bodhisattva should be free of [all other kinds of] association.

[25F][570] "Moreover, O Eminent Householder, the renunciant[571]

---

the statement, according to which the bodhisattva should instead bring forth his roots-of-goodness for the benefit of all. As a result, Bendall and Rouse follow a rather different interpretation, reading "I must not frequent the society of the world, for it is not mine to cultivate the roots of good in [*sic*] a single being" (p. 190; if my interpretation is correct, Bendall and Rouse have also misunderstood the significance of the Sanskrit genitive here).

569 The Tibetan reads "*of* the renunciant bodhisattva," but presumably this is again the result of confusion over the meaning of an underlying Sanskrit genitive.

570 Section §25F is cited in its entirety in *Śikṣ.* 198.6-19:

> *punar aparaṁ gṛhapate pravrajitena bodhisatvenāraṇye viharatā evam upaparīkṣitavyaṁ* | *kim artham aham araṇyam āgataḥ* | *tenaivaṁ mīmāṁsayitavyaṁ* | *bhayabhīto 'smy aham araṇyam āgataḥ* | *kuto bhayabhītaḥ* | *saṁga-ṇikābhayabhītaḥ* | *saṁsargabhayabhīto rāgadveṣamoha-bhayabhīto mānamadamrakṣaparidāhabhaya-bhīto lobherṣyāmātsaryabhayabhītaḥ rūpaśabdagandharasa-sptaṣṭavyabhayabhītaḥ* | *so 'haṁkāramamakārabhaya-bhītaḥ* | *auddhatyavicikitsābhayabhītaḥ* | *skandha-mārabhayabhītaḥ* | *kleśamārabhayabhīto* [sic] | *mṛtyumārabhayabhīto* [sic] | *devaputra-mārabhayabhītaḥ* | *anitye nitya iti viparyāsabhayabhīto 'nātmanyātmeti-viparyāsa-bhayabhīto 'śucau śucir iti viparyāsabhayabhīto* | *duṣkhe* [sic] *sukham iti viparyāsabhayabhītaḥ* | *cittamanovijñānaviparyāsabhayabhīto* | *nivaraṇāvaraṇa-paryutthānabhayabhītaḥ* | *satkāyadṛṣṭibhayabhītaḥ pāpamitrabhayabhīto* [sic] | *lābha-satkārabhayabhīto 'kālamantra-bhayabhīto* | *'dṛṣṭe dṛṣṭam iti bhayabhīto* | *'śrute śrutam iti bhayabhīto 'mate matam iti bhayabhīto 'vijñāte vijñātam iti bhayabhīto 'śramaṇe śramaṇamada-bhayabhīto 'nyonyavidveṣaṇa-bhayabhītaḥ kāmadhāturūpa-dhatvarūpyadhātubhayabhītaḥ sarvabhavagaty-*

bodhisattva who lives in the wilderness should think to himself, 'Why have I come to the wilderness?' And he should reflect as follows: 'I came to the wilderness because of being frightened and afraid.[572] Frightened and afraid of what? Frightened and afraid[573] of noisy gatherings and of associating [with others]; of passion, aversion, and delusion; of pride, intoxication, and anger;[574] of covetousness, envy, and jealousy; of sights,[575] sounds, scents, tastes, and touch-objects; of the Māra of the *skandhas*, the Māra of the defilements, the Māra of death, and of Māra himself;[576] of mistaking the non-eternal for the eternal, the painful for the pleasurable, {the insubstantial for the substantial},[577] the selfless for the self, and the impure for the pure;[578] of thought, mind, and consciousness;[579] of

---

upapattibhayabhīto nirayatiryagyoni-pitṛviṣayabhaya-bhītaḥ saṁkṣepeṇa sarvebhyo 'kuśalebhyo manasikārebhyo bhayabhīta ebhyo hy aham evaṁ rūpebhyo bhayabhaira-vebhyo bhīto 'raṇyāvāsam upagataḥ ||

571 Not in AY or Dh; Dh also omits the word "bodhisattva."

572 Note the reversal of the usual imagery here: ordinarily the wilderness is portrayed as a frightening place, filled with wild animals and other terrors and a place of utter solitude. Here, however, the wilderness (fearful as it is) is portrayed as a place to which the renunciant bodhisattva flees for safety, fearful of dangers of another kind.

573 In the Tibetan and in the underlying Sanskrit the phrase "frightened and afraid" is repeated before each of the items in the following list. I have omitted this redundancy for the sake of readability in English.

574 For the last item AY substitutes "bad friends."

575 Tib. *gzugs*, Skt. *rūpa*, usually translated as "form," but in the present context the term refers specifically to "objects of sight."

576 Lit., "of Māra the *devaputra*" (so the extant Sanskrit, confirmed by the Tibetan and AY; Dh and R read just *t'ien*, presumably a translation only of *deva*, not *devaputra*). Sakurabe takes the Tibetan has *lha'i bu'i bdud* as a plural, but I see no justification in the Tibetan or Sanskrit text (or in the sense) for doing so. On the four Māras see Wayman 1959, especially "Part III: The Four Māras" (pp. 112-125).

For the list as a whole Dh offers an interesting variant: "the Māra of the body (*shen* 身), the Māra of desire (*yü* 欲), the Māra of transgressions (*tsui* 罪) and Māra the deva (*t'ien* 天). Both Dh and R use the standard term *mo* 魔 to translate "Māra," while AY uses *hsieh* 邪 "evil one" (reading with n. 37 in the Taishō edition).

577 Dh only.

578 These four items are not mentioned in AY; Dh omits the last ("mistaking the impure for the pure") but adds an extra item ("mistaking the insubstantial for the substantial"). The sequence in the Tibetan differs from that of the Sanskrit, which has "non-eternal, selfless, impure, and painful," while R

craving and *saṁsāra*; of hindrances, obstructions, and obsessions;[580] of a false view of individuality; of taking things as "me" and "mine";[581] of being unruly, of having doubts and second thoughts; of bad teachers;[582] of profit and honor; of unvirtuous friends;[583] of thinking I have seen what I have not seen, heard what I have not heard, remembered what I have not remembered,[584] discerned what I have not discerned, and cognized what I have not cognized;[585] of the impurities of the *śramaṇa*; of mutual hostility;[586] of the desire realm, the form realm, and the formless realm; of dying and being reborn in all[587] {five}[588] realms of beings; of going to the realm of the hell-beings, the animal rebirth, or the

---

has "non-eternal, selfless, painful, and impure."

579 Tib. *sems* (Skt. *citta*), *yid* (*manas*), and *rnam-par shes-pa* (*vijñāna*).

580 Tib only. "Hindrances" translates Tib. *sgrib-pa*, Skt. *nivaraṇa*; "obstructions" renders Tib. *chod-pa*, Skt. *āvaraṇa*; and "obsessions" translates Tib. *kun-nas ldang-ba*, Skt. *paryutthāna*. For the latter translation (which seems to capture the sense well) see *MDPPL*, p. 256.

581 R and Tib only.

582 Tib. *sdig-pa'i grogs-po*, Skt. *pāpamitra* (lit., "evil friend," but the implication is not of a horizontal relationship but rather of a senior friend or mentor who might lead one astray).

583 Not in AY or Dh. Tib. has *mi-dge-ba'i bshes-gnyen* (lit., "unvirtuous friend"), while the Skt. reads *akālamantra* "untimely mantra" (!), an unexpected reading but apparently paralleled in R, which has *fei-shih yü* 非時語 "untimely speech."

584 Tib. *dran-pa*. Tib and R (which reads *nien* 念 "remember, call to mind") appear to be translating from a text that read *smṛta* "remembered," while AY and Dh are apparently attempting to render the word *muta* "thought, sensed." The latter is the expected form, for we have here an early list of three (later four) means of acquiring knowledge, viz., what is seen (*dṛṣṭa*), heard (*śruta*), sensed (*muta*), and comprehended (*vijñāta*); cf. PTSD 536b. The extant Sanskrit (cited in *Śikṣ.*) has *mata*, either an error for or a near variant of *muta*. The Tibetan in fact has five items in its list (while all three Chinese versions have four), and seems to include both **smṛta* and **muta* or **mata* (translating the latter as *bye-brag phyed*).

585 Tib only.

586 Not in R. AY reads "mutual jealousy," Dh "fear of all sorts of conduct," Skt. "mutual hostility" (*anyonyavidveṣaṇa*).

587 R and Tib only.

588 AY and Dh only. Although AY and Dh specify five *gatis* and R and Tib do not give a number, Sakurabe adds the figure "six," which is standard in East Asia but is found in no version of the sūtra itself. On the five and six *gatis* in Buddhist literature cf. above, §14D, n. 317.

pretas;[589] and of the {eight}[590] inauspicious situations[591]—in short, being frightened and afraid of paying attention to all unvirtuous things.[592] Being frightened by such frightening and fearful things as these,[593] I have come to the wilderness.

[25G] "'One cannot be freed from such frightening and fearful things as these by living at home, living in the midst of noisy gatherings, living without making efforts and without exerting oneself in yogic practice,[594] and while directing one's attention improperly.[595] All the bodhisattva-mahāsattvas who have appeared in the past have been liberated from all fear after dwelling in the wilderness, and thus they have attained the fearless state of Supreme Perfect Enlightenment.[596] All the bodhisattva-mahāsattvas who will appear in the future will be liberated from all fear after dwelling in the wilderness, and thus they will attain the fearless state of Supreme Perfect Enlightenment. All the bodhisattva-mahāsattvas who appear in the present are liberated from all fear after dwelling in the wilderness, and thus they attain the fearless state of Supreme Perfect Enlightenment.[597] This being the case, I too—being frightened and afraid and desiring to leave all fears behind and to attain the the fearless state of Supreme Perfect Enlightenment[598]—should dwell in the wilderness.' Thus should he reflect.[599]

---

[589] For this last item the Tibetan has *yi-dags* (the usual equivalent of Skt. *preta*), but the extant Sanskrit text reads *pitṛviṣaya* "realm of the fathers."

[590] Dh only.

[591] Not in AY, R, or the extant Sanskrit. The standard list of inauspicious situations (Tib. *mi-khom-pa*, Skt. *akṣaṇa*) consists of birth in hell, in the animal realm, as a *preta*, as a long-lived god, in a border region, as a non-Buddhist, with defective mental faculties, and in a time when there is no Buddha (see BHSD 2b-3a).

[592] R omits "and of the eight inauspicious situations ... unvirtuous things." Several of the items in this paragraph appear in a different sequence in AY, but all are present unless otherwise indicated.

[593] Not in AY or Dh.

[594] For "living without ... yogic practice," AY reads "doing deeds which are not in harmony with the Way." Dh has no equivalent.

[595] Not in AY. Dh reads "In meditation one is mindful of emptiness" (*nien k'ung* 念空), but no other version refers to emptiness here.

[596] AY "attained that fearless state which is called self-so (*tzu-jan* 自然.)" Both Dh and R, however, refer explicitly to Buddhahood.

[597] Not in AY; Dh combines these two sentences into one.

[598] Tib only.

[599] Not in AY or Dh.

[25H][600] "Moreover, O Eminent Householder, the renunciant bodhisattvā who, frightened and afraid,[601] lives in a wilderness dwelling-place, should train himself to think as follows:[602] 'Whatever few[603] fears may arise, all those have arisen from grasping at a self.[604] They arise from adhering to a self, grasping at a self, the thirst for a self, the concept of a self, grasping at the teaching of a self, the belief in a self, the establishment of a self, the mental construction of a self, and the defense of a self.[605] If I live in the wilderness but do not give up the assumption of a self, the adherence to a self, the grasping at a self, the basis of a self, the thirst for a self, the concept of a self, the grasping at the teaching of a self, the belief in a self, the establishment of a self, the mental construction of a self, and the defense of a self, then even though I live in the wilderness it will be in vain.[606] For there is no wilderness-dwelling

---

600 The following lines are cited in *Śikṣ.* 198.19-21:

punar aparaṁ gṛhapate pravrajitena
bodhisatvenāraṇyavāsasthitena bhītena vā trastena vā
evaṁ śikṣitavyaṁ | yāni kānicid bhayānyutpadyante sarvāṇi
tāny-ātmagrāhata utpadyante ||

601 R "not frightened and not afraid" (*sic!*).

602 Not in AY or Dh.

603 Tib only.

604 The various translators appear to have taken an underlying **ātmagrāha* (perhaps earlier **ātmagraha*) in various ways: AY "the arising [of the notion of] a self," Dh "accepting [the notion of] a self," R "attachment to a self."

605 The citation in *Śikṣ.* resumes with the following sentence (198.21-199.2):

sacet punar aham araṇye prativasannātmagrāhaṁ
parityajeyam nātmābhiniveśaṁ nātmaparigrahaṁ
nātmanidānaṁ nātmatṛṣṇāṁ nātmasaṁjñāṁ
nātmavādopādānaṁ nātmadṛṣṭiṁ nātmādhiṣṭhānaṁ
nātmaparikalpanāṁ nātmarakṣāṁ parityajeyaṁ |
nirarthako me 'raṇyavāsaḥ syād | api tu khalu punar
gṛhapate nāsty ātmasaṁjñino 'raṇyavāso [sic] | *nāsti*
parasaṁjñinaḥ ||

Slight variations in this sentence (and in the preceding, which contains the same list of items) among the various Chinese translations can all be explained as varying interpretations of (and minor differences in sequence in) the same underlying Indic text.

606 Tib. *don med-pa*, Skt. *nirarthaka*. Choosing another of the many meanings of the term *don*, Sakurabe reads *imi ga nai* "meaningless."

for one who conceives of a 'self' or an 'other.'[607] There is no wilderness-dwelling for one who inclines toward taking things as 'me' and 'mine.'[608] There is no wilderness-dwelling for one who takes anything as a basis, and there is no wilderness-dwelling for one who has mistaken views.[609] O Eminent Householder, if there is no wilderness-dwelling even for one who has the concept of *nirvāṇa*,[610] how much less so for one who has the concept of all[611] the *kleṣas*?

[25I][612] "O Eminent Householder,[613] 'wilderness-dwelling' means to dwell[614] without relying on anything.[615] It is to dwell without grasping at anything.[616] {All delight is also without grasping.}[617] {Pitying and protecting those who dwell in the triple world,}[618] it is to dwell without being desirous of any mark.[619] It is to dwell without relying on any form. It is to dwell without relying on any[620] sound, smell, taste, or touch-object. It is

---

607 R "If the wilderness-dweller does not have the concept of a self, that is wilderness-dwelling."

608 Not in AY or Dh.

609 R omits the first part of this sentence and reads "If he does not have attachments to views, that is wilderness-dwelling."

610 AY *wu-wei* 無為 "the unconditioned"; Dh and R simply transliterate the term.

611 Tib only.

612 The following two sentences are cited in *Śikṣ.* 199.2-3: *araṇyavāso nāma gṛhapate ucyate sarvadharmeṣv asambhava-vāsaḥ sarvadharmeṣv asaṁgavāsaḥ.*

613 Not in AY or Dh.

614 Alone of all the extant versions, AY lacks any equivalent of Skt. *-vāsa* "dwelling," which is repeated in each of the following sentences. AY contains, however, an extra character *tsai* 哉 (used as an emphatic particle) at the end of each sentence, which has no equivalent in the other versions. Could *tsai* 哉 be an error of transcription for the nearly homophonous *tsai* 在 "to dwell in, be at"?

615 AY "Wilderness dwelling means all dharmas are quieted and calmed."

616 AY "All dharmas are without grasping." There are numerous small discrepancies in translation in this paragraph among the various versions of the sūtra; these do not affect the overall sense of the passage, however, and most will therefore not be noted here.

617 AY only. The word *le* 樂 "delight" could also be read as *yao* "desiring."

618 Dh only.

619 AY and Dh can be brought into rough conformity to the other versions if we assume that *hsiang* 想 "idea" is an error for *hsiang* 相 "mark."

620 Tib only.

to dwell without being mistaken about the sameness[621] of all dharmas. It is to dwell with the mind fully calmed and fully purified.[622] It is to dwell fearlessly, having cast off all {the heavy burdens of}[623] fear. It is to dwell having forded the stream, by being liberated from all the defilements.[624] It is to dwell relying.[625] Being satisfied with anything at all[626] and having few desires, it is to dwell delighting in the noble traditions.[627] Being easily filled and easily nourished, it is to dwell in satisfaction. By applying oneself properly for the sake of insight, it is to dwell in what one has learned. By investigating the doors to liberation—viz., emptiness, the signless, and the wishless[628]—it is to dwell in liberation. By breaking all the bonds, it is to dwell in release. By being in accord with dependent origination, it is to dwell pacifying those who are unruly.[629] By being fully purified, it is to dwell in the state of having done what is to be done.[630]

[25J][631] "O Eminent Householder, it is like this: for example,

---

[621] Interestingly, AY and Dh both reflect an underlying *samādhi*, not "sameness" (*samatā*).

[622] Tib only.

[623] AY and Dh only. Has this phrase been edited out on the grounds of a perceived conflict between this statement and the idea that the bodhisattva voluntarily "takes up" the burden of the five *skandha*s? (Cf. above, §2C, n. 36.)

[624] It seems likely, based on the readings found in the three Chinese translations (and supported by *Dbhv.* 26.113c11-12), that older versions of the text referred to the *āsrava*s "outflows," not to the *kleśa*s.

[625] Tib only. Even in the Tibetan, this phrase is not found in all versions; it does not occur, for example, in P.

[626] Tib. *ngan-ngon*, lit., "the inferior," presumably from Skt. *itaretara* "any old, any at all." Cf. above, §23A, n. 492.

[627] See above, §23 and n. 491.

[628] For "By investigating ... wishless" AY reads simply "thoroughly (*pen-mo* 本末) practicing the liberation[s]."

[629] Not in AY. Dh understands that the bodhisattva himself is entering into a state of peacefulness, not pacifying others, while R has "dwelling at the limit" (*sic*).

[630] Not in AY or Dh.

[631] The following lines are cited in *Śikṣ.* 199.3-12:

> *tad yathā gṛhapate 'raṇye tṛṇagulmauṣadhivanaspatayaḥ prativasanto na bibhyati nottrasyanti na saṁtrasyanti na saṁtrāsam āpadyante | evam eva gṛhapate pravrajitena bodhisatvenāraṇye viharatā tṛṇagulmauṣadhivanaspati kāṣṭhakudyavad ātma-pratibhāvasat saṁjñā kāye utpāda-yitavyā | māyāsamatā cittasyotpādayitavyā | ko 'tra bibheti*

grasses, shrubs, and trees, {wild oxen, elephants, and horses}[632] live in the wilderness[633] but are not afraid, frightened, or terrified. O Eminent Householder, in the same way the renunciant bodhisattva who lives in the wilderness should bring forth the idea of his body as like grass, shrubs, medicinal herbs, a wall, a piece of wood,[634] a mountain,[635] or an illusion.[636] And he should bring forth the thought 'Who is afraid here? Who is terrified here?' And when he sees that he is afraid and frightened, he should turn his attention to his body in the following way: 'In this body there is no self, no being, no soul, no creature, no personality,[637] no man, no person, no human being, and no young man.[638] Thus this thing called "fear" is an unreal and mentally constructed thing. Therefore I should not construct such an unreal and mentally constructed thing. Just as the grass, shrubs, medicinal herbs, trees, {and wild oxen}[639] that live in the wilderness are devoid of a sense of 'mine' and devoid of grasping, just so should the bodhisattva who is devoid of a sense of 'mine' and of grasping realize that[640] "all things are the wilderness" and dwell in that apprehension. And why? To live in the

---

| ko 'sminn uttrasyati | tena bhayabhītena vā trastena vā evaṁ yoniśaḥ kāya upaparīkṣitavyaḥ | nāsty atra kāye ātmā vā satvo vā jīvo vā poṣo vā pudgalo vā manujo vā mānavo vā | abhūtaparikalpa eṣa yad uta bhayaṁ nāma | sa mayā 'bhūtaparikalpo na parikalpayitavyaḥ | tena yathāraṇye tṛṇagulamauṣadhi-vanaspatayaḥ prativasanti amamā aparigrahāḥ | evam evāmamenāparigraheṇa-araṇyam eva sarvadharmā iti jñātvā upasampadya vihartavyaṁ | tat kasya hetoḥ | raṇachedo 'raṇyavāso 'mamo 'parigrahaḥ ||

632 Dh only.

633 Note that Dh has been using the character *hsien* 閑 "leisure, peaceful seclusion" to translate *araṇya* when it refers to the renunciant bodhisattva's dwelling place, but switches to *shan-tse* 山澤 "mountain and marsh" when *araṇya* refers to the dwelling-place of wild plants (and, in his version, wild animals). It seems clear that Dh was picturing a more elegant meditational environment than the wild and terrifying wilderness intended by the Indian composers of our text.

634 Tib only. AY substitutes "stones," Dh *wu-mao-fa* 無毛髮 "hairless [things]" (?). R has no equivalent.

635 Tib only.

636 Not in AY or Dh.

637 Tib only. Note that the extant citation in *Śikṣ.* also has no equivalent.

638 The items in this list vary considerably from one version to another.

639 Dh only.

640 Tib only.

wilderness is to cut off the defilements,[641] to be devoid of a sense of "mine," and to be without grasping.'

[25K] "Moreover, O Eminent Householder,[642] the renunciant bodhisattva who lives in the wilderness should train himself to think as follows. 'Living in the wilderness, one conforms to the *śīla-skandha*. Living in the wilderness, one remains absorbed in the *samādhi-skandha*. Living in the wilderness, one assembles the *prajñā-skandha*. Living in the wilderness, the *vimokṣa-skandha* is accomplished. Living in the wilderness, the *vimokṣa-jñāna-darśana-skandha* comes forth.[643] Living in the wilderness, one adheres to the elements conducive to enlightenment. Living in the wilderness, one assembles the twelve ascetic qualities.[644] Living in the wilderness, one examines the [Four Noble] Truths. Living in the wilderness, one comprehends the [five] *skandhas*. Living in the wilderness, one weighs the realms of the senses as equal to the dharma-realm. Living in the wilderness, one cleanses the sense doors.[645] Living in the wilderness, one does not forget the spirit of enlightenment. Living in the wilderness, one is without fear, due to the contemplation of emptiness. Living in the wilderness, one acquires the Dharma. Living in the wilderness, one does not destroy one's roots-of-goodness.[646] Living in the wilderness, one is lauded by the Buddhas. Living in the

---

641 Note the underlying pun here between "wilderness" (*araṇya*) and "defilement" (*raṇa*). The pun would have been more effective in those Prakrits that do not distinguish between intervocalic *-ny-* and *-ṇ-*.

642 Not in AY or Dh (AY also omits "the renunciant bodhisattva").

643 Not in AY. For this list of five "pure *skandhas*" see above, §9B, n. 204. Note that the last two items (unlike the preceding three) are expressed in the Tibetan using an intransitive verb. It is a widespread assumption in Indian religions (not just Buddhism) that liberation—expressed by such terms as *mokṣa*, *vimokṣa*, *nirvāṇa*, and so on—cannot be "created" by the practitioner in transitive fashion.

644 For "assembles the twelve ascetic qualities" Dh reads "cuts off the twelve envoys" (*tuan shih-erh shih* 斷十二使)! This very unexpected reading apparently stems from a confusion between *dhutaguṇa* "ascetic qualities"—the term which certainly was the source of the wording in all other versions of the text, and an expression with which Dh has had difficulty before (see §22A and n. 473)—and **dūta-lūna* "messenger-cut"! That Dharmarakṣa should make such a bizarre error—even when the number "twelve," which should surely have been a tipoff, is given in the text—makes it clear that he was entirely unfamiliar with these practices. Taken in combination with his translation of *araṇya* as *hsien* 閑, this strongly suggests that Dharmarakṣa's understanding of Buddhist practice was far from ascetic in orientation.

645 Skt. *āyatana*, i.e., the six sense organs and their respective objects.

646 Not in AY.

wilderness, one is praised by the bodhisattvas.[647] Living in the wilderness, one is esteemed by the noble ones. Living in the wilderness, one is relied upon by those who desire liberation.[648] As to living in the wilderness, one is propitiated [by those who seek] to awaken to the knowledge of[649] Omniscience.[650]

[25L] "Moreover, O Eminent Householder,[651] the renunciant bodhisattva who lives in the wilderness will be able to accomplish the cultivation of the six perfections with little difficulty.[652] And why?

(1) "The bodhisattva who lives in the wilderness has no regard for his body and life. Thus he will accomplish the cultivation of the wilderness-dweller's[653] perfection of giving.

(2) "O Eminent Householder, how does one accomplish the cultivation of the perfection of morality of the wilderness-dwelling renunciant bodhisattva? O Eminent Householder, the renunciant bodhisattva who lives in the wilderness[654] gains full possession of the three restraints[655] by becoming firmly grounded in the ascetic qualities and the austerities.[656] Thus will he accomplish the cultivation of the wilderness-dweller's[657] perfection of morality.

(3) "O Eminent Householder, how does one accomplish the cultivation of the perfection of endurance of the wilderness-dwelling renunciant bodhisattva? O Eminent Householder, the renunciant bodhisattva who lives in the wilderness[658] bears no malice toward living beings,[659] but produces loving-kindness toward all

---

647 Not in AY or Dh.

648 AY "Living in mountain and marsh, one unleashes the method of achieving Omniscience"; Dh "Living in leisurely seclusion, one is emancipated from fondness."

649 Tib only.

650 Dh "one enters into Omniscience," R "one who desires Omniscience ought to dwell in this place."

651 Not in AY.

652 For "with little difficulty" AY reads "in a short time."

653 Not in AY or Dh.

654 Not in AY or Dh.

655 Tib. *sdom-pa gsum*, Skt. *trisaṁvara*, i.e., the restraint of body, speech, and mind.

656 Tib only.

657 Not in AY or Dh.

658 Not in AY or Dh.

659 Or, reading with P and D, "has no malice in his heart." AY reads "if his mind is not confused."

beings and can endure Omniscience.[660] Thus will he accomplish the cultivation of the wilderness-dweller's[661] perfection of endurance.

(4) "O Eminent Householder, how does one accomplish the cultivation of the perfection of exertion of the wilderness-dwelling renunciant bodhisattva? O Eminent Householder, the renunciant bodhisattva who lives in the wilderness trains himself to think,[662] 'In order to attain the ability to endure the non-arising [of things],[663] I will not turn back from the wilderness.' Thus will he accomplish the cultivation of the wilderness-dweller's[664] perfection of exertion.

(5) "O Eminent Householder, how does one accomplish the cultivation of the perfection of concentration[665] of the wilderness-dwelling renunciant bodhisattva? O Eminent Householder, the renunciant bodhisattva who lives in the wilderness,[666] fully acquiring the perfection of concentration, is not indifferent to the maturing of beings, but[667] devotes himself to amassing the roots-of-goodness. Thus will he accomplish the cultivation of the wilderness-dweller's[668] perfection of concentration.

(6) "O Eminent Householder, how does one accomplish the cultivation of the perfection of insight of the wilderness-dwelling renunciant bodhisattva? O Eminent Householder, the renunciant bodhisattva who lives in the wilderness trains himself to think[669] 'My body is just like the wilderness, and as is the body, just such is enlightenment,'[670] and through [the practice of] suchness[671] he

---

660 AY omits "produces loving-kindness toward all beings" and adds "does not follow another Way."

661 Not in AY or Dh.

662 Not in AY or Dh.

663 Of the Tibetan versions consulted, only N supplies the material in brackets, though it is certainly implied in all. For the expression *anutpattika-dharma-kṣānti* cf. above, §11G(3), n. 240.

664 Not in AY or Dh.

665 Here AY suddenly uses the expression *i-hsin* 一心 "single-minded," which is not his usual translation of *dhyāna*. Is this just for variety, or has some emendation of the text taken place?

666 Not in AY or Dh.

667 Not in AY or Dh.

668 Not in AY or Dh.

669 Not in AY or Dh.

670 Tib. *byang-chub*, Skt. *bodhi*. Sakurabe discusses at length the idea that

does not engage in discriminating or divisive thought.[672] Thus will he accomplish the cultivation of the wilderness-dweller's[673] perfection of insight.

"O Eminent Householder, in this way the renunciant bodhisattva who lives in the wilderness accomplishes the cultivation of the six perfections with little effort.[674]

[25M] "O Eminent Householder, if a renunciant bodhisattva possesses four things, he is allowed to live in the wilderness. And what are the four?

(1) "O Eminent Householder,[675] if he is learned and remembers what he has heard,[676] if he is skilled in the exegesis of the Dharma,[677] if he exerts himself in attentiveness and accomplishes the Dharma and what is in accord with the Dharma, he should live in the wilderness.

(2)[678] "Moreover, O Eminent Householder, a renunciant bodhisattva who has many defilements should live in the wilderness without companions in order to subdue the defilements, and he should annihilate the defilements.

(3) "Moreover, O Eminent Householder, a renunciant bodhisattva who has attained the five paranormal powers[679] should live in the wilderness in order to mature gods, *nāgas*, *yakṣas*, and *gandharvas*.[680]

(4)[681] "Moreover, O Eminent Householder, the renunciant

---

both the wilderness and the body are empty, but in fact the text does not discuss "emptiness" here at all. Sakurabe has apparently again been diverted by R, which gives a reference to "emptiness" not found in any other version of the text at this point. It is clearly "suchness" (*tathatā*)—not translated at all by Sakurabe—rather than "emptiness" (which has not yet been separated from the other two doors of liberation in our text) which is the operative concept here.

671 Not in AY or Dh.

672 Skt. *kalpa* and *vikalpa*; AY has apparently dropped the negative here.

673 Not in AY or Dh.

674 Not in AY or Dh.

675 Not in AY.

676 Not in AY.

677 Tib. *chos rnam-par nges-pa*, Skt. **dharmaviniścaya*.

678 The sequence of (2) and (3) is reversed in AY.

679 Cf. above, §25B, n. 552.

680 Not in AY.

681 The following sentences are cited in *Śikṣ.* 199.12-15:

punar aparaṁ gṛhapate pravrajitena bodhisatvena
buddhānujñāto 'raṇyavāsa iti jñātvā 'raṇye vastavyaṁ |

bodhisattva who knows that the Buddha has sanctioned wilderness-dwelling should live in the wilderness, and there he will perfect all the virtuous qualities. Afterwards, supported by those roots-of-goodness, he should enter villages, towns, cities, realms, kingdoms, and capitals to preach the Dharma.

"O Eminent Householder, if a renunciant bodhisattva possesses these four things, then he is permitted to live in the wilderness.[682]

[§26. INTERACTING WITH OTHER MONKS AND TEACHERS]

[26A][683] "O Eminent Householder,[684] if the renunciant bodhisattva {who lives in the wilderness}[685] enters an assembly[686] for the purpose of

---

> *atra hi śukladharmaparipūrir bhavati | upastabdhakūśala-mūlaḥ paścād grāma-nagara-nigama-rāṣtra-rājadhānīṣv avatīrya dharmaṁ deśayiṣyāmi ||*

682 Throughout the Tibetan (and the sole line from this passage that is extant in Sanskrit; see the citation from *Śikṣ.* in the previous note) states that, under certain circumstances, the bodhisattva *should* live in the wilderness (*gnas-par bya'o*), but here in the concluding passage the text states that he is *permitted* to do so (*gnas-par gnang-ngo*). AY, by contrast, states throughout that a bodhisattva who satisfies these conditions *may* live (*k'o chü* 可居) in the wilderness. (Dh and R are too divergent to be called upon to adjudicate.) Is this simply a difference of interpretation, or has the endorsement of wilderness-dwelling been strengthened over time?

683 The following lines are cited in *Śikṣ.* 199.15-200.4:

> *sacet punar gṛhapate pravrajito bodhisatva uddeśa-svādhyāyārthaṁ gaṇaṁ avatarati | tena tatra sagauravena bhavitavyaṁ sapratīsenācāryopādhyāyeṣu sthaviramadhya-navakeṣu bhikṣuṣu pradakṣina bhavitavyam analasena svayaṁkāriṇā 'paropatāpinā na ca tenopasthānagurukeṇa bhavitavyaṁ | evaṁ cānenopaparīkṣitavyaṁ | tathāgato 'py arhan samyaksaṁbuddhaḥ sadevasya lokasya samārakasya sabrahmakasya saśramaṇabrāhmaṇikāyāḥ prajāyāḥ pujito dakṣinīyaḥ sarvasatvānāṁ | so 'pi tāvan na kasyacit-sakāśād upasthānaṁ svīkaroti | kiṁ punar asmābhir aśikṣitaiḥ śikṣitukāmaiḥ | api tu vayam eva sarvasatvānām upasthāyakā bhaviṣyāmaḥ | vayaṁ eva pareṣāṁ upasthāna paricaryāṁ kariṣyāmo na ca punaḥ kasyacit sakāśād upasthāna paricaryāṁ svīkariṣyāmaḥ |*

684 Not in AY or Dh.

685 AY only.

686 Tib. *tshogs*, Skt. *gaṇa*.

receiving exhortation or recitation,[687] he should conduct himself there with respect. Toward teachers and preceptors, and toward elder, middle-rank, and junior monks, he should act with courtesy and propriety. He should not be lackadaisical but should be self-reliant, and should not cause trouble to others. And he should not long for service. He should reflect as follows: 'If the Tathāgata, the Arhat, the Samyaksambuddha—who is venerated by the entire world with all its creatures, including gods, Māras,[688] Brahmās, {Śakras,}[689] *śramaṇas*, and *brāhmaṇas*,[690] and with its gods, humans, and asuras,[691] and is an object of donations for them—did not require service for himself from any being whatsoever, how much less so should those of us who are unlearned and still desire to learn? Rather, I should perform service for all beings, and should not require service from anyone.'

[26B][692] "And why? O Eminent Householder, the monk who longs for service squanders the good qualities he has acquired, and those who have been attracted by him will think: 'He has attracted us in order to get our service, and not for the sake of the Dharma.' And their faith will be squandered. Those who do perform service for him with worldly goods will not receive great benefit or great fruit. And even when he approaches his teacher or preceptor, he should think, 'If the teacher discerns even a bit of lack of faith in me, he will not benefit me by exhortation or reciting or teaching.' And so thinking, he should conduct himself with skillful body and mind and with a docile mind.[693] For

---

687 AY and Dh say simply that the bodhisattva joins with the community to participate in Dharma-recitation; R, like Tib, states that his purpose is to receive (perhaps "listen to"?) such recitation. Tib is alone in mentioning "exhortation."

688 Not in AY.

689 AY only (though Dh mentions Śakras below).

690 Not in AY or Dh.

691 Not in AY; Dh goes on to provide a much longer list, including all eight varieties of nonhuman beings (*nāgas*, *yakṣas*, etc.) as well as several varieties of gods.

692 The following lines are cited in *Śikṣ*. 200.4-6:

> *tat kasya hetoḥ | upasthānagurukasya hi gṛhapate bhikṣor*
> *guṇadharmānugraho naśyati | yeṣāṁ ca saṁgrahaṁ karoti*
> *teṣāṁ evaṁ bhavati | upasthānahetor eṣo 'smākaṁ*
> *saṁgrahaṁ karoti ||*

693 Tib only. Reading with P alone (which has *sems-can shes-pas* vs. *sems cang-shes-pas* in the other versions), Sakurabe interprets this passage as meaning "knowing the nature (*shishitsu* 資質) of sentient beings." On the term *cang-shes-pa* itself see above, §17B, n. 343.

the sake of receiving exhortation and recitation, he should have no regard for his body and life. Out of desire for the Dharma he should fulfill the wishes of his teacher and preceptor. For the sake of attaining good qualities, he should not desire any gain, reverence, or fame.

[26C][694] "O Eminent Householder, if a bodhisattva who wishes to get instruction or to participate in recitation hears, receives an explanation of, or[695] learns from someone a single four-line verse connected with giving, morality, endurance, exertion, meditation, and insight, {with loving-kindness, compassion, sympathetic joy and equanimity},[696] or with the equipment[697] of the bodhisattva path and so on,[698] he should venerate the teacher from whom he has correctly received it. And for as many words, syllables, and letters as there are in that verse, for that many eons he should serve and attend that teacher without hypocrisy, and should honor and serve him with all kinds of goods, worship, and adoration. O Eminent Householder, if even then his veneration of the teacher as teacher would be incomplete, how much more so is his service to the Dharma![699]

[26D] "O Eminent Householder, to the extent that the mind and mental factors[700] of the one who enters with faith into the cultivation and recitation of what he hears come into association with what is virtuous, or with the Buddha, or with the Dharma, or with the Sangha, or into dissociation from anxiety and desire, or into association

---

694 The following lines are cited in *Śikṣ*. 37.7-12:
sacet punar gṛhapate pāṭhasvādhyāyārthiko bodhisatvaḥ kasyacid antikāc catuṣpādikāṁ gāthāṁ śṛṇuyād uddiśed vā udgṛhṇīyād dānaśīlakṣāntivīryadhyāna-prajñāsaṁprayuktāṁ bodhisatvasaṁbhāropacayaṁ vā tena tasminn ācārye dharmagauravaṁ karaṇīyaṁ yāvadbhir nāmapada-vyañja[nakāya] gāthoddiṣṭā | yadi tāvata evaṁ kalpāṁs tasyācāryasyopasthānaparicaryāṁ kuryād aśaṭhatayā sarvalābhasatkārapūjayā | adyāpi gṛhapate na pratipūritam ācāryasyācārya-gauravaṁ bhavati | kaḥ punar vādodharma [gauravaṁ] ||

695 Tib only.

696 Dh only.

697 Skt. *sambhāra*. Cf. above, §24A, n. 520.

698 Not in AY.

699 Following N, which is far more coherent (and closer to the extant Sanskrit) here than the other Tibetan editions consulted thus far.

700 Tib only.

with purity, discipline, and calm,[701] O Eminent Householder, even if one were to undertake to perform service to one's teacher for that many eons, even then the reverence that should be done to one's teacher as teacher will not be fulfilled. And in the same way, O Eminent Householder, the dharmas to be matured and the knowledge to which one will awaken should be known to be immeasurable.[702] O Eminent Householder, this being the case, thinking 'Because of having asked [him] about the immeasurable dharmas to be matured and the immeasurable knowledge to be awakened to, my teacher is also immeasurable,'[703] the bodhisattva should offer immeasurable veneration to the Dharma.[704]

[§27. THE PURE MORALITY OF THE RENUNCIANT BODHISATTVA]

[27A] "Moreover, O Eminent Householder, the renunciant bodhisattva should dwell in the accomplishments of the renunciant. O Eminent Householder, how should the renunciant bodhisattva dwell in the accomplishments of the renunciant?[705] O Eminent Householder,[706] the renunciant bodhisattva, when he hears about pure morality, should train himself in it. The following four things constitute pure morality. And what are the four? They are (1) dwelling in the noble traditions, (2) delighting in the ascetic practices and austerities,[707] (3) not mixing with householders or renunciants,[708] and (4) living in the wilderness without hypocrisy. These four comprise pure morality.

[27B] "Moreover, O Eminent Householder, there are [another] four items of pure morality. And what are the four? They are (1) restraining the body without imagining[709] a 'body,' (2) restraining the

---

701 Tib only.

702 The tense is not clear in the Tibetan (nor, of course, in the Chinese), but what is clearly at issue here is the need to develop the two immense prerequisites of Buddhahood, viz., merit (*puṇya*, referred to explicitly in AY and Dh as *fu-te* 福德 and *fu* 福, respectively) and knowledge (*jñāna*).

703 Tib only. Sakurabe offers a more interpretive translation: "Because of asking about the limitless existence which is [the result of] the fruition of karma and about the acquisition of limitless wisdom by which one cuts off attachments, one should think of one's teacher as also being without limits" (p. 303).

704 Dh is quite different here.

705 Not in AY.

706 Tib only.

707 Tib only.

708 For (3) Dh substitutes "not delighting in the household."

709 AY "without the obstacle (*kua-ai* 罣礙) of the body," Dh and R "without apprehending (*te* 得) a body," and so on for speech and mind. This

voice without imagining a 'voice,' (3) restraining the mind without imagining a 'mind,' and (4) devoid of views, to arouse the spirit of Omniscience. These four comprise pure morality.

[27C] "Moreover, O Eminent Householder, there are another four items of pure morality. And what are the four? They are (1) to abandon grasping at things as 'me,' (2) to discard grasping at things as 'mine,' (3) to be devoid of [concepts of] annihilation or eternity, and (4) to enter into the teaching of causality.[710] These four comprise pure morality.

[27D] "Moreover, O Eminent Householder, there are another four items of pure morality. And what are the four? They are (1) to consider the *skandha*s as arising and passing away,[711] (2) to weigh the realms of the senses as equal to the dharma-realm,[712] (3) to conceive of the sense doors as an empty city,[713] and (4) not to incline

---

wide variety of renditions suggests an underlying confusion in the Indic texts between **upalambha* "imagination" (represented in Tib as *dmigs-pa*), **upalabdha* "obtained, apprehended" reflected in Dh and R, and perhaps even **uparodha* "obstacle, obstruction" reflected by AY's unexpected translation.

[710] Tib. *rten-pa'i chos*, a phrase whose meaning is less than transparent. All three Chinese versions, however, agree that this is a reference to "the teaching (*dharma*) of causality" (*yin-yüan fa* 因緣法) though they differ on how the bodhisattva should relate to this teaching: AY, like the Tibetan, states that he should "enter into" it (*hsia* 下, literally "descend," perhaps used here as a translation of some form of *avatārati* "enters" but also "descends"), Dh that he should "abandon" it (捨), and R that he should "understand" it (解).

[711] AY "to take the *skandha*s as illusory dharmas," Dh "[to understand] one's own body as one with the Dharma," R "[to understand] the *skandha*s as non-existent (*wu-so-yu* 無所有)."

[712] The equation being made here is between the eighteen sense fields or realms (*dhātu*)—comprising the six sense organs including the mind, the objects of those six organs, and the six corresponding forms of consciousness—and the dharma-realm (*dharmadhātu*). The latter is one of the most elusive terms in the Buddhist lexicon; in the present case it appears to mean simply the realm of all existing or potentially existing things (*dharma*).

[713] "Sense doors" translates Skt. *āyatana* (Tib. *skye-mched*), a term used to refer to a subset of the eighteen *dhātu*s, viz., the six sense organs and their corresponding objects. Since the Sanskrit word also means "house, dwelling place," the application of the idea of no-self yields the image of the *āyatana*s as empty houses (i.e., houses with no resident) and by extension as an empty city.

toward provisional designations.[714] These four comprise pure morality.

[27E] "Moreover, O Eminent Householder, there are another four items of pure morality. And what are the four? They are (1) by conceptualizing the self as selfless, to avoid praising oneself; (2) by not imagining an 'other,' to avoid blaming others; (3) by thoroughly cleansing the mind, to be without conceit; and (4) by virtue of the sameness of all dharmas, to be unwavering.[715] These four comprise pure morality.

[27F] "Moreover, O Eminent Householder, there are another four items of pure morality. And what are the four? They are (1) delighting in emptiness, (2) not being frightened by signlessness, (3) being greatly compassionate toward all beings,[716] and (4) being able to endure selflessness. These four comprise pure morality.

[§28. THE PURE MEDITATION OF THE RENUNCIANT BODHISATTVA]

"Moreover, O Eminent Householder, when the renunciant bodhisattva hears about pure *samādhi*, he should train himself in it. And what is perfectly pure *samādhi*? It is to be effortless with respect to all dharmas;[717] to be free of dualism, because of the sameness of all dharmas; to have a dextrous mind, a one-pointed mind, a mind that has gone forth,[718] a mind that is not scattered, an unwandering mind, a mind that does not dwell anywhere, and a mind that is established in meditation; to be in control of one's mind; to have a mind that is not attached to desirable qualities; and to have a mind that contemplates things as illusory. Just as the *dharmadhātu* is uneffected, and just as it is unborn, unarisen, and characterized by sameness, just so, O

---

[714] Tib. *tha-snyad btags-pa*, Skt. *vyavahāra-prajñapti*. AY and R are in close agreement, while Dh offers the quite different reading "obtaining wisdom and reaching non-dwelling."

[715] Not in AY, who takes each of the two components of items (1) and (2) as separate, thus arriving at a total of four items without the inclusion of (3) and (4). R conforms at least tangentially to Tib, while Dh (as is often the case) is difficult to harmonize with any of the other versions.

[716] One would have expected here a reference to the "wishless" rather than to compassion for all beings, but the reading found in Tib is confirmed by all three Chinese versions.

[717] AY states that he should "thoroughly understand all dharmas," Dh that he should "respectfully receive" them, and R that he should understand that "all dharmas are nonexistent" (cf. above, §27D, n. 711). Other differences in this section are fairly minor.

[718] Tib only.

Eminent Householder, does the renunciant bodhisattva contemplate pure *samādhi*.

[§29. THE PURE INSIGHT OF THE RENUNCIANT BODHISATTVA]

[29A] "Moreover, O Eminent Householder, when the renunciant bodhisattva hears of pure insight,[719] he should train himself in it.[720] And what is pure insight? It is to be thoroughly reflected upon as follows: it is (1) knowing all dharmas directly,[721] (2) knowing how to discern them,[722] (3) knowing how to enter into special knowledge,[723] and (4) knowing how to cause other beings to understand the Dharma[s]. O Eminent Householder, in this way does the renunciant bodhisattva analyze pure insight.[724]

[29B] "Moreover, O Eminent Householder, the renunciant bodhisattva trains himself to think as follows: 'Because this insight has no body, it is marked by being unimpeded.[725] Because it does not wander about, it is marked by not being grasped. Because it is unborn, it is marked by not dwelling anywhere. Because it has the nature of space, it is marked by being uneffected.' O Eminent Householder, this being the case, the contemplation of dharma[s] in this way is the practice of the renunciant bodhisattva."[726]

---

719 The text actually reads "perfection of insight" (Tib. *shes-rab-kyi pha-rol-tu phyin-pa*, Skt. *prajñāpāramitā*), but this is clearly a copyist's error (if not a deliberate editorial emendation) of an original that read simply *prajñā*. Throughout the rest of this section the text consistently refers only to *prajñā*, not to *prajñāpāramitā*, and there is no equivalent of the word *pāramitā* in any Chinese version of the text. In any event, we have to do with a discussion based on the three components of the eightfold path, viz., *śīla* (§27), *samādhi* (§28), and *prajñā* (§29).

720 Tib only.

721 Not in AY.

722 Note that this is the definition of *prajñā* given in the *Abhidharmakośa* (Ch. 1, §2a), viz., "*prajñā* is the discernment of dharmas (*dharmapravicaya*)." AY, in fact, gives only this part of the definition, stating simply that *prajñā* (*hui* 慧) is "the discernment of dharmas" (*chu-fa zhi tse-chih* 諸法之擇智).

723 Tib. *so-so yang-dag-par rig-pa*, Skt. *pratisaṁvid*. There are four of these "special knowledges," viz., *dharma*, *artha*, *nirukti*, and *pratibhāna* (see *Abhidharmakośa* Ch. 7, §37c-40b, and *Visuddhimagga*, 440-443). This phrase is not in AY.

724 Not in AY.

725 Not in AY.

726 R has divided these sentences somewhat differently; Dh seems quite garbled at this point.

[§30. THE ORDINATION OF UGRA AND HIS FRIENDS (version 2)]

[30A] When the Blessed One had taught this Dharma-text, one hundred thousand creatures[727] aroused the spirit of Supreme Perfect Enlightenment. Those eminent householders all attained the ability to endure the non-arising of things, and thirty-two thousand creatures[728] attained the dust-free, stainless, pure eye of the Dharma toward dharmas.[729]

[30B] {Then Ugra and the other eminent householders with one voice said, "It is unprecedented, O Blessed One, that the Tathāgata has spoken so well in this way about the bad qualities of the household life and about the practice of heavy burdens there, and also about the good qualities of going forth from the household. O respectworthy Blessed One, now that you have clarified the many bad qualities of living at home and the innumerable good qualities of going forth from the household, please let us receive the precepts of the renunciant from the Blessed One and attain the conduct of the monk!" The Blessed One replied, "Going forth from the household, O Eminent Householders, is extremely difficult. You must be able to be very pure [and to receive and uphold the teaching." The eminent householders again said to the Buddha, "O Blessed One, the renunciant life may be very difficult and burdensome, but even so, would the Tathāgata permit us to go forth from the household to practice the Way?"

[30C] The Blessed One then told Maitreya bodhisattva and All Pure Conduct bodhisattva to ordain those eminent householders. Maitreya bodhisattva ordained two hundred eminent householders, and All Pure Conduct bodhisattva ordained three hundred eminent householders, into going forth from the household to practice the Way.}[730]

[§31. HOW THE HOUSEHOLDER BODHISATTVA CAN LIVE AS A RENUNCIANT]

[31A] Then Ugra the Eminent Householder, rejoicing, delighted, elated, and glad, presented the Blessed One with pairs of colored cloths[731] valued at 100,000 [coins], and spoke as follows: "O Blessed One, this root-of-goodness of mine I bestow on all beings.[732] By this root-of-goodness of mine, may those who are householder

---

727 AY "five hundred people," Dh "eight thousand people," R "eight thousand living beings." Note the apparent confusion between "eight" (*aṣṭa*) and "one hundred" (*śata*) thousand, which may be yet another indicator of the transmission of the text in Prakrit.

728 Dh "gods and humans," R "living beings."

729 Not in AY.

730 AY only. For a discussion of the significance of the placement of the ordination scene here in the earliest version of the text see Chapter 2, pp. 62-63.

731 That is, the upper and lower monastic robes. (I would like to thank Thanissaro Bhikkhu for clarifying the meaning of this expression.)

732 Dh "on all bodhisattvas."

bodhisattvas completely fulfill whatever training has been designated for householder bodhisattvas, and may those who are renunciant bodhisattvas completely fulfill whatever training the Blessed One has designated for renunciant bodhisattvas. And there is something else that I wish to ask the Blessed One. O Blessed One, how many dharmas must a householder bodhisattva who lives at home possess if he is to train himself in the training of the renunciant bodhisattva?"[733]

[31B] When he had spoken those words, the Blessed One replied to Ugra the Eminent Householder as follows: "O Eminent Householder, if a householder-bodhisattva who lives at home possesses five things, he trains in the training of the renunciant. And what are the five?

(1) "O Eminent Householder, the householder bodhisattva who lives at home gives away all things without regard. Possessing the spirit of Omniscience,[734] he does not hope for the ripening [of his action].[735]

(2) "Moreover, O Eminent Householder, the householder bodhisattva who lives at home is pure in his practice of celibacy. He does not act on desires even in his mind; how much less so does he actually participate in sexual intercourse or enter into erotic love?[736]

(3) "Moreover, O Eminent Householder, the householder bodhisattva who lives at home, not having experienced a fixed course with respect to what is correct,[737] goes into an empty house, and calling forth his tactical skill, absorbs himself in the four *dhyānas*.[738]

(4) "Moreover, O Eminent Householder, the householder bodhisattva who lives at home exerts himself in order to make all beings happy.[739] He exerts himself to become

---

[733] Not in AY. The wording varies slightly in Dh and R, but the overall purport is the same.

[734] For "spirit of Omniscience" Dh reads "great vehicle."

[735] That is, for a reward for his gifts.

[736] Precisely the same wording is used above; see §7A and n. 144. The final phrase "or enter into erotic love" again occurs here in Tib only.

[737] Tib. *yang-dag-pa skyon med-pa*, Skt. **samyaktva-niyama*. Cf. above, §25B and n. 559 as well as the following note.

[738] For a convenient discussion of the four *dhyānas* see Harvey 1990, pp. 250-252. Note also that "tactical skill" (*upāya-kauśalya*) is mentioned in connection with the bodhisattva's own meditative practice, and has nothing to do with techniques used in teaching others. (R states explicitly that it is by means of his *upāya* that the bodhisattva avoids entering into a fixed state with respect to what is correct [*cheng-wei* 正位]—i.e., that he uses his tactical skill to avoid becoming irreversible from Arhatship.) For a detailed discussion of the meaning of the term *upāya* in the *Ugra* and certain other sūtras see Chapter 6, pp. 154-156.

[739] Dh and R state that he directs loving-kindness toward all beings.

established[740] by means of the perfection of insight.[741]

(5) "Moreover, O Eminent Householder, the householder bodhisattva who lives at home upholds the True Dharma himself and causes others to practice it as well.

"O Eminent Householder, if a householder bodhisattva who lives at home possesses these five things, then he trains in the training of the renunciant."

Then Ugra the Eminent Householder spoke to the Blessed One as follows: "O Blessed One, I will act in accordance with the word of the Buddhas. I will train myself in the training of the renunciant, and in this way I will enter into the sameness of [all] phenomena.[742]

[§32. DIALOGUE WITH ĀNANDA]

[32A] Then at that time the Blessed One smiled. Now it is the nature of things[743] that whenever the Buddhas, the Blessed Ones, smile, at that time rays of light of many and various colors come forth from the Blessed One's mouth (colors such as blue, yellow, red, white, reddish orange, crystal, and silver)[744] and by them the entire limitless, endless world-system is pervaded with light. And having risen up as far as the Brahma-heaven they return, circle the Blessed One three times,[745] and disappear into the Blessed One's *uṣṇīṣa*.[746]

[32B] Then by the Buddha's power[747] Ānanda arose from his seat, arranged his upper robe on one shoulder, pressed his right knee to the ground, made the gesture of *añjali* toward the Blessed One,[748] and addressed the Blessed One as follows: "O Blessed One, not without reason, not without cause, do the Tathāgatas smile. For what reason, for

---

740 Reading with N, which omits *'byung-ba*.

741 Dh "he exerts himself to understand the perfection of insight," R "he exerts himself to train in the perfection of insight."

742 The entirety of §31B has no equivalent in AY. The final phrase, "and in this way ... [all] phenomena," occurs in Tib only.

743 Skt. **dharmatā*. Dh and R apparently did not recognize this expression, and translated as if this were "the dharma of all Buddhas" rather than the nature of the universe itself. Because this is a standard expression in this context, there is little doubt about how the underlying Indic text would have read.

744 This parenthetical list of colors appears only in R (in a shorter form) and Tib.

745 The reference to "circling the Blessed One three times" occurs only in R and Tib.

746 The entirety of §32A has no equivalent in AY.

747 This expression occurs only in Tib. Cf. above, §2A, n. 25.

748 The actions from "arranged his upper robe" to "the gesture of *añjali*" are absent from Dh.

what cause, do you smile?" When he had spoken thus, the Blessed One replied to Ānanda as follows: "O Ānanda, did you see the Eminent Householder Ugra make an offering to the Tathāgata and bring forth the lion's roar in order to accomplish the Dharma?" Ānanda replied, "Yes, O Blessed One, I saw it. Yes, O Sugata, I saw it."[749] Then the Blessed One said "O Ānanda, Ugra the Eminent Householder will serve all the Tathāgatas[750] who appear in this good eon.[751] He will worship them with all sorts of worship and veneration. And he will uphold the True Dharma. Though he will continually be a householder,[752] he will dwell in the training of the renunciant, and he will cause the *bodhi* of the Tathāgata to spread."[753]

[32C] Then the Venerable Ānanda addressed Ugra the Eminent Householder as follows: "O Eminent Householder, for what reason, for what cause, do you delight in dwelling in the dust of the household?" Ugra replied, "Reverend Ānanda, there is no dust whatsoever. Out of great compassion,[754] I do not hope for pleasure for myself. Reverend Ānanda, the bodhisattva endures the affliction caused by all suffering, and does not abandon beings."[755]

---

[749] The sentence "Yes, O Sugata, I saw it" does not occur in Dh.

[750] R "the Tathāgatas, the Arhats, the Samyaksaṁbuddhas."

[751] Skt. *bhadrakalpa*. On the idea that the present eon is one in which an especially large number of Buddhas will appear see Nattier 1991, pp. 21-25.

[752] The Tibetan reads "Eminent Householder," but Dh and R have only "householder" (which is surely the preferred reading). Presumably the Tibetan as we have it is the result of an editorial hypercorrection.

[753] For "will cause ... to spread" R reads "will extensively hear." The entirety of §32B has no equivalent in AY.

[754] Not in AY (see the following note).

[755] Not in AY. Dh and R are in rough conformity with Tib, but AY's version of §32B is substantially different:

> At that time the Venerable Ānanda addressed Ugra the Eminent Householder (lit., "house-manager"), saying, "What is it that you see in dwelling in a country, [or] dwelling in the household? The Dharma in which one can take pleasure is the sagely path of leaving home." Ugra the Eminent Householder replied to Ānanda, "It is not that I am desirous of my own happiness; it is because I desire to bring about the happiness of [all] living beings that I live at home. Moreover, the Tathāgata himself has explained to me 'While dwelling at home, be resolute in [the Dharma] that you have accepted.'"

[32D] When he had spoken thus, the Blessed One spoke to the Venerable Ānanda as follows: {"Do you see Ugra the Eminent Householder?" Ānanda replied, "Yes, Blessed One, I see Ugra the Eminent Householder."}[756] "O Ānanda, while dwelling at the household stage,[757] Ugra the Eminent Householder will mature a great many beings {into becoming renunciant bodhisattvas}[758] in this good eon; a renunciant bodhisattva would not be able to do so in a thousand or a hundred thousand eons.[759] And why? O Ānanda, you could not find the good qualities this Eminent Householder possesses in a thousand[760] renunciant bodhisattvas."

[§33. THE TITLE OF THE TEXT]

[33A] Then the Venerable[761] Ānanda spoke to the Blessed One as follows: "O Blessed One, what is the name of this Dharma-text? How should we remember it?"[762] The Blessed One replied, "O Ānanda, remember this Dharma-text as *The Inquiry of Ugra*. Remember it as *The Accomplishment of the Training of the Householder and the Renunciant*. Remember it as *Resolutely Venerating the Teacher*.[763] O

---

756 This standard formulaic exchange occurs in AY only.

757 Not in AY.

758 AY only.

759 Not in AY, which reads "in a hundred eons there will be no one else like him." Dh, which as is so often the case is rather garbled here, makes no mention of a number of eons but states that he "surpasses a hundred thousand teachers who are renunciant bodhisattvas." R agrees with Tib (though the number "one thousand" is given by R as "one hundred").

760 Dh and R "one hundred thousand." AY agrees with Tib.

761 Not in AY or Dh.

762 Lit., "how should we uphold it?", but √*dhṛ* in the sense of "remember" is well established.

763 No two versions of the sūtra agree on the titles, though three alternatives are offered in each. AY reads (1) *The Discourse* (*pien* 變, **parivarta*) *on the Householder and the Renunciant*, (2) *The Discourse* (id.) *on the Qualities of One's Inner Nature* [?], and (3) *The Inquiry of Ugra*. Dh has (1) *The Inquiry of Ugra the Gṛhapati*, (2) *The Discourse* (*p'in* 品, **parivarta*) *on the Householder and the Renunciant*, and (3) *Famous for His Qualities of Maintaining Single-Mindedness and Sitting in Meditation*. R offers (1) *The Inquiry of Ugra the Gṛhapati*, (2) *The Precepts of Householder and Renunciant Bodhisattvas*, and (3) *The Long Discourse* (*p'in* 品, **parivarta*) *on Venerating and Making Offerings to the Teacher*. On the use of the term *parivarta* in the sense of "discourse" see Chapter 2, pp. 32-33, n. 54.

Ānanda, as soon as one hears this Dharma-text, one will attain the virtues, the stamina,[764] and the many qualities (dharmas) of the bodhisattva, whereas one whose exertion is weak could not do so by practicing celibacy for a hundred eons.[765] Therefore, O Ānanda, one who wishes to bring forth exertion in himself and to incite others to exertion, and who wishes to dwell in the sameness of all the dharma-qualities[766] and to establish others in the sameness of all the dharma-qualities[767] should listen to this Dharma-text, master it, recite it, and teach it widely to others.[768] O Ānanda, I entrust this Dharma-text to you, so that it may be widely taught. And why? Because the Tathāgata has taught that within this Dharma-text are assembled all good qualities.[769]

[33B] "O Ānanda, the bodhisattva who does not dwell apart from this Dharma-text will not be deprived of the appearance of the Buddhas. O Ānanda, the bodhisattva who listens to, remembers, and recites this Dharma-text will not be deprived of the appearance of all the Buddhas and of seeing all the Buddhas. And why? Because the Tathāgata has taught that within this Dharma-text all good qualities are assembled, and within this Dharma-text all the good qualities of the path of accomplishing the training are brought together.[770]

[33C] "O Ānanda, even if this trimegachiliocosm were filled with fire, the gentleman or lady who seeks Supreme Perfect Enlightenment should wade through it so as to listen to and master this Dharma-text.[771] O Ānanda, rather than filling this whole trimegachiliocosm with the seven jewels and offering them reverently to one's teacher, one should instead listen to and master this Dharma-text.[772]

[33D] "O Ānanda, if a bodhisattva worships the stūpas[773] of the past Buddhas, the Blessed Ones, with jewels of various kinds and with all sorts of worship, and in the same way offers service throughout his life to the Buddha, the Blessed One of the present and to his Sangha of *śrāvaka*s with all sorts of pleasing goods, and pledges himself as a

---

764 More commonly translated "exertion" (*vīrya*).

765 Not in AY.

766 Not in AY.

767 Not in AY.

768 AY reads simply "receive and practice it."

769 AY substitutes "for the correct practice of many qualities."

770 The entirety of §33B has no parallel in AY. The last sentence is found in Tib only.

771 For another appearance of what must have been a common trope cf. the larger *Sukhāvatīvyūha*, §43 (Müller 1881, p. 68; Gómez 1996, p. 108).

772 The entirety of §33C has no parallel in AY.

773 The reference to the stūpa occurs in R and Tib only.

servant and disciple of the Buddhas and bodhisattvas of the future, to fully serve them, but does not accept, remember, read, master, and enter into this Dharma-text, and does not abide in this accomplishment, O Ānanda, that bodhisattva will not actually be worshipping the Buddhas of the past, future, and present.[774]

[33E] "O Ānanda, if a bodhisattva listens to and masters this Dharma-text, and in order to make the True Dharma long endure, and in order not to cut off the lineage of the Buddhas,[775] also teaches it widely to others, and also abides in this accomplishment, O Ānanda, this bodhisattva will be able to worship the Buddhas of the past, future, and present, and will serve them with reverence."[776]

[§34. THE FINAL REACTION OF THE AUDIENCE]

When the Blessed One had spoken these words, the Venerable Ānanda and Ugra the Eminent Householder and the monks and bodhisattvas[777] and the whole world with its[778] gods and humans, asuras, and gandharvas[779] rejoiced and praised the words of the Blessed One.[780]

[§35. TITLE AND COLOPHON][781]

The Nineteenth Assembly,[782] called *The Inquiry of Ugra*, from the *Noble Great Ratnakūṭa* Dharma-text in one hundred thousand chapters, is completed. Nine hundred

---

774 The entirety of §33D has no parallel in AY. Virtually all of this section is absent from Dh as well, which reads only "O Ānanda, if there is a bodhisattva who makes offerings to the Buddhas, the Blessed Ones, of the past, future, and present, and does so until the end of his life, but does not accept this sūtra-dharma and is not able to recite it and does not cultivate the various good qualities within it, this is equivalent to not making offerings to the Buddhas of the past, future, and present." R agrees with Dh in reading "this is the equivalent of not making offerings" etc.

775 The last phrase ("in order not to cut off the lineage of the Buddhas") occurs only in Tib. On this concept cf. above, §2C, n. 44.

776 The entirety of §33E is absent from AY. Dh and R again read "this is the equivalent of making offerings" etc.

777 Tib only.

778 Not in AY.

779 Not in AY, which however adds a reference to "witnessing faithful kings."

780 For "praised the words of the Blessed One" AY reads "concentrated on what the Blessed One had taught."

781 This section occurs in Tib only.

782 Among the Tibetan versions S and N (which read *'dus-pa* "assembly") clearly reflect the Chinese *hui* 會 "assembly" found solely in R; P eliminates the word, while D replaces it with *le'u* "chapter." For further discussion see Chapter 2, pp. 35-36.

ślokas, three sections.[783] Translated and edited by the Indian preceptor Surendrabodhi and the learned translator Zhang[784] Ye-shes-sde; corrected according to the new language[785] and set down.

[783] The reference to "nine hundred *ślokas*, three sections" occurs in S and N (that is, in Tibetan texts from the western branch of the Kanjur tradition) but not in P and D. The 9th-century catalogue *Ldan-kar-ma* states that the *Ugra* consists of seven hundred fifty *ślokas* and two sections (see Lalou 1953, p. 320, text no. 43). What the word *śloka* "verse" might have meant in reference to a text which is entirely in prose (as are many of the sūtras catalogued in the *Ldan-kar-ma*) remains unclear.

[784] P and D substitute *ban-de* for the clan name Zhang.

[785] P "edited twice," *lan gnyis zhu-sto* [*sic*].

APPENDICES

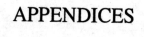

APPENDIX 1

Synoptic Tables of Versions of the *Ugrapariprcchā*

For those who wish to consult the *Ugra* in its Asian-language originals, this section contains synoptic tables providing page and line numbers of the extant Tibetan and Chinese translations, listed according to the section divisions used in the English translation above. For the sole Tibetan version I have provided references in Part A to four of the most widely available versions: the Peking, Derge, Narthang, and Stog Palace editions.[1] Because some scholars will have access to the first three of these in their original xylograph editions, while others will rely on modern reprint editions, I have given the pagination of the original xylographs (which is included in both medieval and modern versions) rather than the modern pagination, which is added only in the reprint editions. For the Chinese text references are provided in Part B for all three of the extant translations: those of An Hsüan and Yen Fo-t'iao (AY), Dharmarakṣa (Dh), and the version of uncertain authorship which is found in the Ratnakūṭa section of the canon (R), using the page, register, and line numbers of the standard *Taishō* edition. In addition I have provided a list of all citations from the scripture contained in the Sanskrit *Śikṣāsamuccaya* (*Śikṣ.*) and in the Chinese translation of the *Daśabhūmikavibhāṣā* (*Dbhv.*). These are included in Part B, not because they are necessarily more closely related to the Chinese versions than to the Tibetan, but simply for reasons of space.

---

[1] A complete critical edition of the Tibetan text based on these four versions, which I prepared as a preliminary step in this study and which served as the basis for the English translation given above, has been eliminated from this volume in order to keep publication costs to a minimum.

Part A: Tibetan Texts

§	Peking 760(19) (vol. 53)[2]	Derge 63 (vol. 42)	Narthang 74[1] (vol. 39)	Stog 11(19) (vol. 39)
Title	296b6	257a7-b2	1b1-3	2.1-3.1
0	296b6-7	257b2	1b3-4	3.1-2
1A	296b7-297a3	257b2-4	1b4-2b2	3.2-4.5
1B	297a3-b1	257b4-258a2	2b3-3b2	4.5-6.3
2A	297b1-6	258a2-5	3b2-4a1	6.3-7.2
2B	297b6-8	258a5-6	4a1-4	7.2-4
2C	297b8-298a8	258a6-b4	4a4-b6	7.4-8.6
2D	298a8-b3	258b5-7	4b6-5a3	8.6-9.3
2E	298b3-6	258b7-259a2	5a3-7	9.3-7
3A	298b6-7	259a2-3	5a7-b1	9.7-10.1
3B	298b8-299a2	259a3-5	5b1-4	10.1-4
3C	299a2-7	259a5-b1	5b4-6a2	10.4-11.2
3D	299a7-b4	259b1-5	6a2-7	11.2-7
4A	299b4-6	259b5-6	6b1-3	12.1-3
4B	299b6-8	259b6-260a1	6b3-6	12.3-6
4C	300a1-4	260a1-3	6b6-7a2	12.6-13.2
4D	300a4-6	260a3-5	7a2-5	13.2-5
4E	300a6-8	260a5-6	7a5-7	13.5-7
5A	300a8-b4	260a6-b2	7a7-b4	13.7-14.5
5B	300b4-301a1	260b2-6	7b5-8a3	14.5-15.4
5C	301a1-6	260b6-261a2	8a3-b1	15.4-16.1
5D	301a6-7	261a2-3	8b1-3	16.1-3

[1] No. 74 in the Lokesh Chandra reprint edition.
[2] Vol. 23 of the Ōtani reprint edition.

§	Peking 760(19)	Derge 63	Narthang 74	Stog 11(19)
6A	301a7-b3	261a3-6	8b4-9a1	16.3-7
6B	301b3-302a2	261a6-b4	9a1-b2	16.7-18.1
7A	302a2-303a1	261b4-262a7	9b2-10b5	18.1-20.2
7B	303a1-5	262a7-b4	10b5-11a4	20.3-21.1
8A	303a6-b4	262b4-263a1	11a4-b4	21.1-22.1
8B	303b4-7	263a1-3	11b4-7	22.1-4
8C	303b7-304a2	263a3-5	11b7-12a3	22.4-7
8D	304a2-8	263a5-b2	12a3-12b3	22.7-23.7
9A	304a8-b4	263b2-5	12b3-13a1	23.7-24.4
9B	302b4-305a2	263b5-264a3	13a1-b1	24.4-25.5
9C	305a2-5	264a3-5	13b1-5	25.5-26.2
9D	305a5-b2	264a5-b1	13b5-14a3	26.2-6
9E	305b2-5	264b1-3	14a3-7	26.6-27.2
9F	305b5-7	264b3-5	14a7-b3	27.2-5
10A	305b7-306a4	264b5-265a1	14b3-15a2	27.5-28.3
10B	306a4-8	265a1-4	15a2-6	28.3-7
11A	306a8-b2	265a4-5	15a6-b1	28.7-29.3
11B	306b2-4	265a6-7	15b1-3	29.3-5
11C	306b4-5	265a7-b1	15b3-5	29.5-7
11D	306b6-7	265b1-3	15b5-7	29.7-30.2
11E	306b8-307a1	265b3-4	16a1-2	30.2-4
11F	307a1-6	265b4-6	16a2-6	30.4-31.1
11G	307a6-b6	265b6-266a5	16a6-17a1	31.1-32.2
12A	307b6-308a2	266a5-b1	17a2-6	32.2-6
12B	308a2-7	266b1-4	17a6-b4	32.6-33.4
12C	308a7-b2	266b4-7	17b4-18a1	33.5-34.1
13A	308b2-3	266b7-267a1	18a1-3	34.1-2
13B	308b3-6	267a1-3	18a3-6	34.3-5
13C	308b6-7	267a3	18a6-7	34.5-6

§	Peking 760(19)	Derge 63	Narthang 74	Stog 11(19)
13D	308b7-8	267a4	18b1-2	34.6-35.1
13E	308b8-309a1	267a4-5	18b2-3	35.1-2
13F	309a1-2	267a5-6	18b3-4	35.2-3
13F'	---	---	---	---
13G	309a2-3	267a6-7	18b4-6	35.3-4
13H	309a3-4	267a7-b1	18b6-7	35.4-6
13I	309a4-6	267b1-2	18b7-19a2	35.6-7
13J	309a6-7	267b2-3	19a2-4	35.7-36.1
13K	309a7-b1	267b3-4	19a4-5	36.1-3
13L	309b1-2	267b4-5	19a5-7	36.3-4
13M	309b2-3	267b5-6	19a7-b1	36.4-6
13N	309b3-4	267b6	19b1-3	36.6-7
13O	309b4-5	267b6-7	19b3-4	36.7-37.1
13P	309b5-6	267b7-268a1	19b4-5	37.1-2
13Q	309b6-7	268a1-2	19b5-6	37.2-3
13R	309b7-8	268a2-3	19b6-20a1	37.3-4
13S	309b8-310a2	268a3-4	20a1-2	37.4-6
13T	310a2-3	268a4	20a2-4	37.6-7
13U	310a3-4	268a4-5	20a4-5	37.7-38.2
13V	310a4-5	268a5-6	20a5-7	38.2-3
13W	310a5-6	268a6-7	20a7-b1	38.3-4
13W'	---	---	---	---
13X	310a6-7	268a7-b1	20b1-2	38.4-5
13Y	310a7-8	268b1-2	20b2-3	38.5-6
13Z	310a8-b1	268b2	20b4-5	38.7-39.1
13AA	310b1-2	268b2-3	20b5-6	39.1-2
13BB	310b2-3	268b3-4	20b6-7	39.2-3
13CC	310b3-4	268b4-5	20b7-21a2	39.3-4
13DD	310b4-5	268b5-6	21a2-3	39.4-5

§	Peking 760(19)	Derge 63	Narthang 74	Stog 11(19)
13EE	310b5-7	268b6-7	21a3-5	39.6-7
13FF	310b7-8	268b7	21a5-6	39.7-40.1
13GG	310b8-311a1	268b7-269a1	21a6-7	40.1-2
13HH	311a1-3	269a1-3	21a7-b2	40.2-3
14A	311a3-7	269a3-6	21b3-7	40.3-41.1
14B	311a7-b1	269a6-7	22a1-2	41.1-3
14C	311b1-3	269a7-b2	22a2-5	41.3-5
14D	311b3-6	269b2-4	22a5-b1	41.5-42.1
14E	311b6-8	269b4-5	22b1-3	42.1-3
15A	311b8-312a3	269b5-270a1	22b3-7	42.3-7
15B	312a3-7	270a1-3	22b7-23a4	42.7-43.4
16A	312a7-b1	270a3-6	23a4-7	43.4-7
16B	312b1-6	270a6-b2	23a7-b6	43.7-44.6
17A	312b6-313a3	270b2-6	23b6-24a5	44.6-45.4
17B	313a3-7	270b6-271a2	24a5-b3	45.4-46.2
17C	313a7-b2	271a2-3	24b3-5	46.2-4
18A	313b2-8	271a3-7	24b5-25a4	46.4-47.3
18B	313b8-314a3	271a7-b2	25a4-7	47.3-5
19A	314a3-6	271b2-4	25a7-b3	47.5-48.1
19B	314a6-8	271b4-5	25b3-5	48.1-3
19C	314a8-b2	271b5-7	25b5-26a1	48.3-5
19D	314b2-5	271b7-272a1	26a1-3	48.5-49.1
19E	314b5-7	272a1-3	26a3-5	49.1-3
19F	314b7-315a1	272a3-4	26a5-b1	49.3-5
19G	315a1-4	272a4-6	26b1-4	49.5-7
19H	315a4-7	272a6-b1	26b4-6	50.1-3
19I	315a7-b1	272b1-2	26b7-27a2	50.3-5
19J	315b2-4	272b2-3	27a2-4	50.5-7
19K	315b4-6	272b3-5	27a4-7	50-7-51.2

§	Peking 760(19)	Derge 63	Narthang 74	Stog 11(19)
19L	315b6-8	272b5-7	27a7-b2	51.2-5
19M	315b8-316a3	272b7-273a1	27b3-4	51.5-52.1
19N	316a3-5	273a1-3	27b4-7	52.1-3
19O	316a5-7	273a3-4	27b7-28a2	52.3-5
19P	316a7-b2	273a4-6	28a2-5	52.5-53.1
19Q	316b2-5	273a6-b1	28a5-7	53.1-4
19R	316b5-7	273b1-2	28a7-b2	53.4-6
19S	316b7-317a1	273b2-4	28b2-5	53.6-54.1
19T	317a1-3	273b4-5	28b5-7	54.1-3
19U	317a3-6	273b5-7	28b7-29a4	54.3-6
20A	317a6-b2	273b7-274a3	29a4-b1	54.6-55.3
20B	317b2-5	274a3-5	29b1-4	55.3-6
20C	317b5-318a1	274a5-b1	29b4-30a2	55.7-56.4
20D	318a1-4	274b1-3	30a2-6	56.4-57.1
20E	318a4-b4	274b3-275a2	30a6-31a2	57.1-58.3
20F	318b4-8	275a2-5	31a2-6	58.3-6
20G	318b8-319a3	275a5-7	31a6-b2	58.7-59.2
21A	319a3-b2	275a7-b5	31b2-32a3	59.2-60.3
21B	319b2-4	275b5-6	32a3-5	60.3-5
21C	319b4-5	275b6-7	32a6-7	60.5-6
22A	319b6-320a1	275b7-276a3	32a7-b4	60.7-61.4
22B	320a2-5	276a3-5	32b4-33a2	61.4-7
22C	320a5-7	276a5-7	33a2-4	61.7-62.3
23A	320a7-b3	276a7-b2	33a4-7	62.3-6
23B	320b3-6	276b2-5	33a7-b3	62.7-63.3
23C	320b6-321a1	276b5-7	33b3-6	63.3-6
23D	321a1-5	276b7-277a2	34b6-34a3	63.6-64.3
23E	321a5-b1	277a2-5	34a3-b1	64.3-7
24A	321b1-6	277a5-b2	34b1-35a1	64.7-65.7

§	Peking 760(19)	Derge 63	Narthang 74	Stog 11(19)
24B	321b6-322a5	277b2-278a1	35a1-b3	65.7-67.2
24C	322a5-b3	278a1-5	35b4-36a2	67.2-7
24D	322b3-7	278a5-b1	36a2-7	67.7-68.5
24E	322b7-323a1	278b1-3	36a7-b3	68.5-69.1
25A	323a2-4	278b3-5	36b3-6	69.1-4
25B	323a4-8	278b5-279a1	36b6-37a5	69.4-70.2
25C	323a8-b2	279a1-3	37a5-b1	70.2-5
25D	323b3-5	279a3-5	37b1-4	70.5-71.1
25E	323b5-324a1	279a5-b1	37b4-38a2	71.1-6
25F	324a1-b6	279b1-280a4	38a2-39a2	71.7-73.7
25G	324b6-325a4	280a4-b1	39a2-b2	73.7-74.6
25H	325a4-b2	280b2-6	39b2-40a2	74.7-76.1
25I	325b2-7	280b6-281a4	40a2-b2	76.1-77.1
25J	325b7-326a5	281a4-b2	40b2-41a2	77.1-78.2
25K	326a6-b5	281b2-7	41a3-b4	78.2-79.2
25L	326b5-327b3	281b7-282b4	41b4-42b6	79.3-81.4
25M	327b3-328a1	282b4-283a2	42b6-43a7	81.4-82.4
26A	328a2-7	283a2-5	43a7-b5	82.4-83.3
26B	328a7-b4	283a5-b2	43b5-44a4	83.3-84.1
26C	328b4-8	283b2-5	44a4-b1	84.1-5
26D	328b8-329a4	283b5-284a2	44b1-5	84.5-85.2
27A	329a4-8	284a2-4	44b5-45a2	85.3-6
27B	329a8-b1	284a4-6	45a2-4	85.6-86.1
27C	329b1-2	284a6-7	45a4-6	86.1-3
27D	329b2-4	284a7-b1	45a6-b1	86.3-5
27E	329b4-6	284b1-3	45b1-3	86.5-7
27F	329b6-7	284b3-4	45b3-4	86.7-87.1
28	329b7-330a3	284b4-7	45b4-46a2	87.2-6
29A	330a4-6	284b7-285a2	46a2-4	87.6-88.1

§	Peking 760(19)	Derge 63	Narthang 74	Stog 11(19)
29B	330a6-8	285a2-4	46a5-7	88.2-4
30A	330a8-b2	285a4-5	46a7-b2	88.4-6
30B	---	---	---	---
30C	---	---	---	---
31A	330b2-6	285a5-b1	46b2-7	88.6-89.4
31B	330b7-331a7	285b2-286a1	46b7-47b3	89.4-90.6
32A	331a7-b2	286a1-4	47b3-6	90.6-91.2
32B	331b3-332a1	286a4-b2	47b6-48a7	91.2-92.2
32C	332a1-3	286b2-4	48a7-b3	92.2-5
32D	332a3-5	286b4-6	48b3-6	92.5-93.1
33A	332a5-b3	286b6-287a5	48b6-49a7	93.1-94.2
33B	332b3-6	287a5-b1	49a7-b3	94.2-5
33C	332b6-8	287b1-3	49b3-5	94.5-7
33D	332b8-333a4	287b3-6	49b5-50a4	94.7-95.5
33E	333a4-7	287b6-288a1	50a4-7	95.5-7
34	333a7-b1	288a1-3	50a7-b2	95.7-96.2
35	333b1-3	288a3-4	50b2-4	96.2-4

Part B: Chinese Texts and Citations in Other Sources

§	AY (vol. 12)	Dh (vol. 12)	R (vol. 11)	*Śikṣ.* (Bendall ed.)	*Dbhv.* (vol. 26)
0	---	---	---	---	---
1A	15b5-9	23a16-19	472b8-13	---	---
1B	15b9-17	23a20-27	472b13-22	---	---
2A	15b17-23	23a27-b2	472b22-26	---	---
2B	15b23-26	23b2-5	472b26-c1	---	---
2C	15b26-c7	23b5-14	472c1-11	---	---
2D	15c7-14	23b14-19	472c11-16	---	---
2E	15c14-18	23b19-22	472c16-20	---	---
3A	15c18-21	23b22-25	472c20-21	---	54c8-11
3B	15c21-16a1	23b26-29	472c21-25	---	---
3C	16a1-5	23b29-c5	472c25-473a2	---	---
3D	16a5-12	23c5-12	473a2-9	---	---
4A	16a13-17	23c13-16	473a9-12	---	54c15-17
4B	16a17-22	23c17-21	473a12-16	---	54c27-28
4C	16a22-28	23c22-27	473a16-21	---	55a6-11
4D	16a28-b2	23c28-24a1	473a21-24	---	55b8-12
4E	16b3-6	24a2-4	473a24-27	---	---
5A	16b6-12	24a5-10	473a27-b5	267.12-13, 144.5-6	55c29-56a2
5B	16b12-21	24a10-18	473b5-12	180.14	56a3, 12, 14-15
5C	16b21-28	24a19-25	473b12-18	145.10	56a12-13, b5-16
5D	16b28-c2	24a25-29	473b18-21	---	56b16-20
6A	16c2-9	24a29-b5	473b21-26	---	56b20-25

§	AY	Dh	R	*Śikṣ.*	*Dbhv.*
6B	16c9-19	24b5-12	473b26-c4	---	56b25-26
7A	16c19-17a13	24b13-c7	473c4-25	78.7-13, 120.3-5, 271.9-11	56b29-c19
7B	17a13-21	24c7-13	473c25-474a3	---	56c22
8A	17a21-29	24c14-25	474a3-12	---	56c27-57a4
8B	17b1-5	24c25-25a1	474a12-16	---	57a10-13
8C	17b5-11	25a1-4	474a16-19	---	---
8D	17b11-20	25a4-12	474a19-26	---	57b4-5
9A	17b20-26	25a13-21	474a26-b3	---	57b18-24
9B	17b26-c5	25a21-b1	474b3-11	---	57b24-c4
9C	17c5-12	25b1-6	474b11-15	---	57c4-8
9D	17c12-17	25b6-12	474b16-21	---	57c8-14
9E	17c17-22	25b13-18	474b21-24	---	57c14-18
9F	17c22-26	25b18-21	474b24-27	---	57c18-22
10A	17c26-18a2	25b22-c2	474b27-c4	19.1-3	57c23-24, 26-27, 58b1-8
10B	18a2-7	25c2-9	474c4-9	19.3-7	58b8-12
11A	18a7-9	25c9-11	474c9-11	----	57c28-58a1
11B	----	25c11-13	----	----	58a1-2
11C	18a9-11	25c13-15	474c11-12	----	58a2-4
11D	----	25c15-17	474c12-14	----	58a4-5
11E	----	25c17-19	474c14-16	----	58a5-6
11F	18a11-16	25c19-23	474c16-20	----	58a6-10
11G	18a16-25	25c23-26a3	474c20-475a2	147.20	58a11, 16-24
12A	18a25-b2	26a4-9	475a2-9	180.1-6	58b16-21
12B	----	----	475a9-14	----	58b24-28
12C	18b2-8	26a9-14	475a14-16	----	58c1-2
13A	18b8-10	26a14-16	475a16-19	----	58c5-6
13B	18b10-13	26a16-19	475a19-22	78.14-16	58c6-8

§	AY	Dh	R	*Śikṣ.*	*Dbhv.*
13C	---	26a19-21	475a22-24	---	58c8
13D	---	---	475a24-25	---	58c8-9
13E	18b16-17[1]	26a21-23	475a25-26	---	58c9-10
13F	---	26a23-25	---	---	---
13F'	---	26a25-27	---	---	---
13G	18b14-16	26a27-28	---	---	58c10-11
13H	18b13-14	26a29-b1	---	---	58c11-12
13I	18b17-19	26b1-3	475a26-27	---	58c12-13
13J	---	---	475a27-29	---	58c13-14
13K	---	---	475a29-b1	---	58c14-15
13L	---	---	475b1-2	---	58c15-16
13M	---	---	475b2-4	78.17	58c16-17
13N	---	---	475b4-5	---	58c17-18
13O	---	---	475b5-6	---	58c18-19
13P	---	---	475b6-7	---	58c19-20
13Q	---	---	475b7-8	---	58c20
13R	---	---	475b8-9	---	58c20-21
13S	---	---	475b9-10	---	58c21-22
13T	---	---	475b10-11	---	58c22-23
13U	---	---	475b11-12	---	58c23-24
13V	---	---	475b12-13	---	58c24-25
13W	---	---	---	---	58c25-26
13W'	---	---	475b13	---	---
13X	---	---	475b13-14	78.17-18	58c26-27
13Y	---	---	475b14-15	---	58c27
13Z	---	---	475b15-16	---	58c28

[1] Here and in §13G-I AY is out of sequence with respect to the other versions.

§	AY	Dh	R	*Śikṣ.*	*Dbhv.*
13AA	----	----	475b16-17	----	58c28-29
13BB	----	----	475b17	----	58c29-59a1
13CC	----	----	475b17-18	----	59a1-2
13DD	----	----	----	----	59a2-3
13EE	----	----	475b18-19	----	59a3-4
13FF	----	----	475b19-20	----	59a4-5
13GG	----	----	475b20-21	----	59a5-6
13HH	18b19-20	26b4-5	475b21-23	----	59a6-8
14A	18b20-25	26b5-9	475b23-c1	19.8-14	59a13-21
14B	18b26-27	26b9-11	475c1-2	----	59a21-24
14C	18b27-c2	26b11-14	475c2-5	19.14-17	59a25-59b5
14D	18c2-7	26b14-18	475c5-9	----	59b5-6, 11-14
14E	18c7-11	26b18-23	475c9-13	19.17-19	59b14-16, 25-26
15A	18c11-16	26b23-27	475c13-18	19.19-20.3	59c4-11
15B	18c16-23	26b27-c3	475c18-23	20.3-9	59c11-18
16A	18c23-27	26c3-7	475c23-26	----	----
16B	18c27-19a1	26c7-14	475c26-476a3	315.14-15	----
17A	19a1-7	26c14-22	476a3-9	----	59c29-60a1, 60b9-14, 23-24
17B	19a7-12	26c22-28	476a9-15	----	60b23-24, 61b18-26
17C	19a12-15	26c28-27a3	476a15-17	----	61a16-18, b26-29
18A	19a15-20	27a4-10	476a18-23	----	61c3-6
18B	19a21-22	27a10-11	476a23-24	----	----
19A	19a22-23	27a12	476a24-26	----	61c16-19
19B	----	----	476a26-29	----	61c19-22

§	AY	Dh	R	*Śikṣ.*	*Dbhv.*
19C	----	----	476a29-b3	----	61c22-26
19D	----	----	476b3-5	----	61c26-29
19E	----	----	476b5-8	----	61c29-62a3
19F	----	----	476b8-10	----	62a3-6
19G	----	----	476b10-14	----	62a6-10
19H	----	----	476b14-16	----	62a10-13
19I	----	----	476b16-19	----	62a13-17
19J	----	----	476b19-21	----	62a17-19
19K	----	----	476b21-24	----	62a19-23
19L	----	----	476b24-26	----	62a23-25
19M	----	----	476b26-29	----	62a25-29
19N	----	----	476b29-c2	----	62a29-b2
19O	----	----	476c2-4	----	62b3-4
19P	----	----	476c4-8	----	62b4-10
19Q	----	----	476c8-11	----	62b10-13
19R	----	----	476c11-13	----	62b13-17
19S	----	----	476c13-16	----	62b17-20
19T	----	----	476c16-19	----	62b20-24
19U	----	----	476c19-21	----	62b24-27
20A	19a22-27	27a13-17	476c21-24	----	61c12-13
20B	----	27a17-20	476c25-29	----	62c22-28
20C	19a27-b5	27a20-27	476c29-477a5	----	63a2-8
20D	19b5-8, 11-15[2]	27a27-b3	477a5-9	----	63a28-b7
20E	19b8-11	27b3-8	477a9-13	----	----
20F	19b15-21	27b8-14	477a13-18	----	63b13-17
20G	19b21-24	27b14-16	477a18-22	----	----

[2] AY is again out of sequence here with respect to the other versions.

§	AY	Dh	R	*Śikṣ.*	*Dbhv.*
21A	----[3]	27b17-26	477a22-28	----	---
21B	----[4]	27b26-c1	477a28-b2	----	---
21C	19b24-27	27c1-3	477b2-3	----	---
22A	19b27-c4	27c4-11	477b3-6	----	---
22B	19c4-8	27c11-13	477b6-8	----	---
22C	19c8-10	27c14-17	477b8-11	----	---
23A	19c10-11	27c18	477b11-16	----	---
23B	19c12	27c18-19	477b16-21	----	---
23C	19c12	27c18-19	[same][5]	----	---
23D	19c12	27c20-22	----	----	---
23E	19c12-14	27c22-23	477b21-22	----	---
24A	19c14-23	27c23-28a4	477b22-c2	136.1-7	111c1-0
24B	19c23-20a14	28a5-17	477c2-13	131.10-12	---
24C	----	28b2-9[6]	----	----	---
24D	20a14-21	28a18-25	477c13-19	----	111c28-112a6
24E	20a21-25	28a25-b1	477c19-24	200.7-11	112a7-8, 13-18, 115b20-22
25A	20a25-b3	28b10?-17	477c24-29	198.1-6	112b1-8
25B	20b3-11	28b17-23	477c29-478a5	----	112b8-15
25C	20b11-15	28b24-28	478a5-9	----	112b15-22
25D	20b15-19	28c1-7	478a9-12	----	112b22-27
25E	20b19-26	28c1-7	478a12-20	196.7-8	113b28-c2
25F	20b26-c6	28c8-21	478a20-b3	198.6-19	---
25G	20c6-11	28c21-26	478b3-11	----	---

[3] Cf. §30B below.
[4] Cf. §30C below.
[5] §23B and C are combined in R.
[6] Dh is out of sequence here

§	AY	Dh	R	*Śikṣ.*	*Dbhv.*
25H	20c11-19	28c26-29a4	478b11-19	198.19-199.2	---
25I	20c19-21a6	29a4-13	478b19-26	199.2-3	113c5-19
25J	21a6-17	29a13-22	478b27-c6	199.3-12	---
25K	21a17-23	29a22-b4	478c6-18	----	113c19-28
25L	21a23-b3	29b5-13	478c19-479a12	----	113c28-114a9
25M	21b3-12	29b14-24	479a12-21	199.12-15	114a10-21
26A	21b12-21	29b24-c4	479a21-28	199.15-200.4	115b25-c5
26B	21b21-c1	29c4-12	479a28-b5	200.4-6	115c14-17
26C	21c2-7	29c12-18	479b5-10	37.7-12	115c18-21
26D	21c7-13	29c18-22	479b10-14	----	---
27A	21c13-17	29c22-28	479b14-18	----	116b20-22
27B	21c18-21	29c28-30a3	479b18-22	----	116a28-b4
27C	22a4-7[7]	30a3-5	479b22-25	----	116b12-15
27D	22a1-4	30a5-7	479b25-27	----	116c4-8
27E	21c21-22a1[8]	30a7-10	479b28-c2	----	117b12-15
27F	22a7-10	30a10-12	479c2-5	----	118a10-13
28	22a10-17	30a12-19	479c5-12	----	---
29A	22a17-18	30a19-22	479c12-16	----	---
29B	22a18-21	30a22-25	479c16-20	----	---
30A	22a21-22	30a26-29	479c20-22	----	---
30B	22a22-b1[9]	----	----	----	---
30C	22b1-4[10]	----	----	----	---
31A	----	30a29-b6	479c22-28	----	---

7 §27C and §27E are reversed in AY.
8 See previous note.
9 AY only (cf. §21A above).
10 AY only (cf. §21B above).

§	AY	Dh	R	*Śikṣ.*	*Dbhv.*
31B	----	30b6-19	479c28-480a11	----	---
32A	----	30b19-21	480a11-14	----	---
32B	----	30b21-28	480a14-22	----	---
32C	22b4-8	30b28-c3	480a22-26	----	---
32D	22b8-13	30c3-7	480a26-29	----	---
33A	22b13-24	30c7-15	480b1-10	----	---
33B	----	30c15-18	480b10-14	----	---
33C	----	30c18-21	480b14-17	----	---
33D	----	30c21-24	480b18-23	----	---
33E	----	30c24-28	480b23-26	----	---
34	22b24-26	30c28-31a1	480b26-28	----	---
35	22b27	31a2	480b29	----	---

APPENDIX 2

Bodhisattva Names in the *Ugrapariprcchā*

Several well-known bodhisattvas, together with one quite obscure one, are listed at the beginning of the *Ugrapariprcchā* as members of the audience. An additional and even more obscure bodhisattva, whose name can be reconstructed (though not with any degree of certainty) as *Sarvacaryāviśuddha, is later called upon together with Maitreya to preside over the ordination of Ugra and his friends. Since none of these bodhisattvas is ever mentioned at any other point in the sūtra, they can hardly be described as central characters in the narrative. Yet the treatment of their names in the various versions of the text is, in itself, of considerable interest. Not only do these renditions demonstrate the variety of ways in which these terms were handled by early Chinese Buddhist translators, but in some cases they can even help to reconstruct an Indic original different from (and older than) what would eventually become the standard Sankrit form. In tabular form, the names of these bodhisattvas are the following:

Sanskrit	AY	Dh	R	Tib
Maitreya	慈氏	慈氏, 彌勒[1]	彌勒	Byams-pa
Mañjuśrī	敬首	軟首	文殊師利	Gzhon-nu dpal
Apāyajaha	殆[2]棄	除惡	斷正道	Ngan-song spong
Avalokiteśvara	闚音	光世音	觀世音	Spyan-ras-gzigs dbang-phyug
Mahāsthāma-prāpta	—	—	得大勢	Mthu-chen thobs
*Sarvacaryā-viśuddha	一切行淨	諸行清淨	一切淨	Spyod-pa thams-cad rnam-par dag-pa

---

[1] The first form appears at the beginning of the sūtra (12.23a17), while the second is used in the ordination scene in the middle of the text (27b26 and 28).

[2] Var. 始.

Since the forms of all names exhibit interesting features, they will be discussed individually below.

Maitreya. The name of this bodhisattva seems at first glance unproblematic; both the translated version of his name (*tz'u-shih* 慈氏 "the compassion-clan," found in AY and at the beginning of Dh) and the transliterated rendition (*mi-le* 彌勒 [Early Middle Chinese *mji-lək*], found in R and later in Dh) would become standard in East Asia. Neither of these renditions, however, can be traced directly to Skt. *Maitreya*. Rather, both certainly were based on an Indic form such as **Maitraka* (or **Metraka*, or **Mitraka*), in which *-ka* seems to have been understood as an adjectival suffix indicating belonging (hence its translation as Ch. *shih* 氏 "clan, tribe, group"). Such a form is not unattested in Indian texts, for Edgerton cites the occurrence of *Maitraka* in the verse portions (though not in the prose) of the *Gaṇḍavyūha* (BHSD 439b).[3] A Prakrit form such as **Metraka* may be reflected in the Bactrian spelling *METRAYO* found on a small number of coins of Kanishka I;[4] it is certainly the basis both of Tokharian A *Metrak*[5] and of Sogdian *Mytr'k*.[6]

Mañjuśrī. Here again the two earliest Chinese versions offer translations of this name, while the later version opts for transliteration. AY's *ching-shou* 敬首 "foremost in respect" and Dh's *juan-shou* 軟首 "foremost in softness" appear quite peculiar until we realize that the syllable *-śrī* "glory" has been misinterpreted as Skt./Pkt. **śiras*

---

3 Gv 488.25, 489.7. Edgerton suggests that this spelling is due to the constraints of meter; it seems at least equally plausible, however, that the verses preserve an older form that has been successfully Sanskritized in the prose. Edgerton would in this case be correct in asserting that the presence of the form *Maitraka* is due to meter, but the metric form would then be the original one, which could not be changed due precisely to those constraints.

The apparent alternation between *-eya* (in the standard Sanskrit form) and *-aka* (in the Prakrit) offers an interesting parallel, though not an exact one, to the fluctuation between *-aya* and *-eka* in the name of the second vehicle of Buddhist practice, that of the *pratyeka-buddha* (a figure who appears also in the spelling *pratyaya-buddha*, a form reflected in the Chinese translation *yüan-chüeh* 緣覺 "enlightened [to] causation"). For instances of the appearance of *pratyaya-buddha* and related terms in Indian texts see Norman 1983b. For another example of the confusion between intervocalic *-k-* and *-y-* in the Gāndhārī language see Brough 1962, pp. 45-48, where the term *udaya* "arising" is confused with *udaka* "water," with ludicrous results.

4 See for example Göbl 1984, coin types 790-793 (p. 79 of plates).

5 See for example Thomas 1964, p. 126.

6 See for example Benveniste 1940, p. 259b.

"head," a confusion discussed by Karashima in his admirable study of the Chinese translations of the *Lotus Sūtra*.[7] Dh's *juan* "soft" can then be explained without difficulty as a translation of *mañju* "soft, pliable." AY's *ching* "respect," on the other hand, appears to be based on an interpretation of *mañju* as a form of the verb *mañyate* "honors, esteems."[8] Both renditions, though admittedly exceptional, occur in a number of early Chinese translations,[9] but it appears that by the beginning of the 5th century they had been definitively superseded by the transliterated form *Wen-shu shih-li* 文殊師利 first introduced by Lokakṣema in the late 2nd century.[10]

Apāyajaha. This bodhisattva is a rather obscure character, though his name (which can be reconstructed on the basis of the Tibetan version) is registered by Edgerton (BHSD 46b). The individual components, though not the name as a whole, are also registered in *Mvy*. (nos. 535, 567, and 4747). The name given in Dh, *ch'u-e* 除惡 "discarding the bad," can be derived without difficulty from the Sanskrit, which consists of *apāya* "evil state" plus *jaha* "discard, abandon." AY's *tai-ch'i* 殆棄 "danger-abandonment" can also be derived from this name, though here there may have been a

---

[7] See Karashima 1992, p. 27. The development of *śrī* to *śiri* is unproblematic, as it is widespread in the Prakrit languages (see Pischel 1955, §98); for the name of Mañjuśrī as such, Edgerton (BHSD 414b) notes variants in *-śiri* and *-śirī*, but not *-śiras*.

[8] This association seems first to have been proposed by Hisao Inagaki (1987, p. 43); cf. also Klaus Wille, 2000, §1.3.2.9, who notes the occurence of spellings of the name of this bodhisattva as *manyuśrī* and *manyugho(ṣa)* in a manuscript of the *Saddharmapuṇḍarīka-sūtra* from Khādaliq. I am grateful to KARASHIMA Seishi for calling these references to my attention.

[9] With the exception of its appearance in AY's *Ugra*, the form *ching-shou* seems to be used almost exclusively in the translations of Chih Ch'ien (T 225, 8.478b25; T 281, 446c19 and *passim*; and T 1011, 19.680b12) and others that are dependent upon them (T 441, T 570, and in particular T 1485, an indigenous Chinese scripture that reproduces the list of Buddhas and bodhisattvas found in T 281). *Juan-shou* appears to be equally localized, restricted (with only one exception) to works translated by Dharmarakṣa (T 324, 12.02c21; T 598, 15.132a5; T 627, 15.406b28 and *passim*; T 635, 15.502c16 and *passim*; and T 817, 17.817c4, 824c14) and Chü Fo-nien 竺佛念 (T 384, 12.1049c19 and 1050a22; T 656, 16.28c2 and *passim*). The sole exception is a tantric text (T 1015, 19.692a24) attributed to the 6th-century translator Buddhaśānta.

[10] E.g., in his translation of the *Aṣṭa* (T 224, 8.425c8 and *passim*). The term is ubiquitous in his corpus.

confusion between *apāya* and *bhaya* "danger, fear." R's *tuan cheng-tao* 斷正道 "cutting off the correct way" (*sic*), however, remains difficult to explain.

Avalokiteśvara. Though Avalokiteśvara is doubtless the most popular bodhisattva in all of East Asia, the meaning of his name is still not fully understood. AY's *k'uei-yin* 闚音 "observing the sound" is the earliest attested Chinese translation, but it never seems to have gained wide currency; the only other occurrences identified thus far are in two of Chih Ch'ien's translations.[11] The name *K'uei-yin* cannot be derived from the standard Sanskrit version of the name, which consists of *avalokita* "glance" + *īśvara* "lord." It can, however, be derived from what now appears to be an earlier form of the name, **avaloka* or **avalokita* (both of which mean "glance") + *svara* "sound, voice." The form *Avalokitasvara* has in fact been documented in some Sanskrit manuscripts of the *Lotus Sūtra*,[12] and according to Karashima it is this form that should be seen as the antecedent of both *k'uei-yin* and the form *kuang-shih-yin* 光世音 "light-world-sound" regularly used by Dharmarakṣa. Karashima explains this rendition as the result of Dharmarakṣa's misunderstanding of *avalokita* as consisting of **ābhā* "light" + *lokita*, and a further misunderstanding of the latter as a derivative of *loka* "world."[13] An interpretation of *ava* as *ābhā* is less problematic than it might appear; confusions between long and short vowels are ubiquitous in early Chinese translations, while alternations betwen *-v-* and *-bh-* are also attested and are relatively easy to explain.[14] I am less certain, however, that

---

[11] T 474, 14.519b16 and T 1011, 19.680b13.

[12] An important early discussion can be found in Mironov 1927, pp. 241-252, in which the author points out that this bodhisattva's name appears in the form *Avalokitasvara* in the Ōtani manuscript of the *Saddharmapuṇḍarīka-sūtra*. According to Mironov, "It cannot be doubted that *Avalokitasvara* was the original form, later supplanted by *Avalokiteśvara*" (p. 243). Even without the evidence supplied by this manuscript it would have been reasonable to postulate the existence of a form of the name ending in *-svara*, for bodhisattva names of this type are quite common; in the *Lotus Sūtra* alone we find nearly a dozen such forms (viz., Bhīṣmagarjitasvararāja, Bhīṣmasvara, Gadgadasvara, Jaladharagarjitaghoṣa-susvara-nakṣatrarāja-saṅkusumita-abhijña, Madhurasvara, Mañjusvara, Megha-dundubhi-svararāja, Meghasvara, Meghasvara-pradīpa, and Meghasvararāja; for references see the index to Kern's English translation of the text).

[13] See the detailed discussion in Karashima 1999.

[14] The most likely explanation is the influence of local (most probably

Dharmarakṣa would have been likely to interpret *avalokita* "glance" as a form of *loka* "world." It seems more reasonable to assume that he was working from a text that read **avalokasvara*, which could much more easily lead to the mistaken reading *ābhā* + *loka* than could a postulated **avalokitasvara*. Happily we now have at least partial corroboration of the existence of this shorter form in a Bactrian manuscript, where the form λωγοαφαρο, presumably from **Lokasvara*, appears at a point in the text where the name of Avalokiteśvara would be expected.[15]

Surprisingly, of all the forms of this name found in the *Ugra* it is only the now standard *Kuan-shih-yin* 觀世音 "regard-world-sound," made famous by the translations of Kumārajīva (and found here in R alone), which cannot be derived from any known or plausible Indic antecedent. Had there been a direct Indic source for this term it would have to be something like **avaloka-* (or *avalokita-*) *-loka-svara*. It seems far more likely, however, that this Chinese rendition is not a direct translation of any Indian term but is the result of a further intra-Chinese development. That is, it appears to be a hybrid form based both on an Indic **avalok(it)a-svara* and on the form *kuang-shih-yin* 光世音 which was by then well established through its wide circulation in the works of Dharmarakṣa.[16]

Mahāsthāmaprāpta. This bodhisattva was clearly the last to be added to the list of members of the audience, for he does not appear in either of the first two Chinese translations. He is fairly well known, however, as a cohort of Avalokiteśvara in a number of Mahāyāna texts, and may well have been added to later recensions of our text for this reason.

The form *te-ta-shih* 得大勢 "gainer of great strength" found in

---

Iranian) pronunciation in the northwest border regions of India. Von Hinüber has recently drawn attention to a number of cases of the writing of *v* for *bh* and vice versa in the Gilgit manuscripts which he attributes to the local pronunciation of *-bh-* as *-β.-* (von Hinüber 1989, p. 358).

[15] See Sims-Williams 2000, p. 277.

[16] The widespread use of the form *Kuang-shih-yin* 光世音, even in texts dating from somewhat later than Kumārajīva's time, may be evidence of the influence of the Avalokiteśvara chapter of Dharmarakṣa's translation of the *Lotus* in which this form was used. See for instance the tale collections cited in Campany 1993, pp. 270-271, where the name of Avalokiteśvara appears as *Kuang-shih-yin* in two collections dating from the late 4th to mid-5th centuries but is changed to *Kuan-shih-yin* 觀世音 in a collection dating from the beginning of the 6th century.

R—the sole Chinese version of the *Ugra* to contain a reference to this bodhisattva—is amply attested in the translations of Kumārajīva, Dharmakṣema, Bodhiruci I, and others. It may well have been introduced by Dharmarakṣa, however, for it also occurs in three of his translations.[17]

***Sarvacaryāviśuddha.** The most obscure bodhisattva mentioned in the *Ugra* is this figure, who seems to be virtually unknown in other texts. The only other occurrences of his name that I have been able to locate in other scriptures are in T 441 (*Fo-ming ching* 佛名經, the "Buddha-Names Sūtra," which consists of a long list of Buddha and bodhisattva names, 14.258b16 and 309a14), and T 1521 (the **Daśabhūmikavibhāṣā*, 26.45a3), where the name occurs in a long list of bodhisattva names. What seems certain, though, is that this is the name of an individual and not of a category of bodhisattvas, given the clear parallelism between this name and that of Maitreya in the narrative.

---

[17] See T 325, 12.37c3; T 342, 12.134a27; and T 585, 15.17b15.

APPENDIX 3

Monastic Specialties Recorded in the *Ugraparipṛcchā*

All extant versions of the *Ugra* contain a long and varied list of types of monks—that is, of specialists pursuing various roles within the monastery—whom the lay bodhisattva might meet during a visit to the *vihāra*. These lists vary in length from twelve such roles in the oldest version (translated by An Hsüan and Yen Fo-t'iao) to seventeen in the most recent version (the Tibetan). An even longer list is found in the *Daśabhūmikavibhāṣā*, which adds to the *Ugra*'s list the entire group of twelve *dhūtaguṇa*s, yielding a total (even though several items found in various versions of the *Ugra* are missing here) of twenty-one.

The items contained in these lists fall quite naturally into three distinct categories: (1) textual learning, (2) ascetic practices, and (3) official positions within the monastery. In what appears to be the oldest list—the one found in AY—these consist of the following:[1]

Textual learning

1. "greatly learned one" (*bahuśruta*)[2]
2. "dharma-preacher" (*dharmabhāṇaka*)[3]
3. "upholder of the vinaya" (*vinayadhara*)
4. "upholder of the producers" (*mātṛkādhara*)[4]

---

[1] Since this passage is apparently not cited in any extant Sanskrit text, all of the Indic terms given here are reconstructions based on the Chinese and Tibetan translations.

[2] Though this is a general expression, given its place in the list it seems likely that *bahuśruta* here refers to a monastic who knows more than one (perhaps all three, or even four) of the *piṭaka*s.

[3] Given its place in this list, this term appears to refer to a monk who specializes in the recitation of the sūtras. This is not a surprising usage in retrospect, given the well-established pairing of "Dharma and Vinaya" in early Buddhist literature.

[4] Though the expression used in AY (for which see the chart below) is non-standard, the versions found in the *Daśabhūmikavibhāṣā* and in the Tibetan clearly refer to one who upholds the *mātṛkā*s, i.e., the lists that gradually evolved into the Abhidharma-piṭaka.

5. "upholder of the *bodhisattva-piṭaka*" (*bodhisattvapiṭakadhara*)

Ascetic practices

6. "wilderness-dweller" (*āraṇyaka*)
7. "alms-receiver" (*paiṇḍapātika*)[5]
8. "yoga-practitioner" (*yogācāra*)[6]
9. "meditator" (*dhyānin*)
10. "member of the bodhisattva vehicle" (*bodhisattvayānika*)[7]

Official monastic positions

11. "supervisor of repairs" (*navakarmika*)
12. "administrator" (*vaiyāpṛtyakara*)[8]

While additional items are added to this list in later translations of the *Ugra*, none of these additions fall outside the three basic categories given above.

The variations in these lists, however, offer a number items of interest. A synoptic table of their occurrences is provided below.

---

[5] That is, one who lives on almsfood alone and does not accept invitations to meals.

[6] That is, one who exerts himself in the practice of yoga, generally understood in Buddhist texts as referring to meditation. For a detailed discussion of the term *yogācāra-bhikṣu* see Silk 2000 (a revised version of Silk 1994a, pp. 97-142) and 1997b. Usually this expression refers to monks who are engaged in intensive meditation practice; it is not clear what the distinction between a *yogācāra* monk and a *dhyānin* would have been.

[7] Unless we wish to treat this item as belonging to a category of its own, it would seem to fit most naturally as the culmination of the category of "ascetic practices." In this connection it is worth remembering that bodhisattvas are regularly referred to in early Mahāyāna literature as "doers of what is hard" (*duṣkarakāraka*).

[8] For an extended discussion of this figure and his role in the monastery see Silk 1994, pp. 215-254.

Skt. (reconstructed)	AY	Dh	R	Dbhv.	Tib
bahuśruta	多聞 (1)	多智者 (1)	多聞 (1)	---	mang-du thos-pa (1)
dharmabhāṇaka[1]	明經者 (2)	解法者 (2)	說法 (2)	說法者 (1)	chos brjod-pa (2)
vinayadhara	奉律者 (3)	持律者 (3)	持律 (3)	持律者 (2)	'dul-ba 'dzin-pa (3)
sūtradhara?[2]	---	---	持阿含(4)	讀修多羅者 (3)	---
mātṛkādhara[3]	奉使者 (4)	住法者 (4)	---	讀摩多羅迦者 (4)	ma-mo 'dzin-pa (4)
bodhisattvapiṭaka-dhara	開士奉藏者 (5)	持菩薩品者 (5)	持菩薩藏 (5)	讀菩薩藏者 (5)	byang-chub sems-dpa'i sde-snod 'dzin-pa (5)
āraṇyaka	山澤者 (6)	閑居行者 (6)	阿練兒 (6)	作阿練若者 (6)	dgon-pa-pa (6)
paiṇḍapātika	行受供者 (7)	分衛者 (7)	乞食 (8)	乞食者 (8)	bsod-snyoms-pa (7)
pāṁśukūlika	---	服五衲衣者[4] (8)	著糞掃衣 (9)	著納衣者 (7)	phyag-dar khrod-pa (8)
---	---	---	---	(9-17)[5]	---
alpeccha	---	---	少欲 (7)	少欲者 (18)	'dod-pa chung-ba (9)
saṁtuṣṭa	---	知止足者 (9)	離欲 (11)	知足者 (19)	chog shes-pa (10)
pravivikta	---	獨行者 (10)	獨處 (10)	遠離者 (20)	rab-tu dben-pa (11)
yogācāra	道行者 (9)	精進者 (13)	修行 (12)	勸化者[6] (22)	rnal-'byor spyod-pa (12)
dhyānin	思惟者[7] (8)	坐禪者 (11)	坐禪 (13)	坐禪者 (21)[8]	bsam-gtan-pa (13)
bodhisattvayānika	開士道者 (10)	大乘者 (12)	–	---	byang-chub sems-dpa'i theg-pa-pa (14)
navakarmika	佐助者 (11)	–	–	---	lag-gi bla (15)
vaiyāpṛtyakara	主事者 (12)	典寺者 (14)	營事 (14)	---	zhal-ta byed-pa (16)
vihārasvāmin?[9]			寺主 (15)[10]	---	dpon-sna byed-pa (17)

[1] Though the *Mahāvyutpatti* gives another expression, viz., *chos smra-ba*, as the standard equivalent of *dharmabhāṇaka* (no. 2764), the latter is probably also the underlying Indian term here. AY has "who clarifies the sūtras" (*ming ching-che*); Dh "who explains the Dharma" (*chieh fa-che*), R "who preaches the Dharma" (*shuo fa*).

[2] R is alone in referring to a monk "who upholds the *āgamas*" (though *Dbhv*'s *tu hsiu-to-lo-che* "one who reads the sūtras" may stem from a related tradition). It is possible—though far from certain—that, given its place in this list and the absence of any reference to the *mātṛkās* in R, that this is the result of a confusion, at some point in the transmission of the text, between *āgama* and *abhidharma* (cf. the following item in the list).

[3] The term *mātṛkā-dhara* refers to one who has memorized the analytical lists (*mātṛkā*) that gradually evolved into the Abhidharma-piṭaka (see BHSD 428b). The underlying Sanskrit is confirmed by *Dbhv*., which reads "the one who reads the *mātṛkā*" (*tu mo-to-lo-che*), as well as by the Tibetan. Sakurabe (p. 278) interprets this term as a reference to the Vinaya-mātṛkā, though he does not provide any justification for such a reading.

[4] Note Dharmarakṣa's odd translation here: he has apparently understood *pāṁśu* "dust, refuse" as *pañca* "five," and translated "one who wears a five-patched robe"!

[5] Here *Dbhv*. introduces a long list of items which have no parallel in any other version of the text, apparently in an attempt to fill out the complete list of twelve (sometimes thirteen) ascetic practices known as the *dhūtaguṇas*. Of these items only two—*āraṇyaka* "wilderness-dweller" and *paiṇḍapātika* "one who lives on almsfood"—are included in all versions of our text; a third, *pāṁśukūlika* "wearer of robes from a refuse heap," appears in all versions except AY. To these *Dbhv*. adds the remaining nine: eating only one meal [per day] (9), constantly sitting up (10), not drinking thick fluids after noon (11), having only three robes (12), wearing a wool robe (13), taking any seat that is offered (14), living at the foot of a tree (15), living in a graveyard (16), and living in the open air (17).

[6] Hirakawa considers this term (which means "to exhort and convert") to be the equivalent of Tib. *dbon-sna byed-pa* (*sic*, for *dpon-sna byed-pa*), but it seems more likely that it is an error for *ch'in-hsing* 勤行 "assiduous practice," which would correspond to other renditions of *yogācārin*.

[7] Hirakawa (1990b, p. 132) equates this expression with "solitary practitioner" (*tu-hsing-che* 獨行者) or "solitary dwelling" (*tu-ch'u* 獨處) in Dh and R, respectively, but *ssu-wei* 思惟 "contemplation, reflection" is well established as a term for "meditation" in the work of several early Chinese translators. In fact, it occurs a number of times elsewhere in AY in this sense, including one occurrence in a list of the six *pāramitās*, where its equivalence with *dhyāna* is secure (§26c,

12.21c3). It seems quite unproblematic, therefore, to equate this term with the expressions for "(seated) meditation" found in the other versions.

8 The citation in *Dbhv*. ends here, omitting any reference to monastery officials.

9 The Tibetan term *dpon-sna byed-pa* does not appear in the *Mahāvyutpatti* or in Lokesh Chandra, and what the corresponding Sanskrit would have been is unclear. I have only tentatively aligned this expression with R's 寺主 "temple head," and in turn with the.reconstructed Sanskrit **vihārasvāmin*.

10 Hirakawa (*loc. cit.*) moves these last two items up one notch, equating R's 營事 with AY's 佐助者, and R's 寺主 with AY's 主事者.

Bibliography

Almond, Philip, 1986. "The Buddha in the West: From Myth to History." *Religion*, vol. 16, pp. 305-322.

_____, 1988. *The British Discovery of Buddhism*. Cambridge: Cambridge University Press.

Babb, Lawrence A., 1998. "Ritual Culture and the Distinctiveness of Jainism." In John E. Cort, ed., *Open Boundaries: Jain Communities and Cultures in Indian History* (Albany: State University of New York Press), pp. 139-162.

Bareau, André, 1955. *Les sectes bouddhiques du petit véhicule*. Saïgon: École Française d'Extrême-Orient.

Barnes, Nancy J. (= Schuster), 1993. "The *Triskandha*, Practice in Three Parts: Study of an Early Mahāyāna Buddhist Ritual." In N. K. Wagle and F. Watanabe, eds., *Studies on Buddhism in Honour of Professor A. K. Warder*. South Asian Studies Papers, no. 5. Toronto: University of Toronto Centre for South Asian Studies.

Beal, Samuel, 1906. *Si-yu-ki: Buddhist Records of the Western World* (London: Kegan Paul, Trench, Trübner & Co. Reprint. 2 vols. in 1. New York: Paragon, 1968.

Bendall, Cecil, ed., 1897-1902. *Çikshāsamuccaya: A Compendium of Buddhistic Teaching Compiled by Çāntideva, Chiefly from Earlier Mahāyāna-sūtras*. Biblitheca Buddhica, vol. 1. St. Petersburg: Imperial Academy. Reprint. Osnabrück: Biblio Verlag, 1970.

Bendall, Cecil, and W. H. D. Rouse, trans., 1922. *Śikshā-samuccaya: A Compendium of Buddhist Doctrine*. London. Reprint. Delhi: Motilal Banarsidass, 1971.

Benveniste, E., 1940. *Textes sogdiens: édités, traduits et commentés*. Paris: Librairie Orientaliste Paul Geuthner.

Bernhard, Franz, 1970. "Gāndhārī and the Buddhist Mission in Central Asia." In J. Tilakasiri, ed., *Añjali: Felicitation Volume Presented to Oliver Hector de Alewis Wijesekera on his Sixtieth Birthday* (Peradeniya: University of Ceylon), pp. 55-69.

Bloch, Jules, 1950. *Les inscriptions d'Asoka*. Paris: Société d'Édition "Les Belles Lettres."

Bongard-Levin, Gregory, Daniel J. Boucher, Takamichi Fukita, and Klaus Wille, 1996. *The Nagaropamasūtra: An Apotropaic Text from the Saṁyuktāgama. A Transliteration, Reconstruction, and Translation of the Central Asian Sanskrit Manuscripts, in Sanskrit-Wörterbuch der buddhistischen Texte aus den Turfan-Funden*. Beiheft 6. Göttingen: Vandenhoeck & Ruprecht.

Boucher, Daniel J., 1996. "Buddhist Translation Procedures in Third-Century China: A Study of Dharmarakṣa and His Translation Idiom." Ph.D. diss., University of Pennsylvania.

_____, 1998. "Gāndhārī and the Early Chinese Buddhist Translations Reconsidered: The Case of the *Saddharmapuṇḍarīkasūtra*." *Journal of the American Oriental Society*, vol. 118, no. 4, pp. 471-506.

_____, 1999. "The Textual History of the *Rāṣṭrapālaparipṛcchā*: Notes on Its Third-Century Chinese Translation." Paper presented at the meeting of the International Association of Buddhist Studies, Lausanne.

Brear, Douglas, 1975. "Early Assumptions in Western Buddhist Studies." *Religion*, vol. 5, pp. 136-159.

Brough, John, 1950. "Thus Have I Heard...." *Bulletin of the School of Oriental and African Studies*, vol. 13, pp. 416-426.

_____, ed., 1962. *The Gāndhārī Dharmapada*. London: Oxford University Press.

Burtt, E. A., ed., 1955. *The Teachings of the Compassionate Buddha*. New York: Signet.

Cabezón, José Ignacio, 1992. *A Dose of Emptiness: An Annotated Translation of the sTong thun chen mo of mKhas grub dGe legs dpal bzang*. Albany: State University of New York Press.

Campany, Robert F., 1993. "The Real Presence." *History of Religions*, vol. 32, no. 3, pp. 233-272.

_____, 1996. *Strange Writing: Anomaly Accounts in Early Medieval China*. Albany: State University of New York Press.

Chakravarti, Uma, 1987. *Social Dimensions of Early Buddhism*. Delhi: Oxford University Press.

Chang, Garma C. C., 1983. *A Treasury of Mahāyāna Sūtras: Selections from the Mahāratnakūṭa Sūtra*. University Park: Pennsylvania State University Press.

Chavannes, Édouard, 1910. *Cinq cents contes et apologues extraits du tripiṭaka chinois*. Vol. 1. Paris: Ernest Leroux.

Clausen, Christopher, 1975. "Victorian Buddhism and the Origins of Comparative Religion." *Religion*, vol. 5, pp. 1-15.

Coblin, W. South, 1983. *A Handbook of Eastern Han Sound Glosses*. Hong Kong: Chinese University Press.

Cohen, Richard S., 1995. "Discontented Categories: Hīnayāna and Mahāyāna in Indian History." *Journal of the American Academy of Religion*, vol. 63, no. 1, pp. 1-25.

Collins, Steven, 1990. "On the Very Idea of the Pali Canon." *Journal of the Pali Text Society*, vol. 15, pp. 89-126.

_____, 1992. "Problems with Pacceka-Buddhas." Review of *Ascetic Figures before and in Early Buddhism* by Martin G. Wiltshire. *Religion*, vol. 22, pp. 271-278.

Conze, Edward, ed. and trans., 1958. *Buddhist Wisdom Books: The Diamond Sutra, the Heart Sutra.* Allen & Unwin. Reprint. New York: Harper Torchbooks, 1972.

_____, 1959. *Buddhist Scriptures.* London: Penguin.

_____, 1962. *Buddhist Thought in India.* London. Reprint. Ann Arbor: University of Michigan, 1967.

_____, 1967a. *Materials for a Dictionary of the Prajñāpāramitā Literature.* Tokyo: Suzuki Research Foundation.

_____, 1967b. *Thirty Years of Buddhist Studies.* London: Bruno Cassirer.

_____, trans., 1973. *The Perfection of Wisdom in Eight Thousand Lines.* San Francisco: Four Seasons Foundation.

_____, trans., 1975. *The Large Sutra on Perfect Wisdom with the Divisions of the Abhisamayālaṅkāra.* Berkeley: University of California Press.

_____, 1978. *The Prajñāpāramitā Literature.* 2nd ed., rev. and enl. Bibliographia Philologica Buddhica, Series Maior, I. Tokyo: The Reiyukai.

Conze, Edward, I. B. Horner, David Snellgrove, and Arthur Waley, ed. and trans., 1954. *Buddhist Texts through the Ages.* London. Reprint. New York: Harper & Row, 1964.

Crosby, Kate, and Andrew Skilton, trans., 1996. *Śāntideva: The Bodhicaryāvatara.* New York: Oxford University Press.

Dantinne, Jean, trans., 1983. *La splendeur de l'Inébranlable (Akṣobhyavyūha).* Tome I (Chapitres I-III): *Les auditeurs (śrāvaka).* Louvain-la-neuve: Institut Orientaliste.

_____, 1991. *Les Qualités de l'ascete (dhutaguṇa): Étude sémantique et doctrinale.* Brussels: Thanh-Long.

Dayal, Har, 1932. *The Bodhisattva Doctrine in Buddhist Sanskrit Literature.* London: Kegan Paul, Trench, Trübner & Co.

de Bary, William Theodore, ed., 1969. *The Buddhist Tradition in India, China, and Japan.* New York: Random House.

Demiéville, Paul, 1970. *Récents travaux sur Touen-houang.* Leiden: E. J. Brill.

Durt, Hubert, 1967. "Note sur l'origine de l'Anavalokitamūrdhatā." *Indogaku bukkyōgaku kenkyū* 印度学仏教学研究, vol. 16, no. 1, pp. 443-450.

_____, 1991. "Bodhisattva and Layman in the Early Mahāyāna." *Japanese Religions*, vol. 16, no. 3, pp. 1-16.

_____, 1994. "Daijō." In Paul Demiéville, Hubert Durt, and Anna Seidel, eds., *Hōbōgirin*, vol. 7 (Paris: Librairie d'Amérique et d'Orient), pp. 768-801.

Dutt, Nalinaksha, ed., 1934. *The Pañcaviṁśatisāhasrikā Prajñāpāramitā, edited with critical notes and introduction.* Calcutta Oriental Series, no. 28. London: Luzac & Co.

Eckel, Malcolm David, 1992. *To See the Buddha: A Philosopher's Quest for the Meaning of Emptiness.* San Francisco: HarperSanFrancisco. Reprint. Princeton: Princeton University Press, 1994.

Eimer, Helmut, 1978. *Bodhipathapradīpa, ein Lehrgedicht des Atiśa (Dīpaṁkaraśrījñāna) in der tibetischen Überlieferung.* Wiesbaden: Otto Harrassowitz.

_____, 1980. "Einige Hinweise zur Edition tibetischer kanonischer Texte—Beobachtungen zur Überlieferung in Blockdrucken." *Zentralasiatische Studien*, vol. 14, no. 1, pp. 195-209.

_____, 1983a. "Some Results of Recent Kanjur Research." In Dieter Schuh and Michael Weiers, eds., *Archiv für zentralasiatische Geschichtsforschung*, Heft 1 (Sankt Augustin: VGH Wissenschafts-Verlag), pp. 5-25.

_____, 1983b. *Rab tu 'byuṅ ba'i gẑi: Die tibetische Übersetzung des Pravrajyāvastu im Vinaya der Mūlasarvāstivādins.* 2 vols. Asiatische Forschungen, 82. Wiesbaden: Otto Harrasowitz.

_____, 1988. "A Note on the History of the Tibetan Kanjur." *Central Asiatic Journal*, vol. 32, nos. 1-2, pp. 64-72.

Ensink, J., trans., 1952. *The Question of Rāṣṭrapāla.* Zwolle: J. J. Tijl.

Fick, Richard, 1920. *The Social Organisation of North-East India in Buddha's Time.* Translated from the German edition of c. 1900 by Shishirkumar Maitra. Calcutta: University of Calcutta Press.

Finot, L., ed., 1901. *Rāṣṭrapālaparipṛcchā, sūtra du Mahāyāna.* Bibliotheca Buddhica, vol. 2. St. Petersburg: Imperial Academy. Reprinted as Indo-Iranian Reprints, II. The Hague: Mouton & Co., 1957.

Fischer, David Hackett, 1970. *Historians' Fallacies: Toward a Logic of Historical Thought.* New York: Harper & Row.

Fronsdal, Egil, 1998. "The Dawn of the Bodhisattva Path: Studies in a Religious Ideal of Ancient Indian Buddhists with a Particular Emphasis on the Earliest Extant Perfection of Wisdom Sutra." Ph.D. diss., Stanford University.

FUJITA Kōtatsu 藤田宏達, 1988. "Genshi bukkyō ni okeru nehan—*nibbāna* to *parinibbāna*" 原始仏教における涅槃—nibbāna と parinibbāna—[*Nibbāna* and *parinibbāna* in Early Buddhism]. *Indogaku bukkyōgaku kenkyū* 印度学仏教学研究, vol. 37, no. 1, pp. 1-12.

Garfield, Jay L., 1995. *The Fundamental Wisdom of the Middle Way: Nāgārjuna's Mūlamadhyamakakārikā.* New York: Oxford University Press.

Gethin, Rupert, 1992. *The Buddhist Path to Awakening: A Study of the Bodhi-Pakkhiyā Dhammā*. Leiden: E. J. Brill.

_____, 1998. *The Foundations of Buddhism*. Oxford: Oxford University Press.

Göbl, Robert, 1984. *System und Chronologie der Münzprägung des Kušānreiches*. Wien: Verlag der Österreichischen Akademie der Wissenschaften.

Gombrich, Richard, 1990. "How the Mahāyāna Began." *The Buddhist Forum*, vol. 1, pp. 21-30.

Gómez, Luis O., 1996. *Land of Bliss: The Paradise of the Buddha of Measureless Light*. Honolulu: University of Hawai'i Press.

Gómez, Luis O., and Jonathan A. Silk, eds., 1989. *Studies in the Literature of the Great Vehicle: Three Mahāyāna Buddhist Texts*. Ann Arbor: Center for South and Southeast Asian Studies, The University of Michigan.

Graham, Mark W., 1998. "Self-Inflicted Violence and the Quest for the Perfected Body: A Re-reading of Some Bodhisattva Narratives." Unpublished paper, Indiana University.

Graham, William A., 1987. *Beyond the Written Word: Oral Aspects of Scripture in the History of Religion*. Cambridge: Cambridge University Press.

Hallisey, Charles, 1988. *Devotion in the Buddhist Literature of Medieval Sri Lanka*. Ph.D. diss., University of Chicago.

Harrison, Paul M., 1978a. *The Tibetan Text of the Pratyutpanna-Buddha-Saṃmukhāvasthita-Samādhi-Sūtra*. Tokyo: The Reiyukai Library.

_____, 1982. "Sanskrit Fragments of a Lokottaravādin Tradition." In L. A. Hercus et al., eds., *Indological and Buddhist Studies: Volume in Honor of Professor J. W. de Jong on his Sixtieth Birthday* (Canberra: Faculty of Asian Studies), pp. 211-234.

_____, 1978b. "Buddhānusmṛti in the *Pratyutpanna-buddha-saṃmukhāva-sthita-samādhi-sūtra*." *Journal of Indian Philosophy*, vol. 6, pp. 35-57.

_____, 1987. "Who Gets to Ride in the Great Vehicle? Self-Image and Identity Among the Followers of the Early Mahāyāna." *Journal of the International Association of Buddhist Studies*, vol. 10, no. 1, pp. 67-89.

_____, trans., 1990. *The Samādhi of Direct Encounter with the Buddhas of the Present*. Tokyo: The International Institute of Buddhist Studies.

_____, 1992a. "Meritorious Activity or a Waste of Time? Some Remarks on the Editing of Texts in the Tibetan Kanjur." In *Tibetan Studies, Proceedings of the 5th Seminar of the International Association of Tibetan Studies, Narita 1989* (Narita: Naritasan), pp. 77-93.

_____, 1992b. *Druma-kinnara-rāja-paripṛcchā-sūtra: A Critical Edition of the Tibetan Text*. Studia Philologica Buddhica Monograph Series, VII. Tokyo: International Institute for Buddhist Studies.

_____, 1992c. "Commemoration and Identification in Buddhānusmṛti." In Janet Gyatso, ed., *In the Mirror of Memory: Reflections on Mindfulness and Remembrance in Indian and Tibetan Buddhism* (Albany: State University of New York Press), pp. 215-238.

_____, 1992d. "Is the Dharma-kāya the Real 'Phantom Body' of the Buddha?" *Journal of the International Association of Buddhist Studies*, vol. 15, no. 1, pp. 44-94.

_____, 1993. "The Earliest Chinese Translations of Mahāyāna Buddhist Sūtras: Some Notes on the Works of Lokakṣema." *Buddhist Studies Review*, vol. 10, no. 2, pp. 135-177.

_____, 1995. "Searching for the Origins of the Mahāyāna: What Are We Looking For?", *Eastern Buddhist*, n.s., vol. 28, no. 1, pp. 48-69.

_____, 1998. "Women in the Pure Land: Some Reflections on the Textual Sources." *Journal of Indian Philosophy*, vol. 26, pp. 553-572.

Harrison, Paul, Jens-Uwe Hartmann, and Kazunobu Matsuda, 2002. "Larger Sukhāvatīvyūha." In Jens Braarvig, ed., *Manuscripts in the Schøyen Collection*, III: *Buddhist Manuscripts*, vol. 2 (Oslo: Hermes Publishing), pp. 179-214.

Harvey, Peter, 1990. *An Introduction to Buddhism: Teachings, History and Practices.* Cambridge: Cambridge University Press.

Hikata, Ryusho, ed., 1958. *Suvikrāntavikrāmi-paripṛcchā-prajñāpāramitā-sūtra.* Fukuoka: Kyushu University.

von Hinüber, Oskar, 1982. "Pāli as an Artificial Language." *Indologica Taurinensia*, vol. 10, pp. 133-140.

_____, 1989. "Origin and Varieties of Buddhist Sanskrit." In Collette Caillat, ed., *Dialectes dans les littératures indo-aryennes* (Paris: Institut de Civilisation Indienne), pp. 341-367.

HIRAKAWA Akira 平川彰, 1957a. "Jūjūbibasharon no chakusha ni tsuite" 十住毘婆沙論について. *Indogaku bukkyōgaku kenkyū* 印度学仏教学研究, vol. 5, pp. 504-510.

_____, 1957b. "Shoki daijō kyōdan ni okeru tōji no imi" 初期大乗教団における塔寺の意味. *Shūkyō kenkyū* 宗教研究, no. 153, pp. 151-172.

_____, 1963. "The Rise of Mahāyāna Buddhism and Its Relationship to the Worship of Stūpas." Translated from the Japanese by Taitetsu Unno. *Memoirs of the Research Department of the Tōyō Bunko*, 22, pp. 57-106.

_____, 1964. *Genshi bukkyō no kenkyū* 原始仏教の研究. Tokyo: Shunjūsha.

_____, 1968. *Shoki daijō bukkyō no kenkyū* 初期大乗仏教の研究. Tokyo: Shunjūsha. Reissued in revised form as Hirakawa 1989 and 1990b.

_____, 1987. "Stupa Worship." In Mircea Eliade, ed., *Encyclopedia of Religion* (New York: Macmillan), vol. 14, pp. 92-96.

_____, 1989. *Shoki daijō bukkyō no kenkyū* 初期大乗仏教の研究, I. Hirakawa Akira Chosakushū 平川彰著作集, vol. 3. Tokyo: Shunjūsha.

_____, 1990a. *A History of Indian Buddhism from Śākyamuni to Early Mahāyāna.*

Translated from the Japanese edition of 1974 and edited by Paul Groner. Honolulu: University of Hawai'i Press.

_____, 1990b. *Shoki daijō bukkyō no kenkyū* 初期大乗仏教の研究, II. Hirakawa Akira Chosakushū 平川彰著作集, vol. 4. Tokyo: Shunjūsha.

Horner, I. B., trans., 1951. *The Book of the Discipline.* London: The Pali Text Society.

Huntington, Susan L., 1985. *The Art of Ancient India.* New York: Weatherhill.

Imaeda, Yoshiro, 1977. "Mise au point concernant les éditions chinoises du Kanjur et du Tanjur tibétains." In Ariane Macdonald et al., eds., *Essais sur l'art du Tibet*, pp. 23-51. Paris: Librairie d'Amérique et d'Orient.

Inagaki, Hisao, 1987. *The Anantamukhanirhāra-dhāraṇī-sūtra and Jñānagarbha's Commentary: A Study and the Tibetan Text.* Kyoto: Nagata Bunshodo.

IWAMATSU Asao 岩松浅夫, 1985. " 'Tenchūten' kō" 「天中天」考 [An Examination of the Epithet 'Devātideva']. *Tōhō* 東方, 1, pp. 201-219.

Jaini, P. S., 1970. "Śramaṇas: Their Conflict with Brāhmaṇical Society." In J. W. Elder, ed., *Chapters in Indian Civilization*, vol. 1 (Dubuque, Iowa: Kendall/Hunt Publishing Co.), pp. 40-81.

de Jong, J. W., 1953. Review of *The Question of Rāṣṭrapāla* by Jacob Ensink. *Journal Asiatique*, vol. 241, pp. 545-549. Reprinted in Schopen 1979a, pp. 407-411.

_____, 1954. "L'Épisode d'Asita dans le Lalitavistara." In *Asiatica: Festschrift Friedrich Weller* (Leipzig: Otto Harrassowitz), pp. 312-325. Reprinted in Schopen 1979a, pp. 459-473.

_____, 1977. "Sanskrit Fragments of the Kāśyapaparivarta." In *Beiträge zur Indien-Forschung, Ernst Waldschmidt zum 80. Geburtstag gewidmet* (Berlin: Museum für Indische Kunst), pp. 247-255. Reprinted in Schopen 1979a, pp. 513-521.

_____, 1997. *A Brief History of Buddhist Studies in Europe and America.* Rev. ed. Tokyo: Kōsei Publishing.

KAGAWA Takao 香川孝雄, 1984. *Muryōjukyō no shohon taishō kenkyū* 無量寿経の諸本対照研究 [A Comparative Study of the Texts of the Larger Sukhāvatīvyūha-sūtra]. Kyoto: Nagata Bunshodo.

_____, 1989. "Shi guzeigan no genryū" 四弘誓願の源流. [The origins of the four universal vows]. *Indogaku bukkyōgaku kenkyū* 印度学仏教学研究, vol. 30, no. 1, pp. 294-302.

Kajiyama, Yuichi, 1989. "Transfer and Transformation of Merits in Relation to Emptiness." In Katsumi Mimaki et al., eds., *Y. Kajiyama, Studies in Buddhist Philosophy (Selected Papers)* (Kyoto: Rinsen Book Company), pp. 1-20.

KARASHIMA Seishi 辛島静志, 1992. *The Textual Study of the Chinese Versions of the Saddharma-puṇḍarīka-sūtra in the Light of the Sanskrit and Tibetan Versions.* Tokyo: Sankibo.

_____, 1993. "Hokekyō ni okeru jō (*yāna*) to chie (*jñāna*): Daijō bukkyō ni okeru *yāna* no gainen no kigen ni tsuite" 法華経における乗 (yāna)と智慧 (jñāna)—大乗仏教における yāna の概念の起源について [Vehicle (*yāna*) and Wisdom (*jñāna*) in the Lotus Sūtra: On the Origin of the Concept of *Yāna* in Mahāyāna Buddhism]. In TAGA Ryūgen 田賀龍彦, ed., *Hokekyō no juyō to tenkai* 法華経の受容と展開 [The Acceptance and Development of the Lotus Sūtra] (Kyoto), pp. 137-197.

_____, 1998. *A Glossary of Dharmarakṣa's Translation of the Lotus Sutra.* Bibliotheca Philologica et Philosophica Buddhica, I. Tokyo: The International Research Institute for Advanced Buddhology, Soka University.

_____, 1999. "Hokekyō no bunkengakuteki kenkyū (2): Kannon 'Avalokitasvara' no gogi kaishaku" 法華経の文献的研究 (2): 観音 'Avalokitasvara' の語義解釈. In *Annual Report of the International Research Institute for Advanced Buddhology,* vol. 2, pp. 39-66.

Keith, A. B., ed., 1919. *Aitareya-Āraṇyaka.* Anecdota Oxoniensia, Aryan Series, vol. 9. Reprint. Oxford: Clarendon Press, 1969.

Kern, Hendrik, and Bunyiu Nanjio, 1908-1912. *Saddharmapuṇḍarīka.* Bibliotheca Buddhica, vol. 10. St Petersburg: Imperial Academy. Reprint. Osnabrück: Biblio Verlag, 1970.

KINO Kazuyoshi 紀野一義, 1957. "Kodai meimon ni arawareta chōja koji ni tsuite" 古代銘文にあらわれた長者居士について [On the Gṛhapati Layman in Ancient Inscriptions]. *Indogaku bukkyōgaku kenkyū* 印度学仏教学研究, vol. 5, no. 1, pp. 166-167.

Kiyota, Minoru, 1984. "Modern Japanese Buddhology: Its History and Problematics." *Journal of the International Association of Buddhist Studies,* vol. 7, pp. 17-36.

Kloppenborg, Ria, 1974. *The Paccekabuddha, A Buddhist Ascetic.* Leiden: E. J. Brill.

Konow, Sten, 1929. *Kharoshṭhî Inscriptions with the Exception of Those of Aśoka.* Corpus Inscriptionum Indicarum, vol. 2, pt. 1. Calcutta: Government of India.

Lalou, Marcelle, 1927. "La Version tibétaine du Ratnakūṭa." *Journal Asiatique,* vol. 211, pp. 233-259.

_____, 1953. "Les textes bouddhiques au temps du roi Khri-sroṅ-lde-bcan." *Journal Asiatique,* vol. 241, pp. 313-353.

Lamotte, Étienne, trans., 1944-1980. *Le Traité de la grande vertu de sagesse.* 5

vols. Publications de l'Institut Orientaliste de Louvain. Louvain: Université de Louvain.

_____, 1954. "Sur la formation du Mahāyāna." In *Asiataica, Festschrift F. Weller* (Leipzig: Otto Harrassowitz), pp. 377-396.

_____, 1976. *The Teaching of Vimalakīrti (Vimalakīrtinirdeśa).* Translated from the French version of 1962 by Sara Boin. London: The Pali Text Society.

_____, 1988a. *History of Indian Buddhism from the Origins to the Śaka Era.* Translated from the French edition of 1958 by Sara Webb-Boin. Louvain: Institut Orientaliste, 1988.

_____, 1988b. "The Assessment of Textual Interpretation in Buddhism." Translated from the French by Sara Boin-Webb. In Donald S. Lopez, Jr., ed., *Buddhist Hermeneutics* (Honolulu: University of Hawai'i Press), pp. 11-27.

Lancaster, Lewis, 1987. "Buddhist Studies." In Mircea Eliade, ed., *The Encyclopedia of Religion* (New York: Macmillan), vol. 2, pp. 554-560.

Lancaster, Lewis, and Sung-bae Park, eds., 1979. *The Korean Buddhist Canon: A Descriptive Catalogue.* Berkeley: University of California Press.

La Vallée Poussin, Louis de, 1925. "Notes bouddhiques, VI, §3: Les fidèles laïcs ou Upāsakas." *Académie Royal de Belgique, Bulletins de la class des lettres et des sciences morales et politiques,* 5e série, tome 11, pp. 15-34.

_____, 1927. *La morale bouddhique.* Paris: Nouvelle Librairie Nationale.

Legge, James, trans., 1886. *A Record of Buddhistic Kingdoms.* Reprint. New York: Dover, 1965.

Lévi, Sylvain, and Édouard Chavannes, 1915. "Quelques titres énigmatiques dans la hiérarchie ecclésiastique du bouddhisme indien." Parts 1 and 2. *Journal Asiatique*, vol. 5, pp. 193-223; vol. 6, pp. 307-310.

Lokesh Chandra, 1959-1961. *Tibetan-Sanskrit Dictionary.* 12 vols. New Delhi: International Academy of Indian Culture. Reprint. 12 vols. in 1. Tokyo: Rinsen Book Company, 1990.

Lopez, Donald S., Jr., ed., 1995. *Curators of the Buddha: The Study of Buddhism under Colonialism.* Chicago: University of Chicago Press.

_____, 1996. *Buddhism in Practice.* Princeton: Princeton University Press.

MacQueen, Graeme, 1981. "Inspired Speech in Early Mahāyāna Buddhism I." *Religion*, vol. 11, pp. 303-319.

_____, 1982. "Inspired Speech in Early Mahāyāna Buddhism II." *Religion*, vol. 12, pp. 49-65.

Malalasekera, G. P., 1937. *A Dictionary of Pāli Proper Names.* 2 vols. London: Pali Text Society.

May, Jacques, 1967. "Chōja." In Paul Demiéville, Hubert Durt, and Anna

Seidel, eds., *Hōbōgirin*, vol. 4 (Paris: Librairie d'Amérique et d'Orient), pp. 347-353.

McRae, John R., 1986. *The Northern School and the Formation of Early Ch'an Buddhism.* Kuroda Institute Studies in East Asian Buddhism 3. Honolulu: University of Hawai'i Press.

Meadows, Carol, 1986. *Ārya-Śūra's Compendium of the Perfections: Text, Translation, and Analysis of the Pāramitāsamāsa.* Bonn: Indica et Tibetica Verlag.

Meeks, Wayne, 1983. *The First Urban Christians.* New Haven: Yale University Press.

Mirecki, Paul, 1994. "The Coptic Manichaean Synaxeis Codex." In H. Preißler and H. Seiwert, eds., *Gnosisforschung und Religionsgeschichte: Festschrift für Kurt Randolph zum 65. Geburtstag.* Marburg: diagonal-Verlag, pp. 199-207.

Mironov, N. D., 1927. "Buddhist Miscellanea." *Journal of the Royal Asiatic Society*, pp. 241-252.

Mitchiner, Michael, 1975-1976. *Indo-Greek and Indo-Scythian Coinage.* 9 vols. London: Hawkins Publications.

MIYAMOTO Shōson 宮本正尊, 1954. *Daijō bukkyō no seiritsushiteki kenkyū* 大乗仏教の成立史的研究. Tokyo: Sanseidō. Reprint of the 1933 edition.

MOCHIZUKI Ryōkō 望月良晃, 1988. "Daijō bosatsu no shūkyō seikatsu—'Ikuka chōja kyō' no kōsatsu" 大乗菩薩の宗教性格一郁伽長者経の考察. In his *Daijō nehangyō no kenkyū—kyōdanshiteki kōsatsu* (Tokyo: Shunjūsha), pp. 221-350.

Morton, A. Q., 1978. *Literary Detection: How to Prove Authorship and Fraud in Literature and Documents.* Epping, England: Bowker.

Müller, F. Max, ed., 1881. *Buddhist Texts from Japan.* Anecdota Oxoniensia, Aryan Series, vol. 1, pt. 1. Oxford: Clarendon Press.

NAGAI Makoto 長井真琴, trans., 1932. "Ikuka chōjae" 郁伽長者会. In *Kokuyaku Issaikyō* 国訳一切経, vol. 42, Hōshakubu 宝積部 5 (Tokyo: Daitō Shuppansha), pp. 1-31.

NAGAO Gadjin. 長尾雅人, 1973. "'Kashōbon' no shohon to 'Daihōshakkyō' seiritsu no mondai" 『迦葉本』の諸本と『大宝積経』成立の問題. *Suzuki gakujutsu zaidan kenkyū nenpō* 鈴木学術財団研究年報, no. 10, pp. 13-25.

_____, 1979. "Presidential Address by Professor Gadjin M. Nagao." *Journal of the International Association of Buddhist Studies*, vol. 1, no. 2, pp. 79-85.

NAKAMURA Hajime 中村元, 1980. *Indian Buddhism: A Survey with Bibliographical Notes.* Tokyo. Reprint. Delhi: Motilal Banarsidass, 1987.

_____, 1981. *Bukkyōgo daijiten* 仏教語大辞典. Tokyo: Tōkyō Shoseki.

Nanjio, Bunyiu (= NANJŌ Bun'yū), 1883. *A Catalogue of the Chinese Translation of the Buddhist Tripitaka*. Oxford: Clarendon Press.

Nattier, Jan, 1988. "The Meanings of the Maitreya Myth: A Typological Analysis." In Alan Sponberg and Helen Hardacre, eds., *Maitreya, the Future Buddha* (Cambridge: Cambridge University Press), pp. 23-47.

_____, 1990. "Church Language and Vernacular Language in Central Asian Buddhism." *Numen*, vol. 37, pp. 195-219.

_____, 1991. *Once Upon a Future Time: Studies in a Buddhist Prophecy of Decline*. Berkeley: Asian Humanities Press.

_____, 1992. "The Heart Sūtra: A Chinese Apocryphal Text?" *Journal of the International Association of Buddhist Studies*, vol. 15, no. 2, pp. 153-223.

_____, 1994. "Namowa buddhay-a: Sources of Mongolian Buddhism." Unpublished manuscript.

_____, 1996. "Hierarchy and Status Dissonance in Early Indian Buddhism." Paper presented at Harvard University and Princeton University.

_____, 1997. "The Lotus Sūtra: Good News for Whom?" Paper presented at the Third International Lotus Sūtra Conference, sponsored by the Risshō Kōseikai, Tokyo, Japan.

_____, 1999. "Arhats in the Pure Land: A New Look at the Place of the Śrāvaka Vehicle in Early Mahāyāna Texts." Paper presented at the meeting of the International Association of Buddhist Studies, Lausanne, Switzerland.

_____, 2000a. "The Realm of Akṣobhya: A Missing Piece in the History of Pure Land Buddhism." *Journal of the International Association of Buddhist Studies*, vol. 23, no. 1, pp. 71-102.

_____, 2000b. "*The Teaching of Vimalakīrti* (*Vimalakīrtinirdeśa*): A Review of Four English Translations." *Buddhist Literature*, vol. 2, pp. 234-258.

_____, 2002. "The 'Eleven Precepts' for Laity in the *Ugraparipṛcchā*." In The Sakurabe Ronshu Committee, ed., *Early Buddhism and Abhidharma Thought in Honour of Dr. Hajime Sakurabe on His Seventy-seventh Birthday* (Kyoto, Japan: Heirakuji shoten, 2002), pp. 33-43 [horizontal section].

Nihon Bukkyō Gakkai 日本仏教学会, eds., 1995. *Bukkyō ni okeru seigan* 仏教における誓願. Kyoto: Heirakuji Shoten.

Norman, K. R., 1983a. *Pāli Literature*. Wiesbaden: Otto Harrasowitz.

_____, 1983b. "The Pratyeka-Buddha in Buddhism and Jainism." In Philip Denwood and Alexander Piatigorsky, eds., *Buddhist Studies Ancient and Modern, Collected Papers on South Asia*, no. 4 (London: Centre of South Asian Studies, University of London), pp. 92-106.

_____, 1997. *A Philological Approach to Buddhism*. The Bukkyō Dendō Kyōkai Lectures 1994. The Buddhist Forum, vol. 5. London: School of Oriental and African Studies, University of London.

ŌCHŌ Enichi 横超慧日, 1958. "Kumarajū no hon'yaku" 鳩磨羅什の翻訳. *Ōtani daigaku gakuhō* 大谷大学学報, vol. 38, no. 4, pp. 1-25.

Ohnuma, Reiko, 1997. "*Dehadāna*: The "Gift of the Body" in Indian Buddhist Narrative Literature." Ph.D. diss., University of Michigan.

OKADA Yukihiro 岡田行弘, 1986. "Nandikasūtra no kan'yaku" Nandikasūtra の漢訳 [The Chinese translation of the Nandikasūtra]. *Indogaku bukkyōgaku kenkyū* 印度学仏教学研究, vol. 35, no. 1, pp. 35-37.

Pagel, Ulrich, 1995. *The Bodhisattvapitaka: Its Doctrines, Practices and Their Position in Mahayana Literature*. Tring, England: Institute of Buddhist Studies.

Pāsādika, Bhikkhu, 1989. *Nāgārjuna's Sūtrasamuccaya: A Critical Edition of the mDo kun las btus pa*. Copenhagen: Akademisk Forlag.

Paul, Diana Y., 1985. *Women in Buddhism: Images of the Feminine in Mahayana Tradition*. 2nd ed., rev. Berkeley: University of California Press.

Pedersen, K. Priscilla, 1980. "Notes on the Ratnakūṭa Collection." *Journal of the International Association of Buddhist Studies*, vol. 3, no. 2, pp. 60-66.

Pischel, R., 1955. *A Grammar of the Prakrit Languages*. 2nd ed., rev. Translated from the German by Subhadra Jhā. Reprint. Delhi: Motilal Banarsidass, 1981.

Pulleyblank, Edwin G., 1991. *Lexicon of Reconstructed Pronunciation in Early Middle Chinese, Late Middle Chinese, and Early Mandarin*. Vancouver: University of British Columbia Press.

Pye, Michael, 1978. *Skilful Means: A Concept in Mahayana Buddhism*. London: Duckworth.

Python, Pierre, 1973. *Vinaya-viniścaya-upāli-paripṛcchā: Enquête d'Upāli pour une exégèse de la discipline*. Paris: Adrien-Maisonneuve.

_____, 1981. "Le rituel du culte Mahāyānique et le traité tibétain *'Phags pa Phuṅ pu gsum-pa* (sanscrit: *Ārya-Triskandhaka*)." *Asiatische Studien*, vol. 35, no. 2, pp. 169-183.

Ray, Reginald A., 1994. *Buddhist Saints in India: A Study in Buddhist Values & Orientations*. New York: Oxford University Press.

Régamey, Konstanty, ed. and trans., 1938. *The Bhadramāyākāravyākaraṇa: Introduction, Tibetan Text, Translation and Notes*. Warsaw. Reprint. Delhi: Motilal Banarsidass, 1990.

Rhys Davids, C. A. F., and Sūriyagoḍa Sumangala Thera, trans., 1917. *The Book of Kindred Sayings*, Part I. Reprint. London: Luzac & Co., 1971.

Robinson, Richard H., 1965-1966. "The Ethic of the Householder Bodhisattva." *Bhāratī: Bulletin of the College of Indology*, no. 9, pt. 2, pp. 25-56.

Robinson, Richard H., and Willard L. Johnson, with Sandra A. Wawrytko and Thanissaro Bhikkhu, 1997. *The Buddhist Religion: A Historical Introduction.* 4th ed. Belmont, Ca.: Wadsworth.

Ruegg, D. Seyfort, 1992. "Some Observations on the Present and Future of Buddhist Studies." *Journal of the International Association of Buddhist Studies*, vol. 15, pp. 104-117.

Sachau, E., 1879. *The Chronology of Ancient Nations: An English Version of the Arabic Text of the Athâr-ul-bâkiya of Albîrûnî.* London: W. H. Allen & Co.

SAKURABE Bunkyō 桜部文鏡, 1930. "Seizōyaku Daihōshakkyō no kenkyū" 西蔵訳大宝積経の研究. *Ōtani gakuhō* 大谷学報, vol. 11, no. 3, pp. 134-175.

SAKURABE Hajime 桜部建, trans., 1974. "Ikuka chōja shomongyō" 郁伽長者諸問経. In *Daijō butten* 大乗仏典, vol. 9, *Hōshakubu kyōten* 宝積部経典 (Tokyo: Chūō kōronsha), pp. 231-335.

Salomon, Richard, 1999. "A Stone Inscription in Central Asian Gāndhārī from Endere (Xinjiang)." *Bulletin of the Asia Institute*, vol. 13, pp. 1-13.

_____, 2002. "A Fragment of a Collection of Buddhist Legends, with a Reference to King Huviṣka as a Follower of the Mahāyāna." In Jens Braarvig, ed., *Manuscripts in the Schøyen Collection*, III: *Buddhist Manuscripts*, vol. 2 (Oslo: Hermes Publishing), pp. 255-267.

SASAKI Shizuka 佐々木閑, 1995. "Daijō bukkyō zaike kigen setsu no mondaiten [Problematic issues in the theory of the lay origins of the Mahāyāna]" 大乗仏教在家起源説の問題点. *Hanazono daigaku bungakubu kenkyū kiyō* 花園大学文学部研究紀要, no. 27, pp. 29-62.

_____, 1997a. "A Study on the Origin of Mahāyāna Buddhism." A revised English version of Sasaki 1995. *The Eastern Buddhist*, n.s., vol. 30, no. 1, pp. 79-113.

_____, 1997b. "Upajjhāya and Ācariya." Paper presented at the annual meeting of the American Academy of Religion, San Francisco, California.

_____, 1997c. "Oshō to ajari" 和尚と阿闍梨. *Hanazono daigaku bungakubu kenkyū kiyō* 花園大学文学部研究紀要, no. 29, pp. 1-43.

_____, 1999. "The Mahāparinirvāṇa Sūtra and the Origins of Mahāyāna Buddhism." Review of *Nehangyō no kenkyū* by SHIMODA Masahiro. *Japanese Journal of Religious Studies*, vol. 26, nos. 1-2, pp. 189-197.

Scholem, Gershom, 1974. *Kabbalah.* New York: New American Library.

Schopen, Gregory, 1975. "The Phrase *'sa pṛthivīpradeśaś caityabhūto bhavet'* in the *Vajracchedikā*: Notes on the Cult of the Book in Mahāyāna." *Indo-Iranian Journal*, vol. 27, pp. 147-181.

_____, 1977. "Sukhāvatī as a Generalized Religious Goal in Sanskrit Mahāyāṇa Sūtra Literature." *Indo-Iranian Journal*, vol. 19, pp. 177-210.

_____, ed., 1979a. *Buddhist Studies by J. W. de Jong*. Berkeley: Asian Humanities Press.

_____, 1979b. "Mahāyāna in Indian Inscriptions." *Indo-Iranian Journal*, vol. 21, pp. 1-19.

_____, 1984. "Two Problems in the History of Indian Buddhism: The Layman/Monk Distinction and the Doctrines of the Transference of Merit." *Studien zur Indologie und Iranistik*, vol. 10, pp. 9-47. Reprinted in Schopen 1997, pp. 23-55.

_____, 1987. "Burial 'Ad Sanctos' and the Physical Presence of the Buddha in Early Indian Buddhism: A Study in the Archeology of Religion." *Religion*, vol. 17, pp. 193-225. Reprinted in Schopen 1997, pp. 114-147.

_____, 1988-1989. "On Monks, Nuns and 'Vulgar' Practices: The Introduction of the Image Cult into Indian Buddhism." *Artibus Asiae*, vol. 49, nos. 1-2, pp. 153-168. Reprinted in Schopen 1997, pp. 238-257.

_____, 1989. "The Manuscript of the *Vajracchedikā* Found at Gilgit." In Luis O. Gómez and Jonathan A. Silk, eds., *Studies in the Literature of the Great Vehicle: Three Mahāyāna Buddhist Texts*, pp. 89-139. Ann Arbor: Center for South and Southeast Asian Studies, The University of Michigan.

_____, 1991. "Archaeology and Protestant Presuppositions in the Study of Indian Buddhism." *History of Religions*, vol. 31, no. 1, pp. 1-23. Reprinted in Schopen 1997, pp. 1-22.

_____, 1997. *Bones, Stones, and Buddhist Monks*. Honolulu: University of Hawai'i Press.

Schuster, Nancy J., 1976. "The *Ugrapariprcchā*, the *Mahāratnakūṭasūtra* and Early Mahāyāna Buddhism." 2 vols. Ph.D. diss., University of Toronto.

_____, 1981. "Changing the Female Body: Wise Women and the Bodhisattva Career in Some Mahāratnakūṭasūtras." *Journal of the International Association of Buddhist Studies*, vol. 4, no. 1, pp. 24-69.

_____, 1985. "The *Bodhisattva* Figure in the *Ugrapariprcchā*." In Anthony K. Warder, ed., *New Paths in Buddhist Research* (Durham, North Carolina: The Acorn Press), pp. 26-56.

Senart, Émile, 1930. *Caste in India: The Facts and the System*. Translated from the French edition of c. 1900 by Sir E. Denison Ross. London. Reprint. Delhi: Motilal Banarsidass, 1975.

SHI Chikai (= Ching-mei Shyu), 2000. "Zhi Qian's Translation Style: A

Study of the Formative Period of Chinese Buddhist Literature." M.A. thesis, University of Hawai'i.

SHIMODA Masahiro 下田正弘, 1997. *Nehangyō no kenkyū: Daijō kyōten no kenkyū hōhō shiron* 涅槃経の研究：大乗経典の研究方法始論. Tokyo: Shunjūsha.

SHIZUTANI Masao 静谷正雄, 1957. "Shoki no daijō kyōdan ni tsuite" 初期の大乗教団について [Early Mahāyāna Saṅgha]. *Indogaku bukkyōgaku kenkyū* 印度学仏教学研究, vol. 5, no. 2, pp. 429-437.

_____, 1974. *Shoki daijō bukkyō no seiritsu katei* 初期大乗仏教の成立過程. Kyoto: Hyakkaen.

Silk, Jonathan, 1989. "A Note on the Opening Formula of Buddhist Sūtras." *Journal of the International Association of Buddhist Studies*, vol. 12, pp. 158-163.

_____, 1992. "A Bibliography on Ancient Indian Slavery." *Studien zur Indologie und Iranistik*, vol. 16, pp. 277-285.

_____, 1994a. "The Origins and Early History of the *Mahāratnakūṭa* Tradition of Mahāyāna Buddhism with a Study of the *Ratnarāśisūtra* and Related Materials." Ph.D. diss., University of Michigan.

_____, 1994b. "The Victorian Creation of Buddhism." *Journal of Indian Philosophy*, vol. 22, pp. 171-196.

_____, 1997a. "The Problem of Slavery in Indian Buddhism." Paper presented at the annual meeting of the American Academy of Religion, San Francisco, California.

_____, 1997b. "Further Remarks on the *yogācāra bhikṣu*." In Bhikkhu Pāsādika and Bhikkhu Tampalawela Dhammaratana, eds., *Dharmadūta: Mélanges offerts au Vénérable Thích Huyền-Vi à l'occasion de son soixante-dixième anniversaire* (Paris: Éditions You Feng), pp. 233-250.

_____, 2000. "The *Yogācāra Bhikṣu*." In Jonathan A. Silk, ed., *Wisdom, Compassion, and the Search for Understanding: The Buddhist Studies Legacy of Gadjin M. Nagao* (Honolulu: University of Hawai'i Press), pp. 265-314.

Sims-Williams, Nicholas, 2000. "A Bactrian Buddhist Manuscript." In Jens Braarvig, ed., *Buddhist Manuscripts*, vol. 1 (Oslo: Hermes Publishing Co.), pp. 275-277.

Snellgrove, David L., 1973. "Śākyamuni's Final Nirvāṇa." *Bulletin of the School of Oriental and African Studies*, vol. 36, pp. 399-411.

Soothill, William Edward, and Lewis Hodous, 1937. *A Dictionary of Chinese Buddhist Terms*. Reprint. Delhi: Motilal Banarsidass, 1977.

Stache-Rosen, Valentina, ed., 1968. *Dogmatische Begriffsreihen im älteren Buddhismus II: Das Saṅgītisūtra und sein Kommentar Saṅgītiparyāya*. Berlin: Akademie-Verlag.

von Staël Holstein, Alexander, 1926. *The Kāśyapaparivarta: A Mahāyānasūtra of the Ratnakūṭa Class.* Shanghai: Commercial Press.

_____, 1933. "On a Peking edition of the Tibetan Kanjur which seems to be unknown in the West." Peking. Privately printed.

Stark, Rodney, and William Sims Bainbridge, 1985. *The Future of Religion: Secularization, Revival, and Cult Formation.* Berkeley: University of California Press.

Strong, John S., ed. and trans., 1995. *The Experience of Buddhism.* Belmont, Ca.: Wadsworth.

TAKASAKI Jikidō 高崎直道, 1967. "Shōshu *āryav356* to shushō *gotra*" 聖種 āryavaṃśa と 種姓 gotra. *Nihon'bukkyō gakkai nenpo* 日本仏教学会年報, no. 32, pp. 1-21.

Tambiah, Stanley J., 1984. *The Buddhist Saints of the Forest and the Cult of Amulets.* Cambridge: Cambridge University Press.

Thomas, E. J., 1947. "Nirvāṇa and Parinirvāṇa." In *India Antiqua: A Volume of Oriental Studies Presented by his Friends and Pupils to Jean Philippe Vogel, C.I.E., on the occasion of the Fiftieth Anniversary of his Doctorate* (Leyden: E. J. Brill), pp. 294-295.

Thomas, Werner, 1964. *Tocharisches Elementarbuch.* Band 2: *Texte und Glossar.* Heidelberg: Carl Winter Universitätsverlag.

Thurman, Robert A. F., trans., 1976. *The Holy Teaching of Vimalakīrti: A Mahāyāna Scripture.* University Park: Pennsylvania State University Press.

TODA Hirofumi, ed., 1981. *Saddharmapuṇḍarīkasūtra, Central Asian Manuscripts Romanized Text.* Tokushima: Kyoiku Shuppan Center.

Troeltsch, Ernst, 1960. *The Social Teaching of the Christian Churches.* 2 vols. Translated from the original German edition of 1911 by Olive Wyon. Chicago: University of Chicago Press.

UEYAMA Daishun 上山大峻, 1967-1968. "DaiBan-koku daitoku sanzō hōshi shamon Hōjō no kenkyū" 大蕃国大徳三蔵沙門法成の研究 [A Study of the Life and Works of Fa-ch'eng 法成 (Ḥgo Chos grub), a Translator of the Buddhist Texts at Tunhuang under Tibetan Rule], *Tōhō gakuhō* 東方学報, vol. 38, pp. 133-198 and vol. 39, pp. 119-222.

URYŪZU Ryūshin 瓜生津隆真, 1994-1995. *Jūjūbibasharon* 十住毘婆沙論. In *Shin kokuyaku daizōkyō* 新国訳大蔵経, series 14, *Shakkyōronbu* 釈経論部, vols. 12-13. Tokyo: Daizō Shuppansha.

Vaidya, P. L., ed., 1960. *Aṣṭasāhasrikā Prajñāpāramitā with Haribhadra's Commentary Called Āloka.* Buddhist Sanskrit Texts, No. 4. Darbhanga: The Mithila Institute of Post-Graduate Studies and Research in Sanskrit Learning.

Walleser, Max, 1914. *Prajñāpāramitā: Die Vollkommenheit der Erkenntnis nach indischen, tibetischen und chinesischen Quellen.* Göttingen: Vandenhoeck & Ruprecht.

Walshe, Maurice, trans., 1987. *Thus Have I Heard: The Long Discourses of the Buddha.* London: Wisdom.

Warren, Henry Clarke, 1896. *Buddhism in Translations.* Cambridge, Mass. Reprint. New York: Atheneum, 1974.

Wayman, Alex, 1959. "Studies in Yama and Māra." Parts 1 and 2. *Iranian Journal,* vol. 3, pp. 44-73; pp. 112-131.

_____, 1974. "The Mirror as a Pan-Buddhist Metaphor-Simile." *History of Religions,* vol. 13, no. 4, pp. 251-269.

_____, 1985. "Some Observations on Dualistic Mirror Symbolism in Western Philosophy and in the Upaniṣads." *Aligarh Journal of Oriental Studies,* vol. 2, nos. 1-2, pp. 113-116.

Wickremeratne, Ananda, 1985. *The Genesis of an Orientalist: Thomas William Rhys Davids and Buddhism in Sri Lanka.* Columbia, Mo.: South Asia Books.

Wille, Klaus, ed., 2000. *Fragments of a Manuscript of the Saddharmapuṇḍarīka-sūtra from Khādaliq.* Tokyo: Soka Gakkai.

Williams, Paul, 1989. *Mahāyāna Buddhism: The Doctrinal Foundations.* London: Routledge.

Wilson, Elizabeth, 1996. *Charming Cadavers: Horrific Figurations of the Feminine in Indian Buddhist Hagiographic Literature.* Chicago: University of Chicago Press.

Wolski, J., 1990. "Le titre de 'roi des rois' dan l'idéologie monarchique des Arsacides." In J. Harmatta, ed., *From Alexander the Great to Kül Tegin. Studies in Bactrian, Pahlavi, Sanskrit, Arabic, Aramaic, Armenian, Chinese, Türk, Greek and Latin Sources for the History of Pre-Islamic Central Asia* (Budapest: Akadémiai Kiadó), pp. 11-18.

Zürcher, Erik, 1959. *The Buddhist Conquest of China.* Reprint. 2 vols. Leiden: E. J. Brill, 1972.

_____, 1979. "Late Han Vernacular Elements in the Earliest Buddhist Translations." *Journal of the Chinese Languages Teachers Association,* vol. 12, no. 3, pp. 177-203.

_____, 1991. "A New Look at the Earliest Chinese Buddhist Texts." In Koichi Shinohara and Gregory Schopen, eds., *From Benares to Beijing: Essays on Buddhism and Chinese Religion in Honour of Prof. Jan Yün-hua* (Oakville, Ontario: Mosaic Press), pp. 277-304.

Zysk, Kenneth G., 1991. *Asceticism and Healing in Ancient India: Medicine in the Buddhist Monastery.* New York: Oxford University Press.

Index

abhidharma, 193; specialist in (*mātṛkādhara*), 274 and n. 430, 276, 347 and n. 4, 349, 350 nn. 2 and 3. See also *mātṛkā*
Abhidharmakośa, 128 n. 47, 213 n. 36, 313 n. 722
Abhirati, 178, 188; visions of, 180-181 n. 19
ācārya, 79, 83, 131
adhiṣṭhāna (designation), 273 n. 427
ādikarmika (beginner), 151
Aitareya-āraṇyaka, 59 n. 11
ājāneya (well-bred), 263 n. 343
Ajaṇṭā, 195 n. 3
Akṣayamati-nirdeśa, 33 n. 54
Akṣayamati-paripṛcchā-sūtra, 32, 33 n. 54
Akṣobhya, 49, 178, 187. *See also* Abhirati; *Akṣobhyavyūha*; celestial Buddhas
Akṣobhyavyūha, 45, 86, 187, 191; on Arhatship as desirable, 175, 180, 191; interpolation in, 180-181 n. 19; recommended to *śrāvakas*, 81 n. 15. *See also* Abhirati; Akṣobhya
alcohol, precept against. *See* intoxicants
All Pure Conduct (**Sarvacaryā-viśuddha*), 122-124, 278 and n. 458; Chinese and Tibetan translations of the name, 122-123, n. 40; 341, 346
ambition, 134 n. 61, 146-147
Amitābha, 147, 158 n. 47, 178, 187, 189 n. 33; death of, 189 n. 33. *See also* celestial Buddhas; Sukhāvatī; *Sukhāvatīvyūha-sūtra*
amulets, 105 and n. 4
Ānanda, 125, 180-181 n. 19, 210 n. 24, 316-317
ānantarya offenses, 120 and n. 35
Anāthapiṇḍada, 207, 209, 210 and n. 24
anātman, 136, 161 n. 52, 180, 288, 290 n. 543, 299-300, 302, 311, 312
Aṅguttara-nikāya, 128 n. 47
An Hsüan and Yen Fo-t'iao, 17, 39, 201
An Shih-kao, 119, 270 n. 401
anubhāva (lingering influence), 210 n. 25
anusmṛti, 130, 159 and n. 48, 167-168, 222 and n. 89, 293; equated with taking refuge, 167, 222-223
anuttarasamyaksaṁbodhi, 215 n. 45
Apāyajaha, 189, 208; Chinese and Tibetan translations of, 341, 343-344
apocryphal scriptures, 12
Aramaic, 292 n. 549
araṇya, 72, 94. *See also* wilderness-dwelling
arapacana syllabary, 292 n. 549
Arhatship, 81 n. 15, 88, 217 n. 57, 221 n. 86; accessibility of, 100, 145, 147; avoidance of, 155, 156, 172, 315 n. 738; desirability of, 105 and n. 4, 175, 180, 219; M.A. degree as analogous to, 85-86. *See also* Buddha, job description of; *śrāvakas*; three vehicles
armor (*saṁnāha*), 99, 148 and n. 24, 213 n. 35, 235
artha, Chinese translations of, 72, 217 n. 58
Āryaśūra, 143 n. 15
āryavaṁśas, 46-47, 56 and n. 7, 282-290; Chinese translations of the term, 127-128 n. 45; meaning of the term, 127 n. 45; Tibetan list of five, 129. *See also names of individual Nikāya schools*
aśaikṣa (no longer in training), 263 n. 344
asceticism, elided in Dharmarakṣa's translation, 291 n. 544, 302 n. 633,

not equivalent to "Nikāya," 195-196 n. 3; sequence of development of the term, 173; Tibetan translation of, 173 n. 4
Hinduism, 159, 177 n. 13. See also *bhakti*; Kṛṣṇa; mystical union; *prasāda*; Śiva; Vaiṣṇavism; Viṣṇu
Hindu literature, impact on Mahāyāna sūtras, 44 n. 73
HIRAKAWA Akira: on the bodhisattva path as a lay practice, 74 n. 2; equation of *bhikṣus* with *śrāvakas*, 124 and n. 41; on laity and renunciants in the *Ugra*, 74 n. 2; on the ordination of Ugra and his friends, 122-124; on the origins of the Mahāyāna, 73, 89-93; on relations between bodhisattvas and *śrāvakas*, 84-86
historical writing (India), 68
homage: as act of worship, 158, 162-163; formula used in Mongolian, 27-28; formulas in Buddhist sūtras, 26-28 and nn. 34-36;
home-dwelling, disadvantages of, 237-240, 266-272. *See also* householder
horizontal relationships. See *bodhisattva-gaṇa*; congregationalism
householder (*gṛhin*), 74; bodhisattva as, 103, 106-121; devotional practice and, 161; Ugra as, 125-127, 317. See also *gṛhin*
hsiao-sheng (small vehicle), 173 n. 4
Hsüan-tsang, 32-33, 50 and n. 3, 80 and n. 13; version of the *Aṣṭa* by, 108 n. 9
hui (as term for divisions within the Ratnakūṭa section), 29, 35, 320 n. 782

ideals, impact of, 105
illness, 131, 159, 275, 277, 288, 290 and n. 540
images, bodhisattva. *See* bodhisattvas, artistic representations of
individualism, 195 n. 2
Indra, 134 n. 58
inflation, terminological, 215 n. 45
inscriptions, 68 and n. 32; at Ajaṇṭā, 195 n. 3; formulaic quality of, 104 n. 3; of King Aśoka, 183 n. 23; Mahāyāna in, 63 and n. 22, 100, 183 n. 23; Mathurā lion capital inscription, 160 n. 50; at stūpa sites, 183 n. 23; Taxila copper plate inscription, 160 n. 50; value of, 103-105
interpolations: "club sandwich" style of, 62 n. 19; in the *Akṣobhyavyūha*, 180-181 n. 19; as conscious acts, 52; in the *Ugra*, 49-59, 240 n. 217, 247-248 n. 261, 266 n. 370. *See also* stratification, textual; "trigger words"
intoxicants, precept against, 109, 110 n. 14, 231-232; conflict with practice of *dāna*, 110, 232
irrelevance, principle of, 66-67, 73
irreversibility. See *avaitartika*
isolation. *See* detachment

**Jagatīṃdhara-sūtra*, 220 n. 76
Jainism, dress of renunciants in, 25 n. 32; non-relational character of, 165-166, 170; ritual offerings in, 165-166
Japan, Buddhism in, 84; influence on Hirakawa's theory, 84, 95 n. 34; influence on western study of the Mahāyāna, 5-6, 7;
Jarāmaraṇa-sutta, 66
jātaka tales, 54 n. 5, 113, 114 n. 22, 144 and nn. 16-17, 186 and n. 29, 188, 190 n. 36, 192
Jeta grove, 209
jhāna. See *dhyāna*
Jōdo Shinshū school, 95 n. 34, 169-170

K'ai-yüan shih-chiao lu, 16 n. 6
Kalhaṇa, 68
Kāma, 231 n. 144
Kanakamuni, 183 n. 23
K'ang Seng-hui, 3, 140 n. 6, 186-187 n. 29; commentary and preface to the *Ugra* by, 21
Kang Seng-k'ai, 17
Kanishka, 44 and n. 75, 342